AI Technology in Medical Image Analysis

AI Technology in Medical Image Analysis

Guest Editors

László Szilágyi
Levente Adalbert Kovács

MDPI

Basel • Beijing • Wuhan • Barcelona • Belgrade • Novi Sad • Cluj • Manchester

Guest Editors
László Szilágyi
PhysCon Lab, University
Research and Innovation Center
Obuda University
Budapest
Hungary

Levente Adalbert Kovács
PhysCon Lab, University
Research and Innovation Center
Obuda University
Budapest
Hungary

Editorial Office
MDPI AG
Grosspeteranlage 5
4052 Basel, Switzerland

This is a reprint of the Special Issue, published open access by the journal *Applied Sciences* (ISSN 2076-3417), freely accessible at: https://www.mdpi.com/journal/applsci/special_issues/316MFJ9Y6G.

For citation purposes, cite each article independently as indicated on the article page online and as indicated below:

Lastname, A.A.; Lastname, B.B. Article Title. *Journal Name* **Year**, *Volume Number*, Page Range.

ISBN 978-3-7258-8267-0 (Hbk)
ISBN 978-3-7258-8268-7 (PDF)
https://doi.org/10.3390/books978-3-7258-8268-7

Contents

About the Editors . . . . **vii**

László Szilágyi and Levente Kovács
Special Issue: Artificial Intelligence Technologies in Medical Image Analysis
Reprinted from: *Appl. Sci.* **2024**, *14*, 2180, https://doi.org/10.3390/app14052180 . . . . **1**

David Clement, Emmanuel Agu, Muhammad A. Suleiman,John Obayemi, Steve Adeshina and Wole Soboyejo
Multi-Class Breast Cancer Histopathological Image Classification Using Multi-Scale Pooled Image Feature Representation (MPIFR) and One-Versus-One Support Vector Machines
Reprinted from: *Appl. Sci.* **2023**, *13*, 156, https://doi.org/10.3390/app13010156 . . . . **6**

Kousuke Usui, Takaaki Yoshimura, Minghui Tang and Hiroyuki Sugimori
Age Estimation from Brain Magnetic Resonance Images Using Deep Learning Techniques in Extensive Age Range
Reprinted from: *Appl. Sci.* **2023**, *13*, 1753, https://doi.org/10.3390/app13031753 . . . . **32**

Daisuke Oura, Shinpe Sato, Yuto Honma, Shiho Kuwajima and Hiroyuki Sugimori
Quality Assurance of Chest X-ray Images with a Combination of Deep Learning Methods
Reprinted from: *Appl. Sci.* **2023**, *13*, 2067, https://doi.org/10.3390/app13042067 . . . . **47**

Jeoung Kun Kim, Yoo Jin Choo, In Sik Park, Jin-Woo Choi, Donghwi Park and Min Cheol Chang
Deep-Learning Algorithms for Prescribing Insoles to Patients with Foot Pain
Reprinted from: *Appl. Sci.* **2023**, *13*, 2208, https://doi.org/10.3390/app13042208 . . . . **59**

Mantas Kundrotas, Edita Mažonienė and Dmitrij Šešok
Automatic Tumor Identification from Scans of Histopathological Tissues
Reprinted from: *Appl. Sci.* **2023**, *13*, 4333, https://doi.org/10.3390/app13074333 . . . . **71**

Gustavo Retuci Pinheiro, Lorenza Brusini, Diedre Carmo, Renata Prôa, Thays Abreu, Simone Appenzeller, et al.
Thalamus Segmentation Using Deep Learning with Diffusion MRI Data: An Open Benchmark
Reprinted from: *Appl. Sci.* **2023**, *13*, 5284, https://doi.org/10.3390/app13095284 . . . . **88**

Bang Xiao and Chunyue Lu
Semi-Supervised Medical Image Classification Combined with Unsupervised Deep Clustering
Reprinted from: *Appl. Sci.* **2023**, *13*, 5520, https://doi.org/10.3390/app13095520 . . . . **109**

Gang Zhang, Zhi-Fei Lai, Yi-Qun Chen, Hong-Tao Liu and Wei-Jun Sun
A Histopathological Image Classification Method Based on Model Fusion in the Weight Space
Reprinted from: *Appl. Sci.* **2023**, *13*, 7009, https://doi.org/10.3390/app13127009 . . . . **123**

Julio Fachrel, Anindya Apriliyanti Pravitasari, Intan Nurma Yulita, Mulya Nurmansyah Ardhisasmita and Fajar Indrayatna
Enhancing an Imbalanced Lung Disease X-ray Image Classification with the CNN-LSTM Model
Reprinted from: *Appl. Sci.* **2023**, *13*, 8227, https://doi.org/10.3390/app13148227 . . . . **143**

Marco Berchiolli, Susann Wolfram, Wamadeva Balachandran and Tat-Hean Gan
Fully Automatic Thoracic Cavity Segmentation in Dynamic Contrast Enhanced Breast MRI Using Deep Convolutional Neural Networks
Reprinted from: *Appl. Sci.* **2023**, *13*, 10160, https://doi.org/10.3390/app131810160 . . . . **162**

Jae-beom Park, Han-sung Lee and Hyun-chong Cho
Investigating Effective Data Augmentation Techniques for Accurate Gastric Classification in the Development of a Deep Learning-Based Computer-Aided Diagnosis System
Reprinted from: *Appl. Sci.* **2023**, *13*, 12325, https://doi.org/10.3390/app132212325 . . . . **178**

About the Editors

László Szilágyi

László Szilágyi received his M.S. degree in electrical engineering from Petru Maior University, Tîrgu Mureş, Romania, in 1998; his Ph.D. degree in electrical engineering from Budapest University of Technology and Economics, Budapest, Hungary, in 2009; and his Habilitation degree from Babeș-Bolyai Universuty of Cluj-Napoca, Romania. Currently, he is a Full Professor at Sapientia Hungarian University of Transylvania, Tîrgu Mureş, Romania, and at Obuda University, Budapest, Hungary. His research interests include deep learning, pattern recognition, fuzzy systems, fuzzy clustering, bioinformatics, protein sequence and interaction networks, medical image and signal processing, and modeling and control in biomedical systems with special attention to the cardiovascular system, infection control and public health. He has published more than 250 articles in peer-reviewed journals and conference proceedings, accumulating an impact factor of over 100 and h-index of 27. He was János Bolyai Research Fellow of the Hungarian Academy of Sciences twice, between 2010 and 2013 and between 2018 and 2021. Since 2022, he has been Consolidator Excellence Researcher of Obuda University.

Levente Adalbert Kovács

Levente Adalbert Kovács received his MSc in Electrical Engineering (2000, Politehnica University of Timisoara) and Biomedical Engineering (2011, Budapest University of Technology and Economics), where he also earned his PhD in 2008. He obtained his DSc from the Hungarian Academy of Sciences in 2024. A Full Professor at Obuda University since 2016, he has served as the university's Rector/President since 2019, where he sits on major doctoral and habilitation committees. His research focuses on modern control theory and physiological controls. He has published over 600 articles and conference papers (h-index = 38, 6,000+ citations, impact factor over 400), placing him in the Stanford top 2% of cited researchers. In 2013, he founded and remains head of the Physiological Controls Research Center at Obuda University. Notably, he was an ERC Starting Grant recipient in 2015 for tumor control, researching personalized therapies via control engineering methods to minimize costs while maximizing patient quality of life. An influential figure in professional societies, Dr. Kovacs has been an IEEE Senior Member since 2018, having chaired the IEEE Hungary Section (2017–2024) and founded its Control Society Chapter. As of 2026, he serves as the Vice President for Conferences and Meetings for the IEEE SMC Society. He is also an active member of IFAC technical committees on biological systems and education. Nationally, he is the Co-President of the Hungarian Rectors Conference and President of the John von Neumann Computer Society. Within the Hungarian Diabetes Association, he founded the Hungarian Artificial Pancreas Working Group and was awarded the lifetime achievement Géza Hetényi Award. His global honors include the Dennis Gabor Award (2022) alongside five Doctor Honoris Causa titles from universities across Romania, Slovakia, and Uzbekistan. He also founded the Cyber-Medical Technical Committee under the IEEE SMC Society.

applied sciences

MDPI

Editorial

Special Issue: Artificial Intelligence Technology in Medical Image Analysis

László Szilágyi [1,2,*] and Levente Kovács [1]

1 Physiological Controls Research Center, Óbuda University, Bécsi út 96/B, 1034 Budapest, Hungary; kovacs@uni-obuda.hu
2 Computational Intelligence Research Group, Sapientia Hungarian University of Transylvania, 540485 Tîrgu Mureș, Romania
* Correspondence: szilagyi.laszlo@uni-obuda.hu or lalo@ms.sapientia.ro; Tel.: +36-70-242-8204

1. Introduction

Artificial intelligence (AI) technologies have significantly advanced the field of medical imaging, revolutionizing diagnostic and therapeutic processes [1]. One notable application is in image interpretation, where machine learning algorithms have demonstrated exceptional capabilities in detecting and diagnosing various medical conditions from imaging data. AI-powered tools have proven particularly effective in the field of radiology, assisting healthcare professionals in identifying abnormalities in X-rays, MRIs (magnetic resonance imaging), and CT (computed tomography) scans with increased speed and accuracy [2–5]. These technologies can analyze vast amounts of medical imaging data much faster than their human counterparts, aiding in early detection and timely intervention.

Moreover, AI plays a crucial role in improving image quality and reducing noise in medical imaging. Image enhancement techniques driven by AI algorithms help produce clearer and more detailed images, leading to improved diagnostic precision [6]. These advancements contribute to better visualizations of anatomical structures and abnormalities, allowing healthcare professionals to make more informed decisions [7]. AI also facilitates the integration of multiple imaging modalities, enabling a comprehensive and holistic view of a patient's condition, which is essential for personalized treatment planning [8–10].

In the realm of medical imaging, AI is instrumental in automating routine tasks, enabling healthcare providers to focus more on patient care. Automated image analysis can streamline the identification of patterns and anomalies, reducing the burden on radiologists and other medical professionals. This increased efficiency not only enhances the speed of diagnosis but also contributes to cost-effectiveness and resource optimization within healthcare systems [11].

Despite the transformative potential of AI in medical imaging, challenges such as data privacy, ethical considerations, and the need for regulatory frameworks remain. As these technologies continue to evolve, addressing these issues is paramount for ensuring their responsible and ethical implementation. The collaboration between healthcare professionals, data scientists, and regulatory bodies is essential in harnessing the full potential of AI in medical imaging, while maintaining patient trust and safeguarding sensitive health information. In the future, further developments in AI technologies are expected to refine and expand their applications in medical imaging, ultimately improving patient outcomes and advancing the overall landscape of healthcare diagnostics and treatment.

2. Contributions

This Special Issue represents a collection of original research papers that bring advancements to automated medical decision support, involving the diagnosis of various abnormal conditions of the human organism, based on a wide range of medical imaging modalities. In the first paper, Clement et al. present an ensemble that incorporates four different versions of deep convolutional neural networks (DCNNs), coupled with a support vector machine (SVM) classifier. The purpose is to classify histopathological images of breast cancer into eight specific classes—four benign and four malignant ones. The methodology harnesses the strengths of DCNNs to extract a highly predictive multi-scale pooled image feature representation, from breast cancer images at four distinct resolutions. These representations are then subjected to classification using SVM. The proposed CNN (convolutional neural network) architecture achieves an impressive 90% accuracy for eight-class breast cancer classification.

In the second paper, Usui et al. introduce a method for estimating age using T1-weighted two-dimensional brain magnetic resonance (MR) images, involving a cohort of 1000 subjects aged between 5 and 79 years. The proposed approach employs a regression model based on the ResNet-50 architecture, which predicts the chronological age of unknown brain MR images using its training on images corresponding to the respective ages. The study's findings reveal a comparable level of correlation to related research, indicating the feasibility of age estimation across a broad age spectrum with enhanced accuracy. This suggests that the proposed method holds promise for accurate age estimation, even in diverse age groups, when utilizing T1-weighted two-dimensional brain MR imaging.

In the third paper, Oura et al. report on the development and evaluation of a quality assurance (QA) system for chest X-ray images, based on deep learning. The QA system includes three classification models and one regression model, developed using a dataset of 23,000 curated images from various sources. The classification method addresses issues such as image orientation correction, left–right reversal, and the estimation of the patient's body position. The regression method focuses on correcting the image angle. Several CNN models are compared, using five cross-fold evaluations. The overall accuracy of the QA system is assessed using clinical images, and the mean correction time of the system is also measured. The deep learning-based QA system demonstrates efficient and accurate corrections of chest X-ray images. The utilization of ResNet-50 for classification and the classical CNN for regression proves to be effective, ensuring precise adjustments for various aspects of image quality.

In the fourth paper, Kim et al. focus on the development and evaluation of deep-learning algorithms designed to automatically recommend orthotic insoles for individuals experiencing foot pain. The input data, gathered from 838 patients, includes details such as the resting calcaneal stance position, pelvic elevation, pelvic tilt, and pelvic rotation. The target data encompasses the foot posture index for the modified root technique, as well as the requirement for interventions such as heel lift, entire lift, and specific supports like lateral wedge, medial wedge, and calcaneocuboid arch. The deep-learning models developed therein, coupled with statistical validation, demonstrate their proficiency in automatically prescribing orthotic insoles for patients with foot pain, achieving commendable accuracy across various parameters.

In the fifth paper, Kundrotas et al. explore various CNN architectures for their effective integration into the automated analysis of histopathological whole slide images. This advancement enhances the capability to detect early stages of diseases, including cancer, thereby contributing to improved health monitoring strategies. Moreover, the predictive abilities of these systems provide opportunities for anticipating and controlling the spread of global diseases, enabling preliminary analyses and viable solutions. The primary objective of the study is to augment the accuracy of machine learning methods in detecting tumor-damaged tissues in histopathological whole slide images. The most promising results were attained through the utilization of a multi-model ensemble, characterized by an impressive AUC (area under the curve) value of 0.97.

In the sixth paper, Pinheiro et al. introduce a foundational multimodality thalamus segmentation pipeline that incorporates diffusion MRI (dMRI) and T1-weighted images through a CNN approach, and can obtain remarkable segmentation accuracy. This marks a significant contribution to the automated diagnosis of various diseases like multiple sclerosis and Parkinson's, where the segmentation and shape assessment of the thalamus play a crucial role. Additionally, the authors established an open benchmark, featuring a substantial, preprocessed, publicly available dataset. This dataset includes co-registered T1-weighted and dMRI images, manual thalamic masks, masks generated by three distinct automated methods, and a STAPLE consensus of the masks. As a result, this initiative opens up new possibilities for advancing research in the field.

In the seventh paper, Xiao and Lu, in response to the dependence of deep neural networks on the large amount of reliable image data, propose a semi-supervised framework for medical image classification that integrates semi-supervised classification with unsupervised deep clustering. The methodology involves the iterative execution of two tasks—semi-supervised classification and unsupervised deep clustering—to attach label information to unlabeled data. This iterative process assists the model in extracting semantic information from unlabeled data, while mitigating the risk of overfitting to the limited labeled data available. To validate their proposed method, the authors conduct a comparative experiment using public benchmark medical image datasets. Compared to earlier solutions, this method enhances model robustness and mitigates the impact of outliers.

In the eighth paper, Zhang et al. introduce a method for optimizing hyperparameters in deep networks employed for automated classification of histopathological images. This method is based on model fusion within the weight space. The authors utilize the cyclical learning rate strategy to fine-tune individual models and suggest a ranking strategy, considering accuracy and diversity, for the selection of candidate models. The fusion of weights from these constituent models is aimed at producing a model with performance levels better aligned with the expected value, potentially enhancing the model's generalization ability. Furthermore, the proposed strategy significantly reduces the proposed model's testing cost. Experiments conducted on two datasets of histopathological images reveal the effectiveness of the proposed model compared to baseline architectures like ResNet, VGG, DenseNet, and their ensemble versions.

In the ninth paper, Fachrel et al. propose a methodology for the effective and accurate classification of lung diseases, specifically targeting COVID-19, pneumonia, and normal cases, based on chest X-ray images. The research focuses on the optimal usage of CNN and LSTM architectures, from the perspective of evaluation metrics and training efficiency. Data augmentation is deployed to overcome the adverse effects of imbalanced datasets. The best performing model, featuring five convolutional blocks and two LSTM layers needs no augmentation and achieves remarkable Dice scores of up to 0.99.

In the tenth paper, Berchiolli et al. propose a segmentation method for the thoracic cavity in dynamic contrast-enhanced NRI data, to assist with the correct diagnosis of breast cancer. The main challenge is the fact that various internal organs can have very similar appearances to malignant breast lesions after the injection of the contrast agent. The proposed approach employs various CNN-based architectures, assessing the effect of several enhancements given to the baseline models. During the evaluation, the proposed methodology is proven to surpass the current state of the art, excelling in both data efficiency and conformity, with expert-made annotations.

Finally, in the eleventh paper, Park et al. address the problem of the accurate detection and effective treatment of gastric cancer. They propose an image-guided solution as an alternative to the usual gastroscopic biopsy, which is time-consuming and may cause delays in diagnosis and subsequent treatment. The proposed computer-aided diagnosis system, called CADx, employs various CNN-based network architectures to produce the diagnosis. Since there are no large image datasets available in this field, the authors proposed an image augmentation technique using cut-and-paste operations and a sliding window-based algorithm. In various classification scenarios, their system achieves an accuracy between 83% and 90%.

3. Conclusions

In conclusion, the integration of AI technology into medical image analysis has ushered in a transformative era in healthcare diagnostics and treatment planning. This Special Issue has explored the multifaceted applications and the profound impact of AI in revolutionizing the way medical professionals interpret and utilize imaging data. From enhancing the accuracy and efficiency of disease detection to facilitating personalized treatment strategies, AI has proven itself as a powerful ally in the medical field.

The rapid evolution of deep learning algorithms, particularly CNNs, has played a pivotal role in the success of AI in medical image analysis. These algorithms exhibit exceptional capabilities in recognizing complex patterns and anomalies within various medical imaging modalities, including X-rays, MRIs, and CT scans. The improved accuracy and speed of diagnosis offered by AI can not only expedite patient care but also contribute to more informed decision-making by healthcare practitioners.

Despite the remarkable strides made in this field, challenges remain, including the need for large, diverse datasets, the need to address ethical considerations, and the need to ensure the seamless integration of AI technologies into existing healthcare workflows. The ongoing collaboration between AI researchers, healthcare professionals, and regulatory bodies is crucial to overcoming these challenges and fostering the responsible and effective deployment of AI in medical image analysis.

As AI continues to evolve and mature, its role in medical image analysis is poised to redefine the landscape of healthcare. The promise of improved diagnostic accuracy, early disease detection, and personalized treatment strategies positions AI as an invaluable tool in advancing the quality of patient care and contributing to the overall well-being of individuals around the world.

Author Contributions: Conceptualization, L.S. and L.K.; writing—original draft preparation, L.S. and L.K.; writing—review and editing, L.S. and L.K. All authors have read and agreed to the published version of the manuscript.

Funding: This work was supported by the Consolidator Researcher Program of Óbuda University.

Conflicts of Interest: The authors declare no conflicts of interest.

List of Contributions:

1. Clement, D.; Agu, E.; Suleiman, M.A.; Obayemi, J.; Adeshina, S.; Soboyejo, W. Multi-Class Breast Cancer Histopathological Image Classification Using Multi-Scale Pooled Image Feature Representation (MPIFR) and One-Versus-One Support Vector Machines. *Appl. Sci.* **2023**, *13*, 156. https://doi.org/10.3390/app13010156.
2. Usui, K.; Yoshimura, T.; Tang, M.H.; Sugimori, H. Age Estimation from Brain Magnetic Resonance Images Using Deep Learning Techniques in Extensive Age Range. *Appl. Sci.* **2023**, *13*, 1753. https://doi.org/10.3390/app13031753.
3. Oura, D.; Sato, S.; Honma, Y.; Kuwajima, S.; Sugimori, H. Quality Assurance of Chest X-ray Images with a Combination of Deep Learning Methods. *Appl. Sci.* **2023**, *13*, 2067. https://doi.org/10.3390/app13042067.
4. Kim, J.K.; Choo, Y.J.; Park, I.S.; Choi, J.W.; Park, D.; Chang, M.C. Deep-Learning Algorithms for Prescribing Insoles to Patients with Foot Pain. *Appl. Sci.* **2023**, *13*, 2208. https://doi.org/10.3390/app13042208.
5. Kundrotas, M., Mažonienė, E.; Šešok, D. Automatic Tumor Identification from Scans of Histopathological Tissues. *Appl. Sci.* **2023**, *13*, 4333. https://doi.org/10.3390/app13074333.
6. Pinheiro, G.R.; Brusini, L.; Carmo, D.; Prôa, R.; Abreu, T., Appenzeller, S.; Menegaz, G.; Rittner, L. Thalamus Segmentation Using Deep Learning with Diffusion MRI Data: An Open Benchmark. *Appl. Sci.* **2023**, *13*, 5284. https://doi.org/10.3390/app13095284.
7. Xiao, B.; Lu, C.Y. Semi-Supervised Medical Image Classification Combined with Unsupervised Deep Clustering. *Appl. Sci.* **2023**, *13*, 5520. https://doi.org/10.3390/app13095520.
8. Zhang, G.; Lai, Z.F.; Chen, Y.Q.; Liu, H.T.; Sun, W.J. A Histopathological Image Classification Method Based on Model Fusion in the Weight Space. *Appl. Sci.* **2023**, *13*, 7009. https://doi.org/10.3390/app13127009.
9. Fachrel, J.; Pravitasari, A.A.; Yulita, I.N.; Ardhisasmita, M.N.; Indrayatna, F. Enhancing an Imbalanced Lung Disease X-ray Image Classification with the CNN-LSTM Model. *Appl. Sci.* **2023**, *13*, 8227. https://doi.org/10.3390/app13148227.

10. Berchiolli, M.; Wolfram, S.; Balachandran, W.; Gan, T.H. Fully Automatic Thoracic Cavity Segmentation in Dynamic Contrast Enhanced Breast MRI Using Deep Convolutional Neural Networks. *Appl. Sci.* **2023**, *13*, 10160. https://doi.org/10.3390/app131810160.
11. Park, J.B.; Lee, H.S.; Cho, H.C. Investigating Effective Data Augmentation Techniques for Accurate Gastric Classification in the Development of a Deep Learning-Based Computer-Aided Diagnosis System. *Appl. Sci.* **2023**, *13*, 12325. https://doi.org/10.3390/app132212325.

References

1. Potočnik, J.; Foley, S.; Thomas, E. Current and potential applications of artificial intelligence in medical imaging practice: A narrative review. *J. Med. Imaging Radiat. Sci.* **2023**, *54*, 376–385. [CrossRef] [PubMed]
2. Messaoudi, H.; Belaid, A.; Ben Salem, D.; Conze, P.H. Cross-dimensional transfer learning in medical image segmentation with deep learning. *Med. Image Anal.* **2023**, *88*, 102868. [CrossRef] [PubMed]
3. Billot, B.; Greve, D.N.; Puonti, O.; Thielscher, A.; Van Leemput, K.; Fischl, B.; Dalca, A.V.; Iglesias, J.E. SynthSeg: Segmentation of brain MRI scans of any contrast and resolution without retraining. *Med. Image Anal.* **2023**, *86*, 102789. [CrossRef]
4. Szepesi, P.; Szilágyi, L. Detection of pneumonia using convolutional neural networks and deep learning. *Biocybern. Biomed. Eng.* **2022**, *42*, 1012–1022. [CrossRef]
5. Prabhu, S.; Prasad, K.; Robels-Kelly, A.; Lu, X.Q. AI-based carcinoma detection and classification using histopathological images: A systematic review. *Comput. Biol. Med.* **2022**, *142*, 105209. [CrossRef] [PubMed]
6. Kaviani, S.; Han, K.J.; Sohn, I. Adversarial attacks and defenses on AI in medical imaging informatics: A survey. *Expert Syst. Appl.* **2022**, *198*, 116815. [CrossRef]
7. Hu, W.M.; Li, X.T.; Li, C.; Li, R.; Jiang, T.; Sun, H.Z.; Huang, X.N.; Grzegorzek, M.; Li, X.Y. A state-of-the-art survey of artificial neural networks for Whole-slide Image analysis: From popular Convolutional Neural Networks to potential visual transformers. *Comput. Biol. Med.* **2023**, *161*, 107034. [CrossRef] [PubMed]
8. Li, J.J.; Han, X.; Qin, Y.M.; Tan, F.; Chen, Y.L.; Wang, Z.K.; Song, H.T.; Zhou, X.; Zhang, Y.; Hu, L.; et al. Artificial intelligence accelerates multi-modal biomedical process: A Survey. *Neurocomputing* **2023**, *558*, 126720. [CrossRef]
9. Altini, N.; Prencipe, B.; Cascarano, G.D.; Brunetti, A.; Brunetti, G.; Triggiani, V.; Carnimeo, L.; Marino, F.; Guerriero, A.; Villani, L.; et al. Liver, kidney and spleen segmentation from CT scans and MRI with deep learning: A survey. *Neurocomputing* **2022**, *490*, 30–53. [CrossRef]
10. Xu, Z.; Wang, Y.Q.; Chen, M.; Zhang Q. Multi-region radiomics for artificially intelligent diagnosis of breast cancer using multimodal ultrasound. *Comput. Biol. Med.* **2022**, *149*, 105920. [CrossRef] [PubMed]
11. Gao, L.; Moodie, M.; Watts, J.J.; Wang, L. Cost-Effectiveness of Osteoporosis Opportunistic Screening Using Computed Tomography in China. *Value Health Reg. Issues* **2023**, *38*, 38–44. [CrossRef] [PubMed]

applied sciences

MDPI

Article

Multi-Class Breast Cancer Histopathological Image Classification Using Multi-Scale Pooled Image Feature Representation (MPIFR) and One-Versus-One Support Vector Machines

David Clement [1,2,3], Emmanuel Agu [2,*], Muhammad A. Suleiman [3], John Obayemi [2] and Steve Adeshina [3] and Wole Soboyejo [2]

1 Department of Computer Science, African University of Science and Technology, Km 10 Umaru Musa Yar'Adua Road, Galadimawa, Abuja 900109, Nigeria
2 Worcester Polytechnic Institute, 100 Institute Road, Worcester, MA 01609-2280, USA
3 Research & Institution Area, Nile University of Nigeria, Plot 681, Cadastral Zone C-OO, Jabi Airport Bypass, Abuja 900001, Nigeria
* Correspondence: emmanuel@wpi.edu

Abstract: Breast cancer (BC) is currently the most common form of cancer diagnosed worldwide with an incidence estimated at 2.26 million in 2020. Additionally, BC is the leading cause of cancer death. Many subtypes of breast cancer exist with distinct biological features and which respond differently to various treatment modalities and have different clinical outcomes. To ensure that sufferers receive lifesaving patients-tailored treatment early, it is crucial to accurately distinguish dangerous malignant (ductal carcinoma, lobular carcinoma, mucinous carcinoma, and papillary carcinoma) subtypes of tumors from adenosis, fibroadenoma, phyllodes tumor, and tubular adenoma benign harmless subtypes. An excellent automated method for detecting malignant subtypes of tumors is desirable since doctors do not identify 10% to 30% of breast cancers during regular examinations. While several computerized methods for breast cancer classification have been proposed, deep convolutional neural networks (DCNNs) have demonstrated superior performance. In this work, we proposed an ensemble of four variants of DCNNs combined with the support vector machines classifier to classify breast cancer histopathological images into eight subtypes classes: four benign and four malignant. The proposed method utilizes the power of DCNNs to extract highly predictive multi-scale pooled image feature representation (MPIFR) from four resolutions (40×, 100×, 200×, and 400×) of BC images that are then classified using SVM. Eight pre-trained DCNN architectures (Inceptionv3, InceptionResNetv2, ResNet18, ResNet50, DenseNet201, EfficientNetb0, shuffleNet, and SqueezeNet) were individually trained and an ensemble of the four best-performing models (ResNet50, ResNet18, DenseNet201, and EfficientNetb0) was utilized for feature extraction. One-versus-one SVM classification was then utilized to model an 8-class breast cancer image classifier. Our work is novel because while some prior work has utilized CNNs for 2- and 4-class breast cancer classification, only one other prior work proposed a solution for 8-class BC histopathological image classification. A 6B-Net deep CNN model was utilized, achieving an accuracy of 90% for 8-class BC classification. In rigorous evaluation, the proposed MPIFR method achieved an average accuracy of 97.77%, with 97.48% sensitivity, and 98.45% precision on the BreakHis histopathological BC image dataset, outperforming the prior state-of-the-art for histopathological breast cancer multi-class classification and a comprehensive set of DCNN baseline models.

Keywords: Breast Cancer; multimodal; SVM; transfer learning; neural networks

1. Introduction

Breast cancer (BC) causes cells in the breast to develop uncontrollably, which can lead to tumor growth and death if not detected early. In 2018, an estimated 627,000 women died from BC, which corresponds to 15% of the total cancer mortality in women [1]. A recent study by the American Cancer Society (ACS) suggests that one in eight women in the US will develop cancer in their lifetime [2]. Globally, BC is a leading type of cancer among women, affecting about 2.1 million women annually, and has been the leading cause of death associated with cancer among women [3]. Early detection and classification of breast cancer subtypes are crucial in deciding the best treatment plan and mitigating the risk of death. According to the World Health Organization (WHO), increasing the survival rates of patients with breast cancer significantly requires early and precise diagnosis of malignancy [4]. There are two kinds of growth in breast tissue, non-harmful (benign) and malignant, with subtypes occurring in each category. Non-harmful (benign) growth patterns include adenosis (A), fibroadenoma (FA), phyllodes tumor (PT), and tubular adenoma (TA), and dangerous (malignant or cancerous) growth patterns include ductal carcinoma (DC), lobular carcinoma (LB), mucinous carcinoma (MC), and papillary carcinoma (PC). These subtypes of BC have distinct biological features, leading to different response patterns to various treatment modalities and thus have varied clinical outcomes. Consequently, to ensure that sufferers receive lifesaving, patient-tailored treatment early, it is very important to accurately distinguish dangerous malignant subtypes of tumors from benign harmless subtypes [5] during patient assessments. Global gene expression profiling (GEP) [6] studies have shown that survival is associated with the classification of distinct biological classes.

As a result of limited knowledge and availability of experts, between 10% and 30% of BCs go undetected during regular screenings. The accuracy of manual BC screening varies according to the pathologist's experience and knowledge, and diagnoses can be incorrect due to human error. Automated computer screening systems for breast cancer classification and identification have been proposed to automatically diagnose malignancy, improving the accuracy and consistency of differentiating the normal vs. abnormal classes of breast tissues by about 10% [7]. Computer aided diagnosis (CAD) systems are accessible, fast, and reliable [8]. Machine learning using handcrafted image features was used in previous image-based breast cancer classification studies [9–11]. Recently, due to their demonstrated impressive performance, deep convolutional neural networks (DCNNs) have become increasingly popular for medical image analysis, segmentation, classification, and ailment prediction [12]. Breast cancer can be detected by automated therapeutic imaging techniques such as histopathological imaging, computed tomography, breast X-rays, sonograms, and magnetic resonance imaging [13]. Currently, histopathological images are considered the best diagnostic images for cancer diagnosis [14]. Several top-down and bottom-up image analyses rely on automated and exact classification of histopathological images, such as classifying nuclei, detecting mitosis, and segmenting glands [15]. Tumor classification, however, is the most critical step in histopathological image examination. A wide range of image analysis tasks can be performed with convolutional neural networks (CNNs), including image classification, disease detection, localization, segmentation [16], and the analyses of histopathological images [12].

Our approach: In this study, a method for multiclass classification of breast cancer using an ensemble of pre-trained deep convolutional neural network (DCNN) and SVM, is proposed. First, four state-of-the-art DCNN backbone models (1) ResNet50 [17], (2) ResNet18 [17], (3) DenseNet201 [18], and (4) EfficientNetb0 [19] were used for feature extraction. The models were used to extract rich multi-resolution features from four resolutions (40×, 100×, 200×, and 400×) of histopathological breast cancer images. The rich multiresolution features were then pooled using global average pooling to create an array of deep multiresolution convolutional features, SVM classifier performs multiclassification (8sub-types) of malignant and benign tumors. SVM algorithms always converge at a global minimum when provided with a suitable feature set irrespective of the dimensionality of the inputs. The target malignant breast cancer classes are ductal carcinoma in situ, lobular carcinoma, mucinous carcinoma, and papillary carcinoma subtypes, and the benign breast cancer target classes are adenosis, fibroadenoma, phyllodes tumor, and tubular adenoma subtypes. Methods for extracting image features fall into three main categories [20]: (1) Automatic feature extraction using deep learning, (2) handcrafted features, and (3) unsupervised feature learning. Manual feature extraction is tedious and error-prone. EffficientNetb0 is the baseline model for EfficientNet, which uses compound scaling, a novel scaling method, to scale the model's dimensions uniformly to increase performance. With ResNet-50, deep residual networks are constructed with 50 layers of residual blocks, which mitigates the vanishing gradient descent problem to maintain accuracy as the depth of the network increases. In contrast to the previously described neural networks, ResNet18 is a gateless or open-gated variant of the highway-net, the first working very deep feedforward neural network. Some layers can be jumped over by using skip connections. In typical implementations, it includes double- or triple-layer skips with nonlinearities and batch normalizations. DenseNet-201 is a convolutional neural network that is 201 layers deep. It utilizes dense connections between layers through dense blocks, where all layers are connected directly. Each layer receives additional inputs from all preceding layers and passes its feature maps to all subsequent layers to preserve the feed-forward nature. The feature extraction step is fundamental to the analysis of medical images using machine learning, and a variety of extraction strategies have been proposed in the past for the classification of various diseases using images [21–24].

In summary, the proposed method utilizes the power of pre-trained, state-of-the-art DCNN models to extract a multi-scale pooled image feature representation (MPIFR) from four resolutions (40×, 100×, 200×, and 400×) of BC images. The proposed MPIFR is a highly predictive auto-learned representation that is then classified using SVM. In rigorous evaluation, the proposed MPIFR achieved an average accuracy of 97.77%, with 97.48% sensitivity, and 98.45% precision on the BreaKHis dataset [25]. The proposed ensemble approach outperforms a comprehensive set of state-of-the-art CNN baselines and the prior state-of-the-art for classifying multiresolution (40×, 100×, 200×, and 400×) histopathological breast cancer images including ResNet18, InceptionV3, DenseNet201, EfficientNetb0, SqueezeNet, and ShuffleNet. Our evaluation demonstrates that every component of MPIFR contributes non-trivially to its superior performance, including transfer learning (pre-training and fine-tuning), deep feature extraction at multiple resolutions into a powerful feature representation and classification using one-versus-one SVM.

Challenges: Firstly, due to the heterogeneous visual texture patterns in breast histopathological images, DCNNs are challenged to reliably classify tumor malignancy, which negatively impacts their performance. Secondly, the most predictive features that discriminate malignant and benign breast cancers in histopathological images may appear at different resolutions, which differ for various BC cases. The proposed MPIFR approach innovatively addresses these two challenges, making it particularly appropriate for discriminating between BC tumor malignancies.

Related work that utilized deep learning and CNNs for breast cancer tumor multi-classification are summarized in Table 1. The deep multiresolution feature representation for 8-classes, which we propose, has not been explored previously for breast cancer classification using neural networks and SVM. Omar et al. in [26] performed multi-class breast cancer classification from histopathology images using 6B-Net deep CNN model, with feature fusion and selection mechanism. The method achieved a multi-class average accuracy of 94.20% for 4-class and 90.00% for 8-class, respectively, on histopathological images. Wei et al. proposed a breast cancer multiclassification from histopathological images with a structured deep learning model [27], the model achieved an accuracy of 93.2%. Murtaza et al. [28] utilized GoogleNet architecture [29] to classify histopathology images into subtypes using majority voting. MUDeRN investigated using ResNet [17] to classify breast cancer images into malignant or benign and further categorized each to its subsequent subtypes using two modules M and B [30]. Ameh Joseph et al. in [31] used handcrafted features extracted to train the DNN classifiers with four dense layers and the SoftMax layer. Xie et al. in [32] performed 4-class classification based on magnification factor, using some deep learning models.

Table 1. Prior models for 2- and 4-class BC classification including performance comparisons. Our proposed approach (in bold) outperforms prior approaches.

Study	Method	Classification Type	Type of Feature Extraction	Accuracy (%)	F1-Score Measure (%)	Specificity (%)	AUC (%)
Al-Haija and Adebanjo (2020) [33]	ResNet-50 CNN	Binary	Automatic unsupervised feature discovery	99	n/a	n/a	n/a
Kassani et al. (2019) [34]	VGG19, MobileNet, DenseNet and multi- layer perceptron classifier	Binary	Automatic feature extraction	98.13	98.64	n/a	n/a
Umer et al. (2022) [26]	6B-Net	4-class | 4-class	Automatic feature extraction	94.20 | 90.10	n/a	n/a	n/a
Z. Han et al. (2017) [27]	CSDCNN End-to-end	8-class	n/a	93.2	n/a	n/a	n/a
Gandomkar et al. (2018) [30]	Variant ResNets models	4-class	Deep Learning for Feature Extraction	96.25	n/a	n/a	n/a
Murtaza et al. (2019) [28]	CNN end- end	4-class	Deep learning for feature extraction	92.45 | 95.48	n/a	91.11 | 96.97	n/a
Proposed MPIFR + SVM Model	Four variant CNN & SVM	8-class	Automatic unsupervised feature discover	**97.77**	**97.92**	**99.57**	**99.00**

Related work that used CNNs to extract deep features from medical images Wichakam et al. proposed an automated mammographic image detection system using a CNN for feature extraction and SVM for classification but did not explore multi-resolution extraction and pooling [35]. Devnath et al. [36] used CNN models to detect pneumoconiosis in X-ray images by extracting deep multi-level features. Devnath et al. [37] present a systematic review of computer-aided diagnosis of coal workers' pneumoconiosis in chest X-rays using machine learning, which included approaches that used CNNs. Devnath et al. [38] used CheXNet-model as part of an ensemble of multi-dimensional deep feature extractors from chest X-rays to detect and visualize pneumoconiosis. To convert the output of the model into one-dimensional vectors, the last layer close to the output layer was removed, then a global average pooling layer was added. Huynh 162 et al. [39] used computer-aided diagnosis (CADx) systems, to examine the optimal point for extracting features from pre-trained CNNs. Zhang et al. [40] proposed ensemble learners for pulmonary nodule classification by combining deep CNNs. Other related research includes work by Yang et al. [41] who previously used adaptive boosting (AdaBoost), an ensemble method, to combine multiple weak classifiers into a single classifier. Using k-means with K = 4000, each tissue image generated 4000-Teton histograms as features. An accuracy of 80% was achieved for multi-class classification (three target classes: I, II, and benign). Al-Haija and Adebanjo [33] proposed a binary classifier using a transfer learning model ResNet-50 CNN and achieved a performance accuracy of 99% using histopathological images. Filipczuk et al. [42] and George et al. [20] previously extracted nuclei feature from fine needle biopsies. First, the circular Hough transform was utilized for detecting nuclei candidates and false-positive reduction, followed by machine learning and Otsu thresholding.

Novelty: Our work is novel because while some prior work has utilized CNNs for 2- and 4-class breast cancer classification, they did not explore using a multi-scale pooled image feature representation (MPIFR) to classify histopathological images into eight (8) BC classes. Specifically, some prior work utilized CNNs for the classification of four (4) BC classes using 6B-Net with deep feature fusion and achieved an accuracy of 94.2%. Innovatively, the proposed ensemble approach leverages several key insights. First, pre-training state-of-the-art DCNNs on huge repositories such as the 14 million image ImageNet repository provides them with the intelligence to learn low-level features such as edges and corners from images of histological breast cancer. Secondly, by extracting features from multiple resolutions of histopathological images, classification accuracy is improved due to the fact that specific visual characteristics may be more visible at different resolutions. Thirdly, the extraction of multiresolution breast cancer features creates a powerful set of features that can be classified using SVM for highly accurate multi-class classification of histopathological images of breast cancer.

2. Proposed Ensemble Model for 8-Class BC Image Classification

2.1. Working Principles of Deep Neural Networks Learning Algorithms

There are many types of deep learning, different kinds of auto-encoder, that vary in architectures and training algorithms. However, one basic element of deep learning is the additional new activation functions such as rectified linear unit (ReLU), SoftMax, and Swish. These are identified to be useful to train deeper networks [43]. Compared to many classical bounded activation functions such as $tanh(x)$ and $\delta(x)$, many of the new activation functions are convex with a large area of non-zeros derivatives [44]. Figure 1 illustrates attributes of new and classical activation functions.

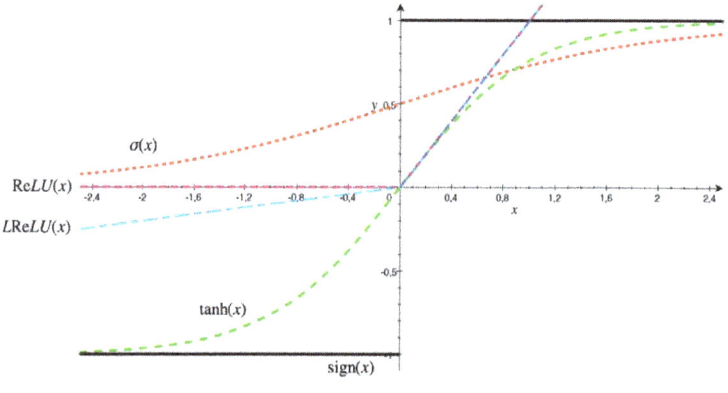

Figure 1. New and classic activation functions.

ReLU was proposed to replace $tanh(x)$ and $\delta(x)$, which are known to be standard ways to model a $neuron's$ output f as a function of its input x. ReLU is non-saturating nonlinearity:

$$h(x) = max(0,\ x) \tag{1}$$

ReLU is a preferred choice of activation function for hidden layers, as it is faster and more efficient for deep convolutional neural networks compared to their equivalents with $tanh(x)$units [44]. Leak ReLU was proposed as an improvement of the ReLU activation function. ReLU sometimes destroys some neurons in each iteration, a condition known as the dying ReLU condition:

$$h(x) = \begin{cases} x, & if\, x > 0 \\ 0.01x, & otherwise \end{cases} \tag{2}$$

A more generalized variant of ReLU is parameterized ReLU:

$$h(x) = \begin{cases} x, & if\, x > 0 \\ ax, & otherwise \end{cases} \tag{3}$$

where a is a trainable parameter with the value of $a = 0.01$; parameterized ReLU acts as Leaky ReLU. SoftMax is a generalization of logistic regression. It is usually used in a final output layer to handle a case of a multi-class problem. Recall that the logistic regression learning model is a sigmoid function:

$$h_\theta(x) = \delta(x) = \frac{1}{1 + e^{-\theta^T}X} \tag{4}$$

In logistic regression the output y^i for an input instance i is assumed to belong to binary set, i.e., $y^i \in \{0, 1\}$. With SoftMax y^i belong to multivariate set, i.e., $y^i \in \{1, \ldots K\}$ where K is the number of target classes. Recall that the cost function for the logistic regression model is:

$$J(\theta) = -\frac{1}{m}[\sum_{i=1}^{m} y^i log(h_\theta(x^i)) + (1 - y^i) log(1 - h_\theta(x^i))] + \frac{\lambda}{2m}\sum_{j=1}^{n}\theta_j^2 \tag{5}$$

In SoftMax, the interest is on multi-class classification rather than binary classification as in the case of logistic regression. Thus, given a test input x, the learning model estimates the probability of $p(y = k/x)$ for each value of $k = 1, \ldots, K$. Hence, the learning model will output a K- dimensional vector for which its element is summed up to 1. The SoftMax function for multi-class prediction is of the form:

$$h_\theta(x) = \delta(x) = \frac{1}{1 + e^{-(\theta')^T}X} \tag{6}$$

Equation (6) predicts the probability of one of the classes, and $(1 - \frac{1}{1+e^{-(\theta')^T}X})$ for the other class; where θ' is a single parameter vector.

Equation (7) below describes the cost function for SoftMax regression:

$$J(\theta) = -\left[\sum_{i=1}^{m}\sum_{k=1}^{K} 1\{y^i = k\} log\frac{exp(\theta^{(k)T}x^i)}{\sum_{j=1}^{K} exp(\theta^{(j)T}x^i)}\right] \tag{7}$$

where $1\{.\}$ is an indicator function. i.e., $1\{a\, true\, statement\} = 1$, and $1[\{a\, false\, statement\} = 0$. For example, $1\{1+1\} = 2$ evaluates to 1; while $1\{1+3\} = 5$ evaluates to 0.

As earlier stated, feature identification and processing are performed in an unsupervised fashion in deep learning. We formally define feature extraction using convolution as in [45]. Given some large images of size $r \times c$ called x_l, a sparse auto-encoder is trained on small patches sampled of these x_l. We refer to the small patches as x_s with size $a \times b$. Suppose k is the number of hidden units, we compute a convolved feature as:

$$f_s = \delta(W^l x_s + b^l) \tag{8}$$

where δ is the sigmoid function. These give a total of $k \times (r - a + 1) \times (c - b + 1)$ array of convolved features.

In theory, what follows after feature extraction is classification, but classifying all features extracted results in a huge computational burden and is susceptible to overfitting. To overcome these computational challenges, a pooling process is applied. It is a process of summarizing the output of a neighboring group of neurons in the same kernel map.

This natural approach of aggregating a statistical summary of these features at the various location is referred to as pooling and sometimes means "pooling" or max "pooling" pending the pooling operation used. Formally, the pooling operation involves dividing the array of convolved features into disjoint $m \times n$ regions and applying to mean (or maximum) feature activation over these regions to generate pooled convolved features. Finally, the pooled convolved features with many lower dimensions are used for classification.

Overfitting is one of the generalization problems that are common when there are few input data examples and higher dimensional features. To reduce the overfitting of models to specific image training sets, two processes are now discussed. Data argumentation is the most common method of addressing overfitting in image data [46]. The second method popularly used in deep learning is the dropout method. It involves setting the output of each hidden neuron with the probability of 0.5 to zero. Dropout neurons are not used for both forward pass and backpropagation processes [46,47]. In this paper, image data augmentation is utilized to reduce overfitting. In future work, we will also explore emerging data augmentation methods that utilize generative adversarial networks (GANs) [48,49].

Despite various methods employed to reduce the dimension of input image data and the superior performance of the CNN, they are still computationally too expensive to use on a large scale to high-resolution image [46]. Figure 2 presents CNN architecture from [23]. It consists of eight layers between the input and output layers: the first five convolutional layers and the last three fully connected layers. The ReLU non-linearity was used as an activation function with the output of the first seven layers and the final fully connected layer is fed to 1000 SoftMax to represent 1000 class labels. For a detailed description of CNN architecture in Figure 2, the reader is referred to the [46]. As a CNN deepens with more layers, the training of the neural network becomes difficult, and performance in terms of accuracy starts to saturate and degrade [50]. Hence, many variants of CNN were developed to address these two issues, among which are residual learning (ResNet) and the model scaling method (EfficientNet).

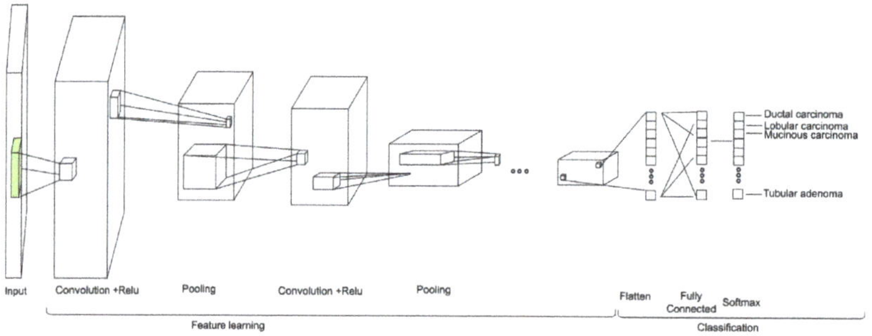

Figure 2. Architecture of a convolutions neural network (CNN) [51].

The residual learning (ResNet) architecture allows features to learn from residual connections rather than the full connection from the preceding layer. The skip connection as in Figure 3 is labeled x identity. This way the stacked layers are designed to learn the desired underlying mapping $H(x)$ without the x identity connection; however, the original mapping is recast by adding the output of the identity mapping to the output of the stacked layers. Details of ResNet and its variants can be found in [17].

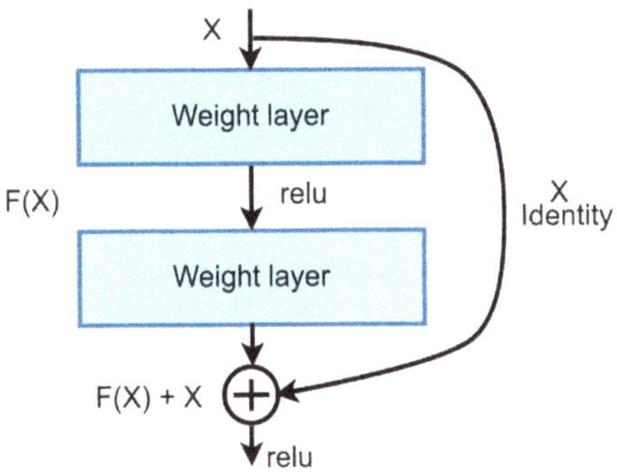

Figure 3. A building block of residual learning from [25].

Tan and Le [19] introduced a compound scaling method to increase the efficiency of a baseline model without altering the layered architecture. Tan and Le [19] named the variant CNN models EfficientNets. Instead of arbitrarily scaling the convNets depth, width, or image size, EfficientNets uniformly scale all three with a constant ratio. Figure 4 illustrates the compound scaling of convNets.

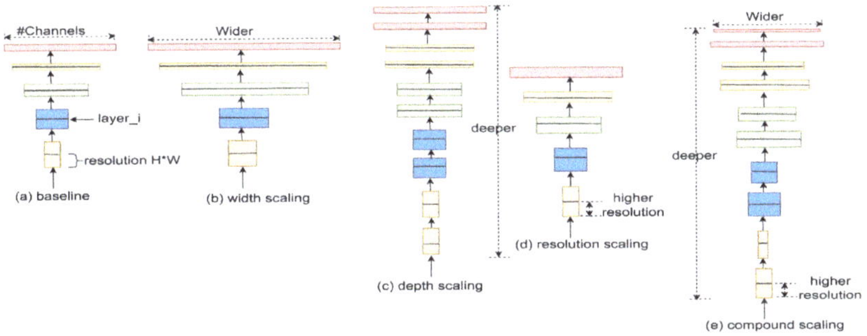

Figure 4. Illustrate model scaling from [29]. (**a**) is a baseline network example; (**b–d**) are conventional scaling that only increases one dimension of network width, depth, or resolution. The compound scaling method (**e**) is the compound scaling method that uniformly scales all three dimensions with a fixed ratio [22].

The main objective of compound model scaling is to maximize model accuracy for given resource constraints. This is formulated in [19] as an optimization problem:

$$\begin{aligned} &\max_{d,w,r} \text{Accuracy}(\mathcal{N}(d,w,r)) \\ &\quad \text{s.t. } \mathcal{N}(d,w,r) = \bigodot_{i=1\ldots s} \hat{\mathcal{F}}_i^{d\cdot\hat{L}_i}\left(X_{\langle r\cdot\hat{H}_i, r\cdot\hat{W}_i, w\cdot\hat{C}_i\rangle}\right) \\ &\quad \text{Memory}(\mathcal{N}) \leq \text{target\_memory} \\ &\quad \text{FLOPS}(\mathcal{N}) \leq \text{target\_flops} \end{aligned} \tag{9}$$

where N is a ConvNet, i a ConvNet layer, F_i is the operator, X_i is input tensor, $\langle r.\widehat{H}_i, r.\widehat{W}_i, r.\widehat{C}_i\rangle$ a tensor shape with spatial dimension H_i by W_i and the channel dimension $\widehat{C}_i.\widehat{F}_i, \widehat{L}_i, \widehat{H}_i, \widehat{W}_i, \widehat{C}_i$, which are predefined parameters in baseline network, and w, d, r are coefficients for scaling network width, depth and resolution, respectively, and $\bigodot$ is the tensor dot product of F_i.

The EfficientNets, such as ResNets, are a family of models, B0 to B7. Of interest to our work is EfficientNet-B0. Details of EfficientNets are in [52].

2.2. Pre-Trained DCNNs for Image Feature Extraction

To create the multi-scale pooled image feature representation (MPIFR) representation, features are extracted from four resolutions (40×, 100×, 200×, and 400×) of histopathological breast cancer images using four (4) state-of-the-art DCNN-based models (1) (Efficientnet-b0), (2) DenseNet201, (3) ResNet50, and (4) ResNet18.

ResNet18 [17] : ResNet has three variants according to its number of layers: ResNet18, ResNet50, and ResNet101 with 18, 50, and 101 layers, respectively. A transfer learning algorithm based on ResNet has been successfully used to classify biomedical images. ResNet18, shown in Figure 5, was used for feature extraction in this paper. The deep neural network layers learn low or high-level features during training, whereas the ResNet layer learns residuals instead.

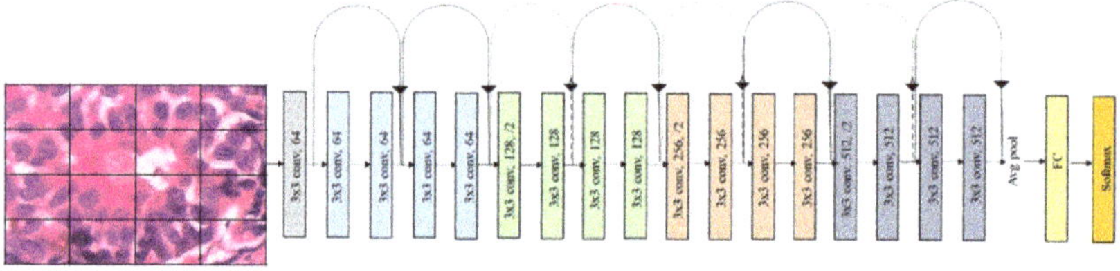

Figure 5. ResNet18 architecture.

EfficientNetB0 [19]: architecture and scaling method utilizes a compound coefficient to uniformly scale all depth, width, and resolution dimensions of the CNN using a set of fixed scale coefficients.In a principled manner, EfficientNet scales network width, depth, and resolution based on a single δ compound coefficient as expressed in Equation (10).

$$\begin{aligned} \text{depth: } d &= \alpha^{\phi} \\ \text{width: } w &= \beta^{\phi} \\ \text{resolution: } r &= \gamma^{\phi} \\ \text{s.t. } \alpha \cdot \beta^2 \cdot \gamma^2 &\approx 2 \\ \alpha \geq 1, \beta \geq 1, \gamma &\geq 1 \end{aligned} \tag{10}$$

For instance, in order to utilize 2N times more computational resources, the network depth can simply be increased by αN, the width by βN, and the image size by γN, where α, β, and γ are constant coefficients determined by a small grid search on the original small model. In order to capture more fine-grained patterns from a larger input image, the compound scaling method uses more layers to increase the receptive field and more channels to capture a larger number of channels. MobileNet-V2's inverted bottleneck residual blocks along with squeeze-and-excite blocks are the basis of EfficientNet-B0's base network. Figure 6 is the architecture for the EfficientNet B0 model.

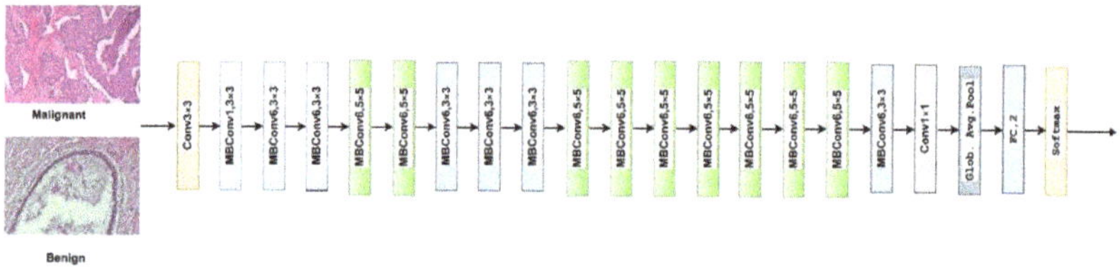

Figure 6. EfficientNetB0 architecture.

DenseNet201 [18]: Compared with conventional CNNs, DenseNet requires fewer parameters because it does not learn redundant feature maps. The DenseNet layers are relatively narrow, (12 filters), which adds a fewer number of new featuremaps. Four variants of DenseNet exist; DenseNet121, DenseNet169, DenseNet201, and DenseNet264. Our paper uses DenseNet201, which has 201 layers, to extract features. In DenseNet (see Figure 7), the input image and gradients from the loss function are accessible directly to each layer. DenseNet is therefore a good choice for image classification due to its reduced computational cost.

ResNet50 [17]: introduced a deep residual learning structure, which reformulates the CNN's layers as learning residual functions of the layer inputs. Correctly denoting the desired underlying mapping as $K(i)$, the stacked non-linear layers were made to fit another mapping of $E(i) := K(i) - i$. ResNet solved the vanishing gradient, whereby the value of the neural network's gradient decreases significantly during backpropagation until its weights barely change. ResNet solved the vanishing gradient problem using a skip connection, by adding the original input to the output of the convolutional block. A skip connection is a direct connection that skips over some of the model layers and can be expressed as $\mathbf{y} = \mathcal{F}(\mathbf{x}, \{W_i\}) + W_s\mathbf{x}$, where $\mathcal{F}(\mathbf{x}, \{W_i\})$ represents the residual mapping to be learned. Resnet utilizes the SGD optimizer with momentum given by Equation (11)

$$v_t = \rho v_{t-1} + \nabla f(x_{t-1}) x_t = x_{t-1} - \alpha v_t \tag{11}$$

where v_{t+1} is the momentum value, ρ is a friction, $\nabla f(x_{t-1})$ is the gradient of the objective function at iteration $t-1$, x_t are parameters and α is the learning rate. ResNet50 [17], which the MPIFR utilized, is a variant of ResNet. It has 48 convolutional layers, 1 MaxPool layer, and an average pool layer. Figure 8 is the architecture for the ResNet50 model.

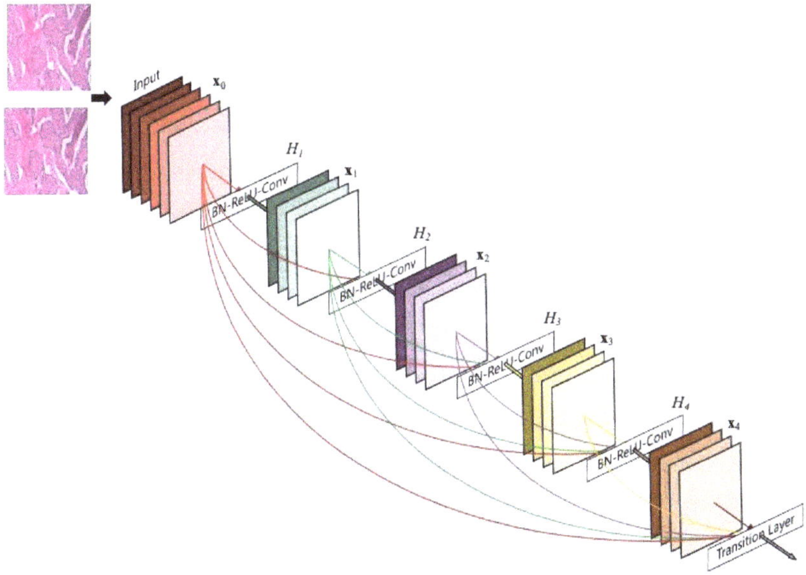

Figure 7. DenseNet201 architecture.

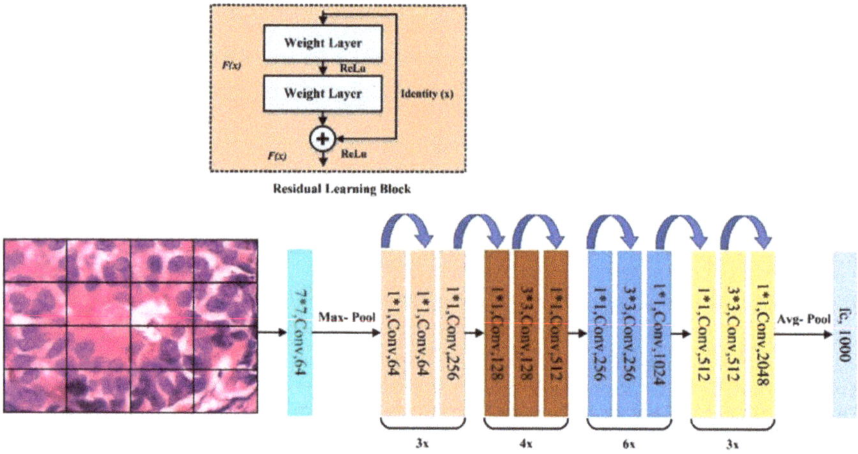

Figure 8. ResNet50 architecture.

2.3. *One-Versus-All Support Vector Machines (SVM) as a Multiple Class Classification Model*

SVM was utilized for the classification of the auto-extracted MPIFR. SVM with a radial basis function (RBF) kernel was utilized because it can represent a wide variety of classification boundaries ranging from simple, almost-linear models to complex, highly non-linear models. We now present the mathematical description and theoretical background of SVM. Further, we briefly described the architecture of two of the variant deep convolutional neural networks used to extract features in this study. By default, SVM is a binary classification algorithm. However, SVM and the related algorithms use a heuristic technique such as one-versus-one or one-versus-the-rest to build a binary classification model for multi-class classification. With eight target classes for the breast cancer BreakHis dataset, a total of 28 SVM classifiers are modeled based on the (k×(k − 1))/2 formula, where k is the number of classes. The details of the one-vs-one technique are presented in the subsequent section of this study. The goals of SVM are to separate data with a hyperplane and to extend this to non-linear boundaries using a kernel trick. Central to the construction of SVM is a small subset of data points extracted during the learning process from the training sample. This small subset of data points is the support vector.

To illustrate the SVM algorithm as a binary classifier, we formularized the task of estimating an f belonging to R^n, using pairs of input–output training data that are independent identically distributed (iid) such that: $f : R^n \to \{-1, +1\}$ according to an unknown probability distribution $p(x, y) : (x_1, y_1), (x_2, y_2), .., (x_n, y_n) \in R^n \times Y$ and $Y \in \{-1, +1\}$. An unseen example belongs to the class +1 if $f(x) \geqslant 0$ and to the class -1 otherwise.

The goal of a machine learning model is to find model parameters that will minimize the model sum of squared errors, which is known as the cost function. The SVM cost function is expressed in Equation (12). It is a modification of the cost function of logistic regression:

$$\min_{\theta} J(\theta) = C\sum_{i=1}^{m}[y^i cost_1(z) + (1-y^i)cost_0(z)] + \frac{1}{2}\sum_{j=1}^{n}\theta_j^2 \tag{12}$$

where θ is unknown parameters $z = \theta^T X$, $cost_1(z) = -\log\frac{1}{1+e^{-z}}$, for $y = 1$, $cost_0(z) = -log(1 - \frac{1}{1+e^{-z}})$, for $y = 0$ and $C = \frac{1}{\lambda}.\lambda$ is the regularization parameter which tends to decrease the model parameters without reducing the feature. This is useful for avoiding over-fitting. So, the SVM minimization cost function is convex, which is why it always converges to a global minimum. The SVM learning model (h) is expressed as:

$$h(x) = \begin{cases} 1, & if\, z \geqslant 0 \\ 0, & if\, z < 0 \end{cases} \quad (13)$$

In the minimization problem in Equation (12), when C is a big value, then it is likely that θ will be chosen to minimize the first term of Equation (12) to a value close to zero. Hence, $cost_1 = 0$ whenever $y = 1$ and $cost_0 = 0$ whenever $y = 0$. By implication, $cost(z)$ will approach zero when θ is found. That is $\theta^T X \geqslant 1$ or $\theta^T X \leqslant -1$. Hence, with the entire first term of the minimization problem being zero, the new minimization problem will be given by Equation (14):

$$\min_{\theta} J(\theta) = \frac{1}{2} \sum_{j=0}^{n} \theta_j^2 \quad (14)$$

Such that $\theta^T X \geqslant 1$, if $y^{(i)} = 1$ or $\theta^T X \leqslant -1$, if $y^{(i)} = 0$. The solution to the minimization problem in Equation (14) gives the decision boundary of SVM with a large margin.

3. Methodology

We now present a description of the dataset of histopathological breast cancer images utilized and the computational implementation of the ensemble model proposed in this study.

3.1. Histopathological Breast Cancer Dataset

We utilized the BreakHis dataset which is a publicly available open image dataset of hematoxylin-eosin (HE) stained histopathological slides. The histopathological images were obtained in four (4) optical intensification factors, specifically 40×, 100×, 200×, and 400× with an efficacious pixel sizes of 0.49 m, at 0.20 m, at 0.10 m, and at 0.0 m. The images were saved in RGB format in true color space. The pathologist spots a distinctive and appropriate region of interest (ROI) for diagnosis in every patient. The unwanted region, for instance, text clarification or dim edge was eliminated, and the images were edited to a component of 700 × 460 pixels. The distribution of benign and malignant images over various subtypes is shown in Table 2, and the sample images of benign and malignant subtypes are shown in Figures 9 and 10, respectively.

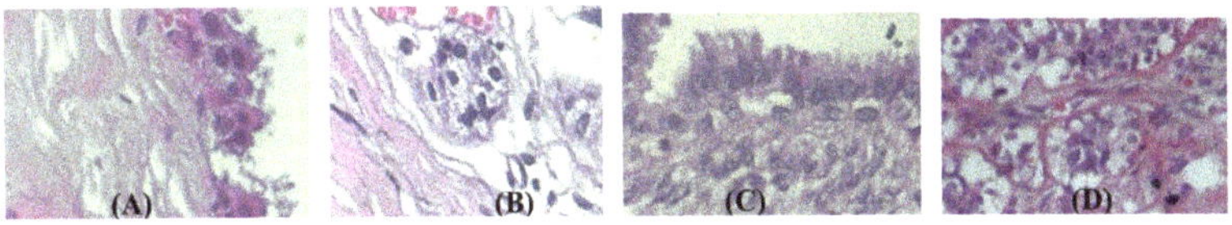

Figure 9. Sample of benign subtypes: (**A**) adenosis; (**B**) fibroadenoma; (**C**) phyllodes tumor; (**D**) tubular adenoma.

Table 2. The distribution of benign and malignant images over various subtypes.

Class	Subtype	No. of Patients	No. of Images
Benign	Adenosis	4	444
	Fibroadenoma	10	1014
	Phyllodes tumor	3	453
	Tubular adenoma	7	569
Malignant	Ductal carcinoma	38	3451
	Lobular carcinoma	5	626
	Mucinous carcinoma	9	792
	Papillary carcinoma	6	560
	Total	82	7909

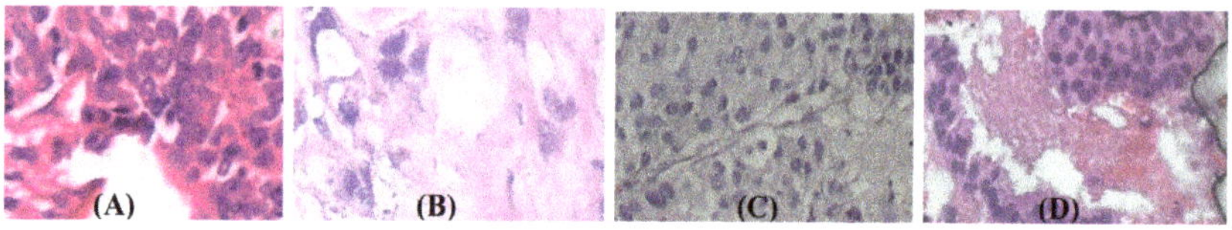

Figure 10. Sample of malignant subtypes: (**A**) ductal carcinoma; (**B**) lobular carcinoma; (**C**) mucinous carcinoma; (**D**) papillary carcinoma.

3.2. Computational Methodology of the Proposed Ensemble Model

In this section, we present our proposed ensemble model for the multi-class classification of breast cancer histopathology images. Four pre-trained DCNNs are utilized as deep feature extractors, namely; ResNet50, DenseNet201, EfficientNet-B0, and ResNet18. Our choice of pre-trained ConvNets was to reduce the training time and leverage the powerful image features learned from training on a large image dataset such as ImageNet. Further, pre-trained ConvNet models were evaluated using the benchmark image dataset, ImageNet [46]. More so, the idea is to bring together the good features generated by variant ConvNets structures (ResNet50, DenseNet201, EfficientNet-B0, and ResNet18) and pooled them as the features input to the SVM model for classification. Figure 11 illustrates the multi-scale pooled image feature representation (MPIFR) method proposed for this study and Figure 12 depicts the complete computational process end-to-end, from input to output.

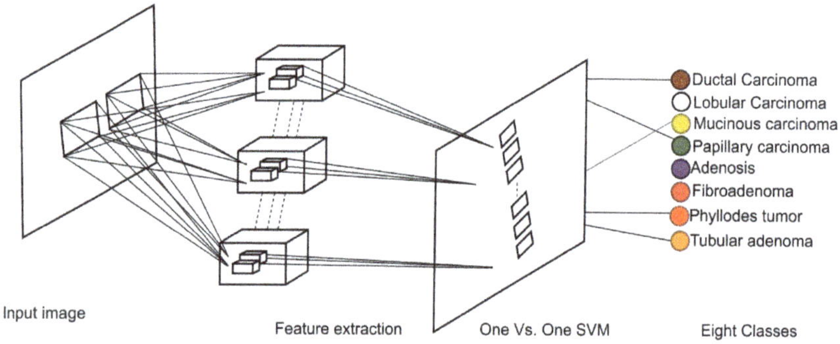

Figure 11. Proposed multi-scale pooled image feature representation (MPIFR) approach for multi-class classification of breast cancer.

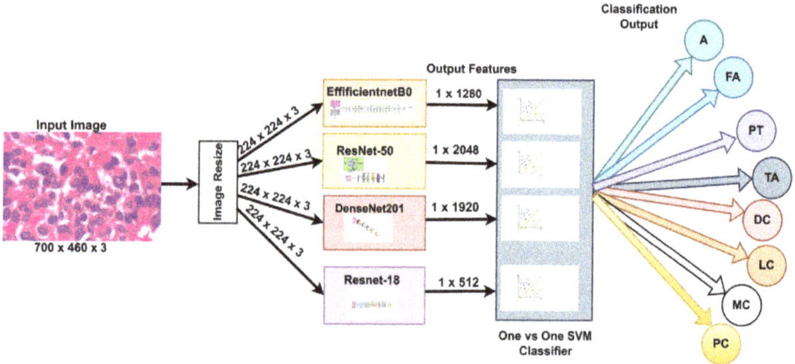

Figure 12. Computational process architecture for the ensemble model.

The cancer images are the input datasets to the three convNet models, which utilize unsupervised learning (as described in Section 2.2) to extract features from the input images. Each of the baseline models utilizes SoftMax as an output function for multi-class problems.

However, in this study, we use the one-vs-one technique with SVM for the eight-class classification of the 8 cancer subtypes from breast cancer images. Recall that SoftMax is a generalization of logistic regression, and logistic regression is susceptible to overfitting. Replacing SoftMax with SVM will guarantee convergence. As it is well known, the cost function of SVM is convex. In the one-vs-one technique, a pairwise SVM classifier of the breast cancer image classes is modeled using the training features extracted. A total of 28 SVM classifiers are built for the 8 classes of breast cancer datasets based on the $\frac{(k\times(k-1))}{2}$ formula where k is the number of classes. Finally, a test breast cancer image is predicted based on the class output of the SVM models with a majority of counts. This model uses a heuristic technique to classify into one target class. This method is different from the previous method in [53], which first classifies input data into benign or malignant binary classes before being further categorized using two modules; one for benign and the other for malignant. Each module contains a ConvNet structure with a decision tree for subclass classification.

To further explain the proposed ensemble model mathematically, consider X_i as a feature vector extracted from an input image by a pre-trained ConvNet baseline i. i is a concatenation of features extracted from the input image by convNet baselines $i = 1, 2..., n$. In this study, $n = 4$ for the four baselines pre-trained convNets used in this study. Recall that in Equation 2, $h(x)$ is defined as the SVM learning model. Thus, $h_j(X) \in H(X)$, where $H(X)$ is the set of SVM learning models, and $h_j(X)$ is an individual SVM classifier for a pair of class (y_d, y_l). $j = 1, 2, ..., m$ indicates the number of classifiers, $d = 1, 2, ..., k-1$, and $l = 1, 2, ..., k$. In this study, $k = 8$ and $m = 28$ indicate the number of breast cancer classes and the total number of SVM classifiers, respectively. Note that $h_j(X)$ does not exist for a pair of classes where $y_d \geqslant y_l$. Table 3 illustrates the matrix for the pairs of classes. A tick indicates the valid pair and blank cells indicate not a valid pairing.

In making a classification, a feature X of an unseen image is input to all binary classifiers and produced a class k for which the corresponding classifier with the majority counts:

$$\hat{y}_l = \underset{l\in 1,\ldots,k}{\operatorname{argmax}} H_l(X) \tag{15}$$

Table 3. The valid number of classifiers for one-versus-one SVM.

	y_1	y_2	y_3	y_4	y_5	y_6	y_7	y_8
y_1		✓	✓	✓	✓	✓	✓	✓
y_2			✓	✓	✓	✓	✓	✓
y_3				✓	✓	✓	✓	✓
y_4					✓	✓	✓	✓
y_5						✓	✓	✓
y_6							✓	✓
y_7								✓

4. Experimental Details

We present the detailed experiment conducted in this study. Starting with the pre-processing and trimming of the assessed dataset, extraction of features using deep CNN baselines, and SVM used for multi-level classification. The experiment was conducted using MATLAB software R2021a on a Windows 10 machine with the following specifications—Processor: Intel Core i7-10750Hcpu@2.6 GHz 2.59 GHz, with RAM of 16 GB DDR4 1TB SSD storage. Further, it comes with a GPU card with 4 GB of GDDR5 and GDDR6 memory clocked at 8 GHz; altogether it has a 128-bit memory interface that creates a bandwidth of 112.1 GB/s.

4.1. Pre-Processing

We provide the details of the image datasets for this study in Section 4.1. Each instance of an image comes in four magnification factors (x40, x100, x200, and x400). To make our learning model more robust in classifying images irrespective of the quality of the BreakHis image, we combine all BreakHis images of the same subtype as one class regardless of their intensification factor. These are shown in Table 2. In total, there are 7909 BreakHis images.

4.2. Image Augmentation

We apply image augmentation to improve learning performance for two reasons. First, looking at the distribution of datasets in Table 2, we observed a class imbalance in the dataset. For example, one class (ductal carcinoma) contains over 3000 instances, and the others (adenosis, phyllodes tumor, papillary carcinoma, etc.) have 500 examples on average. Class imbalance can lead to building a model that is biased and will fail to generalize. In order to augment only the training set of the original dataset and yield a larger training corpus, rotation, and horizontal flip operations were applied. Since we need to consider the class imbalance, the oversampling augmentation was performed to increase the number of instances of all cancer subtypes except ductal carcinoma. Figure 13 shows sample results of data augmentation and Table 4 presents the distribution of images in each target class after applying the oversampling data augmentation technique.

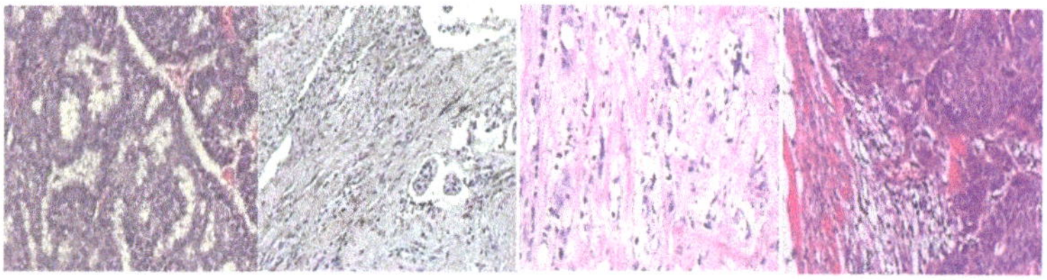

Figure 13. Example images after applying oversampling data augmentation operations.

Table 4. The distribution of benign and malignant images over various subtypes after applying augmentation techniques.

Subtype	Original No. of Instances	No. of Training Instances	No. of Test Instances	No. of Training Instances after Oversampling
Adenosis	444	311	133	2416
Fibroadenoma	1014	710	304	2416
Phyllodes tumor	453	317	136	2416
Tubular adenoma	569	398	171	2416
Ductal carcinoma	3451	2416	1035	2416
Lobular carcinoma	626	438	188	2416
Mucinous carcinoma	792	554	238	2416
Papillary carcinoma	560	392	168	2416
Total	7909	5536	2373	19,328

After the augmentation, the total number of BreakHis images increased to almost three times the original number of images (from 7909 images to 21,701 images). However, it should be noted while this data augmentation step addressed the class imbalance, in terms of pathological processes, the creation of variation in data does not produce variability within the disease itself.

4.3. Image Resizing

The original images have a size of 700 × 460 × 3. However, these were resized to 224 × 224 × 3 size to be suitable for the pre-trained networks. The four pre-trained models (ResNet50, ResNet18, EfficientNetB0, and DenseNet201) have 224 × 224 image input size networks.

4.4. Model Selection

To train the MPIFR architecture, we re-trained eight baseline models with the breast cancer images (namely, inceptionv3, inceptionresnetv2, Resnet18, Resnet50, Densenet201, Efficientnetb0, ShuffleNet, and SqueezeNet) all of which are state-of-the-art pre-trained models. We selected four out of the eight models that performed best to train our ensemble deep learning algorithm. The four-baseline models selected are ResNet50, ResNet18, DenseNet201, and EfficientNetb0. The four models were set up as described in Figures 11 and 12 for feature extraction.

4.5. Feature Extraction

The combined features totaling 5760 were extracted by the four baseline ConvNets. Before data augmentation, the entire datasets were divided into train and test subsets in the ratio of 7:3 (5536: 2373), respectively. Table 5 presents the details of the feature set generated by each baseline model and the combination of the four for the ensemble model. The feature input for the proposed ensemble model is a concatenation of the features generated from four baseline models (ResNet50, DenseNet201, ResNet18, and EfficientNetB0).

Figure 14 presents the one-vs-one coding matrix designed for the eight classes of breast cancer that yield twenty-eight binary classifiers. Each column of the coding matrix is one hot-encoding corresponding to a classifier, and each row corresponds to one of the eight breast cancer classes. For example, the first column of Figure 14 is [1; −1; 0; 0; 0; 0; 0; 0] indicating that the ensemble model trains the first SVM binary classifier using features classifier as Adenosis and Ductal carcinoma because Adenosis corresponds to a positive class; ductal carcinoma corresponds to −1, so it is a negative class. A class output of an unseen breakHis image sample x is determined by the ensemble model using majority voting count as in Equation (16):

$$\hat{y} = \underset{k \in 1,\ldots,8}{\operatorname{argmax}} f_k(x) \tag{16}$$

where $\hat{y}$ is the class with majority count, k is the class label, and $f_k(x)$ is the predicting model for the label k for which the corresponding classifier reports the highest confidence score.

1	1	1	1	1	1	1	0	0	0	0	0	0	0	0	0	0	0	0	0	0	0	0	0	0	0	0	0
-1	0	0	0	0	0	0	1	1	1	1	1	1	0	0	0	0	0	0	0	0	0	0	0	0	0	0	0
0	-1	0	0	0	0	0	-1	0	0	0	0	0	1	1	1	1	1	0	0	0	0	0	0	0	0	0	0
0	0	-1	0	0	0	0	0	-1	0	0	0	0	-1	0	0	0	0	1	1	1	1	0	0	0	0	0	0
0	0	0	-1	0	0	0	0	0	-1	0	0	0	0	-1	0	0	0	-1	0	0	0	1	1	1	0	0	0
0	0	0	0	-1	0	0	0	0	0	-1	0	0	0	0	-1	0	0	0	-1	0	0	-1	0	0	1	1	0
0	0	0	0	0	-1	0	0	0	0	0	-1	0	0	0	0	-1	0	0	0	-1	0	0	-1	0	-1	0	1
0	0	0	0	0	0	-1	0	0	0	0	0	-1	0	0	0	0	-1	0	0	0	-1	0	0	-1	0	-1	-1

Figure 14. Coding matrix for the eight classes of breast cancer.

Table 5. Detail distribution of the dataset and features extracted.

Models	Train Feature Size	Test Features Size
ResNet50	19,328 × 2048	2373 × 2048
ResNet18	19,328 × 512	2373 × 512
DenseNet201	19,328 × 1920	2373 × 1920
EfficientNetB0	19,328 × 1280	2373 × 1280
Ensemble Model	19,328 × 5760	2373 × 5760

4.6. DCNN Model Interpretability Using Grad-CAM

DCNN Model Interpretability using Grad-CAM [54]. This experiment aimed to ensure that breast cancer classification models focus on the appropriate regions of images when analyzing them. In Grad-CAM, the gradient of the ranking score is computed in relation to the DCNN characteristics map, highlighting specific ROIs based on the greatest gradient score. Grad-CAM computes gradients with respect to feature maps of a convolutional layer that are then global-average-pooled to determine importance weights α_k^c, which represents a partial linearization of the deep network downstream from A, capturing the importance of feature map k for a target class c:

$$\alpha_k^c = \overbrace{\frac{1}{Z}\sum_i\sum_j}^{\text{global average pooling}} \qquad \underbrace{\frac{\partial y^c}{\partial A_{i,j}^k}}_{\text{gradients via backprop}} \tag{17}$$

is the gradient of the score for class c, y^c , with respect to feature maps A^k of a convolutional layer. A Grad-CAM heat-map is then generated as a weighted combination of forward activation feature maps, but followed by a ReLU activation function:

$$L_{Grad-CAM}^c = ReLU \quad \underbrace{\left(\sum_k \alpha_k^c A^k\right)}_{\text{linear combination}} \tag{18}$$

where $L_{Grad-CAM}^c$ is the class-discriminative localization map Grad-CAM that was applied to produce a coarse localized map highlighting the most important ROIs in the histopathological images to classify the images as benign or malignant. Sample Grad-CAM results are shown in Figures 15 and 16.

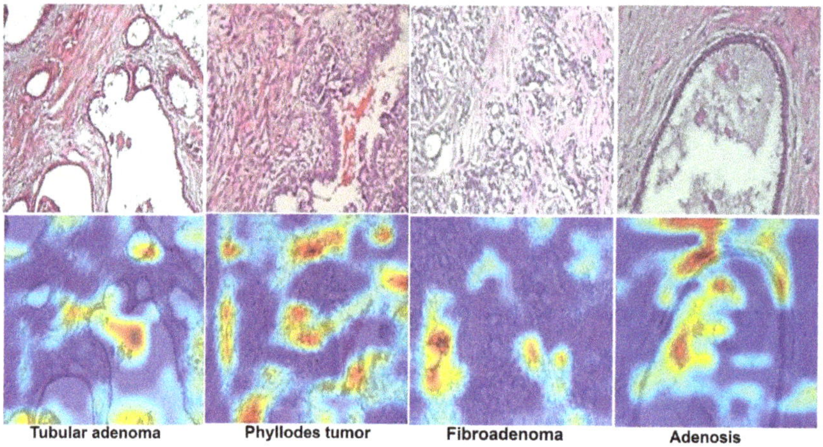

Figure 15. Sample of regions of interest generated by Grad-CAM (top = benign subtypes original images, bottom = benign Grad-CAM heatmap.

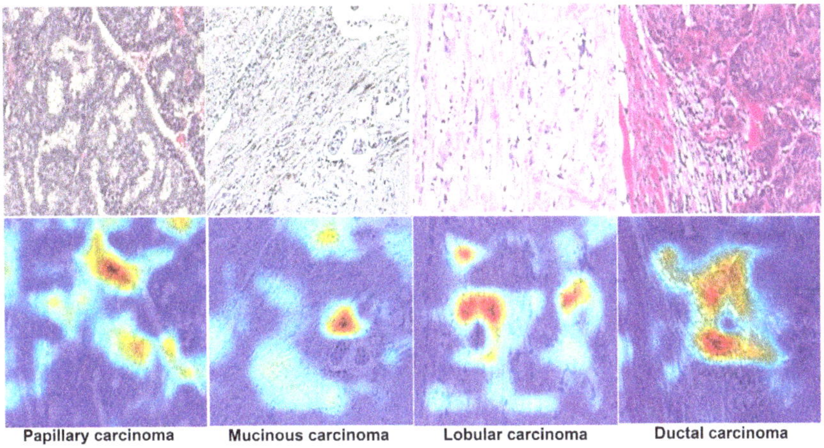

Figure 16. Sample of regions of interest generated by Grad-CAM (top = malignant subtypes original images, bottom = malignant Grad-CAM heatmap.

4.7. Classifying the MPIFR Representation Using Different Machine Learning Classifiers

The goal of this experiment was to compare the performance of the one vs. one support vector machines (SVM) with other traditional machine learning (ML) classifiers for the task of classifying the MPIFR representation into target labels of malignant (ductal carcinoma, lobular carcinoma, mucinous carcinoma, and papillary carcinoma) subtypes of tumors from (adenosis, fibroadenoma, phyllodes tumor, and tubular adenoma benign harmless subtypes. Results in Table 6 show that one vs. one SVM outperformed all other ML classifiers on all metrics except sensitivity for this 8-class classification task, likely because one vs. one SVM was designed to perform well on multiclassification tasks.

Table 6. Results of classifying the MPIFR with various machine learning (ML) classifiers.

Models	Accuracy	Sensitivity	Precision	Specificity	F1-Score	AUC
K-Nearest Neighbor (KNN)	95.85	97.48	92.85	98.84	94.91	97.52
Generalized Additive Model	94.45	92.50	96.17	99.02	92.69	95.25
Naïve Bayes	95.15	98.80	91.18	97.98	93.83	96.89
Gradient Boosted Machines (GBM)	96.55	95.73	97.17	98.64	95.91	97.61
MPIFR	97.77	97.48	98.45	99.57	97.92	99.00

5. Results

We present the results of various experiments we have conducted in this study. To evaluate the performance of our proposed ensemble architecture, individual baseline models were trained first that would serve as a basis for comparison of our eventual method and also to discover which DCNN architectures performed best. Out of the eight models, the four best-performing baseline models were selected to evaluate the performance of our ensemble architecture. Table 7 shows the performance of the baseline models.

Table 7. Performance of the eight pre-trained models.

Models	Accuracy of the Pre-Trained Baseline Models (%)	Elapsed Training Time (Hours)
Efficientnetb0	92.08	8.89
ResNet50	92.84	5.9
Inceptionresnetv2	90.43	33.46
Inceptionv3	90.73	0.71
ResNet18	91.32	2.33
DenseNet201	93.34	33.95
Squeezenet	85.92	1.47
Shufflenet	90.60	3.25

Only baseline models with accuracy above 90% were selected, which include ResNet50, ResNet18, DenseNet201, and EfficientNetb0. The selected models were pre-trained models using the hyperparameter values presented in Table 8. We trained the MPIFR by first combining the selected baseline models in pairs, in threes, and all four selected models.

Table 8. Set of hyper-parameters for training baseline models using transfer learning.

Hyperparameter	Value
Train-Test ratio	70:30
Activation function	ReLU
Mini Batch Size	20
Max Epochs	30
Initial Learn Rate	0.00125
Learn-Rate Drop Factor	0.1
Learn-Rate Drop Period	20

The result of combining the selected baseline models are presented in Table 9. The result shows significant improvement from a combined pair of baseline models in comparison to all four selected baseline models. However, model training takes more time when a large number of models are combined as indicated by the training time in hours presented in Table 9. The ensemble model took more than two (2) days to train because the final training time was that combined training time for all four models utilized in our MPIFR method. Further, we note that while the MPIFR model training time is large in some cases, training time is incurred once during model development. Test time is typically faster and is more important when the model is deployed and operationalized. We believe that it is reasonable to trade off higher training time to achieve higher performance.

Table 9. Performance of the different combination of baseline models.

Modes	Accuracy (%)	Time (Hours)
Densenet201_Resnet50	0.9684	39.87
Densenet201_Efficientnetb0	0.9562	42.99
Densenet201_Resnet18	0.9617	36.28
Resnet18_ Resnet50	0.9633	8.23
Resnet50_Efficientnetb0	0.9676	14.8
Resnet18_Efficientnetb0	0.9587	11.225
Resnet18_Efficientnetb0_Densenet	0.9676	45.17
Resnet18_Efficientnetb0_Resnet50	0.9730	17.12
Efficientnetb0_Densenet_Resnet50	0.9739	48.74
Resnet50_Densenet_Resnet18	0.9735	42.18
Ensemble model	**0.9777**	50.79

The ensemble model in Table 9 combines the four selected baseline models namely ResNet50, DenseNet201, ResNet18, and EfficientNetb0. The resulting performance is the best of the state-of-the-art multi-class models of the histopathological breast cancer classification based on BreakHis images.

Confusion Matrix: In order to determine which classes were confounded by other classes, we analyzed the confusion matrix. Figure 17 shows the confusion matrix of the top-performing technique. Columns correspond to targeted classes and rows to output classes. Diagonal cells correspond to correctly classified observations. Off-diagonal cells are referred to as incorrect classifications. There is also a percentage of the overall number of observations and a number of observations for each cell. On the extreme right, you can see the proportion of incorrectly predicted classifications (red color) and correctly predicted classifications (green color). In statistics, these metrics are called false discovery rate and positive predictive value. The lowest row indicates the percentage of incorrectly classified and correctly classified results, referred to as false negative rate (FNR) and true positive rate (TPR). In the bottom-most right cell, you can see the general precision. Column-normalized column summaries show the percentage of correctly classified observations for every predicted class. Using row-standardized row summaries, you can see how many observations are incorrectly classified and how many are correctly classified. As can be seen in the confusion matrix, the majority of results fall on the leading diagonal with very few off the diagonal, demonstrating that the proposed approach did not confuse benign and malignant cells.

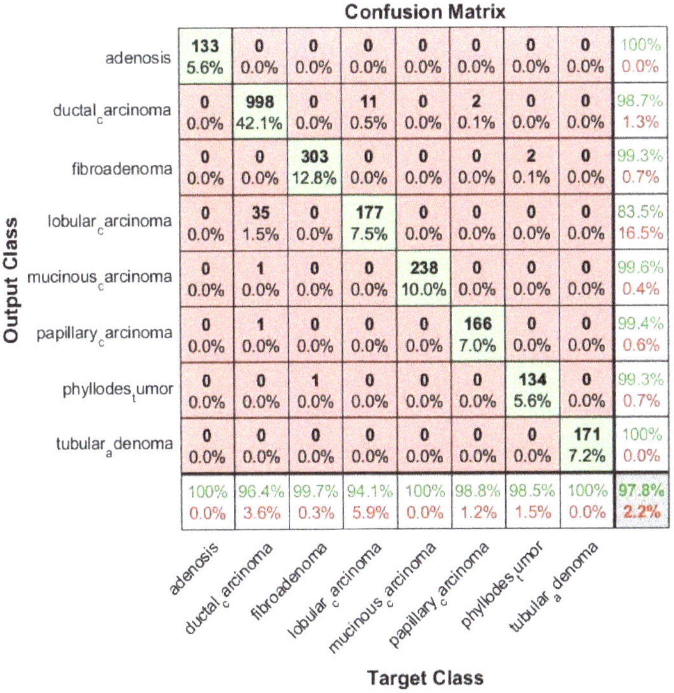

Figure 17. Confusion matrix displaying the performance of the proposed ensemble approach.

The MPIFR model classified all eight cancer subtypes with 97.77% accuracy and 99.57% specificity on average. This means that for a specific subtype, the individual classifier in our proposed model has a high ability to discriminate one class of BC subtype from another. The classifier SVM performance was evaluated with ten-fold cross-validation with a cross-validation error of 0.0432. This is a good indication of the significance and consistency of the results of classifiers of the corresponding individual cancer subtypes. Further, to demonstrate that the difference in performance between the MPIFR and other ensemble baselines was statistically significant, the Nemenyi post hoc test [55] was performed. At a confidence level of a = 0.05, the critical distance (CD) is 1.2536. Our model F1-score is 97.92%. The F1-score is the harmonic average of precision and sensitivity. While precision measures the extent of the error caused by false positives and sensitivity measures the extent of the error caused by the false negative. Figure 18 is a T-SNE plot that illustrates that our proposed MPIFR method adequately discriminates between the eight target BC classes in feature space.

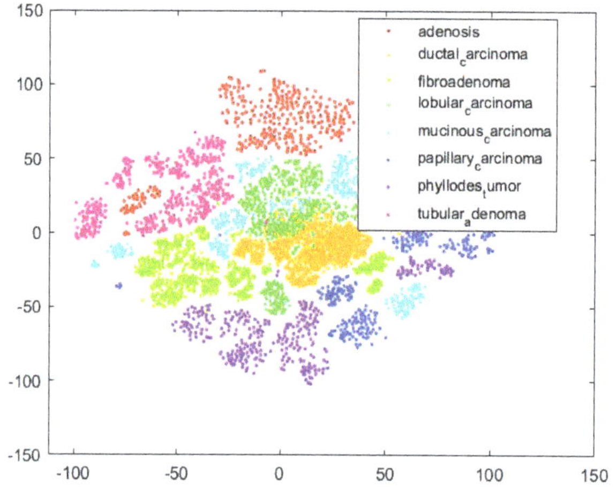

Figure 18. T-SNE visualization to illustrate that our proposed MPIFR method adequately discriminates between the eight target BC classes in feature space .

AUC is an effective way to summarize the overall accuracy of the test. In general, an AUC of 0.5 suggests no discrimination (i.e., the ability to diagnose patients with or without the BC based on the test), 0.7 to 0.8 is considered acceptable, 0.8 to 0.9 is considered excellent, and more than 0.9 is considered outstanding. The MPIFR has an AUC of 0.99 (99%). Table 10 presents detailed results of the performance of the ensemble model.

Table 10. Performance of ensemble model for each of the eight classes.

Disease	Accuracy (%)	Precision (%)	Sensitivity (%)	Specificity (%)	F1-Score (%)	AUC (%)
Adenosis	100	100	100	100	100	100
Ductal Carcinoma	98.7	96.43	98.71	97.28	97.56	98.00
Fibroadenoma	99.3	99.67	99.34	99.95	99.51	99.65
Lobular Carcinoma	83.5	94.15	83.49	99.49	88.50	91.49
Mucinous Carcinoma	99.6	100	99.58	100	99.79	99.79
Papillary Carcinoma	99.4	98.81	99.40	99.91	99.10	99.66
Phyllodes Tumor	99.3	98.53	99.26	99.91	98.89	99.58
Tubular Adenoma	100	100	100	100	100	100

6. Discussion

As shown in Table 10, in rigorous evaluation experiments, the proposed MPIFR outperformed a comprehensive set of baseline models and also previous state-of-the-art techniques for both binary and multiclassification (Table 1) of histopathological images. Our results also demonstrate that all key components of our approach contribute non-trivially to its superior results, including:

Transfer learning by pre-training on a large image repository (ImageNet) with fine-tuning on the BreakHis breast cancer image dataset: that enables the CNN feature extractors models to learn a robust image representation from the large image repository. Fine-tuning on the BreakHis breast cancer dataset transfers the learned intelligence to the task of analyzing and classifying breast cancer. This conclusion is evident in Table 9.

Using an ensemble of DCNNs for deep feature extractors: This step also facilitates downstream classification with traditional machine learning algorithms such as SVM. Deep MPIFRs are a powerful representation, which had the best performance for all combinations of the DCNN model explored in this study as shown in Table 7. The proposed technique of using MPIFR features, combined and classified using SVM outperformed single DCNN models approaches in Table 6. Compared with a single pre-trained CNN, it achieves superior performance for feature extraction (see Tables 6 and 8). While SVM is utilized for final classification, pre-trained CNNs were utilized for feature extraction. SVM, a classic machine learning algorithm was utilized for classification because the features extracted by the CNN are relatively small for each of the target classes. We also show in Table 8 that the four state-of-the-art CNN models (ResNet50, ResNet18, DenseNet201, and EfficientNetb0), which were discovered through extensive experimentation and employed to extract features, outperform other CNN combinations and ensembles. The features extracted by each DCNN are slightly different intuitively. Multi-CNN feature extraction produces a superset of features that outperforms single-CNN feature extraction.

One-versus-one SVM effectively performs 8-class Bc classification: was used as a heuristic technique such as a one-versus-one binary classification model for multi-class classification. With eight target classes for the breast cancer BreakHis dataset, a total of 28 SVM classifiers are modeled based on the $(k(k-1))/2$ formula, where k is the number of classes. The result of the one-vs-one technique is presented in Figure 17.

Our proposed MPIFR method outperforms the state-of-the-art for 8-class BC classification: as shown in Table 1 in which various proposed BC image classification models are compared in terms of the proposed method, classification type, accuracy, F1-score, specificity, and AUC. All models in the table utilize the BreakHis breast cancer image datasets. As seen in Table 1, the proposed MPIFR model built for 8-class classification performed better than the other state-of-the-art multi-class models. Multiclassification of breast cancer images into eight (8) subtypes of malignant and benign are much more challenging [39]. It can be the basis of a computer-aided grading diagnosis system for BC histopathology. Compared to Murtaza et al. [28], Gandomkar et al. [30] etc., the proposed ensemble model outperformed (97.77%) the other state-of-the-art multi-class BC classifiers.

Besides that, our study and that of Han et al. are the only ones to perform eight (8) class classifications. The other studies performed four (4) class classifications. Han et al., in their study, used the structured deep learning model, and did not perform feature extraction using pre-trained DCNNs, achieving an accuracy of 93.2% on histopathological images. However, the proposed ensemble model in this study extract features from four pre-trained models and trains SVM classifiers in a one-vs-one approach. The trained model classifies test subset BreakHis images irrespective of the difference in magnification factor. Hypothetically this means that the proposed ensemble model will classify the image with high accuracy regardless of the difference in magnification of the input image. In addition, despite ensemble architecture consisting of multiple baseline models and multiple classifiers, the built model is a single model with reduced generalization error of the prediction. Except for Murtaza et al. [28], the existing models reported only performance accuracy. Other relevant metrics such as precision, sensitivity, and specificity measures are missing. They are crucial to deciding the consistency and significance of an AI-based BC medical screening and grading system.

We present criteria for selecting machine learning techniques to support the decision of classifying BC from histopathological images in Table 10. One of the objectives of using an AI-based application is to assist medical specialists with rapid screening for disease by assessing medical images and deciding on the presence or absence of a specific medical condition. A more complex AI-based application can further assess medical images and diagnose the extent or grade of a specified medical condition. The former is an AI-based screening system, and the latter is AI-based grading system. Deep learning is a state-of-the-art machine learning (ML) technique, which has been highly successful in various computer vision and image analysis tasks, substantially outperforming all clinical image analysis techniques [25]. Although deep learning models outperform other traditional clinical image analysis techniques, they are still susceptible to false positive and false negative rates. For these reasons, some criteria should be considered when selecting a deep learning model as an AI-based medical system. Table 11 presents criteria for selecting machine learning techniques to support the decision of BC classification from histopathological images.

A deep learning algorithm trained to model BC classification should only be adopted for an AI-based screening or grading system after it has passed a prospective study test. The prospective study is carried out when both a licensed specialist and an AI-based system independently examine BC histopathological images from the same person/patient. The prospective study will compare the diagnostic capability of an AI-based model with respect to actual oncologists evaluating the histopathological image in real-time. In the case of selecting an AI-based model for BC screening in low-incidence regions, in addition to the prospective study, a deep learning model will have high accuracy, sensitivity, and specificity scores with a benchmark histopathological image. It should take a few seconds to run and generate a report and should be lightweight. Such a model should be robust enough to accommodate images of different magnification factors. Lastly, deep learning for grading should score high in all of the selection criteria as indicated in Table 11.

Table 11. Criteria for selecting machine learning techniques to support the decision of classifying BC from histopathological images.

Criteria	AI-Based Screening in Low Incidence of Cancer	AI-Based Screening in High Incidence of Cancer	AI-Based Grading System
Accuracy measure	high	high	high
Sensitivity measure	high	optional	high
Specificity measure	high	optional	high
Model complexity	small	very small	very small
Model robustness	high	high	high
Prospective study	needed	needed	needed

Limitations of this work and potential future work: Some limitations can be addressed in future work. Before deploying classifiers in hospitals, more images with more magnifications could be included in the dataset for more robust classification. Secondly, the MPIFR was based on four existing models. Future performance could be improved by fusing more deeper models. We would also like to validate our results on other histopathological breast cancer datasets. Lastly, mobile devices can be a promising platform for our methods to be implemented.

7. Conclusions

We have proposed a multi-scale pooled image feature representation (MPIFR) deep learning architecture with one-versus-one SVM for 8-class BC histopathological image classification. The proposed method of four pre-trained DCNN architectures (ResNet50, ResNet18, DenseNet201, and EfficientNetb0) to extract highly predictive multi-scale pooled image feature representation (MPIFR) from four resolutions (40X, 100X, 200X, and 400X) of BC images that are then classified using one-versus all SVM has been presented. In rigorous evaluation, the proposed MPIFR method achieved an average accuracy of 97.77%, with 97.48% sensitivity, and 98.45% precision on the BreakHis histopathological BC image dataset, outperforming the prior state-of-the-art for histopathological breast cancer multi-class classification and a comprehensive set of DCNN baseline models.

With an evaluation based on a prospective study, the proposed ensemble model can reliably aid diagnosis for BC histopathology at high precision and sensitivity scores. Model complexity measures indicate how fast the model can take in the histopathological images and produce a classification result. Further, model complexity specification can be in terms of storage space. A lightweight model can be embedded into mobile apps in developing countries. A robust model should be able to accommodate images at a vary magnification factors. An AI-based model with only a high accuracy measure and having passed a prospective study can be considered in high BC incidence regions as a rapid screening system. In a future study, we will investigate other possible pre-trained models, particularly conVNet with fewer connections. This will give a lightweight grading system for use in places with low access to computational resources.

Author Contributions: D.C., E.A., M.A.S. and W.S. conceived the presented idea; D.C., M.A.S. and E.A. developed the theory and performed the computations; E.A., M.A.S. and W.S. verified the analytical methods; E.A., M.A.S. and W.S. encouraged D.C. to investigate the algorithm used for this work and supervised the findings of this work. J.O. and S.A. were involved in the conceptualization and supervision of the research. All authors discussed the results and contributed to the final manuscript. All authors have read and agreed to the published version of the manuscript.

Funding: This research was supported in part by World Bank through the African Centre of Excellence Program hosted by Pan African Materials Institute (AUST/PAMI/2015 5415-NG); the WPI Global Impact Fellowship Program, the WPI Innovation Fellowship, and the African Development Bank (AFDB).

Institutional Review Board Statement: The research utilized a de-identified, public dataset and IRB approval was not necessary.

Informed Consent Statement: The research utilized a de-identified, public dataset and IRB approval was not necessary.

Data Availability Statement: This study is based on the publically available BreakHis dataset from the laboratory of Vision, Robotics, and Imaging (VRI), Federal University of Parana (FUPR). The BreakHis dataset is available at the following URL: https://web.inf.ufpr.br/vri/databases/breast-cancer-histopathological-database-breakhis/ (accessed on 1 November 2022).

Conflicts of Interest: The authors declare no conflict of interest.

References

1. Manon Cairat Nutrition and the Risk of Breast Cancer—IARC. Available online: https://www.iarc.who.int/news-events/video-ms-manon-cairat-on-nutrition-and-the-risk-of-breast-cancer/ (accessed on 7 October 2022).
2. ICA Breast Cancer. Available online: https://en.cancer.org.il/template_e/default.aspx?PageId=7749 (accessed on 1 November 2022).
3. Omar, A.; Bakr, A.; Ibrahim, N. Female medical students' awareness, attitudes, and knowledge about early detection of breast cancer in Syrian Private University, Syria. *Heliyon* **2020**, *6*, e03819. [CrossRef] [PubMed]
4. Murtaza, G.; Shuib, L.; Wahab, A.W.A.; Mujtaba, G.; Nweke, H.F.; Al-Garadi, M.A.; Zulfiqar, F.; Raza, G.; Azmi, N.A.Deep learning-based breast cancer classification through medical imaging modalities: State of the art and research challenges. *Artif. Intell. Rev.* **2019**, *53*, 1655–1720. [CrossRef]
5. Yersal, O.; Barutca, S. Biological subtypes of breast cancer: Prognostic and therapeutic implications.*World J. Clin. Oncol.* **2014**, *5*, 412. [CrossRef]
6. Rakha, E.A.; Ellis, I.O. Modern Classification of Breast Cancer: Should we Stick With Morphology or Convert to Molecular Profile Characteristics. *Adv. Anat. Pathol.* **2011**, *18*, 255–267. [CrossRef] [PubMed]
7. Doi, K. Current status and future potential of computer-aided diagnosis in medical imaging. *J. Radiol.* **2005**, *78*, 21–30. [CrossRef]
8. Salama, M.S.; Eltrass, A.S.; Elkamchouchi, N.H. An Improved Approach for Computer-Aided Diagnosis of Breast Cancer in Digital Mammography. In Proceedings of the 2018 IEEE International Symposium on Medical Measurements and Applications (MeMeA), Rome, Italy, 11–13 June 2018; pp. 1–5.

9. Maglaveras, N.; Chouvarda, I.; de Carvalho, P. Precision Medicine Powered by pHealth and Connected Health. In Proceedings of the ICBHI 2017, Thessaloniki, Greece, 18–21 November 2017; Volume 66.
10. Asri, H.; Mousannif, H.; Al, H.; Noel, T. Using Machine Learning Algorithms for Breast Cancer Risk Prediction and Diagnosis *Procedia Comput. Sci.* **2016**, *83*, 1064–1069. [CrossRef]
11. Amrane, M. Breast cancer classification using machine learning. In Proceedings of the 2018 Electric Electronics, Computer Science, Biomedical Engineerings' Meeting (EBBT), Istanbul, Turkey, 18–19 April 2018; pp. 1–4.
12. Litjens, G.; Kooi, T.; Bejnordi, B.E.; Setio, A.A.A.; Ciompi, F.; Ghafoorian, M.; Van Der Laak, J.A.; Van Ginneken, B.; Sánchez, C.I. A survey on deep learning in medical image analysis. *Med. Image Anal.* **2017**, *42*, 60–88. [CrossRef]
13. Kasban, D.H.S.H.; El-Bendary, M.A.M. A Comparative Study of Brain Imaging Techniques. *Int. J. Inf. Sci. Intell. Syst.* **2015**, *4*, 37–58.
14. He, L.; Long, L.R.; Antani, S.; Thoma, G.R. Histology image analysis for carcinoma detection and grading *Comput. Methods Programs Biomed.* **2011**, *107*, 538–556. [CrossRef] [CrossRef]
15. Yan, R.; Ren, F.; Wang, Z.; Wang, L.; Zhang, T.; Liu, Y.; Rao, X.; Zheng, C.; Zhang, F. Breast cancer histopathological image classification using a hybrid deep neural network. *Methods* **2020**, *173*, 52–60. [CrossRef] [CrossRef]
16. Zhang, Y.; Gorriz, J.M.; Dong, Z. Deep learning in medical image analysis. *J. Imaging* **2021**, *7*, 74. [CrossRef] [CrossRef]
17. He, K.; Zhang, X.; Ren, S.; Sun, J. Deep residual learning for image recognition. In Proceedings of the IEEE Conference 678 on Computer Vision and Pattern Recognition, Las Vegas, NV, USA, 27–30 June 2016; pp. 770–778.
18. Huang, G. Densely connected convolutional networks. In Proceedings of the 2017 IEEE Conference on Computer Vision and Pattern Recognition (CVPR), CVPR 2017, Honolulu, HI, USA, 21–26 July 2017; pp. 2261–2269. [CrossRef]
19. Tan, M.; Le, Q.V. EfficientNet: Rethinking Model Scaling for Convolutional Neural Networks. In Proceedings of the 36th International Conference on Machine Learning, Long Beach, CA, USA, 9–15 June 2019.
20. Cheng, G.; Li, Z.; Yao, X.; Guo, L.; Wei, Z. Remote Sensing Image Scene Classification Using Bag of Convolutional Features. *IEEE Geosci. Remote Sens. Lett.* **2017**, *14*, 1–5. [CrossRef]
21. Eltonsy, N.H.; Tourassi, G.D.; Elmaghraby, A.S. A concentric morphology model for the detection of masses in mammography. *IEEE Trans. Med. Imaging* **2007**, *26*, 880–889. [CrossRef] [CrossRef]
22. Barata, C.; Marques, J.S.; Celebi, M.E. Improving dermoscopy image analysis using color constancy In Proceedings of the 2014 IEEE International Conference on Image Processing (ICIP), Paris, France, 27–30 October 2014; Volume 19, pp. 3527–3531. [CrossRef]
23. Pinto, A.; Pereira, S.; Correia, H.; Oliveira, J.; Rasteiro, D.M.L.D.; Silva, C.A. Brain Tumour Segmentation based on Extremely Randomized Forest with high-level features. In Proceedings of the 2015 37th Annual International Conference of the IEEE Engineering in Medicine and Biology Society (EMBC), Milan, Italy, 25–29 August 2015; pp. 3037–3040. [CrossRef]
24. Nicholas, J.T.; Shrinidhi, K.L.; Wintermark, M.; Christopher, R.D.; Benjamin, M.K.; James C.G.; Murray, C.G.; Brian, B.A. Optimal Symmetric Multimodal Templates and Concatenated Random Forests for Supervised Brain Tumor Segmentation (Simplified) with ANTsR. *Neuroinformatics* **2015**, *13*, 209–225.
25. Spanhol, F.A.; Oliveira, L.S.; Petitjean, C.; Heutte, L. A Dataset for Breast Cancer Histopathological Image Classification. *IEEE Trans. Biomed. Eng.* **2016**, *63*, 1455–1462. [CrossRef] [CrossRef]
26. Umer, M.J. ; Sharif, M.; Kadry, S.; Alharbi, A. Multi-Class Classification of Breast Cancer Using 6B-Net with Deep Feature Fusion and Selection Method. *J. Pers. Med.* **2022**, *12*, 683. [CrossRef] [CrossRef]
27. Han, Z.; Wei, B.; Zheng,Y.; Yin, Y.; Li, K.; Li, S. Breast Cancer Multi-classification from Histopathological Images with Structured Deep Learning Model. *Sci. Rep.* **2017**, *7*, 4172. [CrossRef] [CrossRef]
28. Murtaza, G.; Shuib, L.; Mujtaba, G.; Raza, G. Breast Cancer Multi-classification through Deep Neural Network and Hierarchical Classification Approach. *Multimed. Tools Appl.* **2020**, *79*, 15481–15511. [CrossRef] [CrossRef]
29. Szegedy, Z. Going deeper with convolutions. In Proceedings of the 2015 IEEE Conference on Computer Vision and Pattern Recognition (CVPR), Boston, MA, USA, 7–12 June 2015. [CrossRef]
30. Gandomkar, Z.; Brennan, P.C.; Mello-Thoms, C. MuDeRN: Multi-category classification of breast histopathological image using deep residual networks *Artif. Intell. Med.* **2018**, *88*, 14–24. [CrossRef] [CrossRef]
31. Joseph, A.A.; Abdullahi, M.; Junaidu, S.B.; Ibrahim, H.H.; Chiroma, H. Improved multi-classification of breast cancer histopathological images using handcrafted features and deep neural network (dense layer). *Intell. Syst. Appl.* **2022**, *14*, 200066. [CrossRef] [CrossRef]
32. Xie, J.; Liu, R.; Luttrell, J.; Zhang, C. Deep learning based analysis of histopathological images of breast cancer. *Front. Genet.* **2019**, *10*, 80. [CrossRef] [CrossRef] [PubMed]
33. Al-Haija, Q.A.; Adebanjo, A. Breast Cancer Diagnosis in Histopathological Images Using ResNet-50 Convolutional Neural Network. In Proceedings of the IEEE International IOT, Electronics and Mechatronics Conference (IEMTRONICS), Vancouver, BC, Canada, 9–12 September 2020. [CrossRef]
34. Kassani, S.H.; Kassani, P.H.; Wesolowski, M.J.; Schneider, K.A.; Deters, R. Classification of histopathological biopsy images using ensemble of deep learning networks. *arXiv* **2019**, arXiv:1909.11870.
35. Wichakam, I.; Vateekul, P. Combining Deep Convolutional Networks for Mass Detection on Digital Mammograms. In Proceedings of the 8th International Conference on Knowledge and Smart Technology (KST), Chiang Mai, Thailand, 3–6 February 2016.

6. Devnath, L.; Luo, S.; Summons, P.; Wang, D. Automated detection of pneumoconiosis with multilevel deep features learned from chest X-Ray radiographs. *Comput. Biol. Med.* **2020**, *129*, 104125. [CrossRef] [CrossRef] [PubMed]
7. Devnath, L.; Summons,P.; Luo, S.; Wang, D.; Shaukat, K.; Hameed, I. A.; HAljuaid, H. Computer-Aided Diagnosis of Coal Workers' Pneumoconiosis in Chest X-ray Radiographs Using Machine Learning: A Systematic Literature Review. *Int. J. Environ. Res. Public Health* **2022**, *19*, 6439. [CrossRef] [PubMed]
8. Devnath, L.; Fan, Z.; Luo, S.; Summons, P. Detection and Visualisation of Pneumoconiosis Using an Ensemble of Multi-Dimensional Deep Features Learned from Chest X-rays. *Int. J. Environ. Res. Public Health* **2022**, *19*, 11193. [CrossRef]
9. Huynh, B. Q.; Li, H.; Giger, M. L. Digital mammographic tumor classification using transfer learning from deep convolutional neural networks. *J. Med. Imaging* **2016**, *3*, 034501. [CrossRef] [CrossRef]
0. Zhang, B.; Qi, S.; Monkam, P.; Li, C.; Yang, F.; Yao, Y.-D.; Qian, W. Ensemble learners of multiple deep cnns for pulmonary nodules classification using ct images. *IEEE Access* **2019**, *7*, 110358–110371. [CrossRef] [CrossRef]
1. Yang, L.; Chen, W.; Meer, P.; Salaru, G.; Goodell, L.A.; Berstis, V.; Foran, D.J. Virtual microscopy and grid-enabled decision support for large-scale analysis of imaged pathology specimens. *IEEE Trans. Inf. Technol. Biomed.* **2009**, *13*, 636–644. [CrossRef] [CrossRef]
2. Filipczuk, P.; Fevens, T.; Krzyzak, A.; Monczak, R. Computer-aided breast cancer diagnosis based on the analysis of cytological images of fine needle biopsies. *IEEE Trans. Med. Imaging* **2013**, *32*, 2169–2178. [CrossRef] [CrossRef]
3. Shin, H.-C.; Roth, H. R.; Gao, M.; Lu, L.; Xu, Z.; Nogues, I.; Yao, J.; Mollura, D.; Summers, R. M. Deep Convolutional Neural Networks for Computer-Aided Detection: CNN Architectures, Dataset Characteristics and Transfer Learning. *IEEE Trans. Med. Imaging* **2016**, *35*, 1285–1298. [CrossRef] [CrossRef]
4. Krizhevsky, A.; Sutskever, I.; Hinton, G.E. ImageNet Classification with Deep Convolutional Neural Networks. In Proceedings of the Twenty-sixth Conference proceedings on Neural Information Processing Systems (NIPS2012), Lake Tahoe, NY, USA, 3–6 December 2012.
5. Roy, S.; Menapace, W.; Oei, S.; Luijten, B.; Fini, E.; Saltori, C.; Huijben, I.; Chennakeshava, N.; Mento, F.; Sentelli, A.; et al. Deep Learning for Classification and Localization of COVID-19 Markers in Point-of-Care Lung Ultrasound. *IEEE Trans. Med. Imaging* **2020**, *39*, 2676–2687. [CrossRef] [CrossRef]
6. Krizhevsky A.; Hinton, G.E. ImageNet Classification with Deep Convolutional Neural Networks. *Commun. ACM* **2017**, *60*, 84–90. [CrossRef]
7. Hinton, G.; Srivastava, N.; Krizhevsky, A.; Sutskever, I.; Salakhutdinov, R. Improving neural networks by preventing co-adaptation of feature detectors. *arXiv* **2012**, arXiv:1207.0580.
8. Shah, M.; Vakharia, V.; Chaudhari, R.; Vora, J.; Pimenov, D.Y.; Giasin, K. Tool wear prediction in face milling of stainless steel using singular generative adversarial network and LSTM deep learning models. *Int. J. Adv. Manuf. Technol.* **2022**, *121*, 723–736. [CrossRef]
9. Dumagpi, J.K.; Jeong, Y.-J. Evaluating GAN-Based Image Augmentation for Threat Detection in Large-Scale Xray Security Images. *Appl. Sci.* **2020**, *11*, 36. [CrossRef]
0. Navab, N.; Hornegger, J.; Wells, W.M.; Frangi, A.F.; Hutchison, D. Medical Image Computing and Computer-Assisted Intervention. In Proceedings of the MICCAI 2015 18th International Conference, Munich, Germany, 5–9 October 2015.
1. Torheim, T.; Malinen, E.; Kvaal, K.; Lyng, H.; Indahl, U.G.; Andersen, E.K.F.; Futsaether, C.M. Classification of Dynamic Contrast Enhanced MR Images of Cervical Cancers Using Texture Analysis and Support Vector Machines. *IEEE Trans. Med. Imaging* **2014**, *33*, 1648–16566. [CrossRef] [CrossRef]
2. Huang, C.; Han, H.; Yao, Q.; Zhu, S.; Zhou, K. S. *3D U2-Net: A 3D Universal U-Net for Multi-domain Medical Image Segmentation.* In *Medical Image Computing and Computer Assisted Intervention, Proceedings of the 22nd International Conference, Shenzhen, China, 13–17 October 2019*; Springer: Cham, Switzerland, 2019; Volume 1, pp. 291–299. [CrossRef]
3. Araujo, T.; Aresta, G.; Castro, E.M.; Rouco, J.; Aguiar, P.; Eloy, C.; Polónia, A.; Campilho, A. Classification of breast cancer histology images using convolutional neural networks. *PLoS ONE* **2017**, *12*, 1–14. [CrossRef] [CrossRef]
4. Selvaraju, R.R.; Cogswell, M.; Das, A.; Vedantam, R.; Parikh, D.; Batra, D. Grad-cam: Why did you say that? Visual explanations from deep networks via gradient-based localization. *Rev. Hosp. Das* **2016**, *17*, 331–336.
5. Nemenyi, P.B. Distribution-Free Multiple Comparisons. Ph.D. Thesis, Princeton University, Princeton, NJ, USA, 1963.

applied sciences

MDPI

Article

Age Estimation from Brain Magnetic Resonance Images Using Deep Learning Techniques in Extensive Age Range

Kousuke Usui [1], Takaaki Yoshimura [2,3,4,5], Minghui Tang [5,6] and Hiroyuki Sugimori [4,5,7,*]

1 Graduate School of Health Sciences, Hokkaido University, Sapporo 060-0812, Japan
2 Department of Health Sciences and Technology, Faculty of Health Sciences, Hokkaido University, Sapporo 060-0812, Japan
3 Department of Medical Physics, Hokkaido University Hospital, Sapporo 060-8648, Japan
4 Global Center for Biomedical Science and Engineering, Faculty of Medicine, Hokkaido University, Sapporo 060-8648, Japan
5 Clinical AI Human Resources Development Program, Faculty of Medicine, Hokkaido University, Sapporo 060-8648, Japan
6 Department of Diagnostic Imaging, Faculty of Medicine and Graduate School of Medicine, Hokkaido University, Sapporo 060-8638, Japan
7 Department of Biomedical Science and Engineering, Faculty of Health Sciences, Hokkaido University, Sapporo 060-0812, Japan
* Correspondence: sugimori@hs.hokudai.ac.jp; Tel.: +81-11-706-3410

Abstract: Estimation of human age is important in the fields of forensic medicine and the detection of neurodegenerative diseases of the brain. Particularly, the age estimation methods using brain magnetic resonance (MR) images are greatly significant because these methods not only are noninvasive but also do not lead to radiation exposure. Although several age estimation methods using brain MR images have already been investigated using deep learning, there are no reports involving younger subjects such as children. This study investigated the age estimation method using T1-weighted (sagittal plane) two-dimensional brain MR imaging (MRI) of 1000 subjects aged 5–79 (31.64 $\pm$ 18.04) years. This method uses a regression model based on ResNet-50, which estimates the chronological age (CA) of unknown brain MR images by training brain MR images corresponding to the CA. The correlation coefficient, coefficient of determination, mean absolute error, and root mean squared error were used as the evaluation indices of this model, and the results were 0.9643, 0.9299, 5.251, and 6.422, respectively. The present study showed the same degree of correlation as those of related studies, demonstrating that age estimation can be performed for a wide range of ages with higher estimation accuracy.

Keywords: deep learning; age estimation; regression model; machine learning; ResNet-50

1. Introduction

The human brain develops and atrophies during growth and aging, resulting in structural changes in the brain [1,2]. These changes in the brain structure can be confirmed with the human eye using medical images. Particularly, noninvasive and radiation-free magnetic resonance (MR) imaging (MRI) of the brain is a useful method for confirming structural changes. Thus, human age can be estimated by using brain structures that change with age, and this type of age estimation technique can be applied to two major fields: forensic medicine and early detection of neurodegenerative diseases of the brain.

As for the application to the field of forensic science, both living and deceased subjects can be targeted [3,4]. In the case of the living subject, it is expected to be applied to situations where identification is required, such as asylum applications, criminal lawsuits, and youth sports [3], whereas in the case of the corpse, it is expected to be applied to the identification of the unidentified corpse [4]. In such applications, since previous studies have attempted to estimate the age with other parts of the body, such as the teeth, clavicles, hands, and knees, the reliability of the age estimation will be improved by using this method together with these techniques. As for the application to the early detection of neurodegenerative diseases of the brain, it is based on the fact that brain morphology changes with aging (atrophy due to linear decrease in gray matter volume) and these neurodegenerative diseases cause brain atrophy that is greater than that of normal aging [5]. Since patients with neurodegenerative diseases develop brain atrophy caused by systematic loss of nerve cells in the central nervous system, such changes can be confirmed through MRI and computed tomography (CT) images [6,7]. Therefore, patients with neurodegenerative diseases are assumed to show a larger discrepancy between their chronological age and estimated age based on their brain structures, and this discrepancy can be used for the early detection of neurodegenerative diseases. Furthermore, considering the aging of the population on a global scale and the fact that "aging" is considered a risk factor for neurodegenerative diseases, this type of technology is expected to be increasingly utilized in the future [8,9]. Early detection of these diseases is greatly significant since these diseases affect not only the patients themselves, but also the quality of life of their families [10,11].

In related works, regarding the methodology used to estimate age, in order to improve the identification of age-related developmental disorders as significant, an investigation was conducted based on a dental examination that included the determination of the X-ray image of the left hand and dental status and X-ray images of the dentition [12], however, if the skeletal formation of the hand has been completed, an additional X-ray examination of the clavicles was required. These results indicate that it is difficult to estimate age using the same physical indicators. In addition, another paper has been reported [13] that suggests a problem with the use of X-rays in age estimation because of the radiation exposure involved in age estimation, and as the international atomic energy agency (IAEA) regulates the use and possible abuse of X-rays, it is desirable to perform this non-invasive method. Moreover, a paper has been reported [14] that shows the usefulness of MRI-based methods as an alternative to age estimation methods that involve radiation exposure, and a report examining the degree to which imaging time can be reduced in age estimation methods using MR images of the hand and wrist joint. However, the method has the disadvantage that it is not applicable to a wide range of age groups because the number of subjects is small and the age range of the subjects is limited. In summarizing these reports, noninvasive and identical body part-based age estimation is required.

Recently, deep learning technology has continued to develop and has been applied to several medical image analyses [15–20] besides classification [21], including semantic segmentation [22,23], and object detection [24,25] using convolutional neural networks (CNNs) and regression tasks [26,27]. This study attempted to estimate human age from brain MR images using regression analysis. Although medical methods are more useful than nonmedical methods for human age estimation [28] and age estimation methods using brain MR images via deep learning [29–32] have already been reported, studies on young subjects such as minors have not been confirmed. However, no study on young subjects, such as minors, has been reported. Moreover, previous studies reported that sagittal images should be used for age estimation using two-dimensional (2D) brain MR images [32] and that central regions of the brain are better than peripheral regions [31] as the target regions. Therefore, this study aimed to examine the accuracy of age estimation by using 2D CNN, a type of deep learning technique, for a wider age range than previous studies, including from infants to elderly individuals, using brain MR images.

2. Materials and Methods

2.1. Subjects

Images from two public databases were used. One database is the Decoded Neurofeedback (DecNef) Project Brain Data Repository (https://bicr-resource.atr.jp/srpbsopen/ (accessed on 28 December 2022)), which is part of the Japanese Strategic Research Program of Brain Sciences (SRPBS) supported by the Japanese Advanced Research and Development Programs for Medical Innovation (AMED) [33]. Another one is the "Healthy Brain

Network" published by the Child Mind Institute (http://fcon_1000.projects.nitrc.org/indi/cmi_healthy_brain_network/ (accessed on 28 December 2022)) [34]. This study obtained T1-weighted images of 1000 subjects (men = 500, women = 500) aged 5–79 years from these databases (Table 1). The images were sourced from multiple centers. Therefore, the minimum to maximum width and height of the images used in this study ranged from 180–320 mm and 138–320 mm, respectively. When the same number of male and female data was obtained, care was taken to adjust the distribution of the number of persons by age to be as uniform as possible.

Table 1. Age information of subjects.

Subjects	Age				
	Mean	SD	Median	Q1	Q3
Total: 1000 subjects	31.64	18.04	30.00	16.00	45.00
500 Male subjects	30.97	17.52	30.00	16.00	44.00
500 Female subjects	32.30	18.52	31.00	16.00	46.00

SD: standard deviation, Q1: first quartile, Q3: third quartile.

2.2. Preprocessing

Since all data acquired in this study were in the Neuroimaging Informatics Technology Initiative (NIfTI) format and this study targets 2D images (sagittal plane), the data were converted to Joint Photographic Experts Group (JPEG) format. The accuracy of age estimation using 2D brain MR images is higher when the central region of the brain is targeted than the peripheral regions. Therefore, in this study, we used a total of 11 images from each subject, consisting of the central value of the total number of images after conversion from NIfTI format to JPEG format and five images before and after the central value.

Since the lower limit of the subject age was set lower than that of previous studies, it cannot be denied that the age estimation in the present study is based on the size of the cranium and brain, not on the structural differences of the brain. Since the proportion of the brain in the MRI image can be changed by setting the field of view (FOV) and other factors, the size of the head in the MRI image tends to be the same to some extent, if we simply consider the size of the head in the image. However, considering the fact that there is a difference in the standardization of the head size, it cannot be eliminated that the age estimation is based only on the size of the cranium and the brain. To exclude the influence of the head size, the data augmentation of brain size rescaling was performed. Since the results of the actual measurement of head standards (Figures 1 and 2) and images that included a part of the brain (Figure 3) are missing due to magnification, scaling factors of data augmentations as 0.8, 0.9, and 1.0 were conducted in this study. The measured angles of the subcallosal line (the line connects the inferior surface of the genu of the corpus callosum to the inferior surface of the splenium of the corpus callosum) showed normality in the variation of the angle of the head (mean = $-1.0°$). Therefore, in this study, data augmentation on rotation was not conducted. Data augmentation by scaling down or equalizing was conducted.

2.3. Architecture and Training

To construct a regression model for estimating chronological age (CA) from brain MR images, we developed a regression CNN based on ResNet-50 [35]. Originally, ResNet-50 has a structure in which the softmax layer outputs the input data as values ranging from 0 to 1, and the classification layer shows the final classification result. However, in this study, since the estimated age is the output, the regression model is created by introducing a regression layer instead of these layers, which can output the estimated value before it is converted to a value between 0 and 1 by the softmax layer. Using this model, we created three age estimation models (Table 2). The CNN conditions used during training were the stochastic gradient descent with momentum optimizer, and the initial learning rate, max Epochs, and mini-batch size were set to 0.0001, 10, and 512, respectively.

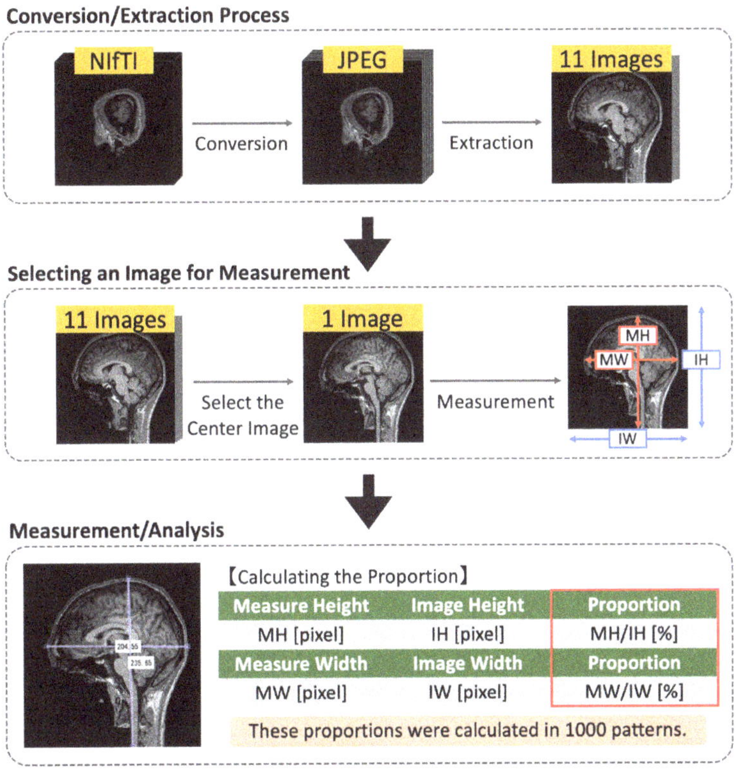

Figure 1. Measured head standard in a brain MR image. (MH: Measured Height, IH: Image Height, MW: Measured Width, IW: Image Width).

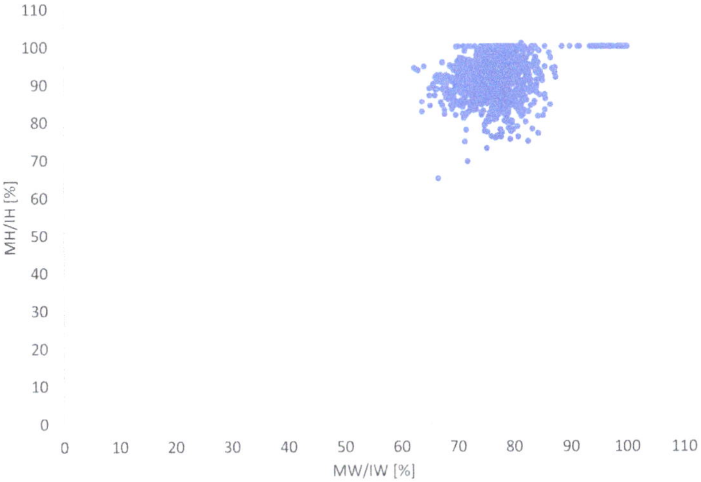

Figure 2. Measured results of head standard. (MH: Measured Height, IH: Image Height, MW: Measured Width, IW: Image Width).

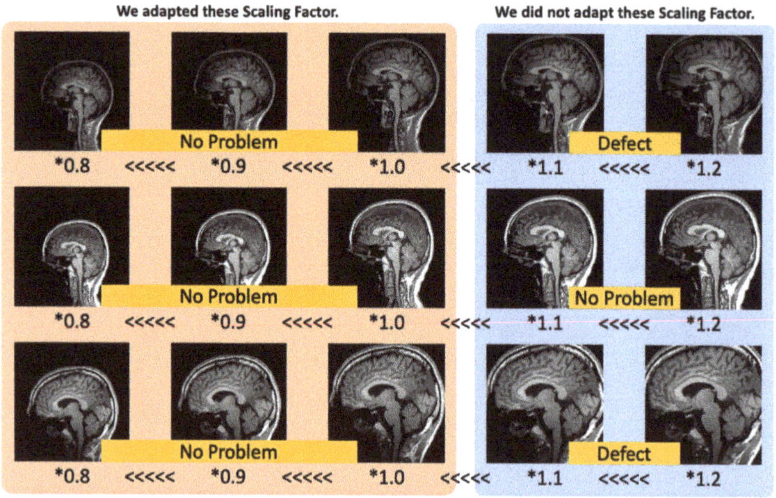

Figure 3. Images missing due to data augmentation. *: magnification factor.

Table 2. Age estimation model.

Model	Content
ALL_Model	Training/evaluation using images of a total of 1000 subjects
Male_Model	Training/evaluation using images of 500 male subjects
Female_Model	Training/evaluation using images of 500 female subjects

A fivefold cross-validation (train:test = 4:1) was used in training the data. In this study, we defined a subset as one of the five divisions of the dataset, and we adjusted the distribution of the number of persons in each age group to be as uniform as possible before creating the subset, so as not to bias the age distribution within each dataset. These pre-adjustments and the five-fold cross validation are performed to avoid overfitting of specific data to the created predictor. Table 3 shows the software and computer specification used for the training of these CNNs.

Table 3. Software/equipment used in the study.

Environment	Content
Software	MATLAB 2021a (developed by MathWorks)
OS	Windows 10
CPU	Intel core i9-10980XE 3.0 GHz
GPU	NDIVIA RTX A6000 48 GB × 2
Memory	DDR4 2933 Quad-Channel 64 GB

2.4. Evaluating the Created Regression Models

The regression models were used to estimate CA from brain MR images in the test data. Since training and evaluation were conducted using fivefold cross-validation in this study, the average performance of the five regression models was evaluated as the performance of this method.

Mean absolute error (MAE), root mean squared error (RMSE), correlation coefficient (R), and coefficient of determination (R^2) were used as evaluation indices. Since linear regression is used in this study, we calculated the R^2 value by squaring R which was obtained from linear regression and used it as an evaluation index. R, MAE, and RMSE are calculated using the following equations:

$$R = \frac{\frac{1}{n}\sum_{i=1}\left(y_{obs,\ i} - \overline{y_{obs}}\right)\left(y_{pred,\ i} - \overline{y_{pred}}\right)}{\sqrt{\frac{1}{n}\sum_{i=1}\left(y_{obs,\ i} - \overline{y_{obs}}\right)^2} \times \sqrt{\frac{1}{n}\sum_{i=1}\left(y_{pred,\ i} - \overline{y_{pred}}\right)^2}} \quad (1)$$

$$MAE = \frac{\sum_i \left|y_{obs,\ i} - y_{pred,\ i}\right|}{n}$$

$$RMSE = \sqrt{\frac{\sum_i \left(y_{obs,\ i} - y_{pred,\ i}\right)^2}{n}}$$

where $y_{obs,i}$ is the real age, $y_{pred,i}$ is the estimated age, $\overline{y_{obs}}$ is the average of $y_{obs,\ i}$, $\overline{y_{pred}}$ is the average of $y_{pred,\ i}$, and n is the number of samples in the case.

2.5. Evaluation of the Significant Region in Age Estimation

The results of previous studies showed that central regions of the brain have a better effect on age estimation than peripheral regions of the brain [31]. A detailed examination of the visualization map of the basis for this report shows that the MAE is smaller in the corpus callosum region. This indicates that the corpus callosum region is a useful region for age estimation.

In this study, based on the results of the previous study, we created an image in which the corpus callosum region is removed (Figure 4). By determining how the accuracy of the estimation changes before and after the removal of the corpus callosum region, it is possible to examine whether the corpus callosum region is a useful region for age estimation in this method. As a specific analysis procedure, we used the method for examining significant differences as described in Section 2.6.

2.6. Statistical Analysis

In this method, three adjustments were considered when collecting data and creating a dataset/subset: (1) adjusting the distribution of the number of persons by age to be as uniform as possible between men and women, (2) adjusting the number of data to be as uniform as possible between men and women, and (3) adjusting the distribution of the number of persons by age to be as uniform as possible between each subset. Therefore, the five age estimation models A, B, C, D, and E, which were created using the fivefold cross-validation, are models that each learn the same number of data with similar age distributions, which contributes to showing similar age distribution trends for both Male_Model A–E and Female_Model A–E.

Based on this trend, we conducted a statistical significance study using the absolute error (AE) of each test data. The AE of 200 subjects for ALL_Model and the AE of 100 subjects for Male_Model and Female_Model were used to confirm the normality by the Shapiro–Wilk test, and when the normality was found, the F test and *t*-test were used to examine the statistical significance. In the case of nonnormality, the Wilcoxon rank sum test was used to examine the significance of the difference. A p value less than 0.05 was considered statistically significant. Specifically, we used this method to examine whether there is a statistically significant difference in the accuracy of age estimation between Male_Model and Female_Model and whether there is a statistically significant difference in the accuracy of age estimation before and after the deletion of the corpus callosum region. In the former case, a total of 25 patterns (cross comparison for five patterns of Male_Model (Male_Model A–E) and five patterns of Female_Model (Female_Model A–E)) were examined for statistical significance using AE. Conversely, in the latter case, since the images before and after the deletion of the corpus callosum are paired (the original images are identical before and after the deletion), we examined the statistical significance of AE using five patterns each of ALL_Model, Male_Model, and Female_Model (15 patterns in total). The test data used for the input are images without data augmentation processing and images from which the corpus callosum region is removed.

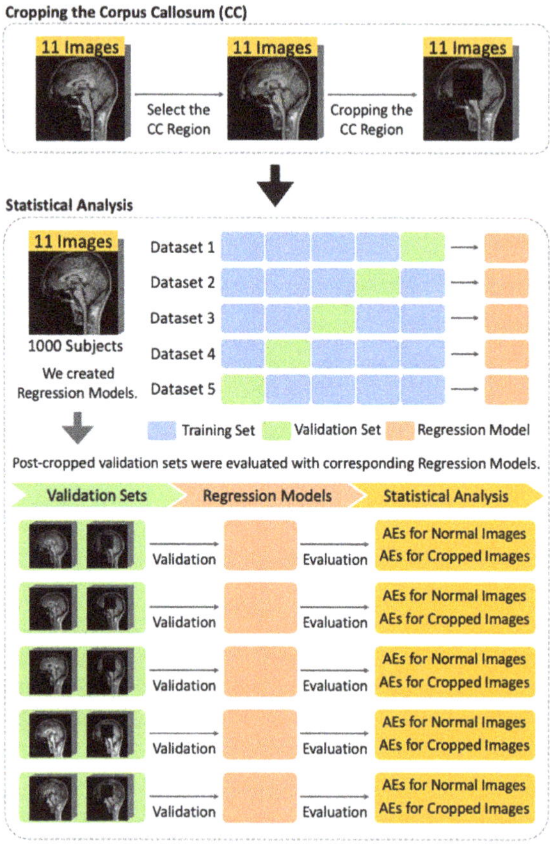

Figure 4. The process of the statistical analysis on the accuracy of age estimation before and after the removal of the corpus callosum (CC) region.

3. Results

3.1. Evaluation of the Accuracy of the Age Estimation Model

Accuracy evaluations for the ALL_Model, Male_Model, and Female_Model age estimation models are shown in Figures 5–8. As for the R and R^2 value, which indicate the degree of correlation, the accuracy of both age estimation models improved before and after data augmentation. Specifically, the R and R^2 value were 0.9643 and 0.9299, respectively, for ALL_Model, and 0.94582 and 0.93945, respectively, for Male_Model and Female_Model, and 0.89513 and 0.88257, respectively, for R^2. As for MAE and RMSE, which indicate the error between the actual age and estimated age, the accuracy improved before and after data augmentation for ALL_Model and Female_Model, but the results for Male_Model were almost the same before and after data augmentation. Specifically, the MAE and RMSE of the ALL_Model were 5.251 and 6.422 years, respectively, whereas the MAE and RMSE of the Male_Model and Female_Model were 6.323 and 5.766 years, respectively, and 7.734 and 7.006 years, respectively. Figure 9 shows examples of age estimation from brain MR images using this method. The upper two rows show examples of highly accurate age estimation, and the lower two rows show examples with estimation errors of about MAE or larger.

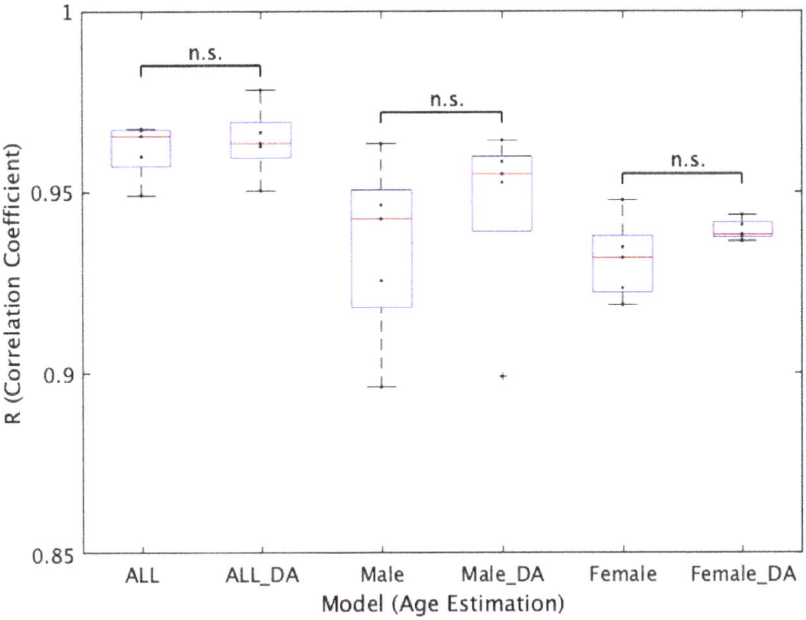

Figure 5. Results for correlation coefficient (R). (DA: Data Augmentation).

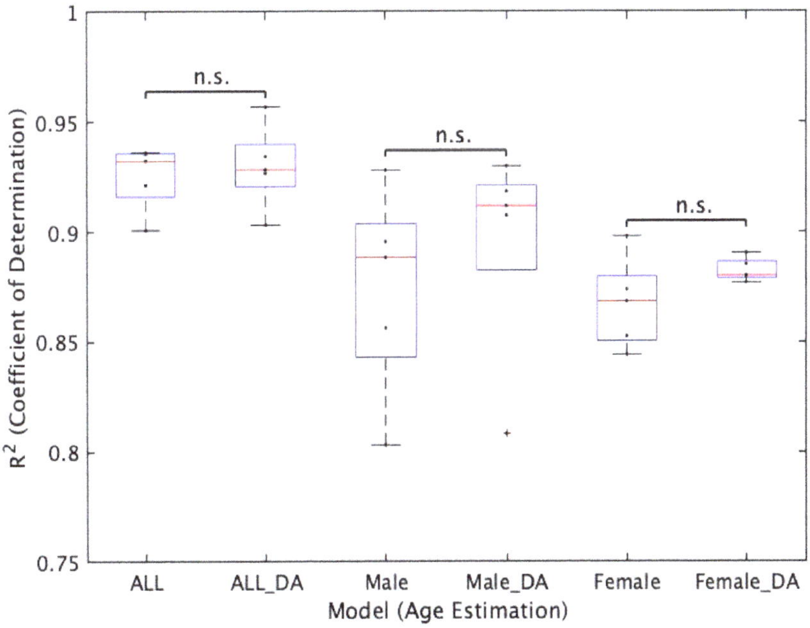

Figure 6. Results for the coefficient of determination (R^2). (DA: Data Augmentation).

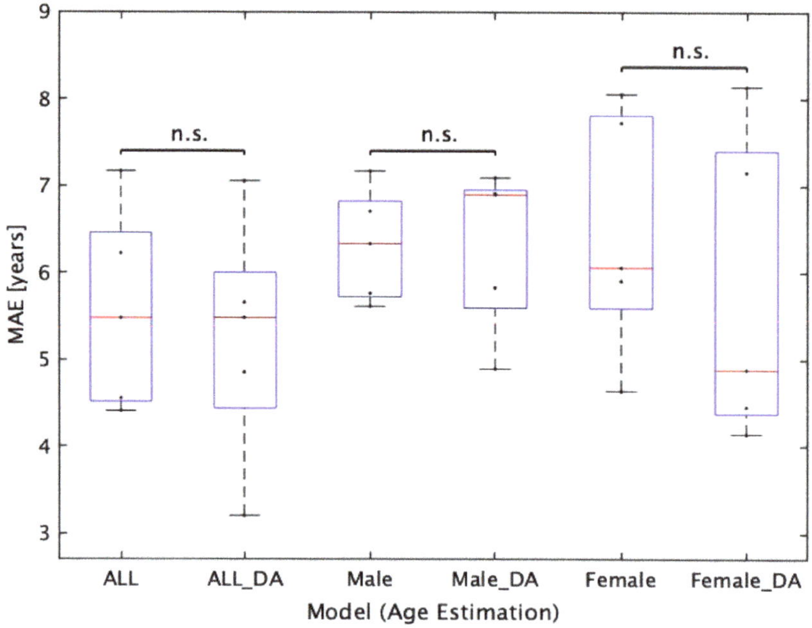

Figure 7. Results for mean absolute error (MAE). (DA: Data Augmentation).

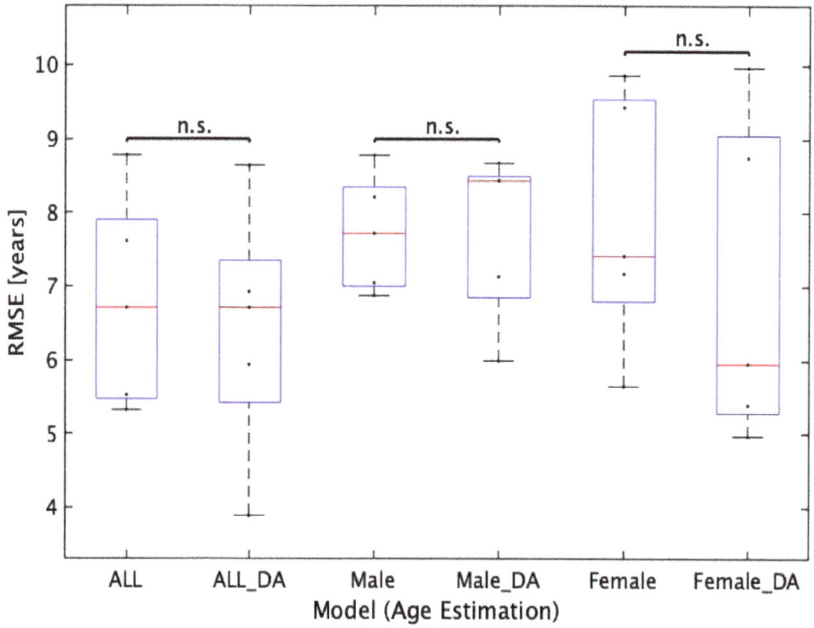

Figure 8. Results for root mean squared error (RMSE). (DA: Data Augmentation).

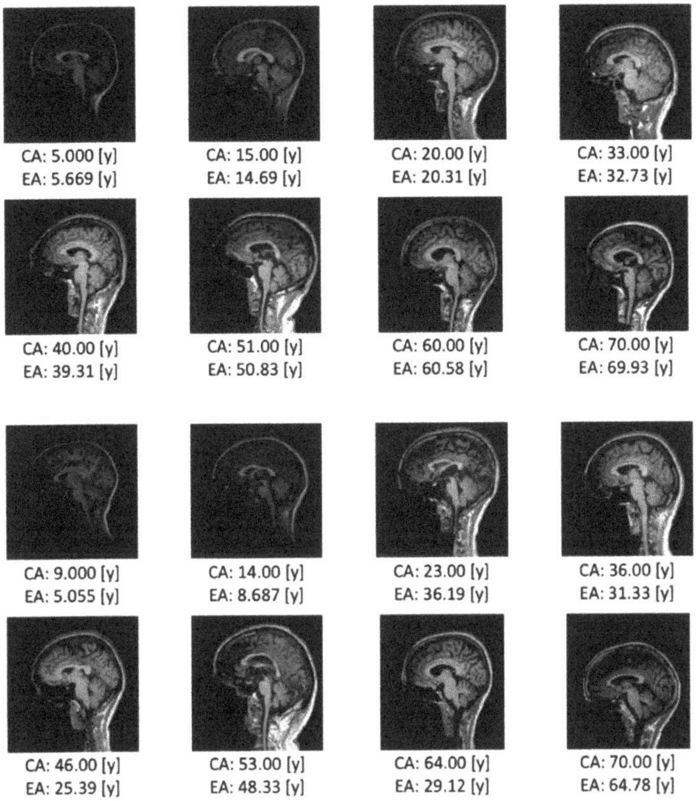

Figure 9. Typical example of this age estimation method. (CA, chronological age; EA, estimated age).

3.2. Evaluation of the Significant Region in Age Estimation

Table 4 shows the results of the Shapiro–Wilk test for the data on AEs obtained in this study. In Table 4, since there is no normality in the data on AEs obtained in this study, it was decided that the statistical significance be examined by using the Wilcoxon rank sum test. Table 5 shows the results of the Wilcoxon rank sum test. This table shows that although there is one case each for Male_Model and Female_Model in which there is no statistically significant difference. In all other cases, there is a statistically significant difference in the accuracy of age estimation before and after the deletion of the corpus callosum region. In sum, the overall results show that the accuracy of age estimation significantly decreases before and after the removal of the corpus callosum region. Table 6 shows the specific values of MAE and other parameters.

Table 4. Results of the Shapiro–Wilk test.

	ALL_Model		Male_Model		Female_Model	
	With CC	**Without CC**	**With CC**	**Without CC**	**With CC**	**Without CC**
Model_A	$p < 0.0001$	$p < 0.0001$	$p < 0.0001$	$p = 0.0024$	$p < 0.0001$	$p = 0.0010$
Model_B	$p < 0.0001$	$p = 0.0003$	$p < 0.0001$	$p = 0.0013$	$p = 0.0145$	$p = 0.0644$
Model_C	$p < 0.0001$	$p = 0.0003$	$p < 0.0001$	$p = 0.0289$	$p < 0.0001$	$p < 0.0001$
Model_D	$p < 0.0001$	$p = 0.0001$	$p < 0.0001$	$p = 0.0090$	$p = 0.0003$	$p = 0.0002$
Model_E	$p < 0.0001$	$p = 0.0005$	$p < 0.0001$	$p = 0.0004$	$p < 0.0001$	$p < 0.0001$

CC: corpus callosum.

Table 5. Results of the Wilcoxon rank sum test.

	ALL_Model	Male_Model	Female_Model
	p Value	*p* Value	*p* Value
Model_A	<0.0001	0.0001	0.2523
Model_B	<0.0001	0.0825	<0.0001
Model_C	<0.0001	<0.0001	<0.0001
Model_D	<0.0001	0.0025	<0.0001
Model_E	<0.0001	0.0048	0.0046

Table 6. Change in accuracy before and after deletion of the corpus callosum region.

	ALL_Model		Male_Model		Female_Model	
	With CC	Without CC	With CC	Without CC	With CC	Without CC
MAE	5.2508	7.7777	6.3234	8.0344	5.7555	8.4124
RMSE	6.4215	9.2961	7.7338	9.6469	7.0057	10.201
Radius	0.96425	0.93054	0.94582	0.91073	0.93945	0.91764
Radius^2	0.92986	0.86602	0.89513	0.82725	0.88257	0.84228
Slope	0.78307	0.62174	0.75018	0.63040	0.75067	0.63020
Intercept	4.7428	11.520	4.9793	11.436	6.0545	9.3505

CC: corpus callosum.

3.3. Results of Statistical Analysis on the Accuracy of Age Estimation between Male and Female Age Estimation Models

As shown in Table 4, the Wilcoxon rank sum test should be used in statistical analysis using AE. Therefore, Table 7 shows the results of the Wilcoxon rank sum test to examine whether there is a statistically significant difference in the accuracy of age estimation between men and women. Table 7 shows that in 17 of 25 cases, the *p* value is higher than the significance level of 0.05, indicating that there is no statistically significant difference between the two cases. In the remaining eight cases, the *p* values are below the significance level of 0.05, indicating that there is a statistically significant difference. These results indicate that there is no statistically significant difference in the age-estimated sex between men and women when evaluated as a whole.

Table 7. Wilcoxon rank sum test.

		Female_Model				
		Model_A	Model_B	Model_C	Model_D	Model_E
Male_Model	Model_A	$p = 0.0007$	$p = 0.6734$	$p = 0.7517$	$p = 0.9815$	$p = 0.0037$
	Model_B	$p = 0.0817$	$p = 0.0328$	$p = 0.1345$	$p = 0.0808$	$p = 0.2647$
	Model_C	$p < 0.0001$	$p = 0.5071$	$p = 0.1957$	$p = 0.2895$	$p = 0.0001$
	Model_D	$p = 0.0537$	$p = 0.0513$	$p = 0.1949$	$p = 0.1147$	$p = 0.1889$
	Model_E	$p = 0.1766$	$p = 0.0017$	$p = 0.0201$	$p = 0.0068$	$p = 0.3877$

4. Discussion

To the best of our knowledge, this is the first study to examine age estimation methods based on brain MR images using deep learning over a wide age range from young people, including infants, to elderly individuals. Therefore, we were concerned that the age estimation would be affected by the difference in the head standard due to the age range of the target population, but we did not observe any decrease in accuracy even after data augmentation by scaling down/equalizing the images. In fact, the accuracy of age estimation improved as the number of data increased with the implementation of data augmentation, and we expect further improvement in accuracy by adding more data, including data in age ranges where data are lacking, and increasing the number of data through further implementation of data augmentation methods. A further increase in the number of data is expected to improve the accuracy.

Compared with previous studies, the results of MAE are inferior to those of the previous studies, whereas the results of correlation coefficients are comparable to those of previous studies. Jiang et al. [32] reported the results of age estimation using 2D images segmented into gray matter and white matter in the axial, sagittal, and coronal sections. The results show that the best estimation accuracy is obtained for the combination of sagittal and GM, recording 3.57 years, which exceeds the MAE of 5.25 years in the present study. Hepp et al. [31] also reported an age estimation method for 10,691 subjects, which is 10 times larger than the present study, although using 3D brain MR images. In this report, the MAE was 3.21 years, which is approximately two years less than that of the present study. This may be due to the fact that more features can be obtained from each subject using 3D images rather than using 2D images and that more features can be obtained from each subject per age than in the present study because more subjects were included in the study. The reason for this may be that the number of features that can be obtained from each age group is larger than that of the present study. Conversely, Masaru et al. [30] reported an age estimation method using 3D brain MR images for 1101 subjects aged 20–80 years. In this report, the correlation coefficient was 0.96, which was equivalent to that of the present study, although the MAE was 3.67 years, which was approximately 1.6 years smaller than that of the present study. Although the differences in MAE may be attributed to the differences in the number of subjects and the image format, an overview of the estimated age against CA suggests that this method already has the performance to show the same trend as the previous studies.

The abovementioned comparison with previous studies suggests that the estimation accuracy of the present method will be further improved with an increase in the number of data and similar analysis using 3D-CNN.

Next, as for the analysis of the significant region, the accuracy of age estimation significantly decreased before and after the deletion of the corpus callosum region in the overall evaluation of this method. This result suggests that the corpus callosum is a useful region for age estimation, and the results show a similar trend to those obtained in previous studies. The corpus callosum connects the left and right cerebral hemispheres, which are separated by the median longitudinal fissure, and therefore plays a role in the transmission of information between the two hemispheres, as it is composed of more than 190 million axons. Cognitive functions are affected by cerebral corpus callosum dysplasia and cerebral corpus callosum disconnection [36,37], and considering this, it can be said that the corpus callosum plays a role in brain functions corresponding to higher brain dysfunction and cognitive dysfunction. Thus, taking into account that brain atrophy and cognitive decline progress with aging, it is considered that some morphological changes have occurred in the corpus callosum region due to aging and that the AI focused on these changes to estimate the age of the subjects. However, although we focused only on the corpus callosum region in this study, we cannot deny that other regions may have had a significant impact on age estimation. Therefore, the influence of other regions on age estimation should be examined by using heat mapping techniques, such as Grad-CAM [38] and occlusion sensitivity [39].

Finally, regarding the accuracy of age estimation between Male_Model and Female_Model, no statistically significant difference in estimation accuracy was found in 17 of 25 cases in this study, and significant differences were found in eight cases. Therefore, since no statistically significant differences were found overall, the results suggest the possibility of data collection methods that focus on age distribution regardless of sex in the field of research on age estimation by combining deep learning techniques and brain MR images. For example, the results indicate that the brain MR images of a "42-year-old man" and a "42-year-old woman" can be treated as data of a 42-year-old person. Therefore, this result supports the fact that it is possible to collect data more easily without falling into the data shortage caused by the consideration of the sex ratio at the time of data collection, as in the present study.

However, in eight of 25 cases (32%), there was a significant difference in the accuracy of age estimation. There are various theories regarding anatomical differences in brain structure. In particular, morphological differences in the corpus callosum between men and women were raised by Lacoste-Utamsing and Holloway [40], but their truth or falsehood has been debated due to the recent spread of MRI and CT equipment [41–43]. Therefore, it is difficult to explain the eight cases in which significant differences were found between men and women because of the difference in brain structures between sexes, but some structural differences indeed caused the significant differences. Therefore, it is important to confirm how the current results will change when the volume of data is increased and to examine how the results are represented by heat mapping techniques, such as Grad-CAM and occlusion sensitivity, as described above.

There was a limitation in this study. Even though ResNet-50 was used in this study, original network models, rather than pre-trained models, are considered to be important in order to create an age estimation model with higher performance. Considering the fact that previous study [17] has already confirmed the use of original networks, we believe that it will be necessary to consider the network model to be used in order to create an age estimation model that shows higher performance in the future.

5. Conclusions

Although the MAE of this method is lower than that of the previous study, the degree of correlation is comparable to that of the previous study. Since the degree of correlation is already high, it is expected that the estimation accuracy will be higher and the age estimation model with higher generalization performance will become closer by increasing the volume of data through the implementation of the data collection method suggested in this study and further data augmentation methods. In this study, chronological age (CA) estimation was performed using deep learning techniques on brain MR images from individuals across a wide range of ages from young to old, including infants, who had not been included in previous studies. The results showed that age estimation, including young people such as infants, showed correlations equivalent to those in previous studies. In addition, it would be essential to investigate a method to perform age estimation on 3D brain MR images using 3D-CNN in order to improve the accuracy of age estimation in the future.

Author Contributions: K.U. contributed to the data analysis, algorithm construction, and writing and editing of the manuscript. T.Y. and M.T. reviewed and edited the manuscript. H.S. proposed the idea and contributed to the data acquisition, performed supervision and project administration, and reviewed and edited the manuscript. All authors have read and agreed to the published version of the manuscript.

Funding: This research received no external funding.

Institutional Review Board Statement: Not applicable.

Informed Consent Statement: Not applicable.

Data Availability Statement: The created models in this study are available on request from the corresponding author. The source code of this study is available at https://github.com/MIAlaboratory/AgeEstimation (accessed on 16 December 2022).

Acknowledgments: The authors would like to thank the laboratory members of the Medical Image Analysis Laboratory and Yoshimura's laboratory for their help.

Conflicts of Interest: The authors declare that no conflict of interest exists.

References

1. Whitaker, K.J.; Vértes, P.E.; Romero-garcia, R.; Moutoussis, M.; Prabhu, G. Adolescence Is Associated with Genomically Patterned Consolidation of the Hubs of the Human Brain Connectome. *Proc. Natl. Acad. Sci. USA* **2016**, *113*, 9105–9110. [CrossRef] [PubMed]
2. Fjell, A.M.; Walhovd, K.B.; Fennema-notestine, C.; Mcevoy, L.K.; Hagler, D.J.; Holland, D.; Brewer, J.B.; Dale, A.M. One-Year Brain Atrophy Evident in Healthy Aging. *J. Neurosci.* **2009**, *29*, 15223–15231. [CrossRef]
3. der Mauer, M.A.; van Well, E.J.; Herrmann, J.; Groth, M.; Morlock, M.M.; Maas, R.; Säring, D. Automated Age Estimation of Young Individuals Based on 3D Knee MRI Using Deep Learning. *Int. J. Legal Med.* **2021**, *135*, 649–663. [CrossRef] [PubMed]

4. Willems, G.; Moulin-Romsee, C.; Solheim, T. Non-Destructive Dental-Age Calculation Methods in Adults: Intra- and Inter-Observer Effects. *Forensic Sci. Int.* **2002**, *126*, 221–226. [CrossRef] [PubMed]
5. Good, C.D.; Johnsrude, I.S.; Ashburner, J.; Henson, R.N.A.; Friston, K.J.; Frackowiak, R.S.J. A Voxel-Based Morphometric Study of Ageing in 465 Normal Adult Human Brains. *Neuroimage* **2001**, *14*, 21–36. [CrossRef]
6. Seeley, W.W.; Crawford, R.K.; Zhou, J.; Miller, B.L.; Greicius, M.D. Neurodegenerative Diseases Target Large-Scale Human Brain Networks. *Neuron* **2009**, *62*, 42–52. [CrossRef]
7. Bin Zahid, A.; Mikheev, A.; Srivatsa, N.; Babb, J.; Samadani, U.; Rusinek, H. Accelerated Brain Atrophy on Serial Computed Tomography: Potential Marker of the Progression of Alzheimer Disease. *J. Comput. Assist. Tomogr.* **2016**, *40*, 827–832. [CrossRef]
8. Chang, A.Y.; Skirbekk, V.F.; Tyrovolas, S.; Kassebaum, N.J.; Dieleman, J.L. Measuring Population Ageing: An Analysis of the Global Burden of Disease Study 2017. *Lancet Public Health* **2019**, *4*, e159–e167. [CrossRef]
9. Tyas, S.L.; Manfreda, J.; Strain, L.A.; Montgomery, P.R. Risk Factors for Alzheimer's Disease: A Population-Based, Longitudinal Study in Manitoba, Canada. *Int. J. Epidemiol.* **2001**, *30*, 590–597. [CrossRef]
10. Revell, A.J.; Caskie, G.I.L.; Willis, S.L.; Schaie, K.W. Factor Structure and Invariance of the Quality of Life in Alzheimer's Disease (Qol-Ad) Scale. *Exp. Aging Res.* **2009**, *35*, 250–267. [CrossRef]
11. Wimo, A.; Jönsson, L.; Bond, J.; Prince, M.; Winblad, B. The Worldwide Economic Impact of Dementia 2010. *Alzheimer's Dement.* **2013**, *9*, 1–11.e3. [CrossRef] [PubMed]
12. Schmeling, A.; Grundmann, C.; Fuhrmann, A.; Kaatsch, H.-J.; Knell, B.; Ramsthaler, F.; Reisinger, W.; Riepert, T.; Ritz-Timme, S.; Rösing, F.W.; et al. Criteria for Age Estimation in Living Individuals. *Int. J. Legal Med.* **2008**, *122*, 457–460. [CrossRef] [PubMed]
13. De Tobel, J.; Bauwens, J.; Parmentier, G.I.L.; Franco, A.; Pauwels, N.S.; Verstraete, K.L.; Thevissen, P.W. Magnetic Resonance Imaging for Forensic Age Estimation in Living Children and Young Adults: A Systematic Review. *Pediatr. Radiol.* **2020**, *50*, 1691–1708. [CrossRef] [PubMed]
14. Widek, T.; Genet, P.; Ehammer, T.; Schwark, T.; Urschler, M.; Scheurer, E. Bone Age Estimation with the Greulich-Pyle Atlas Using 3T MR Images of Hand and Wrist. *Forensic Sci. Int.* **2021**, *319*, 110654. [CrossRef] [PubMed]
15. Sugimori, H.; Sugiyama, T.; Nakayama, N.; Yamashita, A. Development of a Deep Learning-Based Algorithm to Detect the Distal End of a Surgical Instrument. *Appl. Sci.* **2020**, *10*, 4245. [CrossRef]
16. Sugimori, H. Evaluating the Overall Accuracy of Additional Learning and Automatic Classification System for CT Images. *Appl. Sci.* **2019**, *9*, 682. [CrossRef]
17. Manabe, K.; Asami, Y.; Yamada, T.; Sugimori, H. Improvement in the Convolutional Neural Network for Computed Tomography Images. *Appl. Sci.* **2021**, *11*, 1505. [CrossRef]
18. Sugimori, H.; Hamaguchi, H.; Fujiwara, T.; Ishizaka, K. Classification of Type of Brain Magnetic Resonance Images with Deep Learning Technique. *Magn. Reson. Imaging* **2021**, *77*, 180–185. [CrossRef] [PubMed]
19. Yoshimura, T.; Nishioka, K.; Hashimoto, T.; Mori, T.; Kogame, S.; Seki, K.; Sugimori, H.; Yamashina, H.; Nomura, Y.; Kato, F.; et al. Prostatic Urinary Tract Visualization with Super-Resolution Deep Learning Models. *PLoS ONE* **2022**, *18*, e0280076. [CrossRef]
20. Asami, Y.; Yoshimura, T.; Manabe, K.; Yamada, T.; Sugimori, H. Development of Detection and Volumetric Methods for the Triceps of the Lower Leg Using Magnetic Resonance Images with Deep Learning. *Appl. Sci.* **2021**, *11*, 12006. [CrossRef]
21. Mohsen, H.; El-Dahshan, E.-S.A.; El-Horbaty, E.-S.M.; Salem, A.-B.M. Classification Using Deep Learning Neural Networks for Brain Tumors. *Future Comput. Inform. J.* **2018**, *3*, 68–71. [CrossRef]
22. Chen, H.; Dou, Q.; Yu, L.; Qin, J.; Heng, P.A. VoxResNet: Deep Voxelwise Residual Networks for Brain Segmentation from 3D MR Images. *Neuroimage* **2018**, *170*, 446–455. [CrossRef] [PubMed]
23. Myronenko, A.; Hatamizadeh, A. Robust Semantic Segmentation of Brain Tumor Regions from 3D MRIs. In *Brainlesion: Glioma, Multiple Sclerosis, Stroke and Traumatic Brain Injuries*; Lecture Notes in Computer Science; Springer: Cham, Switzerland, 2020; pp. 82–89. [CrossRef]
24. Zhou, Z.; Sanders, J.W.; Johnson, J.M.; Gule-Monroe, M.K.; Chen, M.M.; Briere, T.M.; Wang, Y.; Bum Son, J.; Pagel, M.D.; Li, J.; et al. Computer-Aided Detection of Brain Metastates in T1-Weighted MRI for Stereotactic Radiosurgery Using Deep Learning Single-Shot Detectors. *Radiology* **2020**, *295*, 407–415. [CrossRef] [PubMed]
25. Chegraoui, H.; Philippe, C.; Dangouloff-ros, V.; Grigis, A.; Calmon, R.; Boddaert, N.; Frouin, F.; Grill, J.; Frouin, V. Object Detection Improves Tumour Segmentation in MR Images of Rare Brain Tumours. *Cancers* **2021**, *13*, 6113. [CrossRef] [PubMed]
26. Jonsson, B.A.; Bjornsdottir, G.; Thorgeirsson, T.E.; Gudbjartsson, D.F.; Stefansson, H.; Stefansson, K.; Ulfarsson, M.O. Brain Age Prediction Using Deep Learning Uncovers Associated Sequence Variants. *Nat. Commun.* **2019**, *10*, 5409. [CrossRef] [PubMed]
27. Ichikawa, S.; Hamada, M.; Sugimori, H. A Deep-Learning Method Using Computed Tomography Scout Images for Estimating Patient Body Weight. *Sci. Rep.* **2021**, *11*, 15627. [CrossRef]
28. Hagen, M.; Schmidt, S.; Rudolf, E.; Schmeling, A. The Significance of Sociopedagogic Age Estimation in Comparison to Forensic Age Assessment. *Rechtsmedizin* **2020**, *30*, 233–240. [CrossRef]
29. Rossi, A.; Vannuccini, G.; Andreini, P.; Bonechi, S.; Giacomini, G.; Scarselli, F.; Bianchini, M. Analysis of Brain NMR Images for Age Estimation with Deep Learning. *Procedia Comput. Sci.* **2019**, *159*, 981–989. [CrossRef]
30. Ueda, M.; Ito, K.; Wu, K.; Sato, K.; Taki, Y.; Fukuda, H.; Aoki, T. An age estimation method using 3D-CNN from brain MRI images. In Proceedings of the 2019 IEEE 16th International Symposium on Biomedical Imaging (ISBI 2019), Venice, Italy, 8–11 April 2019.

31. Hepp, T.; Blum, D.; Armanious, K.; Schölkopf, B.; Stern, D.; Yang, B.; Gatidis, S. Uncertainty Estimation and Explainability in Deep Learning-Based Age Estimation of the Human Brain: Results from the German National Cohort MRI Study. *Comput. Med. Imaging Graph.* **2021**, *92*, 101967. [CrossRef]
32. Jiang, H.; Guo, J.; Du, H.; Xu, J.; Qiu, B. Transfer Learning on T1-Weighted Images for Brain Age Estimation. *Math. Biosci. Eng.* **2019**, *16*, 4382–4398. [CrossRef]
33. Tanaka, S.C.; Yamashita, A.; Yahata, N.; Itahashi, T.; Lisi, G.; Yamada, T.; Ichikawa, N.; Takamura, M.; Yoshihara, Y.; Kunimatsu, A.; et al. A Multi-Site, Multi-Disorder Resting-State Magnetic Resonance Image Database. *Sci. Data* **2021**, *8*, 227. [CrossRef] [PubMed]
34. Alexander, L.M.; Escalera, J.; Ai, L.; Andreotti, C.; Febre, K.; Mangone, A.; Vega-Potler, N.; Langer, N.; Alexander, A.; Kovacs, M.; et al. An Open Resource for Transdiagnostic Research in Pediatric Mental Health and Learning Disorders. *Sci. Data* **2017**, *4*, 1–26. [CrossRef] [PubMed]
35. Kaiming, H.; Xiangyu, Z.; Ren, S.; Sun, J. Deep Residual Learning for Image Recognition. In Proceedings of the IEEE Conference on Computer Vision and Pattern Recognition (CVPR), Las Vegas, NV, USA, 27–30 June 2016; pp. 770–778. [CrossRef]
36. Marco, E.; Harrell, K.; Brown, W.; Hill, S.; Jeremy, R.; Kramer, J.; Sherr, E.; Paul, L. Processing Speed Delays Contribute to Executive Function Deficits in Individuals with Agenesis of the Corpus Callosum. *J. Int. Neuropsychol. Soc.* **2012**, *18*, 521–529. [CrossRef]
37. Huang, X.; Du, X.; Song, H.; Zhang, Q.; Jia, J.; Xiao, T.; Wu, J. Cognitive Impairments Associated with Corpus Callosum Infarction: A Ten Cases Study. *Int. J. Clin. Exp. Med.* **2015**, *8*, 21991–21998. [PubMed]
38. Selvaraju, R.R.; Cogswell, M.; Das, A.; Vedantam, R.; Parikh, D.; Batra, D. Grad-CAM: Visual Explanations From Deep Networks via Gradient-Based Localization. In Proceedings of the IEEE International Conference on Computer Vision (ICCV), Venice, Italy, 22–29 October 2017; pp. 618–626.
39. Zeiler, M.D.; Fergus, R. Visualizing and Understanding Convolutional Networks. In *Computer Vision–ECCV 2014*; Lecture Notes in Computer Science; Springer: Cham, Switzerland, 2014; ISBN 9783319105895.
40. De Lacoste-Utamsing, C.; Holloway, R.L. Sexual Dimorphism in the Human Corpus Callosum. *Am. Assoc. Adv. Sci.* **1982**, *216*, 1431–1432. [CrossRef]
41. Joel, D.; Berman, Z.; Tavor, I.; Wexler, N.; Gaber, O.; Stein, Y.; Shefi, N.; Pool, J. Sex beyond the Genitalia: The Human Brain Mosaic. *Proc. Natl. Acad. Sci. USA* **2015**, *112*, 15468–15473. [CrossRef]
42. Ritchie, S.J.; Cox, S.R.; Shen, X.; Lombardo, M.V.; Reus, L.M.; Alloza, C.; Harris, M.A.; Alderson, H.L.; Hunter, S.; Neilson, E.; et al. Sex Differences in the Adult Human Brain: Evidence from 5216 UK Biobank Participants. *Cereb. Cortex* **2018**, *28*, 2959–2975. [CrossRef]
43. Ingalhalikar, M.; Smith, A.; Parker, D.; Satterthwaite, T.D.; Elliott, M.A.; Ruparel, K.; Hakonarson, H.; Gur, R.E.; Gur, R.C.; Verma, R. Sex Differences in the Structural Connectome of the Human Brain. *Proc. Natl. Acad. Sci. USA* **2014**, *111*, 823–828. [CrossRef]

applied sciences

MDPI

Article

Quality Assurance of Chest X-ray Images with a Combination of Deep Learning Methods

Daisuke Oura [1,2], Shinpe Sato [1], Yuto Honma [1], Shiho Kuwajima [1] and Hiroyuki Sugimori [3,*]

1 Department of Radiology, Otaru General Hospital, Otaru 047-0152, Japan
2 Graduate School of Health Sciences, Hokkaido University, Sapporo 060-0812, Japan
3 Faculty of Health Sciences, Hokkaido University, Sapporo 060-0812, Japan
* Correspondence: sugimori@hs.hokudai.ac.jp

Abstract: Background: Chest X-ray (CXR) imaging is the most common examination; however, no automatic quality assurance (QA) system using deep learning (DL) has been established for CXR. This study aimed to construct a DL-based QA system and assess its usefulness. Method: Datasets were created using over 23,000 images from Chest-14 and clinical images. The QA system consisted of three classification models and one regression model. The classification method was used for the correction of image orientation, left–right reversal, and estimating the patient's position, such as standing, sitting, and lying. The regression method was used for the correction of the image angle. ResNet-50, VGG-16, and the original convolutional neural network (CNN) were compared under five cross-fold evaluations. The overall accuracy of the QA system was tested using clinical images. The mean correction time of the QA system was measured. Result: ResNet-50 demonstrated higher performance in the classification. The original CNN was preferred in the regression. The orientation, angle, and left–right reversal of all images were fully corrected in all images. Moreover, patients' positions were estimated with 96% accuracy. The mean correction time was approximately 0.4 s. Conclusion: The DL-based QA system quickly and accurately corrected CXR images.

Keywords: quality assurance; X-ray; deep learning; artificial intelligence

1. Introduction

Chest X-ray (CXR) imaging has been used for diagnostic imaging since the beginning, and despite the development of diagnostic imaging equipment such as computed tomography (CT) and magnetic resonance imaging (MRI), CXR imaging has still been used for screening for cardiovascular and pulmonary diseases. The cardiothoracic ratio (CTR) measurement using CXR images is an important index to evaluate heart diseases [1–3]. CTR is usually calculated as the ratio of the largest transverse heart dimension to the largest transverse chest dimension in a CXR obtained from posterior irradiation. CXR with posterior irradiation can avoid the enlargement of the cardiac shadow caused by the proximity of the detector and heart, based on the geometry of the X-ray system. Lung water also works as an important index to assess heart and lung diseases and can be evaluated in lung water secondary to increased intravascular hydrostatic pressure due to cardiogenic edema resulting from heart failure, increased permeability of pulmonary microvessels due to acute lung injury or acute respiratory distress syndrome, and other causes [4,5]. Since the beginning of the coronavirus disease-2019 (COVID-19) pandemic, CXR imaging has played a crucial role in the evaluation of lung conditions. It is easily accessed, has a low radiation exposure as a primary screening, and a low cost to assess pneumonia, which is one of the typical symptoms of COVID-19 [6–8]. The importance of the CXR examination in daily medicine is undoubtedly important. However, during CXR imaging, both CTR and the distribution of lung water change with the patient's position. For example, if the patient is able to walk independently, CXR imaging is performed in the standing position; therefore, if lung water is detected, it is concentrated in the lower lung field due to the gravitational effect. However, in a patient with difficulty standing, such as a critically ill patient, CXR imaging is performed in the supine position, and therefore, if lung water is present, it is distributed over the entire dorsal side of the lungs. In other words, the patient's position is an important factor in the accurate assessment of CXR images in clinical practice. Therefore, the patient's position should be reported to readers immediately after CXR imaging.

However, most of these works depend on manual operations by radiological technologists. For example, technologists add a marker that shows the patient's position, such as "standing", "sitting", and "lying", to the free space in the CXR image immediately after CXR imaging. Even though these markers allow the image reader, the radiologist, and the physician in the medical department to identify the imaging status at a glance for a large number of taken clinical images, human errors may occur at some point during this process, and these errors may cause serious incidents by misunderstanding the patient's position in clinical practice [9]. For instance, imaging findings will be confused by a misunderstanding of the patient's position. Moreover, CXR output with left-right reversal is due to the difference in the irradiation direction due to incorrect imaging parameters of the X-ray console between a standing position and another position. Despite the large efforts of radiological technologists, these are quite often encountered in clinical practice. Therefore, an automatic and highly accurate system without manual operation is desired.

Artificial intelligence (AI) has been applied for the automatic assessment of medical images in recent years [10,11]. Amount of image data is needed to construct a high-accuracy model in machine learning (ML) and deep learning (DL). From this view, CXR, which has been traditional and common, may be suitable for attempts to apply ML and DL methods [12]. Meanwhile, Marcus G et al. argue that the difficulty of replacing human workers with AI is from the view of the core frameworks of human knowledge: time, space, causality, and basic knowledge of physical objects and humans and their interactions [13]. Hence, the medical field has been trying to implement AI specialized for specific tasks. We planned to construct DL models to focus on the quality assurance (QA) of CXR.

The previous study reported achieving correction of radiographs using AI [14,15]. We hypothesized that a QA system of CXR could be developed using QA modes. The classification method can estimate the orientation of the CXR and the patient's position. The regression method can assess the angle of the CXR. Therefore, we attempted to construct an automatic QA system combining the classification method and the regression method. We expected that the system would correct the orientation, angle, and left-right reversal of CXR and estimate the patient's position. Finally, the QA system adds the marker demonstrating the patient's position in the free space of the CXR. In other words, manual work by technologists is completely replaced by automation in the QA system. If the QA system offers high accuracy in the management of CXR, the QA system can perform one of the important roles in preventing serious medical accidents and can be one of the most effective techniques to improve the overall quality of medical procedures and contribute to patient safety. This study aimed to construct a DL-based QA system for CXR and assess its usefulness.

2. Materials and Methods

This study was conducted in accordance with the principles of the Declaration of Helsinki and was approved by the local Institutional Review Board of the Otaru General Hospital (04–022). All the patients or their families provided oral or written informed consent to participate in this study.

2.1. Concept of a QA System for CXR

The workflow outline of the QA system is shown in Figure 1. The outline of the datasets is summarized in Table 1. The QA system consisted of four models: (1) correction of orientation, (2) correction of angle, (3) correction of left–right reversal, and (4) judging the patient's position. We used the regression method for the correction of the angle, and another correction was performed using the classification methods.

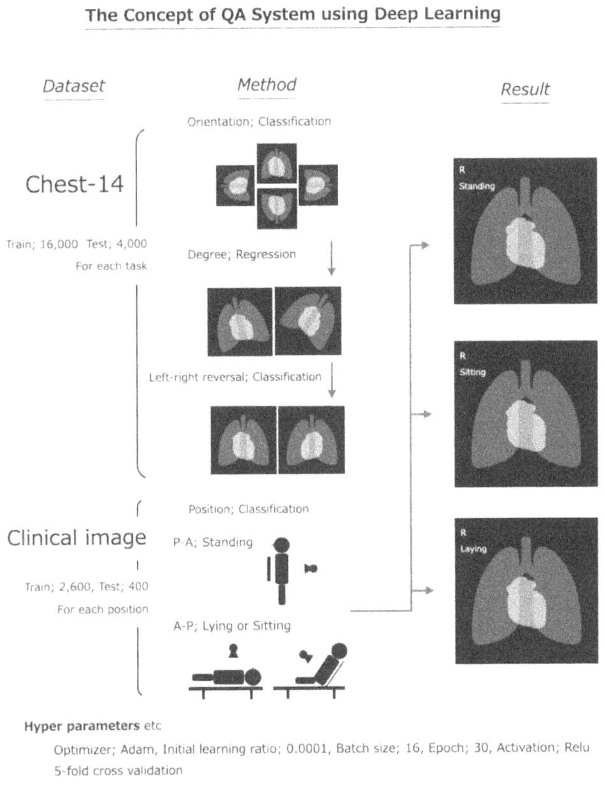

Figure 1. Concept of the QA system.

Table 1. Summary of datasets for each training and the overall test.

Task	Method	Source	Train Images	Test Images	Remarks	Pre-Processing
Orientation	Classification				Including 1/4 each of 0°, 90°, 180°, and 270° rotations.	Excluding images under 15 years old and inappropriate images by visual review
Angle	Regression	Chest-14	16,000	4000	Randomly rotation from −25 degrees to 25 degrees	The first exam of each patient
Left-Right reversal	Classification					Half of the images underwent horizontal flips.
Patient's position	Classification	Clinical image	7800	1200	Including 3000 images of each position, which were standing, sitting, and lying.	
					Including 40 images of each position, which were standing, sitting, and lying.	DICOM images were converted to JPEG format.
Overall test				120	30% of the images underwent horizontal flips.	Maker was masked.
					Randomly rotation from 0 degrees to −359 degrees.	

In this QA system, each image is programmed to undergo correction at each step according to the judgment of each DL model. Finally, the QA system adds the marker in the free space of the CXR to inform readers of the patient's position according to the judgement of the DL model. Makers were added at the right upper corner of the images.

The QA system consisted of four steps. Images were corrected in their orientation, angle, and left–right reversal, then the patient's position was estimated through the QA system. The QA system was constructed by combining the classification method and the regression method. QA, quality assurance.

2.2. Datasets and Preprocessing of Images

Chest-14 data [16–18] and clinical images were used for this study. Only the patients' positions were evaluated using the clinical data of Otaru General Hospital. Other datasets were constructed using Chest-14. To focus on adult patients, data of children aged <15 years from Chest-14 were carefully excluded. Inappropriate images were also excluded from Chest-14 based on the visual review by the four radiological technologists. All images were confirmed as having no subjects with left-right organ reversal by two radiological technologists. All images were converted into a 224-square matrix in Joint Photographic Experts Group (JPEG) format to apply CNNs.

2.3. Dataset for the Orientation Correction

Throughout the above processing, a total of 20,000 images were prepared for the orientation correction model. To avoid training similar images, all images were selected from the first examination of each patient from Chest-14. The images were divided into 16,000 training images and 4000 test images. The dataset included 1/4 of each of 0°, 90°, 180°, and 270° rotations. Half of the images were flipped horizontally.

2.4. Dataset for the Angle Correction

In the same way as the datasets for the correction of orientation, a total of 20,000 images were prepared from the first examination of each patient in Chest-14. Half of the images were flipped horizontally. All images were randomly rotated from −25 degrees to 25 degrees using the computed processing. The images were divided into 16,000 training images and 4000 testing images.

2.5. Dataset for the Left–Right Reversal Correction

A total of 20,000 images were prepared from the first examination of each patient in Chest-14. Half of the images were flipped horizontally with computed processing, and images were divided into 16,000 training images and 4000 testing images.

Horizontal flipping of chest radiographs can occur due to incorrect parameter settings on the X-ray console. For example, if a chest radiograph is taken in the sitting or lying position using the console's parameters for the standing position, the resulting image may be flipped horizontally.

2.6. Dataset for the Judgment of the Patient's Position

Clinical images obtained in Otaru General Hospital were utilized for the dataset for the judgment of the patient's position. A total of 3000 images were prepared for each position: standing, sitting, and lying. A total of 2600 and 400 images were used for training and testing data, respectively. Thus, a total of 7800 images for training and 1200 images for testing data were prepared.

2.7. Dataset for Overall Test

The QA system was constructed by combining the models trained using the above datasets. For the assessment of the overall quality of the QA system, a total of 120 clinical images, including 40 images of each position, were prepared. A random left–right inversion process was applied to 30% of the total images, and all images were randomly rotated from 0 to −359 degrees. Therefore, the dataset contained a mixture of images in various states. We masked the makers informing patient's position in the left upper space of CXR with a black cover in pre-processing of the clinical images.

2.8. Training for Creating Models

The software for building the DL method was developed with in-house MATLAB software (The Mathworks, Inc., Natick, MA, USA), and a desktop computer with an NVIDIA GeForce RTX 3080 graphics card (Nvidia Corporation, Santa Clara, CA, USA) was used. Three convolutional neural networks (CNNs) were used for image training, and they could be selected in MATLAB: VGG-16 (Visual Geometry Group) [19], ResNet-50 (Residual Neural Network) [20], and the original CNN. The original CNN was a simple CNN that was constructed by reducing the convolution layers in VGG-16. The architecture of the original CNN is shown in Figure 2. The classification method was applied, except for the angle correction. The regression method was applied for angle correction. In the regression method, the final layer was replaced with the regression layer, with an output size of 1. The dropout layer was added in front of the regression layer. The optimizer was Adam.

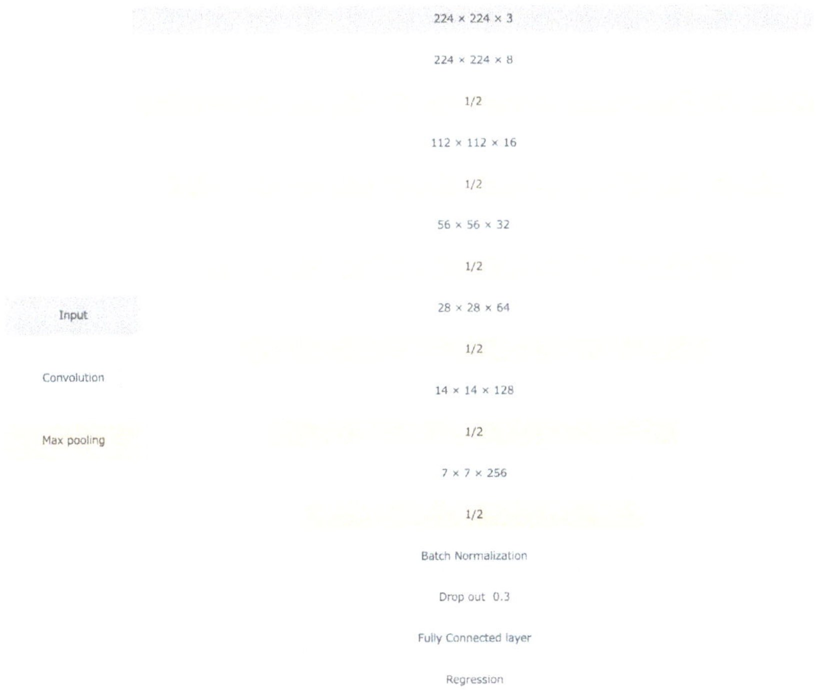

Figure 2. Outline of the original convolutional neural network.

The loss function was cross-entropy for the classification method and half-mean squared error for the regression method. Fivefold cross-validation was performed for all training. The following hyperparameters were used: maximum number of training epochs, 30; initial learning ratio, 0.0001; learning rate drop period, 5; and learning rate drop factor, 0.2. The early stopping method was used. The validation patience was 10 days, and the batch size was 16. In the classification method, the model with the highest area under the curve (AUC) was selected as the best model. In the regression method, the lowest mean absolute error (MAE) was selected as the best model.

2.9. Overall Test

We performed the overall test to evaluate the accuracy of our QA system. The QA system corrected the orientation, left-right reversal, and angle, then estimated the patient's position. Finally, a marker was added to the free space in the upper left corner of the image according to the patient's position. The image correction was confirmed with the visual evaluation by two radiological technologists who had 20 and 5 years of experience. Precision, recall, and overall accuracy in estimating the patient's position were calculated. The mean processing time of the QA system was measured. The dataset included 120 clinical images as described in the above.

2.10. Statistical Analysis

All continuous variables are shown as means ± standard deviations, regardless of the datasets. The Steel–Dwass test was used to compare the performance of the CNN after the Kruskal–Wallis test. A *p*-value < 0.05 was considered statistically significant. R version 4.1.1 was used for all statistical analysis and figure creation.

3. Results

3.1. Training for the Created Models

The accuracy and AUC are compared in Figure 3. In the classification method, ResNet-50 showed a tendency toward higher accuracy and AUC in all corrections. In the regression method, the original CNN showed significantly lower MAE of degrees and higher correlation coefficients among the three CNNs. The performance of the best models is shown in Table 2.

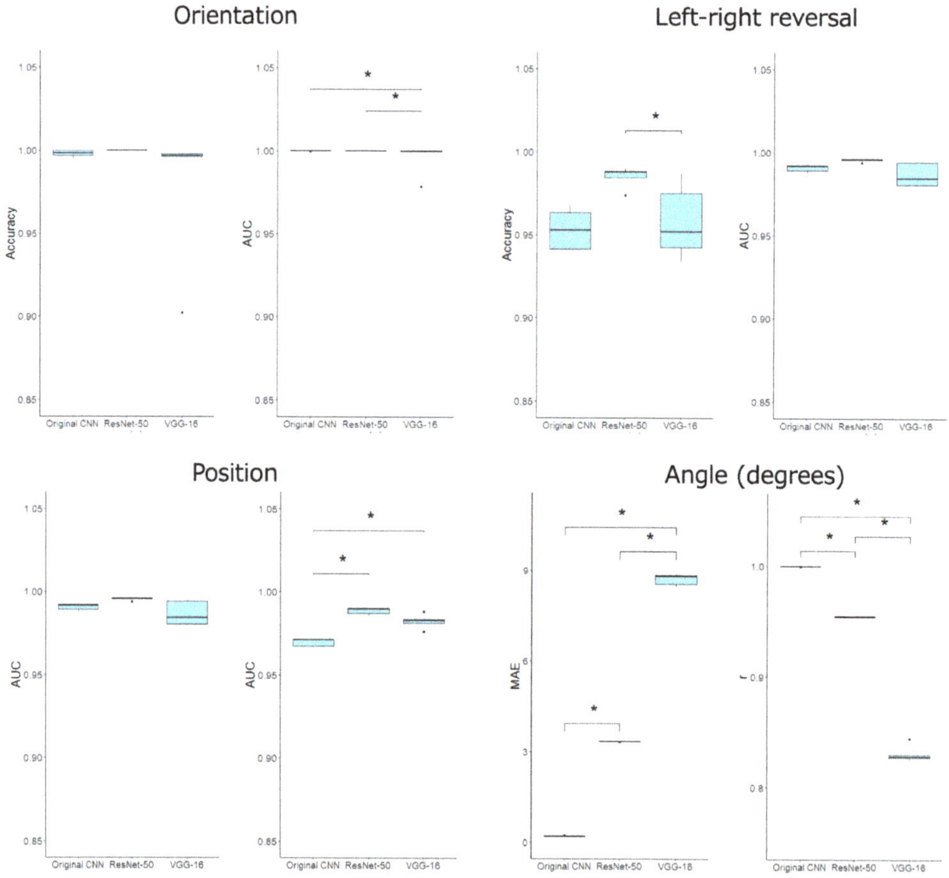

Figure 3. Summary of the accuracy and area under the curve of the receiver operating characteristics analysis. * $p < 0.05$.

Table 2. Summary of the accuracy and area under the curve of the best-performing models.

Method	Task	Best CNN	Accuracy	AUC
Classification	Orientation	ResNet-50	1.0000	1.0000
	Left-right reversal	ResNet-50	0.9895	0.99579
	Position	ResNet-50	0.9525	0.99017
			MAE (degrees)	r
Regression	Degree	Original CNN	0.19020	0.99977

Three CNNs were used: the original CNN, ResNet-50, and VGG-16. Both ResNet-50 and VGG-16 were trained. In the classification, ResNet-50 demonstrated higher accuracy and AUC among the three CNNs. In the regression, the original CNN showed significantly higher performance. CNN, convolutional neural networks.

In the classification method, ResNet-50 was superior. In the regression method, the original CNN demonstrated significantly higher performance. CNN, convolutional neural networks.

3.2. Overall Test

The examples of before–after correction using the QA system are shown in Figure 4. The confusion matrix of the overall test is shown in Figure 5. All images were corrected to normal orientation from various statuses. Makers informing the patient's position when took CXR were automatically added at right upper corner of images. The overall accuracy was 95.8%, and the time for correction was 0.39 ± 0.074 s. All images with standing positions were completely estimated. A few images were confused between the sitting position and the lying position.

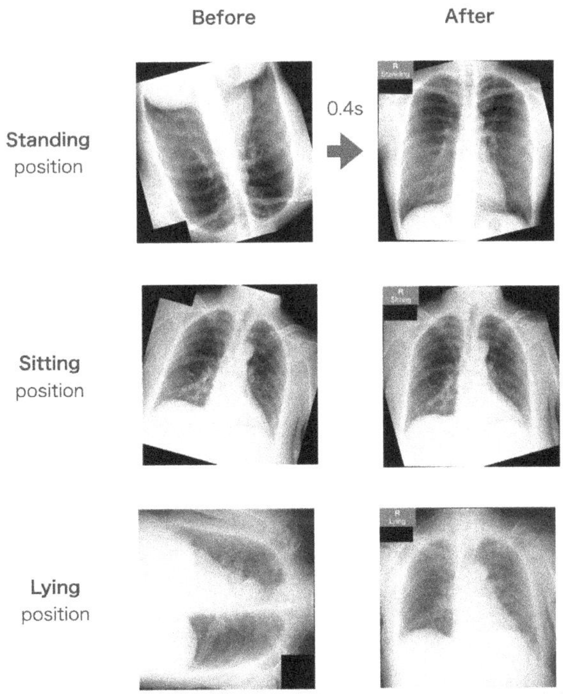

Figure 4. Images of each patient's position before and after evaluation through the QA system.

		True Label			
		Standing	Lying	Sitting	Precision (%)
Predicted Label	Standing	40	0	0	100
	Lying	0	39	4	88.6
	Sitting	0	1	36	97.3
	Recall (%)	100	97.5	90.0	95.8
					Overall accuracy (%)

Figure 5. Confusion matrix of the overall test.

All images were perfectly corrected in their orientation, angle, and left–right reversal. The patient's position was estimated with 96% accuracy within 0.4 s.

4. Discussion

We developed a QA system for CXR imaging using DL methods. The orientation, angle, and left–right reversal of CXR were corrected completely within approximately 0.4 s. In addition, the patient's position, such as standing, sitting, and lying, was estimated with 96% accuracy.

Fonseca A et al. achieved 99.4% accuracy for the orientation correction of pediatric CXR using a machine learning method [14]. In contrast, we acquired 100% accuracy for the correction of orientation, angle, and left-right reversal of CXR. This result suggested the advantage of using CNNs for the correction of CXR. Hržić F et al. reported highly accurate correction of various parts of radiographs using CNNs. They achieved 99.3% accuracy using VGG-16 and 0.02 s of processing with the GPU [15]. Meanwhile, we proposed a specific QA system with 100% geometric correction in CXR. This result showed that it might be better to construct the QA system according to each body part. The processing time will not become a large problem for routine clinical use because under 1 s is clearly faster than manual operation by technologists.

Totally, the main advantage of our study compared to the above studies is that we combined four simple models to construct the QA system. Moreover, we also estimated the patient's position directly related to the imaging findings. We believed that our study could propose a novel, comprehensive QA system for CXR based on the DL method.

The constructed QA system combined classification and regression using CNN. ResNet-50 demonstrated better performance for classification, correct orientation, left-right, and patient position estimation. We have already confirmed good compatibility with classification in medical images and ResNet-50 in magnetic resonance images [21]. The same trend was confirmed in this study.

On the contrary, the original CNN that had simple layers showed significantly higher performance for the regression method for correcting the angle of CXR images. We thought that the original CNN could avoid overtraining compared with other CNNs in the regression of angle correction. ResNet-50 might have too many deep layers to use the angle correction. The accuracy of the entire QA system can be assured by using the appropriate model for each task. In the detection of pneumonia in CXR using DL, Szeppi P et al. achieved extremely high accuracy, such as 97%, using modified VGG-16. This study strongly suggests that VGG-16-like CNNs are compatible with CXR and can exhibit high performance [22]. They showed the efficacy of dropouts on CNN. Our CNNs may be able to be refined according to their method.

QA systems should be built into the X-ray console system. CXR is immediately corrected, and the patient's position's marker is assigned. Then, radiological technologists confirm the corrected CXR and send it to the picture archiving and communication system.

Recently, medical errors have been serious concerns in the clinical scene. In the United States, medical errors claim more lives in hospitals than motor vehicle accidents, breast cancer, or AIDS [10]. According to the Swiss cheese model and Heinrich's law, many minor accidents are hidden behind serious medical accidents. Therefore, the prevention of minor accidents is directly related to the prevention of major accidents.

In the circumstances, artificial intelligence has been employed to develop an automatic QA system in the medical field. Claessens M et al. summarized the current status of the QA system based on AI in radiotherapy. In the radiotherapy field, various technologies using AI have been applied. The examples are auto-segmentation, image registration, auto-planning, CT image generation, patient QA, and machine QA. They suggested the importance of the correct use of case-specific and routine QA in clinical practice [23]. Chan MF et al. reported that machine learning approaches are explored, highlighting specific applications in machine and patient-specific quality assurance (QA). They introduced the clinical usefulness and limitations of machine learning in QA systems. They argued for the necessity of a sanity check and a second check before the clinical use of QA systems based on AI. Additionally, they suggested that we should address the limitations of both data and ML models. [24] Thus, we believe that we should avoid total reliance on AI-based QA systems, especially in the field of radiography, where AI-based QA systems have not been developed in comparison with radiotherapy. In this sense, our QA system for CXR will work as a powerful tool to perform double-checks with radiological technologists.

A large amount of radiography has been taken in daily practice. Therefore, the QA system for radiographs is sure to make a significant contribution to daily clinical practice. However, many studies of radiographs using AI technology have been performed to diagnose using the classification method and to estimate the quantitative value using the regression method. We considered that these techniques should be applied to the construction of a QA system for radiographs. However, no study has reported an automatic QA system for CXR imaging to automatically correct the orientation and angle and estimate the patient's position. Hence, we attempted to develop a QA system for CXR, which is the most common radiograph in clinical practice.

One of the reasons CXR was selected was that a large dataset such as Chest-14, which had over one hundred thousand CXR was available, and many clinical images were also stored on our institution's server. To create a DL model with high accuracy, a large data set is necessary. In addition, the CXR has only one pattern, which the chest is in the center of the image, and the pattern of the image is extremely small compared to other parts, such as the extremities. We did not need to prepare images of many patterns. This fact works as an advantage in the preparation of datasets and the model training process. Therefore, CXR was suitable to attempt to construct a QA system based on AI as a novel study.

We excluded images with the same patients from Chest-14 to avoid training similar images. Many images became unusable, but this process was necessary to avoid overfitting specific images. It seems that the dataset had sufficient size for this task because complete correction was achieved in the orientation, angle, and left-right reversal. Chest-14 does not provide information relating detail patient's position when taking XR, such as standing, sitting, or lying. Therefore, we used the clinical images of our institution as a dataset to train the estimation of the patient's position, even though dataset was small compared with other datasets. As a result, we obtained 96% accuracy in the patient's position estimation. We believe that the data set size was sufficient for this study.

Meanwhile, a few images were confused between the sitting position and the lying position in this system. This is because strict positioning management was not enforced. In addition, in both the sitting and lying positions, X-rays are irradiated from the front side of the patient. Therefore, CXR images in both positions may become very similar. From the clinical perspective, the degree of body raising is adjusted according to the patient's respiratory status. We think that the blurring of the boundary between the sitting position and the lying position is, to some extent, unavoidable.

On the other hand, the standing position was completely classified. Thus, the direction of X-ray irradiation was fully distinguished. The direction of X-ray irradiation is directly related to CXR findings, such as the distribution of pleural effusions, air inclusions and the measurement of CTR. Therefore, an accurate estimation of the irradiation direction is an important factor in CXR management in clinical practice. Moreover, orientation, image angle, and left-right reversal were fully corrected by the QA system. The processing time is clearly faster than a manual operation. These facts proved the usefulness of the QA system.

This study involves several limitations. First, this study was performed at a single institution. Further investigation is desired to evaluate the generalization performance of the QA system. The larger datasets, including another institution's clinical images, should be applied for model training. Moreover, we excluded images of children under 15 from the datasets. This processing may lead to a statistical bias compared with the actual clinical scene. Although this processing is essential to achieving a high-accuracy model for CXR in adult patients [12].

Second, all clinical images were retrospectively prepared. Therefore, a black mask is present in the upper-right corner of the image to hide a previous marker corresponding to the patient's position. This mask might work as a landmark to correct the orientation, angle, and left-right reversal. Further investigation using plain CXR imaging is warranted. Although, the correction model is created from Chest14 data that does not have a mask. Third, all evaluations were performed using a GPU machine. The portable X-ray console PC without a GPU may delay the processing time. The clinical trial should be attempted using a daily-use X-ray console system.

Third, this study aimed to construct a specific AI for the QA of CXR. Hence, this system cannot make fully alternative human work from the perspective of the difference between the AI model and human cognition [13]. Still, furthermore, double-checking should be enforced by both the QA system and technologists.

5. Conclusions

This study showed that the deep learning model could perform quality assurance for CXR. QA system was constructed by combining the classification method and the regression method. The orientation, angle, and left-right reversal were fully corrected. The regression method was used for the correction of the angle. Other corrections were performed using the classification method. Finally, the QA system added the maker demonstrating the patient's position when it took the CXR, such as standing, sitting, and lying. Patient's position was estimated with 96% accuracy. The correction processing was about 0.4 s. This system will make a large contribution to clinical practice.

Author Contributions: Conceptualization, D.O.; methodology, D.O.; software, D.O.; validation, S.S., Y.H. and S.K.; investigation, S.S., Y.H. and S.K.; writing—original draft preparation, D.O.; writing—review and editing, H.S.; visualization, D.O.; supervision, H.S.; project administration, D.O. All authors have read and agreed to the published version of the manuscript.

Funding: This research received no external funding.

Institutional Review Board Statement: This study was conducted in accordance with the principles of the Declaration of Helsinki and was approved by the local Institutional Review Board of the Otaru General Hospital (04–022). All the patients or their families provided oral or written informed consent to participate in this study. All authors had no conflicts of interest.

Informed Consent Statement: Written or oral consent was obtained from all subjects involved in the study.

Data Availability Statement: We used Chest-14 datasets. (https://nihcc.app.box.com/v/ChestXray-NIHCC accessed on 4 January 2023). The clinical images are not available.

Conflicts of Interest: The authors declare no conflict of interest.

Abbreviations

The following abbreviations are used in this manuscript:

AI	Artificial intelligence
AUC	Area under the curve
CNN	Convolution neural network
COVID-19	Coronavirus disease-2019
CT	Computed tomography
CTR	Cardiothoracic ratio
CXR	Chest X-ray
DL	Deep learning
JPEG	Joint Photographic Experts Group
MAE	Mean absolute error
ML	Machine learning
MRI	Magnetic resonance imaging
QA	Quality assurance

References

1. Loomba, R.S.; Shah, P.H.; Nijhawan, K.; Aggarwal, S.; Arora, R. Cardiothoracic ratio for prediction of left ventricular dilation: A systematic review and pooled analysis. *Future Cardiol.* **2015**, *11*, 171–175. [CrossRef] [PubMed]
2. Truszkiewicz, K.; Poręba, M.; Poręba, R.; Gać, P. Radiological Cardiothoracic Ratio as a Potential Predictor of Right Ventricular Enlargement in Patients with Suspected Pulmonary Embolism Due to COVID-19. *J. Clin. Med. Res.* **2021**, *10*, 5703. [CrossRef] [PubMed]
3. Yotsueda, R.; Taniguchi, M.; Tanaka, S.; Eriguchi, M.; Fujisaki, K.; Torisu, K.; Masutani, K.; Hirakata, H.; Kitazono, T.; Tsuruya, K. Cardiothoracic Ratio and All-Cause Mortality and Cardiovascular Disease Events in Hemodialysis Patients: The Q-Cohort Study. *Am. J. Kidney Dis.* **2017**, *70*, 84–92. [CrossRef]
4. Cardinale, L.; Priola, A.M.; Moretti, F.; Volpicelli, G. Effectiveness of chest radiography, lung ultrasound and thoracic computed tomography in the diagnosis of congestive heart failure. *World J. Radiol.* **2014**, *6*, 230–237. [CrossRef] [PubMed]
5. Gupta, R.K.; Newbould, R.D.; Matthews, P.M. Methods of Measuring Lung Water. *Pediatr. Crit. Care Med.* **2012**, *13*, 209–215. [CrossRef]
6. Liu, T.Y.; Rai, A.; Ditkofsky, N.; Deva, D.P.; Dowdell, T.R.; Ackery, A.D.; Mathur, S. Cost benefit analysis of portable chest radiography through glass: Initial experience at a tertiary care centre during COVID-19 pandemic. *J. Med. Imaging Radiat. Sci.* **2021**, *52*, 186–190. [CrossRef]
7. Rorat, M.; Zińczuk, A.; Szymański, W.; Simon, K.; Guziński, M. Usefulness of a portable chest radiograph in the initial diagnosis of coronavirus disease 2019. *Pol. Arch. Intern. Med.* **2020**, *130*, 906–909.
8. Saez de Gordoa, E.; Portella, A.; Escudero-Fernández, J.M.; Andreu Soriano, J. Usefulness of chest X-rays for detecting COVID-19 pneumonia during the SARS-CoV-2 pandemic. *Radiologia* **2022**, *64*, 310–316. [CrossRef]
9. Pescarini, L.; Inches, I. Systematic approach to human error in radiology. *Radiol. Med.* **2006**, *111*, 252–267. [CrossRef]
10. Kora, P.; Ooi, C.P.; Faust, O.; Raghavendra, U.; Gudigar, A.; Chan, W.Y.; Meenakshi, K.; Swaraja, K.; Plawiak, P.; Rajendra Acharya, U. Transfer Learning Techniques for Medical Image Analysis: A Review. *Biocybern. Biomed. Eng.* **2022**, *42*, 79–107. [CrossRef]
11. Mondal, M.R.H.; Bharati, S.; Podder, P. Diagnosis of COVID-19 Using Machine Learning and Deep Learning: A Review. *Curr. Med. Imaging Rev.* **2021**, *17*, 1403–1418. [CrossRef]
12. Roccetti, M.; Delnevo, G.; Casini, L.; Cappiello, G. Is Bigger Always Better? A Controversial Journey to the Center of Machine Learning Design, with Uses and Misuses of Big Data for Predicting Water Meter Failures. *J. Big Data* **2019**, *6*, 1–23. Available online: https://www.proquest.com\T1\guilsinglrightdocview (accessed on 4 January 2023). [CrossRef]
13. Marcus, G.; Davis, E. Insights for AI from the Human Mind. *Commun. ACM* **2020**, *64*, 38–41. [CrossRef]
14. Fonseca, A.; Vieira, G.S.; Felix, J.; Freire Sobrinho, P.; Silva, A.V.P.; Soares, F. Automatic Orientation Identification of Pediatric Chest X-Rays. In Proceedings of the 2020 IEEE 44th Annual Computers, Software, and Applications Conference (COMPSAC), Madrid, Spain, 13–17 July 2020.
15. Hržić, F.; Tschauner, S.; Sorantin, E.; Štajduhar, I. XAOM: A Method for Automatic Alignment and Orientation of Radiographs for Computer-Aided Medical Diagnosis. *Comput. Biol. Med.* **2021**, *132*, 104300. [CrossRef] [PubMed]
16. Sim, J.Z.T.; Ting, Y.-H.; Tang, Y.; Feng, Y.; Lei, X.; Wang, X.; Chen, W.-X.; Huang, S.; Wong, S.-T.; Lu, Z.; et al. Diagnostic Performance of a Deep Learning Model Deployed at a National COVID-19 Screening Facility for Detection of Pneumonia on Frontal Chest Radiographs. *Healthcare* **2022**, *10*, 175. [CrossRef] [PubMed]
17. Lenga, M.; Schulz, H.; Saalbach, A. Continual Learning for Domain Adaptation in Chest X-Ray Classification. In Proceedings of the Third Conference on Medical Imaging with Deep Learning, PMLR, Montreal, QC, Canada, 6–8 July 2020; Volume 121, pp. 413–423.
18. Baltruschat, I.M.; Nickisch, H.; Grass, M.; Knopp, T.; Saalbach, A. Comparison of Deep Learning Approaches for Multi-Label Chest X-Ray Classification. *Sci. Rep.* **2019**, *9*, 1–10. [CrossRef]

19. Simonyan, K.; Zisserman, A. Very Deep Convolutional Networks for Large-Scale Image Recognition. *arXiv* **2014**, arXiv:1409.1556.
20. He, Z.; Ren, S. Deep Residual Learning for Image Recognition. In Proceedings of the 2016 IEEE Conference on Computer Vision and Pattern Recognition (CVPR), Las Vegas, NV, USA, 27–30 June 2016; pp. 770–778.
21. Sugimori, H.; Hamaguchi, H.; Fujiwara, T.; Ishizaka, K. Classification of type of brain magnetic resonance images with deep learning technique. *Magn. Reson. Imaging* **2021**, *77*, 180–185. [CrossRef]
22. Szepesi, P.; Szilágyi, L. Detection of Pneumonia Using Convolutional Neural Networks and Deep Learning. *Biocybern. Biomed. Eng.* **2022**, *42*, 1012–1022. [CrossRef]
23. Claessens, M.; Oria, C.S.; Brouwer, C.L.; Ziemer, B.P.; Scholey, J.E.; Lin, H.; Witztum, A.; Morin, O.; El Naqa, I.; Van Elmpt, W.; et al. Quality Assurance for AI-Based Applications in Radiation Therapy. *Semin. Radiat. Oncol.* **2022**, *2*, 421–431. [CrossRef]
24. Chan, M.F.; Witztum, A.; Valdes, G. Integration of AI and machine learning in radiotherapy QA. *Front. Artif. Intell.* **2020**, *3*, 577620. [CrossRef] [PubMed]

applied sciences

MDPI

rticle

Deep-Learning Algorithms for Prescribing Insoles to Patients with Foot Pain

oung Kun Kim [1], Yoo Jin Choo [2], In Sik Park [3], Jin-Woo Choi [4], Donghwi Park [4,*,†] and Min Cheol Chang [2,*,†]

1 Department of Business Administration, School of Business, Yeungnam University, Gyeongsan-si 38541, Republic of Korea
2 Department of Physical Medicine and Rehabilitation, Yeungnam University Medical Center, College of Medicine, Yeungnam University, 317-1 Daemyungdong, Namku, Daegu 41415, Republic of Korea
3 Korean Podiatry and Pedorthics Institute, Goyang 10442, Republic of Korea
4 Department of Physical Medicine and Rehabilitation, University of Ulsan College of Medicine, Ulsan University Hospital, 877 Bangeojin Sunhwando-ro, Dong-gu, Ulsan 44033, Republic of Korea
* Correspondence: bdome@hanmail.net (D.P.); wheel633@ynu.ac.kr (M.C.C.); Tel.: +82-52-250-7222 (D.P.); +82-53-620-4682 (M.C.C.); Fax: +82-52-250-7228 (D.P.)
† These authors contributed equally to this work.

Abstract: Foot pain is a common musculoskeletal disorder. Orthotic insoles are widely used in patients with foot pain. Inexperienced clinicians have difficulty prescribing orthotic insoles appropriately by considering various factors associated with the alteration of foot alignment. We attempted to develop deep-learning algorithms that can automatically prescribe orthotic insoles to patients with foot pain and assess their accuracy. In total, 838 patients were included in this study; 70% (n = 586) and 30% (n = 252) were used as the training and validation sets, respectively. The resting calcaneal stance position and data related to pelvic elevation, pelvic tilt, and pelvic rotation were used as input data for developing the deep-learning algorithms for insole prescription. The target data were the foot posture index for the modified root technique and the necessity of heel lift, entire lift, and lateral wedge, medial wedge, and calcaneocuboid arch supports. In the results, regarding the foot posture index for the modified root technique, for the left foot, the mean absolute error (MAE) and root mean square error (RMSE) of the validation dataset for the developed model were 1.408 and 3.365, respectively. For the right foot, the MAE and RMSE of the validation dataset for the developed model were 1.601 and 3.549, respectively. The accuracies for heel lift, entire lift, and lateral wedge, medial wedge, and calcaneocuboid arch supports were 89.7%, 94.8%, 72.2%, 98.4%, and 79.8%, respectively. The micro-average area under the receiver operating characteristic curves for heel lift, entire lift, and lateral wedge, medial wedge, and calcaneocuboid arch supports were 0.949, 0.941, 0.826, 0.792, and 0.827, respectively. In conclusion, our deep-learning models automatically prescribed orthotic insoles in patients with foot pain and showed outstanding to acceptable accuracy.

Keywords: insole; foot pain; deep learning; prescription

1. Introduction

Foot pain is common among adults and is frequently observed in patients who visit pain clinics, particularly older adults [1,2]. Its prevalence among adults aged ≥18 years is reported to range from 17 to 24% [3]. It can lead to a diminished ability to perform activities of daily living, problems with balance and gait, and an increased risk of falls [1,2]. Foot pain is reported to significantly impact the quality of daily life and work [1,2]. Therefore, the appropriate treatment of foot pain is important. Despite the use of various therapeutic methods such as oral medication, physical therapy, injections, extracorporeal shockwave therapy, and orthoses, many patients frequently complain of persistent foot pain [1,2,4,5]. The development of foot pain is associated with alterations in foot alignment, which result in abnormally distributed loads on the foot [6,7]. Orthotic insoles are frequently used to correct altered foot alignments [8,9]. The usefulness of orthotic insoles for patients with foot pain has been demonstrated in several previous studies, and they have been widely applied in clinical practice for the treatment of foot pain [10–12].

Additionally, the asymmetrical motion between the right and left lower limbs and pelvic malalignment is kinetically associated with abnormal foot motion [13]. A misalignment can create excessive load on certain foot structures, causing foot pain. To correct the symmetry between the lower limbs and pelvic malalignment, the height of orthotic insoles can be adjusted by lifting the insole. The asymmetric movement of the pelvis can be corrected by applying lateral wedge, medial wedge, and calcaneocuboid arch supports to the insole and lifting the heel [14,15]. The rotation of the pelvis to one side can be blocked using lateral wedge, medial wedge, and calcaneocuboid arch supports. The tilt of one side of the pelvis toward the anterior region can be corrected by a heel lift.

A lot of experience should be accumulated to prescribe orthotic insoles appropriately. To apply the appropriate orthotic insole, clinicians should consider various factors such as foot alignment, pelvic movement, and leg length discrepancy [13,16]. The comprehensive consideration of various factors associated with the alteration of foot alignment is difficult for inexperienced clinicians. An algorithm that automatically prescribes the orthotic insole would be of great help to clinicians treating patients with foot pain.

Machine learning is an artificial intelligence technique that involves system learning rules and patterns from given data [17–19]. It has several advantages for determining the appropriate prescription for patients with various disorders [17–19]. The deep-learning technique is an advanced machine learning approach [20,21]. In particular, it constructs artificial neural networks with functions and structures similar to those of the human brain using a large number of hidden layers [20,21]. Several studies have demonstrated that the deep-learning technique can outperform traditional machine learning techniques [17–19].

We propose that deep learning can be used to develop an algorithm that automatically prescribes orthotic insoles to patients with foot pain, using several measured results as input data. In the current study, we investigated the potential of deep learning to prescribe an appropriate orthotic insole for patients with foot pain.

2. Methods

2.1. Study Design and Population

The data for developing the machine learning algorithms were obtained from a single insole manufacturer (BioMechanics, Goyang-si, Republic of Korea). Insoles were made on the basis of the insole prescription paper on which the results of the physical examination, including the resting calcaneal stance position (RCSP), pelvic elevation, pelvic tilt, and pelvic rotation, were written [22–24]. The prescription paper was written by a podiatrist (ISP) who had more than 25 years of experience in the prescription of orthotic insoles for patients with foot pain. Insole prescriptions were written at five different hospitals. We used the following inclusion criteria: (1) age $\geq$ 20 years, (2) the insole was prescribed for managing foot pain, (3) patients with no neurological disorders, (4) patients with no diabetic foot ulcer, and (5) the presence of an insole prescription paper containing all the information on the RCSP, pelvic elevation, pelvic tilt, and pelvic rotation.

Informed consent was waived by the Institutional Review Board of Yeungnam University Hospital. This study was approved by the Institutional Review Board of Yeungnam University Hospital (2022-06-046). All procedures were carried out in accordance with the relevant guidelines and regulations.

2.2. Input Variables

Resting Calcaneal Stance Position

To measure the RCSP, patients with foot pain were asked to place their foot on the edge of the bed and lay in the prone position on a bed parallel to the ground. The investigator manually inspected the foot and drew a bisector by placing three dots on the top, middle, and bottom of the heel, regardless of the fat surrounding the calcaneus (Figure 1A). The RCSP was measured when the patients stood on their feet placed at a fist-width distance (Figure 1B). Angles were determined between the line of the heel and the surface.

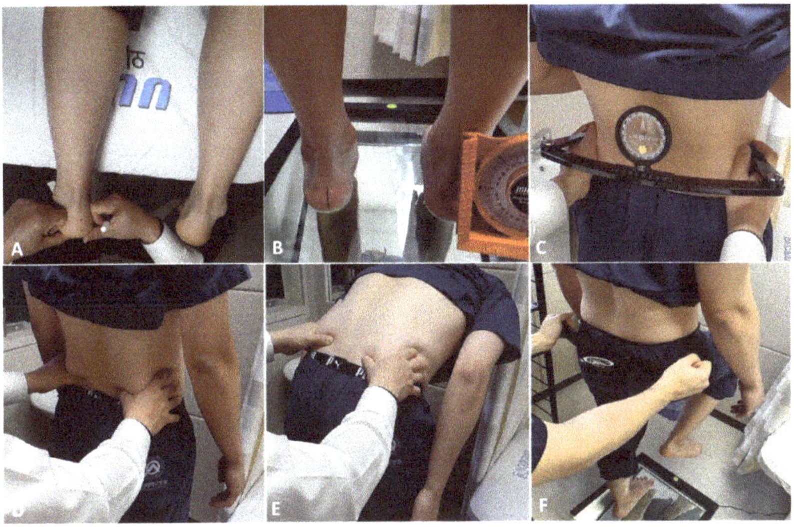

Figure 1. Measurement of the resting calcaneal stance position (RCSP), pelvic elevation, pelvic tilt, and pelvic rotation. Measurements of the (**A**) RCSP in the prone position, (**B**) RCSP in the standing position, (**C**) pelvic elevation, (**D**,**E**) pelvic tilt, and (**F**) pelvic rotation.

2.3. Pelvic Elevation, Pelvic Tilt, and Pelvic Rotation

Pelvic elevation indicated the height difference between the left and right iliac crests. It was measured using an angulometer with the patients standing on their feet placed at a fist-width distance. The right and left blades of the angulometer were placed at the highest point of the iliac crest, and pelvic elevation was measured (Figure 1C). When one iliac crest was elevated relative to the iliac crest of the other side, the value was indicated as a positive value, and a larger value indicated a greater difference in the heights of the left and right pelvis (e.g., when the heights of the left and right iliac crests were the same, it was described as 0-0, and when the height of the left iliac crest was 2 degrees higher than the other side, it was presented as 2-0).

To assess the presence of pelvic tilt, the investigator's thumb was placed on the posterior superior iliac spine (PSIS), and the remaining fingers were placed on the patient's iliac crest (Figure 1D). The investigator then asked the patients to bend their lower back 90 degrees forward and assessed the difference in the degree of anterior tilt of the investigator's thumb (Figure 1E). When the tilt of both PSISs was symmetrical, it was presented as "−,−," and when the tilt of the left PSIS was greater than the left PSIS, it was presented as "+,−."

To measure pelvic rotation, the investigator attached the angulometer to the patients' PSISs, asked the patients to walk in place, and observed the movement of the angulometer (Figure 1F). The investigator assessed whether the degree of the backward movement of the right and left wings of the angulometer was symmetrical. When the angulometer attached to the patients' PSIS moved backward symmetrically, it was described as "−,−," and when the left side moved backward more than the right side, it was described as "+,−."

2.4. Target Variables

The foot posture index for the modified root technique and the application of heel lift, entire lift, and lateral wedge, medial wedge, and calcaneocuboid arch supports were set as the target variables (Figure 2).

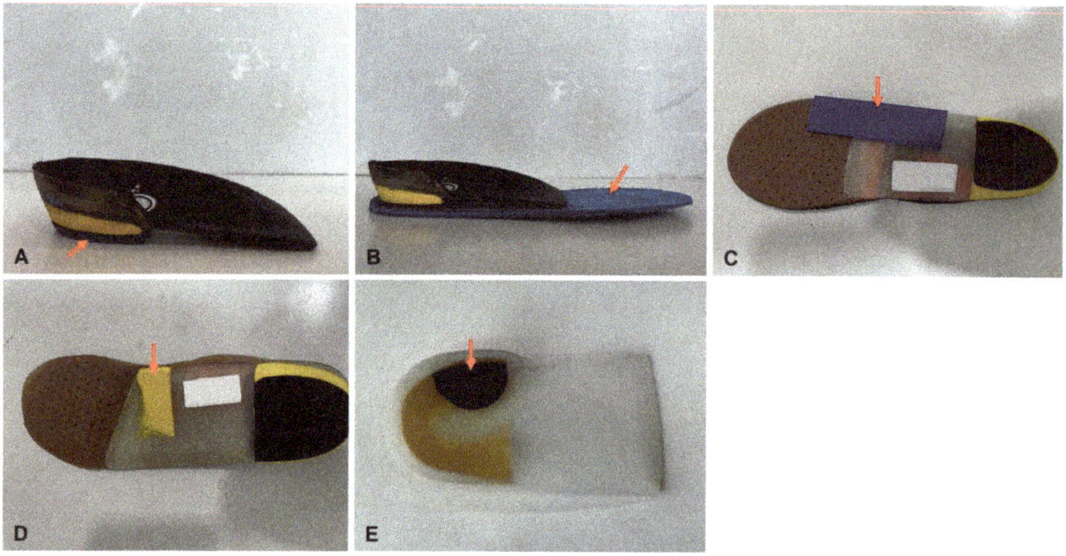

Figure 2. Photographs of (**A**) heel lift, (**B**) entire lift, and (**C**) lateral wedge, (**D**) medial wedge, and (**E**) calcaneocuboid arch supports.

2.5. Deep-Learning Algorithms

Sequential deep neural networks (DNNs) were applied for classification and sequential DNN-based regression algorithms (Supplementary Materials). TensorFlow 2.9.1 with Keras, Python 3.8.1, and Scikit-learn 1.1.1. were used to train two DNN regression models (right and left feet) for automatic prescriptions of the foot posture index for the modified root technique and five DNN classification models to determine the application of heel lift, entire lift, and lateral wedge, medial wedge, and calcaneocuboid arch supports. Among the study population, 70% (n = 586) and 30% (n = 252) were included in the training and validation sets, respectively. The details of each model are listed in Tables 1–6.

Table 1 shows the application of deep-learning regression to determine the foot posture index. This approach is particularly effective because of its capability to handle complex and non-linear associations between inputs and outputs, making it an optimal solution for determining the foot posture index using continuous values. The mean absolute error (MAE) and root mean square error (RMSE) were used to validate the performance of the two regression models.

Table 1. Details of the model for determining the foot posture index for the modified root technique.

	Prescription Left DNN Regression Model	Prescription Right DNN Regression Model
DNN model	- Four hidden layers with 256-128-128-64 neurons - RMSProp optimizer, ReLU activation - Learning rate 1×10^{-5}, batch size 512 - Batch normalization for regularization	- Five hidden layers with 512-512-1024-1024-512 neurons - RMSProp optimizer, ReLU activation - Learning rate 2×10^{-3}, batch size 512 - Batch normalization for regularization
Model performance	- MAE 1.460, RMSE 3.539 for training - MAE 1.408, RMSE 3.365 for validation	- MAE 1.560, RMSE 3.860 for training - MAE 1.601, RMSE 3.549 for validation

DNN, deep neural network; RMSProp, root mean squared propagation; ReLU, rectified linear unit; MAE, mean absolute error; RMSE, root mean square error.

Table 2. Details of the model for determining the application of heel lift.

Sample size and ratio Sample class size and ratio	- 70% for training: 586; 30% for validation: 252; total: 838 - Class 0: 392 (66.9%), class 1: 64 (10.9%), class 2: 130 (22.2%) for training - Class 0: 169 (67.1%), class 1: 28 (11.1%), class 2: 55 (21.8%) for validation					
DNN model	- Five hidden layers with 512-512-1024-1024-512 neurons - Adam optimizer, ReLU activation - Learning rate 1×10^{-2} batch size 32 - Dropout layer for regularization - Training accuracy: 89.1%, validation accuracy: 89.7%					
Model performance (validation data)	Class	Precision	Recall	F1-score	Support	ROC AUC
	0	0.961	0.882	0.920	169	0.942
	1	0.839	0.939	0.881	28	0.993
	2	0.773	0.927	0.843	55	0.950
	Macro average	0.858	0.913	0.881	252	0.961
	Micro average	0.907	0.897	0.899	252	0.949

DNN, deep neural network; Adam, adaptive moment estimation; ReLU, rectified linear unit; ROC, receiver operating characteristic; AUC, area under the curve; class 0, no application; class 1, application of heel lift to the right side; class 2, application of heel lift to the left side.

Table 3. Details of the model for determining the application of entire lift.

Sample size and ratio Sample class size and ratio	- 70% for training: 586; 30% for validation: 252; total: 838 - Class 0: 508 (86.7%), class 1: 23 (3.9%), class 2: 55 (9.4%) for training - Class 0: 218 (86.5%), class 1: 10 (4%), class 2: 24 (9.5%) for validation					
DNN model	- Three hidden layers with 256-256-512 neurons - RMSProp optimizer, ReLU activation - Learning rate 5×10^{-3}, batch size 2 - Dropout layer for regularization - Training accuracy: 94.7%, validation accuracy: 94.8%					
Model performance (validation data)	Class	Precision	Recall	F1-score	Support	ROC AUC
	0	0.977	0.968	0.972	218	0.939
	1	0.750	0.600	0.667	10	0.868
	2	0.786	0.917	0.846	24	0.991
	Macro average	0.838	0.828	0.828	252	0.933
	Micro average	0.950	0.948	0.948	252	0.941

DNN, deep neural network; RMSProp, root mean squared propagation; ReLU, rectified linear unit; ROC, receiver operating characteristic; AUC, area under the curve; class 0, no application; class 1, application of entire lift to the right side; class 2, application of entire lift to the left side.

Table 4. Details of the model for determining the application of lateral wedge support.

Sample size and ratio Sample class size and ratio	- 70% for training: 586; 30% for validation: 252; total: 838 - Class 0: 571 (97.4%), class 1: 9 (0.015%), class 2: 3 (0.005%), class 3: 3 (0.005%) for training - Class 0: 245 (97.2%), class 1: 4 (0.016%), class 2: 1 (0.004%), class 3: 2 (0.008%) for validation					
DNN model	- Two hidden layers with 256-1024 neurons - RMSProp optimizer, ReLU activation - Learning rate 5 × 10^{-4}, batch size 128 - Dropout layer for regularization - Training accuracy: 98.8%, validation accuracy: 98.4%					
Model performance (validation data)	Class	Precision	Recall	F1-score	Support	ROC AUC
	0	0.988	0.996	0.992	245	0.790
	1	0.667	0.500	0.571	4	0.861
	2	1.000	1.000	1.000	1	1.000
	3	1.000	0.500	0.667	2	0.800
	Macro average	0.914	0.749	0.807	252	0.863
	Micro average	0.983	0.984	0.983	252	0.792

DNN, deep neural network; RMSProp, root mean squared propagation; ReLU, rectified linear unit; ROC, receiver operating characteristic; AUC, area under the curve; class 0, no application; class 1, application of medial wedge support to the right side; class 2, application of medial wedge support to the left side; class 3, application of medial wedge support to both sides.

Table 5. Details of the model for determining the application of medial wedge support.

Sample size and ratio Sample class size and ratio	- 70% for training: 586; 30% for validation: 252; total: 838 - Class 0: 289 (49.3%), class 1: 19 (3.2%), class 2: 80 (13.7%), class 3: 198 (33.8%) for training - Class 0: 124 (49.2%), class 1: 8 (3.2%), class 2: 35 (13.9%), class 3: 85 (33.7%) for validation					
DNN model	- Two hidden layers with 256-1024 neurons - Nadam optimizer, ReLU activation - Learning rate 5 × 10^{-5}, batch size 64 - Dropout layer for regularization - Training accuracy: 93.0%, validation accuracy: 72.2%					
Model performance (validation data)	Class	Precision	Recall	F1-score	Support	ROC AUC
	0	0.786	0.798	0.792	124	0.827
	1	0.333	0.250	0.285	8	0.754
	2	0.455	0.429	0.441	35	0.791
	3	0.759	0.776	0.767	85	0.845
	Macro average	0.583	0.583	0.572	252	0.804
	Micro average	0.716	0.722	0.719	252	0.826

DNN, deep neural network; Nadam, Nesterov-accelerated adaptive moment estimation; ReLU, rectified linear unit; ROC, receiver operating characteristic; AUC, area under the curve; class 0, no application; class 1, application of lateral wedge support to the right side; class 2, application of lateral wedge support to the left side; class 3, application of lateral wedge support to both sides.

Tables 2–6 present the results of the multi-class classification models designed to handle more than two classes or categories. The entire lift, lateral wedge support, and calcaneocuboid arch support models used the RMSProp optimizer. The heel lift and medial wedge support models utilized the Adam and Nadam optimizers, respectively. In terms of performance, the heel lift, entire lift, and lateral wedge support models exhibited exceptional results, with accuracy rates surpassing 90% for the validation data. In contrast, the accuracies of the medial wedge support and calcaneocuboid arch support models were moderate, yielding accuracy levels ranging between 72% and 80% for the validation data.

Table 6. Details of the model for determining the application of calcaneocuboid arch support.

Sample size and ratio Sample class size and ratio	- 70% for training: 586; 30% for validation: 252; total: 838 - Class 0: 412 (70.3%), class 1: 36 (6.1%), class 2: 138 (23.6%) for training - Class 0: 177 (70.2%), class 1: 16 (6.4%), class 2: 59 (23.4%) for validation					
DNN model	- Four hidden layers with 1024-512-256-128 neurons - RMSProp optimizer, ReLU activation - Learning rate 2×10^{-3}, batch size 128 - Dropout layer for regularization - Training accuracy: 88.7%, validation accuracy: 79.8%					
Model performance (validation data)	Class	Precision	Recall	F1-score	Support	ROC AUC
	0	0.868	0.853	0.860	177	0.824
	1	0.684	0.812	0.743	16	0.859
	2	0.627	0.627	0.627	59	0.828
	Macro average	0.726	0.764	0.743	252	0.837
	Micro average	0.800	0.798	0.798	252	0.827

DNN, deep neural network; RMSProp, root mean squared propagation; ReLU, rectified linear unit; ROC, receiver operating characteristic; AUC, area under the curve; class 0, no application; class 1, application of calcaneocuboid arch support to the right side; class 2: application of calcaneocuboid arch support to the left side.

3. Statistical Analysis

Receiver operating characteristic (ROC) curve analysis was performed using scikit-learn, and the area under the curve (AUC) was calculated. The one-versus-one (OVO) method was used to calculate accurate multi-class macro- and micro-average ROC AUC values. The OVO method is a commonly used approach for solving multi-class imbalance problems; this method transforms a multi-class problem into a set of two-class sub-problems [25].

4. Results

In total, 838 patients (mean age, 47.7 ± 14.7 years; 323 men, 515 women) were included. Regarding the foot posture index for the modified root technique, for the left foot, the mean absolute error (MAE) and root mean square error (RMSE) of the validation dataset for the developed model were 1.408 and 3.365, respectively (Table 1). For the right foot, the MAE and RMSE of the validation dataset for the developed model were 1.601 and 3.549, respectively (Table 1). The accuracy of applying heel lift was 89.7%, and the macro- and micro-average ROC AUC values were 0.961 and 0.949, respectively (Figure 3A). The accuracy of applying entire lift was 94.8%, and the macro- and micro-average ROC AUC values were 0.933 and 0.941, respectively (Figure 3B). The accuracy of applying lateral wedge support was 72.2%, and the macro- and micro-average ROC AUC values were 0.804 and 0.826, respectively (Figure 3C). The accuracy of applying medial wedge support was 98.4%, and the macro- and micro-average ROC AUC values were 0.863 and 0.792, respectively (Figure 3D). The accuracy of applying calcaneocuboid arch support was 79.8%, and the macro- and micro-average ROC AUC values were 0.837 and 0.827, respectively (Figure 3E).

Figure 4 shows the correct classification and misclassification of the DNN models. The model for the application of heel lift and entire lift correctly classified 226 and 239 of 252 cases, respectively, from the validation dataset. The model for the application of medial and lateral wedge supports correctly classified 182 and 248 of 252 cases, respectively, from the validation dataset. Lastly, the model for the application of calcaneocuboid arch support correctly classified 201 of 252 cases from the validation dataset. It can be concluded that the overall classification accuracy of the five models is good. However, the medial wedge model (Figure 4D) has lower accuracy for classes 1 and 2 due to a small sample size of patients in the validation data for those classes, resulting in inadequate learning.

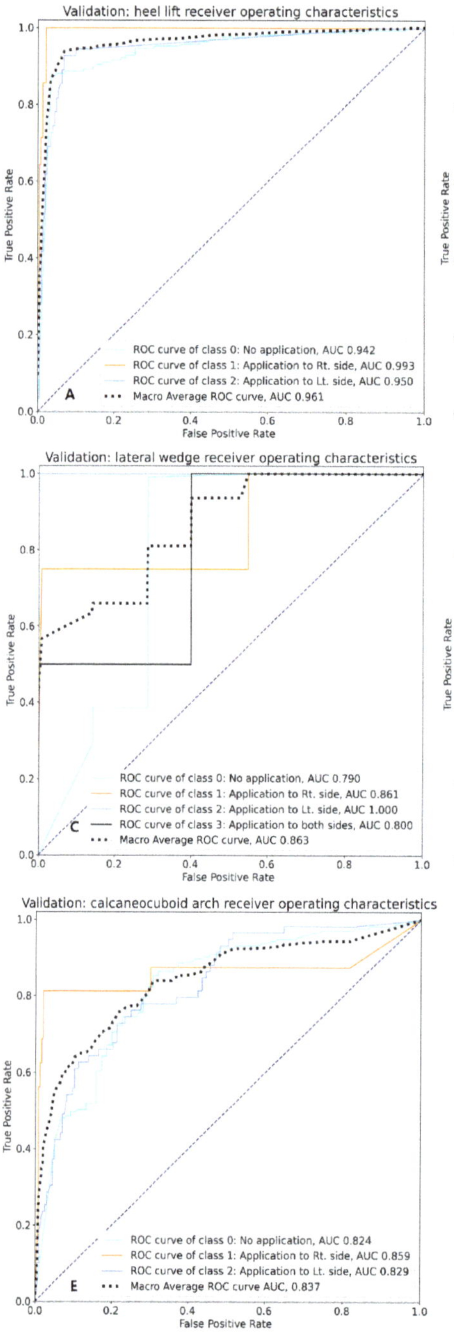

Figure 3. Receiver operating characteristic curve of the validation dataset of the deep-learning models for the prescription of orthotic insoles. (**A**) heel lift (**B**) entire lift (**C**) lateral wedge (**D**) medial wedge (**E**) calcaneocuboid arch.

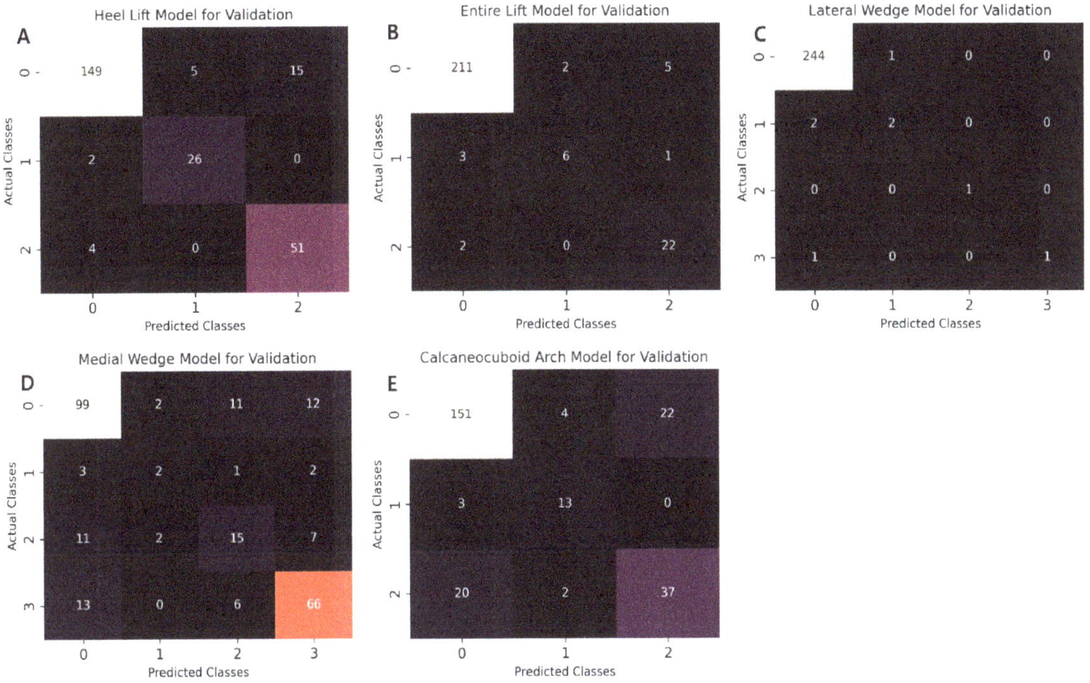

Figure 4. Confusion matrix of the deep-learning model for the prescription of orthotic insoles. (**A**) heel lift (**B**) entire lift (**C**) lateral wedge (**D**) medial wedge (**E**) calcaneocuboid arch.

5. Discussion

In this study, we developed a deep-learning model for prescribing the appropriate orthotic insole for patients with foot pain. Our developed model automatically determined the foot posture index for the modified root technique and the necessity of heel lift, entire lift, and lateral wedge, medial wedge, and calcaneocuboid arch supports. The MAE of the foot posture index for the modified root technique in our model was 1.6. The micro-average ROC AUC values of the models for determining the necessity of applying heel lift and entire lift were >0.9, and those of lateral wedge, medial wedge, and calcaneocuboid arch supports were 0.79–0.83. Considering that ROC AUC values ranging from 0.7 to 0.8 are considered acceptable, those ranging from 0.8 to 0.9 are considered excellent, and those >0.9 are considered outstanding. Therefore, these results indicate that the ability of our developed model to automatically prescribe orthotic insole ranged from outstanding to acceptable, which supports our proposition [26].

Our developed deep-learning models automatically determine the foot posture index for the modified root technique and the necessity of heel lift, entire lift, and lateral wedge, medial wedge, and calcaneocuboid arch supports. The modified root technique considers forefoot-to-rearfoot structural problems and attempts to hold the rearfoot in its neutral position while maintaining the appropriate forefoot-to-rearfoot relation [27–29]. This technique modifies the ground reaction force around the subtalar joint axis [27–29]. The foot posture index is the amount of twisting of the insole to place the rear foot in a neutral position. Heel lift and entire lift are used when the right and left pelvic heights are different [30,31]. In addition, when the side of the pelvic elevation is tilted anteriorly, a heel lift is applied to the other side. When the side of pelvic elevation is not tilted anteriorly, entire lift is applied. Lateral and medial wedge supports are applied to reduce varus and valgus torques, respectively, during walking [14,15]. A calcaneocuboid arch support is used when either side of the pelvis moves backward. A calcaneocuboid arch support is applied to the side on which the pelvis moves more backward than forward. These prescriptions can be helpful for correcting the malalignment of the lower extremities, as they would effectively reduce pain due to malalignment that occurs in any part of the leg, not only limited to the foot.

When prescribing orthotic insoles, clinicians should consider all the data of the RCSP and the static and dynamic states of the pelvis. Without a deep-learning model, clinicians should prescribe orthotic insoles by considering all these results. Therefore, for the appropriate prescription for patients with foot pain, a lot of experience in the field of foot pain and orthotic insoles is necessary. Incorrect prescription leads to the application of inappropriate insoles, which can aggravate patients' foot pain. We used data on insole prescriptions written by podiatrists with abundant experience in prescribing insoles. We believe that the automatic prescription deep-learning model that we developed can relieve the burden on clinicians of appropriately prescribing orthotic insoles.

The DNN model was trained using an artificial neural network structure based on the neural network structure of the human brain [32]. A DNN is a powerful machine learning algorithm that is implemented by stacking hidden layers of neural networks between the input and output layers [20,21]. It attempts high-level abstraction by combining several non-linear transformations [33]. Deep learning uses a large amount of data for training and creating a model capable of processing new data [34]. It has been used to produce advanced results in various fields, including computer vision, natural language processing, voice recognition, and signal/voice processing [33]. The widely recognized benefits of deep learning include its ability to identify interactions between multiple variables and detect useful information in time series, clinical, and imaging data [35]. In particular, deep learning is more useful for analyzing big data and detecting useful information from images [35]. Deep learning can detect rules or relationships among large amounts of data that cannot be found using traditional statistical analysis methods. The DNN detects the correct mathematical manipulation to convert the input into output through a series of hidden layers [20,21]. When input data are fed into a DNN, the input value is multiplied by the weights at the nodes that comprise each layer, and the output data are generated using an activation function [33].

Parameters such as learning rate, loss function, optimizer, number of epochs and iterations, and batch size are varied by researchers and developers to generate a DNN. An optimal model is determined by evaluating and comparing the accuracy and capacity of each developed model [36,37]. Complex networks with multiple layers effectively represent the complex nature of input and output variables [33]. This feature of DNNs enables the analysis of large amounts of clinical data [36,37]. Multiple layers of a DNN appear to be effective in determining the complex nature of orthotic insole prescription in patients with foot pain.

The procedure for developing a deep-learning algorithm with a large amount of clinical data as the input is as follows: First, the clinical data for deep learning are collected. The clinical data are divided into input and target data and then arranged and saved as comma-separated value files [38]. Programming languages such as Python and R and Python-based deep-learning frameworks such as TensorFlow, PyTorch, and Keras are commonly used to develop deep-learning algorithms [39]. The data, divided into input and target data, are loaded onto the platform and converted into the NumPy array format for deep-learning analysis [39]. Subsequently, the data are stacked in a column and standardized. The data are then divided into training and test datasets, and a deep-learning model is trained [39]. The accuracy of the developed deep-learning model is assessed, and the results are usually depicted by the ROC and AUC [39].

In conclusion, we developed DNN models that automatically prescribe orthotic insoles in patients with foot pain. We demonstrated that their accuracies ranged from outstanding to acceptable. However, for the application of our models in real clinical practice, the accuracy of the prescription of orthotic insoles should be further increased. To increase accuracy, more appropriate input and output data are required. In addition, to increase the generosity of the models, data or information on the prescription of insoles from more clinicians or podiatrists should be used for the development of models. Finally, the clinical data used to develop the deep-learning models, including RCSP, pelvic elevation, pelvic tilt, and pelvic rotation, were measured manually and visually. However, their reliability and validity have yet to be well-demonstrated. Therefore, a method or tool that can objectively and accurately measure such data must be developed. Further studies are warranted to address these limitations.

Supplementary Materials: The following supporting information can be downloaded at: https://www.mdpi.com/article/10.3390/app13042208/s1. Source codes of DNN models.

Author Contributions: J.K.K.: data analysis, data curation, and writing the manuscript; Y.J.C.: data curation; I.S.P.: data curation and preparing figures; J.-W.C.: data curation; D.P.: writing and reviewing the manuscript and preparing figures; M.C.C.: writing and reviewing the manuscript, data analysis, and data curation. All authors have read and agreed to the published version of the manuscript.

Funding: This work was supported by the 2022 Yeungnam University Research Grant.

Institutional Review Board Statement: The study was conducted in accordance with the Declaration of Helsinki, and approved by the Institutional Review Board of Yeungnam University Hospital (2022-06-046).

Informed Consent Statement: Patient consent was waived due to the retrospective nature of our study.

Data Availability Statement: The datasets used and/or analyzed during the current study are available from the corresponding author upon reasonable request.

Conflicts of Interest: The authors declare no conflict of interest.

References

1. Choo, Y.J.; Park, C.H.; Chang, M.C. Rearfoot disorders and conservative treatment: A narrative review. *Ann. Palliat. Med.* **2020**, *9*, 3546–3552.
2. Park, C.H.; Chang, M.C. Forefoot disorders and conservative treatment. *Yeungnam Univ. J. Med.* **2019**, *36*, 92–98. [CrossRef]
3. Alqahtani, T.A. The prevalence of foot pain and its associated factors among Saudi school teachers in Abha sector, Saudi Arabia. *Family Med Prim Care.* **2020**, *9*, 4641–4647.
4. Chang, M.C. The blind spot and challenges in pain management. *J. Yeungnam Med. Sci.* **2022**, *39*, 179–180.
5. Park, C.H.; Boudier-Revéret, M.; Chang, M.C. Tarsal tunnel syndrome due to talocalcaneal coalition. *Yeungnam Univ. J. Med.* **2023**, *40*, 106–108. [CrossRef]
6. Chow, T.H.; Chen, Y.S.; Hsu, C.C. Relationships between Plantar Pressure Distribution and Rearfoot Alignment in the Taiwanese College Athletes with Plantar Fasciopathy during Static Standing and Walking. *Int. J. Environ. Res. Public Health* **2021**, *18*, 12942.
7. Menz, H.B.; Dufour, A.B.; Riskowski, J.L.; Hillstrom, H.J.; Hannan, M.T. Association of planus foot posture and pronated foot function are associated with foot pain: The Framingham foot study. *Arthritis Care Res.* **2013**, *65*, 1991–1999.
8. Elattar, O.; Smith, T.; Ferguson, A.; Farber, D.; Wapner, K. Uses of Braces and Orthotics for Conservative Management of Foot and Ankle Disorders. *Foot Ankle Orthop.* **2018**, *3*, 2473011418780700. [CrossRef]
9. Razeghi, M.; Batt, M.E. Biomechanical analysis of the effect of orthotic shoe inserts: A review of the literature. *Sports Med.* **2000**, *29*, 425–438. [CrossRef]
10. Amer, A.O.; Jarl, G.M.; Hermansson, L.N. The effect of insoles on foot pain and daily activities. *Prosthet. Orthot. Int.* **2014**, *38*, 474–480.
11. Gómez Carrión, Á.; Atín Arratibe, M.L.Á.; Morales Lozano, M.R.; Martínez Rincón, C.; Martínez Sebastián, C.; Saura Sempere, Á.; Nuñez-Fernandez, A.; Sánchez-Gómez, R. Changes in the Kinematics of Midfoot and Rearfoot Joints with the Use of Lateral Wedge Insoles. *J. Clin. Med.* **2022**, *11*, 4536.
12. Paterson, K.L.; Hinman, R.S.; Metcalf, B.R.; McManus, F.; Jones, S.E.; Menz, H.B.; Munteanu, S.E.; Bennell, K.L. Effect of foot orthoses vs sham insoles on first metatarsophalangeal joint osteoarthritis symptoms: A randomized controlled trial. *Osteoarthr. Cartil.* **2022**, *30*, 956–964.
13. Khamis, S.; Dar, G.; Peretz, C.; Yizhar, Z. The Relationship Between Foot and Pelvic Alignment While Standing. *J. Hum. Kinet.* **2015**, *46*, 85–97. [CrossRef]
14. Fukuchi, C.A.; Lewinson, R.T.; Worobets, J.T.; Stefanyshyn, D.J. Effects of Lateral and Medial Wedged Insoles on Knee and Ankle Internal Joint Moments During Walking in Healthy Men. *J. Am. Podiatr. Med. Assoc.* **2016**, *106*, 411–418. [CrossRef]

15. Kerrigan, D.C.; Lelas, J.L.; Goggins, J.; Merriman, G.J.; Kaplan, R.J.; Felson, D.T. Effectiveness of a lateral-wedge insole on knee varus torque in patients with knee osteoarthritis. *Arch. Phys. Med. Rehabil.* **2002**, *83*, 889–893.
16. Mahmoud, A.; Abundo, P.; Basile, L.; Albensi, C.; Marasco, M.; Bellizzi, L.; Galasso, F.; Foti, C. Functional leg length discrepancy between theories and reliable instrumental assessment: A study about newly invented NPoS system. *Muscles Ligaments Tendons J.* **2017**, *7*, 293–305.
17. Choo, Y.J.; Kim, J.K.; Kim, J.H.; Chang, M.C.; Park, D. Machine learning analysis to predict the need for ankle foot orthosis in patients with stroke. *Sci. Rep.* **2021**, *11*, 8499. [CrossRef]
18. Kim, J.K.; Choo, Y.J.; Chang, M.C. Prediction of Motor Function in Stroke Patients Using Machine Learning Algorithm: Development of Practical Models. *J. Stroke Cerebrovasc. Dis.* **2021**, *30*, 105856.
19. Kim, J.K.; Lv, Z.; Park, D.; Chang, M.C. Practical Machine Learning Model to Predict the Recovery of Motor Function in Patients with Stroke. *Eur. Neurol.* **2022**, *85*, 273–279.
20. Kim, J.K.; Chang, M.C.; Park, D. Deep Learning Algorithm Trained on Brain Magnetic Resonance Images and Clinical Data to Predict Motor Outcomes of Patients With Corona Radiata Infarct. *Front. Neurosci.* **2022**, *15*, 795553.
21. Shin, H.; Choi, G.S.; Shon, O.J.; Kim, G.B.; Chang, M.C. Development of convolutional neural network model for diagnosing meniscus tear using magnetic resonance image. *BMC Musculoskelet. Disord.* **2022**, *23*, 510. [CrossRef]
22. Cho, Y.; Park, J.W.; Nam, K. The relationship between foot posture index and resting calcaneal stance position in elementary school students. *Gait Posture* **2019**, *74*, 142–147. [CrossRef]
23. Keenan, A.M.; Bach, T.M. Clinicians' assessment of the hindfoot: A study of reliability. *Foot Ankle Int.* **2006**, *27*, 451–460. [CrossRef]
24. Kouhkan, S.; Rahimi, A.; Ghasemi, M.; Naimi, S.S.; Baghban, A.A. Postural Changes during First Pregnancy. *Br. J. Med. Med. Res.* **2015**, *7*, 744–753. [CrossRef]
25. Wang, S.; Minku, L.L. AUC estimation and concept drift detection for imbalanced data streams with multiple classes. In Proceedings of the 2020 International Joint Conference on Neural Networks (IJCNN), Glasgow, UK, 19–24 July 2020; pp. 1–8.
26. Mandrekar, J.N. Receiver operating characteristic curve in diagnostic test assessment. *J. Thorac. Oncol.* **2010**, *5*, 1315–1316. [CrossRef]
27. Buchanan, K.R.; Davis, I. The relationship between forefoot, midfoot, and rearfoot static alignment in pain-free individuals. *J. Orthop. Sports Phys. Ther.* **2005**, *35*, 559–566.
28. Kim, P.J.; Peace, R.; Mieras, J.; Thoms, T.; Freeman, D.; Page, J. Interrater and intrarater reliability in the measurement of ankle joint dorsiflexion is independent of examiner experience and technique used. *J. Am. Podiatr. Med. Assoc.* **2011**, *101*, 407–414.
29. Menz, H.B. Foot orthoses: How much customisation is necessary? *J Foot Ankle Res.* **2009**, *2*, 23. [CrossRef]
30. Severin, A.C.; Gean, R.P.; Barnes, S.G.; Queen, R.; Butler, R.J.; Martin, R.; Barnes, C.L.; Mannen, E.M. Effects of a corrective heel lift with an orthopaedic walking boot on joint mechanics and symmetry during gait. *Gait Posture* **2019**, *73*, 233–238.
31. Yen, S.T.; Andrew, P.D.; Cummings, G.S. Short-term effect of correcting leg length discrepancy on performance of a forceful body extension task in young adults. *Hiroshima J. Med. Sci.* **1998**, *47*, 139–143.
32. Kriegeskorte, N.; Golan, T. Neural network models and deep learning. *Curr. Biol.* **2019**, *29*, R231–R236.
33. Sarker, I.H. Deep learning: A comprehensive overview on techniques, taxonomy, applications and research directions. *SN Comput. Sci.* **2021**, *2*, 420. [CrossRef]
34. LeCun, Y.; Bengio, Y.; Hinton, G. Deep learning. *Nature* **2015**, *521*, 436–444.
35. Rajula, H.S.; Verlato, G.; Manchia, M.; Antonucci, N.; Fanos, V. Comparison of conventional statistical methods with machine learning in medicine: Diagnosis, drug development, and treatment. *Medicina* **2020**, *56*, 455. [CrossRef]
36. Choo, Y.J.; Chang, M.C. Use of Machine Learning in Stroke Rehabilitation: A Narrative Review. *Brain Neurorehabil.* **2022**, *15*, e26.
37. Lee, H.; Song, J. Introduction to convolutional neural network using Keras; an understanding from a statistician. *Commun. Stat. Appl. Methods* **2019**, *26*, 591–610. [CrossRef]
38. Giulia, A.; Anna, S.; Antonia, B.; Dario, P.; Maurizio, C. Extending association rule mining to microbiome pattern analysis: Tools and guidelines to support real applications. *Front. Bioinform.* **2022**, *1*, 794547. [CrossRef]
39. Mendez, K.M.; Pritchard, L.; Reinke, S.N.; Broadhurst, D.I. Toward collaborative open data science in metabolomics using Jupyter Notebooks and cloud computing. *Metabolomics* **2019**, *15*, 125. [CrossRef]

applied sciences

MDPI

Article

Automatic Tumor Identification from Scans of Histopathological Tissues

Mantas Kundrotas, Edita Mažonienė and Dmitrij Šešok *

Department of Information Technologies, Vilnius Gediminas Technical University, Sauletekio Al. 11, LT-10223 Vilnius, Lithuania
* Correspondence: dmitrij.sesok@vilniustech.lt

Abstract: Latest progress in development of artificial intelligence (AI), especially machine learning (ML), allows to develop automated technologies that can eliminate or at least reduce human errors in analyzing health data. Due to the ethics of usage of AI in pathology and laboratory medicine, to the present day, pathologists analyze slides of histopathologic tissues that are stained with hematoxylin and eosin under the microscope; by law it cannot be substituted and must go under visual observation, as pathologists are fully accountable for the result. However, a profuse number of automated systems could solve complex problems that require an extremely fast response, accuracy, or take place on tasks that require both a fast and accurate response at the same time. Such systems that are based on ML algorithms can be adapted to work with medical imaging data, for instance whole slide images (WSIs) that allow clinicians to review a much larger number of health cases in a shorter time and give the ability to identify the preliminary stages of cancer or other diseases improving health monitoring strategies. Moreover, the increased opportunity to forecast and take control of the spread of global diseases could help to create a preliminary analysis and viable solutions. Accurate identification of a tumor, especially at an early stage, requires extensive expert knowledge, so often the cancerous tissue is identified only after experiencing its side effects. The main goal of our study was to expand the ability to find more accurate ML methods and techniques that can lead to detecting tumor damaged tissues in histopathological WSIs. According to the experiments that we conducted, there was a 1% AUC difference between the training and test datasets. Over several training iterations, the U-Net model was able to reduce the model size by almost twice while also improving accuracy from 0.95491 to 0.95515 AUC. Convolutional models worked well on groups of different sizes when properly trained. With the TTA (test time augmentation) method the result improved to 0.96870, and with the addition of the multi-model ensemble, it improved to 0.96977. We found out that flaws in the models can be found and fixed by using specialized analysis techniques. A correction of the image processing parameters was sufficient to raise the AUC by almost 0.3%. The result of the individual model increased to 0.96664 AUC (a more than 1% better result than the previous best model) after additional training data preparation. This is an arduous task due to certain factors: using such systems' applications globally needs to achieve maximum accuracy and improvement in the ethics of AI usage in medicine; furthermore if hospitals could give scientific inquiry validation, while retaining patient data anonymity with clinical information that could be systemically analyzed and improved by scientists, thereby proving AI benefits.

Keywords: machine learning; automatization; histopathology; medical imaging

1. Introduction

Machine learning integration in the medical field, especially image analysis for histopathology and cancer research could make a huge impact due to the possibility of rapid and more accurate results. In recent years, advancements in technology have revolutionized the health system enabling it to use digitized imaging in order review patient data through computer systems and applications. Digital content can be simply stored without losing its quality and reshared between health specialists, especially because of the increasing number of image analysis applications and large image compression tools [1–3]. Unfortunately, switching from glass to digital analysis requires new expensive hardware, extensive memory size and especially trained technicians [4]. To this day a legitimate comparison research method using accepted AI techniques that could be used for histopathology does not exist, especially because of expensive hardware and eligible access to patient data. Additionally, the main challenge is that different WSI's scanners lower the results, and the most significant barrier to the widespread use of AI approaches in the clinic is undoubtedly the limited generalizability of algorithms [5]. Despite this, medical professionals might help develop new techniques that could be applied in clinical practice as the start of implementing AI in histology [4].

A cancer, also called tumor, is a formation of altered, unregulated, unlimitedly proliferating but not clearly defined clusters of abnormal cells that lead to terminal illnesses. There are three main types of tumors: benign, premalignant, and malignant. Benign tumors are defined as less dangerous and harmful due to the fact of being noninvasive, however, certain cases declare that they can become malignant. Malignant tumors usually grow rapidly, penetrating and destroying healthy tissues, spreading to distant organs and finally, metastasize [6,7]. There is a variety tumor identification methods: magnetic resonance imaging (MRI), computed tomography (CT), Single-Photon-Emission Computed Tomography (SPECT), and other medical imaging technologies are used to determine the exact type, location, and level of threat that cancer-damaged tissue has [8,9]. International research for cancer statistics in 2020 showed over 19.3 million new cancer cases from all over the world. Even though the medical field is rapidly growing and progressing, the World Health Organization (WHO) declared that cancer is the main leading cause of death, unfortunately reflecting the size of population [10].

In histopathology analysis, specialists must focus on objective and accurate identification of diagnosis due to the complexity of diseases. Digital imaging allows to analyze histopathological specimens with a quantification of slides technique using machine learning methods as deep learning. Such promising technology of multi-layered artificial neural networks allows to perform a quantity of tasks adapting consistent tasks. Other studies have suggested that using digital histopathological images makes it possible to identify cancer cells [11–13]. To increase the efficiency of tumor identification research with the reduction in errors, automatization using mathematical methods could be a solution. Taking into consideration this relevant case, AI experts [14–17] have already developed a variety of fully exploitable technologies that take place in the medical field. For instance, to detect or identify a brain, spine and chest tumor, the following methods are applicable: K-means, SVM, Level Set, Adaboost, Naive Bayes classifier, ANN classifier, convolutional neural networks, multilayer perceptron neural networks for analyzing magnetic resonance, and computed tomography type data analysis [18–22].

In this article, we use machine learning for recognizing cancer cells that are applied over histopathological images consisting immense number of pixels. We are aware of deep learning methods that can benefit the identification and recognition of tumor cells. The machine learning algorithm goes over the given data, or as in our cases an image, or an image that shows cancer affected tissue, following an algorithm mode to ascertain from the training data and assign to make a prediction for further work. If this algorithm advances and increases the number of executions of improved and correct diagnosis—then we consider it as a learned task [23]. To explain machine learning, we use certain terms: supervised, unsupervised, semi-supervised, and reinforcement learning [24] algorithms [25]. Furthermore, deep learning gives us opportunities to explore wide-ranging data [26]. To gain the best possible accuracy, we must use an artificial neural network (ANN) as one of the machine learning techniques that allows to remove the artifacts (errors) that naturally appear in different types of data. Such errors, especially in the medical field, are one of the most common issues for misinterpretation. An ANN can be explained as assembly of neurons that are arranged in a sequence of multiple layers. The activation of an ANN begins from an input layer whose main aim is to correctly choose the format and transfer data to different layers until it reaches the last or the output layer. Fascinatingly, all other layers have different numbers of neurons and are identified as hidden because they play an important role allowing to learn data structure and give the ability to classify its type. In general, the operation of neural networks is very similar to linear regression, which means that each individual neuron is just like a linear regression model consisting of input data, its weights, bias and finally the output [27,28]. Medical image analysis empowered by deep learning, especially using a convolutional neural network (CNN), and its significant results for different types of cancer detection in histopathology scans (two-dimensional data), has drawn attention from scientists all over the world [29–31]. The main reason is that it gives the ability to clinicians to make correct health diagnoses and receive precise analysis of illnesses that can be compared with previous samples. Training deep learning models, including CNN, demand significant training size and computing resources due to the profuse number of pixels in an image [1,32]. One of the subtypes of CNN, called the residual convolutional neural network (ResNet), can work with large datasets (the training and test material) even if the neural network increases in depth (extend in number of stacked layers), benefiting in a reduction in error rate [33,34]. Another subtype of CNN is the DenseNet, that reduces the vanishing gradient effect in DNN. This network is formed of dense blocks that are detached by a transition layer that minimizes the size of the delivered feature maps that will be transferred to the following layers. To compare ResNet and DenseNet we must understand how data are being directed between the layers. A transition layer, which aims to minimize the size of the generated feature maps that will be sent to the following layers, separates each dense block in a DenseNet network [35]. A residual learning unit is a feature of ResNet, which was created to counteract deep neural network degeneration. This system is built as a feed-forward network with a shortcut link that enables the addition of new inputs and outputs. The main benefit is that it increases the classification accuracy without complicating the model's actual design [36].

Following reviews of different tumor identification systems, it became obvious that selecting the machine learning system that is best suited to produce the desired result based on the current data comes only after the data has been properly analyzed and processed [37–39]. There is a lot of space for improvement because most of the systems that have been presented only process very small amounts of data using straightforward neural networks [40,41]. Applying more recent advancements in data collection and processing, which have been successfully used in other scientific fields, along with a new generation of convolutional neural networks with a more complex structure, guarantees the most accurate outcome for tumor detection.

In this research, we applied machine learning to histopathological images that consisted of immense numbers of pixels to recognize cancer cells. Automatic systems can solve complex problems that require an extremely fast response, accuracy, or take place on tasks that require both a fast and accurate response at the same time. Such systems and image pre-processing that are based on machine learning algorithms can be adapted to work with medical images, especially whole slide images (WSIs), that will allow clinicians to review a much larger number of health cases in a shorter time and give the ability to identify the preliminary stages of cancer or other diseases, thereby improving health monitoring strategies.

The main contributions of this paper are as follows:

- Modern augmentation and image preprocessing methods to analyze WSIs,
- Creating an adaptive U-Net model architecture,
- Adding different optimizers for best outcoming result in AUC.

The paper is organized as follows:

- In Section 2, we did a review of machine learning models, architectures, algorithms, and other techniques that can be used for histopathological WSIs,
- Section 3 outlines the methodology, that step by step describes the machine learning model, dataset, and accuracy requirements for further experiments,
- Section 4 consists of the design of the experiments, the main values, graphical and statistical results,

- In Section 5, we list the major accomplishments and talk about the outcomes,
- In Section 6, we conclude our work and identify potential work directions.

2. Related Work

2.1. Medical Imaging

The field of computer-aided medical image analysis, particularly the recognition of cancer in histopathological images, has received extensive attention from researchers [42–44]. It has been heavily focused on the area of computer-aided medical image analysis, new and improved applications in bioinformatics [45], particularly the identification of cancer in histopathological images as it enhances the benefits of quality diagnostics for patients [46]. One of the medical disciplines that has seen a sizable number of deep learning applications is digital pathology and microscopy, especially as advancements in technology have given us an opportunity in using histopathological scans-digital images [47–49].

Bright prospects have been demonstrated for the detection, segmentation, and classification of diseases, especially finding cancer cells using newly developed techniques that provide pathologists with decision support and most likely are guiding to more accurate results. A new cross-domain field of graph-based deep learning, which seeks to learn informative representations of medical images in an end-to-end manner [50], has emerged because of the increased attention given to the adaptation of deep learning from images. Convolutional neural networks, a deep learning method that excels at tasks like histology segmentation, are being used more frequently in pathology [51,52].

Thus, artificial intelligence tools based on machine learning techniques could fundamentally alter pathologists' and medical professionals' workflow in the future, whether through computer-aided diagnosis or simply by accelerating laborious manual tasks. The current rigid classification and analysis system that enables difficult visual recognition tasks, like separating tumors from normal tissue in slides and classifying different types of tumors [53] may be replaced by a more analytical and flexible model that incorporates radiological, biological, and clinical variables based on deep learning [54,55].

2.2. Machine Learning Models

The study of algorithms and statistical models that computer systems use to accomplish a task without being explicitly programmed is known as ML and its main purpose is to learn from data. Algorithms and statistical models are divided into groups according to the main principle of operation. For instance, a function that maps an input to an output that is learned through supervised learning using sample input-output pairs. Algorithms that require outside assistance are those that fall under the category of supervised machine learning. They use labelled training data made up of a collection of training examples to infer a function [56]. Unsupervised learning undoubtedly is the biggest goal and struggle for medical diagnostic systems [57,58]; unfortunately, most of these models simply cannot be applied as they are capable of working only with a limited amount of imaging data [59].

Our attention was drawn to U-Net model, that is one of the most widely used CNN architectures and differs from the others for two reasons. First, it is made of two parts: first—descends resolution, second, after each block, a maximum signal selection operation is used, which doubles the width and height. After this operation, the number of channels used is doubled. The second part uses the same convolutional blocks, but the local resolution reduction operation uses an up-sample operation that doubles the height and width. Later, this layer is combined with high-frequency information from the dimensionally appropriate first part of the network. By passing information from the left part of the network to the right in this way, the network can gain more detailed and accurate information [60]. The U-Net architecture can surely be implemented for histopathological data for nuclei segmentation and, according to Ibtihaj et al. [61], it significantly improves segmentation performance.

Learning Rate and Planning Algorithms

Another major challenge is the learning rate (LR). While using huge amounts of data such as in histopathological medical images, the training time obviously takes longer and to achieve the most optimal performance we need to choose a learning rate as one of the hyper-parameters [62]. The LR describes any positive number that is less than the integer one; it is also a parameter that controls the weight adjustment [63]. If the learning step is specified as one or very close to one, it means that when the backpropagation calculation is performed, the original weight matrix of the calculated layer will be adjusted using the full error matrix. This means that adjusted model weights for the current data input will return zero error. This is acceptable for one part of the data set from which the gradient is calculated, but this tightening to one set at a time means that if the next set will not likely to be like the current one, output will show an error and subsequently the gradient itself will be very large. Such a process will cause the model to diverge. The opposite of this process would slow the convergence, or the model will turn to stagnation. This happens when too small a learning step is chosen. During this process, the calculated model weight correction matrix is multiplied by a number very close to zero, thus performing an extremely minimal weight correction. Compared to too large a learning step, a small constant close to zero does not cause an impact. The model is learning, but the process is slightly slower than it could be [64].

From a practical perspective, a deep artificial neural model occasionally performs remarkably well on training data but dreadfully on testing data. This behavior happens when the model overlearns; it remembers the numerical values of the model's inputs and classes, nevertheless it fails to learn the necessary features from the training data. Regularization techniques are used to address this issue because a model that has been overtrained cannot be used for real medical cases. Comparing to other machine learning algorithms, regularization is a relatively simple operation. Its purpose is to prevent the model from memorizing incoming data by adjusting the values of the weight matrix throughout the model. Scientists use regularization even as a consistent strategy while analyzing histopathological imaging [61,65].

Another useful idea for using DNN is transfer learning, and the use of this technique to solve such issues as extracting certain features or tuning [66]. Basically, when there is a small amount of labeled data in the target dataset, it is demonstrated to be a powerful tool to combat overfitting. The authors of [67] observed that transfer learning performed successfully full training, achieving this in a shorter period also lowering the labor required for manual data labeling.

Resources are the most common issue when using deep neural networks to solve complex problems. As we said above, it is necessary to wisely choose and use a sufficiently large and complex deep neural network in situations where the data are extremely complex and extensive.

3. Materials and Methods

3.1. Proposed Model

To achieve objective results, it is important to maintain a standardized training process. In the field of machine learning, even small changes can dramatically determine or change the result. For equal initialization of weights, we used Xavier's algorithm [67–69]. It led us to fix a random seed so we could use the same model with the exact same initialization weights for different experiments. We did not limit or fix how long learning can last because the model might have different architectures. The only limitation we set was the verification algorithm that counts the duration of learning; the main reason was that it halts learning if the model has not improved in the previous ten iterations. Besides that, we used the SGD optimizer [70] with acceleration, and a cyclic learning step with warm-up was used for training purposes. For the first 1000 iterations, the model learns with a fixed learning step of 1×10^{-4} and then gradually increases to 5×10^{-3} over 2400 iterations and descends to 5×10^{-5} over 3600 iterations, shown in Figure 1. Warm-up applies only to the first epoch. The total number of iterations per epoch that we used was 6000, while the batch size was 64.

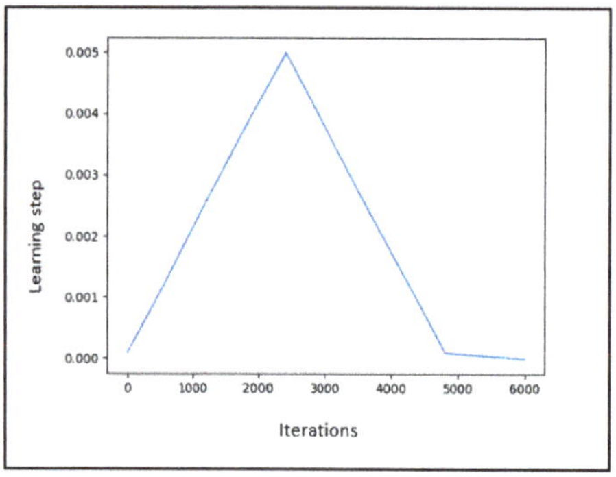

Figure 1. An example model that learns with fixed learning rate.

In the interim, testing and validation data sets were not augmented or otherwise adjusted. Additionally, 5 million artificially augmented images were created from the training dataset for training. In addition to that, for experiments that compare models, but not individual model accuracy by adjusting data or hyper parameters, we used Binary Cross-Entropy objective function as well as AUS metrics. Before creating a new neural network architecture, changing the objective function, or training data, it is necessary to find out whether the data set is suitable. The fastest way to do this is to use trained models. Using this process, it is possible to draw conclusions about how each architecture affects the final accuracy. For this work, the ResNet, DenseNet, MobileNet, EfficientNet, Inception architectures [71–73] were selected from their derived versions from the Tensorflow library. All these models were already trained on the ImageNet dataset [74], which means that each model already had 1000 output classes.

Proper data processing is one of the most crucial components of training deep neural networks. Considering a number of more than 200,000 WSIs seems to be enough for training data, however as we previously stated, larger convolutional models easily remember the statistics of incoming data and tend to retrain. As a result, using augmentation techniques such as cropping, vertical and horizontal conversion, random rotation by 0–360 degrees, and contrast adjustment shown in Figure 2, let us create synthetic data with the same class value but a different representation. The original information was tightly compressed in *.h5 format. For each set type—training, validation, or testing—were divided into two files: actual images, and the values for the classes according to the corresponding index are in the other. These assemblies were scanned using the h5py library. Afterwards, a generator function was created, which simultaneously reads from two files and combines the read values into a pair. Next, these data were appropriately augmented and converted to 32-bit floating point format depending on the type. For final training, the data are typically compressed into some deep learning-friendly data format. Because the Tensorflow library was used in this work, all data were stored in *.tfrecord format. Before the images were sent to the input layer of the model, the data were normalized. Each pixel in the image was given a value between $[-1, 1]$ during normalization; the Equation (1) is shown below.

$$x = x/127.5 - 1 \tag{1}$$

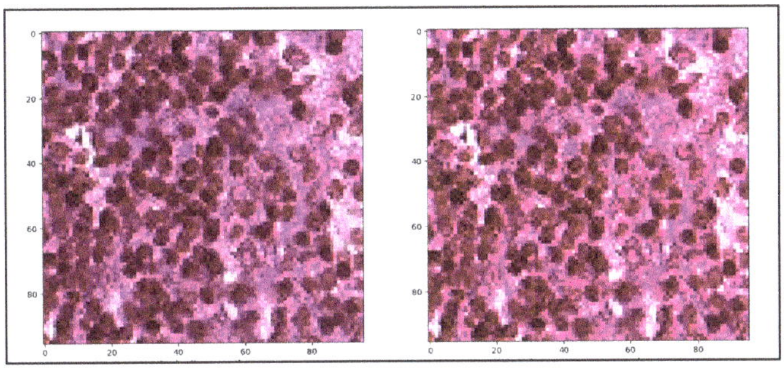

Figure 2. Contrast adjustment applied on image.

3.2. Dataset

We used the PatchCamelyon (https://github.com/basveeling/pcam), 2020 (accessed on 2 January 2022) image classification dataset. It is made up of 327,680 color images (96 × 96 pixels each) that were taken from a histopathologic image of a lymph node section as shown in Figure 3. Each image has a binary label that indicates whether metastatic tissue is present. The entire data set was divided into two parts. The first one was for training only; it consisted of 262,144 photos. The second one was for testing; it contained 32,768 photos. The dataset authors assured that all the splits have an even distribution of positive and negative examples, and there was no overlap in the whole slides images (WSI) between any of the splits. When it comes to labeling, a patch with a positive label has at least one pixel of tumor tissue in its central region. During the experiments, it was observed that excessive sharpening, darkening or contrast enhancement of the image erases all the information identifying the cancer from the histopathological image. Furthermore, it was observed that the influence of heavy data on the total error of the training data set during learning was extremely small.

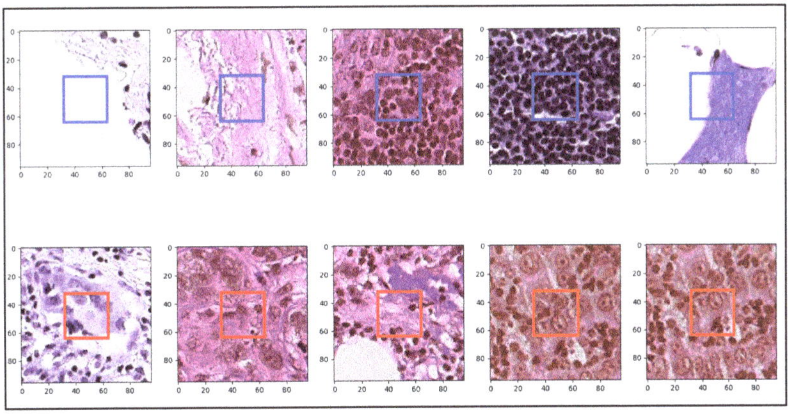

Figure 3. Random samples of the PatchCamelyon dataset that are stained with hematoxylin-eosin (H&E), blue (healthy tissue) and red squares (cancerous tissue) showing central regions.

3.3. Accuracy Calculation

In practice, the performance of a neural network is evaluated by several criteria: calculation speed, overall accuracy, adaptability when applied to a new data set, etc. As it is very important to consider that final accuracy and reliability are the most important factors for medical image analysis, calculation speed and memory space were not evaluated in our work. We considered four estimates, wherein TP stands for true positives, FP for false positives when the model mixes negatives with positive class, and FN for false negatives when the model mixes positive with negative classes (equations listed sequentially):

- Precision using Equation (2),

$$\text{Precision} = \frac{\text{TP}}{\text{TP} + \text{FP}} \tag{2}$$

- Recall using Equation (3),

$$\text{Recall} = \frac{\text{TP}}{\text{FP} + \text{FN}} \tag{3}$$

- F1-score using Equation (4),

$$\text{F1-score} = \frac{2 \cdot \text{Precision} \cdot \text{Recall}}{\text{Precision} + \text{Recall}} \tag{4}$$

- AUC. Measures the quality of the model in terms of sensitivity and accuracy over the entire set of limits.

4. Experiments and Results

4.1. Experimental Setup

As we stated previously, the U-Net type architecture is currently one of the most popular templates to search for a suitable architecture. It allows you to easily check the signal information of different levels individually and by combining high and low frequency signals in separate levels; in our work, we called it the M-model, shown in Figure 4.

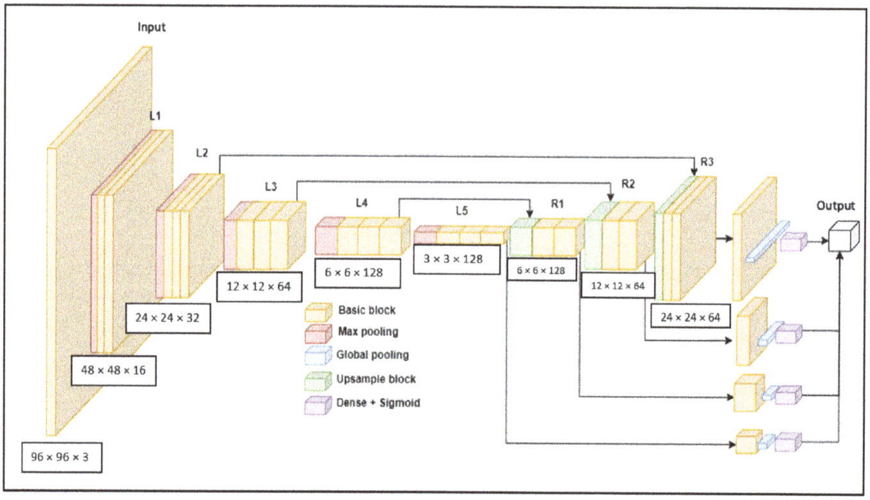

Figure 4. The M-model based on the U-Net network architecture.

By default, U-Net networks form a complete U-shape—they transmit the entire input signal to the output of the model, which is applicable in this work due to efficiency and the type of task itself. Higher resolution output is usually used for image reproduction or segmentation tasks. In this research, classification was performed from low-resolution images, so the high-resolution output will not be superior. The following changes were made to the intermediate modules of the network structure, that we will call the E-Module, shown in Figure 5. Compared to the commonly used standard ResNet module, the E module was more efficient and faster—two 3 × 3 convolutions were changed to one compressed 3 × 3 convolution and one 1 × 1 convolution, with the same number of channels as the number of input layer channels. Furthermore, the typical ReLU (rectified linear unit) activation was changed to PReLU (parametric rectified linear unit) [75]. In this way, the model will be able to apply the best activation for each layer according to the direction of the gradient. Together with this activation function, it was possible to see the behavior of the model by analyzing the values of the activation coefficients. Finally, a Dropout layer was added at the end of the module, which performs a dual regularization: it reduces the signal bandwidth and allows the dropout factor to be increased to 1 at the end of training to discard supposedly unnecessary parts of the model.

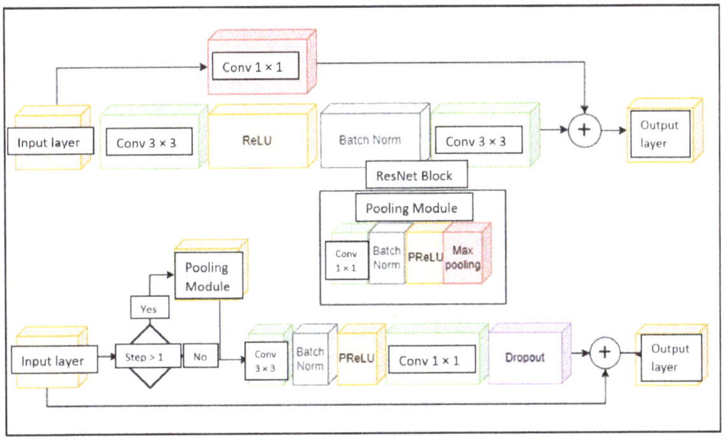

Figure 5. E-module based on ResNet block design.

Additionally, the entire network structure was reworked into a dynamic format. Based on the principle of the EfficientNet architecture [76], the rules for growing the width and length of the network were established and adaptive regularization were applied with Equations (5)–(9) shown below:

- Number of filters (5):

$$\text{Number of filters} = max\left(16, \frac{f \cdot s \cdot F}{h \cdot 2}\right) \cdot g \tag{5}$$

- Number of blocks (6):

$$\text{Number of blocks} = max\left(2, \frac{\text{Number of filters}}{64}\right) \tag{6}$$

- Exclusion factor (7):

$$\text{Exclusion factor} = max\left(0.05, \frac{\text{Number of filters}}{m/2}\right) \tag{7}$$

- L2 regularization (8):

$$\text{L2 regularization} = 1 \times e - 5 + \frac{f}{8} \times 0.0001 \tag{8}$$

where f is the base number of filters, F is the filter multiplier, s is the filter multiplier, h is the height of the network in pixels, g is the number of convolutional groups of the network. The number of blocks indicates how many internal blocks will make up the mesh module after each decrease or increase in height and width of the mesh. Exclusion factor—indicates how many neurons will be turned off in percentage in each block, where m indicates the maximum possible number of filters. The L2 regularization [77,78] specifies the value of the L2 regularization constant for all network convolutions.

To understand whether all the changes made to the model gave advantages compared to ResNet50 or DenseNet121 models, the following experiments were performed. According to the already presented formula for changing the structure of the model, three sizes for f were selected: 8, 16, 32. Sizing allows us to see the areas where the network performs too poorly, overlearns, and where it performs optimally. It is additionally important to find out from which part of the network the best result can be obtained. Therefore, five output layers were added to the already existing network. Accordingly, we noticed a trend while comparing the results of all outputs. All models gave their best performance from the outputs of L5 and R1. This suggests that using a model with such a structure for this task, a higher resolution not only does not provide additional benefits, but also spoils the result. We can be assured that the most suitable model size for this task is $f = 16$, as in the first test, models where $f = 8$ and $f = 32$ performed worse. Among the model outputs, it can also be seen that higher resolution did not provide enough benefits.

Overall, compared to the first experiment, most of the results have improved, especially the output AUC of L5 has increased from 0.95279 to 0.95341. According to these results, it can be confidently stated that the U-Net type architecture did not provide enough benefits for this task. Moreover, comparing the obtained results with ResNet50 and Densenet121, the new model was already superior in terms of accuracy and learning speed—the new model reached the maximum result in eight epochs, which none of the previously described models was able to do when learning with newly initialized weights. According to the results of the first tests, the U-Net model was modified. We removed the right part of U-Net layers and all intermediate connection, also fixed size multiplier $f = 16$. Such pruning not only provided speed, but also allowed to gain greater accuracy due to less information reuse, this improved model will be called the MS-model.

4.2. Results

First, we made additional training validation performed on the artificially augmented and non-augmented datasets. The ResNet and DenseNet networks with ImageNet weights were applied for the test. Both models performed with more than 1% greater accuracy with augmented data than with non-augmented data (Table 1). It can be assumed that these models were too large for such a task and most probably overlearned as a result, however the AUC value on the training data set shown in Table 2 confirmed this. Without augmentation, the AUC was almost at unity at 0.993, while with augmented data it was only 0.975 with the ResNet50 model. Although retraining has occurred, the results show that the data generated for training was fine, and the selected augmentations were useful.

Table 1. Learning from zero with testing data set.

	AUC (Area under the Curve)	
Model	**Using Augmentation**	**Not Using Augmentation**
ResNet50	0.95001	0.93988
DenseNet121	**0.95511**	0.93780

Table 2. Learning from zero with learning data set.

	AUC (Area under the Curve)	
Model	**Using Augmentation**	**Not Using Augmentation**
ResNet50	0.96501	0.99297
DenseNet121	0.98891	0.99971

After making sure that the training environment and data were correct and everything was working as it should, further analysis was performed. Each selected model was trained twice. First, using ImageNet weights and then applying Xavier weights with initialization according to the training protocol, results are shown in Table 3.

Table 3. Model architectures analysis results.

	AUC (Area under the Curve)	
Model	**ImageNet Weights**	**Xavier Initialization Weights**
DenseNet121	0.95672	0.94560
ResNet50	**0.95078**	0.94380
ResNet50 V2	0.95078	0.94380
MobileNetV1	0.94954	0.93855
MobileNetV2	0.95065	0.95395
Inception	0.94697	0.94608
EfficientNetB0	0.95121	0.94608
EfficientNetB1	0.93876	0.94608
EfficientNetB0 V2	0.94570	0.75981
EfficientNetB1 V2	0.94287	0.79871

Comparing with ImageNet weights, DenseNet achieved the best result. According to the learning graph, it exceeded the AUC value of 0.95 after only two epochs. The next best was ResNet50, although it did not show the second result according to the table, but it also exceeded the AUC value of 0.95 after two epochs. Collectively, this means that these two architectures were the most suitable for this task. Furthermore, the ResNetV1 and ResNetV2 models excelled the most. Although their results were not the best, they exceeded 0.94 AUC in just five epochs. This shows that the ResNet-type blocks and persistent connections were well suited for this task due to their fine gradient feedback.

A new training session was performed with the trimmed model called the MS-model. Two tests were selected. The first was by extending the training using the best weights, as shown in Table 4 and gave better results after reusing weights. As the original structure of the network remained the same, weights could easily be transferred from one network to another. The second was to train the same network with ever new weights initialization.

Table 4. MS-model results. New initialization indicates that the model weights were generated by Xavier initialization from a newly chosen random point.

Learning Iteration	AUC
Reusing weights	0.95501
New initialization 1	0.95498
New initialization 2	**0.95508**
New initialization 3	0.95505

A popular way to get a better result is to change the optimization algorithm. Although all training was done with the SGD optimizer, which should potentially be the best for this problem, other methods could potentially find a better solution simply because of the difference in the optimization Hyper parameters. As a result, shown in Table 5, we learned that of several optimizers, the best result was achieved with the AdamW optimizer.

Table 5. Comparison of optimization methods.

Learning Iteration	AUC
SGD	0.95510
Adam	0.95475
AdamW	**0.95515**
Ranger	0.95500

Based on the results of the last test that adding more regularization is better, changes were made to the model and training code. The L2 regularization of the convolutional weights used so far was increased to 1×10^{-4}, and the learning frequency cycle used in the SGD optimizer was converted to cosine. As expected, this teaching principle worked very well. After the fifth iteration, we managed to achieve an AUC of 0.95911, which was almost 0.4% better than the last best model trained with the AdamW optimizer.

In addition to that, we added the TTA [79,80] method, as the training data were adjusted very flexibly—we selected certain featuring: color channel change, vertical flip, horizontal flip, rotate −90 degrees, rotate +90 degrees, lighten the image by 5%, darken the image by 25%; unfortunately, the individually processed images results gained only 0.9590 AUC.

Another approach that did not require model retraining, reengineering, or other changes was model ensemble. This can be done in several ways. We proposed two methods for it. The first one, which combines the outputs of the different models according to the arithmetic mean and returns a single result, and the next one, which combines the weights of the different models into one common list of weight matrices.

5. Discussion

After all strategies and methods, we observed that different training optimizers, more heavily augmented data, learning step graph, or even a well-chosen learning starting point of the model, all influence the overall result when using them combined in an ensemble; it can be argued that the models or weights will converge if their individual performance does not overlap. This means that the models must make different errors among themselves. Therefore, it is obvious that by combining the ensemble methods of the last two experiments, it will be possible to achieve even higher accuracy.

It can be seen in Table 6 that all used methods are models that lead our MS-model to be improved from 0.95918 to 0.96675 AUC.

Table 6. Summary of results. The difference column represents the AUC difference between the type and the first starting point in DenseNet121.

	AUC (Area under the Curve)	
Ensemble Type	**AUC**	**Difference**
DenseNet121	0.95672	-
M-model training 5 outputs together	0.95405	−0.267%
M-model training 5 outputs separately	0.95491	−0.1891%
MS-model	0.95508	−0.164%
MS-model with AdamW	0.95515	−0.157%
MS-model with repeated training	0.95911	0.239%
MS-model TTA	0.96870	1.198%
MS-model ensemble	0.96592	0.920%
MS-model connecting weights	0.96240	0.568%
TTA + weights and models ensemble	0.96922	1.250%
MS-model after corrections	0.96147	0.475%
MS-model after corrections with repeated training	0.96675	1.003%
Group of ensembles from all experiments	0.96977	1.305%
Optimized ensemble based on the best model	**0.97673**	**2.001%**

To sum up, it can be stated that artificial neural networks are able to distinguish tissue areas affected by cancer quite well. The developed MS-model is more accurate and faster than most of the models presented in the "Patch Chameleon" standings as shown in Figure 6. It can be said that such accuracy was most influenced by the effective architecture of the neural network and research on combining and assembling models. As shown in Figure 7, we have reached a maximum **F1 score of 0.924** with a threshold of **0.393**; this score measured on our last best model's accuracy (that is evaluated from precision and recall), as long as the confusion matrix is that shown in Figure 8, giving us a result of meaning how many times our best model gave us correct predictions: true positives—15,096, true negatives—15,189, false negatives—1295, and false positives—1188. According to experiments, even with less-than-ideally prepared training data, the last ensemble method managed to exceed **0.9691 AUC**.

#	User (Team)	Created	AUC	Comment
1st	rezazad68 (LSTM-U-net)	25 June 2019	1.0000	First submission by Reza Azad
1st	JasonHuang	24 May 2019	1.0000	test submission
3rd	Debu (Test123)	19 Sept. 2019	0.9971	
4th	mencco	10 May 2019	0.9968	The first trial
5th	mantaskundrotas2	21 May 2022	0.9767	TTA + ResNet Assembly
6th	zhongqiaoyong (Dr. Strange)	20 May 2019	0.9737	
7th	GeertLitjens	15 June 2019	0.9691	DenseNet with TTA

Figure 6. "Patch Chameleon" standings. The result of this work is in the fifth place—marked 5th.

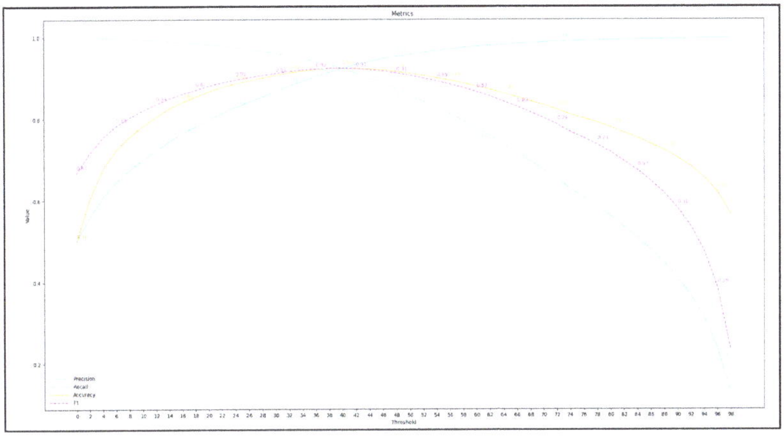

Figure 7. Maximum F1 score reached on an optimized ensemble with the best model (threshold = 0.393).

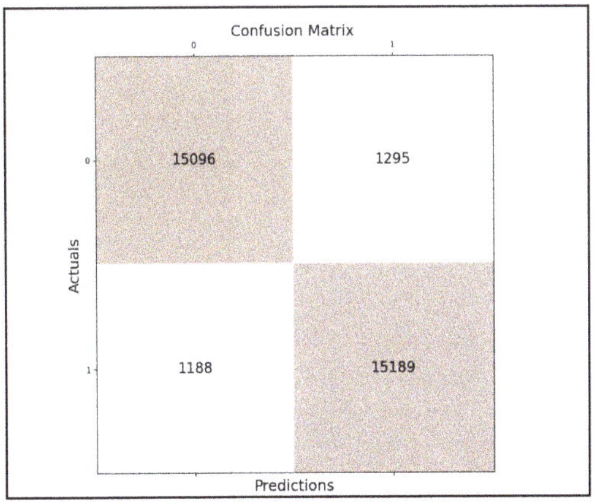

Figure 8. Confusion matrix reached with the best model.

6. Conclusions

In this work, we proposed to use ML and different neural network techniques to find a solution to WSIs histopathological data analysis. Our extensive experiments showed that the application of artificial deep neural networks for the classification of medical images, compared to other classical methods, are superior in almost all criteria. First, the CNN generalize well and perform similarly well on unseen data, even with additional constraints. From the obtained experiments, the AUC difference between the training and testing datasets was about one percent. Second, these models were highly flexible, allowing the size and architecture of the model to be experimentally tailored to the type of task. Using the M-model in several training iterations, we managed to reduce the model size by almost twice and increase the accuracy from 0.95491 to 0.95515 AUC. Third, when properly trained, convolutional models perform well on groups of various sizes. The result increased to 0.96870 with the TTA method, and 0.96977 with the addition of the multi-model ensemble. Fourth, by applying special analysis methods, it was possible to identify the shortcomings of the models and correct them. After finding that excessive and inappropriate image augmentation was detrimental to learning, a correction of the image processing parameters was sufficient to increase the AUC by almost 0.3%. Moreover, after additional training data preparation, the result of the individual model increased to 0.96664 AUC.

Due to the complexity of histopathological images, current image classification methods still lack accuracy and stability, and even the final model ensemble result of 0.97673 was not sufficient for the system to work autonomously. The results are too unpredictable, so this type of system can only be used as a guide as an image analysis tool for the physician.

Nevertheless, even such an achievement is important—it is a step closer to the ideal accuracy that would exceed human resolution.

In future work, not only another optimizing, and DNN techniques and architectures, but also imaging improving unsupervised methods could be used to gain best accurate results that further diagnostics tools for faster and more accurate cancer detection in histopathology imaging.

Author Contributions: Conceptualization, M.K. and D.Š.; methodology, M.K. and E.M.; software, M.K.; writing—original draft preparation, M.K.; visualization, M.K.; investigation, M.K. and E.M.; editing, E.M.; writing—review, supervision, project administration, funding acquisition, D.Š. All authors have read and agreed to the published version of the manuscript.

Funding: This research received no external funding.

Institutional Review Board Statement: Not applicable.

Informed Consent Statement: Not applicable.

Data Availability Statement: Not applicable.

Conflicts of Interest: The authors declare no conflict of interest.

References

1. Ahmed, S.; Shaikh, A.; Alshahrani, H.; Alghamdi, A.; Alrizq, M.; Baber, J.; Bakhtyar, M. Transfer learning approach for classification of histopathology whole slide images. *Sensors* **2021**, *21*, 5361. [CrossRef]
2. Pantanowitz, L.; Dickinson, K.; Evans, A.J.; Hassell, L.A.; Henricks, W.H.; Lennerz, J.K.; Lowe, A.; Parwani, A.V.; Riben, M.; Smith, C.D.; et al. American Telemedicine Association clinical guidelines for telepathology. *J. Pathol. Inform.* **2014**, *5*, 39. [CrossRef]
3. Helin, H.; Tolonen, T.; Ylinen, O.; Tolonen, P.; Napankangas, J.; Isola, J. Optimized JPEG 2000 compression for efficient storage of histopathological whole-slide images. *J. Pathol. Inform.* **2018**, *9*, 20. [CrossRef]
4. Kim, I.; Kang, K.; Song, Y.; Kim, T.J. Application of Artificial Intelligence in Pathology: Trends and Challenges. *Diagnostics* **2022**, *12*, 2794. [CrossRef]
5. Van der Laak, J.; Litjens, G.; Ciompi, F. Deep learning in histopathology: The path to the clinic. *Nat. Med.* **2021**, *27*, 775–784. [CrossRef]
6. Saba, T. Journal of Infection and Public Health. 13 Recent advancement in cancer detection using machine learning: Systematic survey of decades, comparisons, and challenges. *J. Infect. Public Health* **2020**, *13*, 1274–1289. [CrossRef]
7. Lansdowne, L.E. Tumor Biology. Cancer Research from Technology Networks. Accessed August 16, 2022. Available online: http://www.technologynetworks.com/cancer-research/infographics/tumor-biology-359548 (accessed on 1 October 2021).

8. Azhari, E.E.M.; Hatta, M.M.M.; Htike, Z.Z.; Win, S.L. Tumor detection in medical imaging: A survey. *Int. J. Adv. Inf. Technol.* **2014**, *4*, 21.
9. Díaz-Pernas, F.J.; Martínez-Zarzuela, M.; Antón-Rodríguez, M.; González-Ortega, D. A deep learning approach for brain tumor classification and segmentation using a multiscale convolutional neural network. *Healthcare* **2021**, *9*, 153. [CrossRef]
10. Sung, H.; Ferlay, J.; Siegel, R.L.; Laversanne, M.; Soerjomataram, I.; Jemal, A.; Bray, F. Global cancer statistics 2020: GLOBOCAN estimates of incidence and mortality worldwide for 36 cancers in 185 countries. *CA: A Cancer J. Clin.* **2021**, *71*, 209–249. [CrossRef]
11. Litjens, G.; Sánchez, C.I.; Timofeeva, N.; Hermsen, M.; Nagtegaal, I.; Kovacs, I.; Hulsbergen-van de Kaa, C.; Bult, P.; Van Ginneken, B.; Van Der Laak, J. Deep learning as a tool for increased accuracy and efficiency of histopathological diagnosis. *Sci. Rep.* **2016**, *6*, 26286. [CrossRef]
12. He, L.; Long, L.R.; Antani, S.; Thoma, G.R. Histology image analysis for carcinoma detection and grading. *Comput. Methods Programs Biomed.* **2012**, *107*, 538–556. [CrossRef] [PubMed]
13. Pandian, A.P. Identification and classification of cancer cells using capsule network with pathological images. *J. Artif. Intell.* **2019**, *1*, 37–44.
14. Ehteshami, B. Diagnostic Assessment of Deep Learning Algorithms for Detection of Lymph Node Metastases in Women With Breast Cancer. *J. Am. Med. Assoc.* **2017**, *318*, 2199–2210. [CrossRef] [PubMed]
15. Maseer, Z.K.; Yusof, R.; Bahaman, N.; Mostafa, S.A.; Foozy, C.F.M. Benchmarking of machine learning for anomaly based intrusion detection systems in the CICIDS2017 dataset. *IEEE Access* **2021**, *9*, 22351–22370. [CrossRef]
16. Senkamalavalli, R.; Bhuvaneswari, T. Improved classification of breast cancer data using hybrid techniques. *Int. J. Adv. Eng. Res. Sci.* **2017**, *5*, 237467. [CrossRef]
17. Jiang, P.; Peng, J.; Zhang, G.; Cheng, E.; Megalooikonomou, V.; Ling, H. Learning-based automatic breast tumor detection and segmentation in ultrasound images. In Proceedings of the 2012 9th IEEE International Symposium on Biomedical Imaging (ISBI), Barcelona, Spain, 2–5 May 2012; pp. 1587–1590.
18. Parmar, S.; Gondaliya, N. A Survey on Detection and Classification of Brain Tumor from MRI Brain Images using Image Processing Techniques. *Int. Res. J. Eng. Technol. IRJET* **2018**, *5*, 162–166.
19. Jayade, S.; Ingole, D.T.; Ingole, M.D. MRI brain tumor classification using hybrid classifier. In Proceedings of the 2019 International Conference on Innovative Trends and Advances in Engineering and Technology (ICITAET), Shegoaon, India, 27–28 December 2019; pp. 201–205.
20. Peter, R.; Korfiatis, P.; Blezek, D.; Oscar Beitia, A.; Stepan-Buksakowska, I.; Horinek, D.; Flemming, K.D.; Erickson, B.J. A quantitative symmetry-based analysis of hyperacute ischemic stroke lesions in noncontrast computed tomography. *Med. Phys.* **2017**, *44*, 192–199. [CrossRef] [PubMed]
21. Seetha, J.; Raja, S.S. Brain tumor classification using convolutional neural networks. *Biomed. Pharmacol. J.* **2018**, *11*, 1457. [CrossRef]
22. Yu, J.; Li, Q.; Zhang, H.; Meng, Y.; Liu, Y.F.; Jiang, H.; Ma, C.; Liu, F.; Fang, X.; Li, J.; et al. Contrast-enhanced computed tomography radiomics and multilayer perceptron network classifier: An approach for predicting CD20+ B cells in patients with pancreatic ductal adenocarcinoma. *Abdom. Radiol.* **2022**, *47*, 242–253. [CrossRef]
23. Erickson, B.J.; Korfiatis, P.; Akkus, Z.; Kline, T.L. Machine learning for medical imaging. *Radiographics* **2017**, *37*, 505. [CrossRef]
24. Khajuria, R.; Quyoom, A.; Sarwar, A. A comparison of deep reinforcement learning and deep learning for complex image analysis. *J. Multimed. Inf. Syst.* **2020**, *7*, 1–10. [CrossRef]
25. Tyagi, A.K.; Chahal, P. Artificial intelligence and machine learning algorithms. In *Research Anthology on Machine Learning Techniques, Methods, and Applications*; IGI Global: Hershey, PA, USA, 2022; pp. 421–446.
26. Sarker, I.H. Machine learning: Algorithms, real-world applications and research directions. *SN Comput. Sci.* **2021**, *2*, 160. [CrossRef] [PubMed]
27. Montavon, G.; Samek, W.; Müller, K.R. Methods for interpreting and understanding deep neural networks. *Digit. Signal Process.* **2018**, *73*, 1–15. [CrossRef]
28. Rossi, F.; Conan-Guez, B. Functional Multi-Layer Perceptron: A Nonlinear Tool for Functional Data Analysis. *Neural Netw. Off. J. Int. Neural Netw. Soc.* **2005**, *18*, 45–60. [CrossRef]
29. Wahab, N.; Khan, A. Multifaceted fused-CNN based scoring of breast cancer whole-slide histopathology images. *Appl. Soft Comput.* **2020**, *97*, 106808. [CrossRef]
30. Zainudin, Z.; Shamsuddin, S.M.; Hasan, S. Deep layer CNN architecture for breast cancer histopathology image detection. In *International Conference on Advanced Machine Learning Technologies and Applications*; Springer: Cham, Switzerland, 2019; pp. 43–51.
31. Dabeer, S.; Khan, M.M.; Islam, S. Cancer diagnosis in histopathological image: CNN based approach. *Inform. Med. Unlocked* **2019**, *16*, 100231. [CrossRef]
32. Graziani, M.; Lompech, T.; Müller, H.; Andrearczyk, V. Evaluation and comparison of CNN visual explanations for histopathology. In Proceedings of the 35th AAAI Conference on Artificial Intelligence, Virtual Event, 2–9 February 2021; pp. 195–201.
33. Zhang, L.; Wu, Y.; Zheng, B.; Su, L.; Chen, Y.; Ma, S.; Hu, Q.; Zou, X.; Yao, L.; Yang, Y.; et al. Rapid histology of laryngeal squamous cell carcinoma with deep-learning based stimulated Raman scattering microscopy. *Theranostics* **2019**, *9*, 2541. [CrossRef]
34. He, K.; Zhang, X.; Ren, S.; Sun, J. Deep residual learning for image recognition. In Proceedings of the IEEE Conference on Computer Vision and Pattern Recognition, Las Vegas, NV, USA, 27–30 June 2016; pp. 770–778.

35. Lauande, M.G.M.; Teles, A.M.; da Silva, L.L.; Matos, C.E.F.; Junior, G.B.; de Paiva, A.C.; de Almeida, J.S.; Oliveira, R.; Brito, H.; Nascimento, A.; et al. Classification of Histopathological Images of Penile Cancer using DenseNet and Transfer Learning. In Proceedings of the 17th International Joint Conference on Computer Vision, Imaging and Computer Graphics Theory and Applications—Volume 4: VISAPP, Online, 6–8 February 2022; pp. 976–983.
36. Reenadevi, R.; Sathiya, T.; Sathiyabhama, B. Breast cancer histopathological image classification using augmentation based on optimized deep ResNet-152 structure. *Ann. Rom. Soc. Cell Biol.* **2021**, *25*, 5866–5874.
37. Wang, C.-W.; Lee, Y.-C.; Chang, C.-C.; Lin, Y.-J.; Liou, Y.-A.; Hsu, P.-C.; Chang, C.-C.; Sai, A.-K.; Wang, C.-H.; Chao, T.-K. A weakly supervised deep learning method for guiding ovarian cancer treatment and identifying an effective biomarker. *Cancers* **2022**, *14*, 1651. [CrossRef]
38. Samee, N.A.; Atteia, G.; Meshoul, S.; Al-antari, M.A.; Kadah, Y.M. Deep Learning Cascaded Feature Selection Framework for Breast Cancer Classification: Hybrid CNN with Univariate-Based Approach. *Mathematics* **2022**, *10*, 3631. [CrossRef]
39. Allegra, A.; Tonacci, A.; Sciaccotta, R.; Genovese, S.; Musolino, C.; Pioggia, G.; Gangemi, S. Machine learning and deep learning applications in multiple myeloma diagnosis, prognosis, and treatment selection. *Cancers* **2022**, *14*, 606. [CrossRef] [PubMed]
40. Xie, X.; Fu, C.C.; Lv, L.; Ye, Q.; Yu, Y.; Fang, Q.; Zhang, L.; Hou, L.; Wu, C. Deep convolutional neural network-based classification of cancer cells on cytological pleural effusion images. *Mod. Pathol.* **2022**, *35*, 609–614. [CrossRef] [PubMed]
41. Gadermayr, M.; Koller, L.; Tschuchnig, M.; Stangassinger, L.M.; Kreutzer, C.; Couillard-Despres, S.; Oostingh, J.G.; Hittmair, A. MixUp-MIL: Novel Data Augmentation for Multiple Instance Learning and a Study on Thyroid Cancer Diagnosis. *arXiv* **2022**, arXiv:2211.05862.
42. Jimenez-del-Toro, O.; Otálora, S.; Andersson, M.; Eurén, K.; Hedlund, M.; Rousson, M.; Müller, H.; Atzori, M. Analysis of histopathology images: From traditional machine learning. In *Biomedical Texture Analysis*; Academic Press: Cambridge, MA, USA, 2017; pp. 281–314.
43. Komura, D.; Ishikawa, S. Machine learning methods for histopathological image analysis. *Comput. Struct. Biotechnol. J.* **2018**, *16*, 34–42. [CrossRef] [PubMed]
44. Lee, J.; Warner, E.; Shaikhouni, S.; Bitzer, M.; Kretzler, M.; Gipson, D.; Pennathur, S.; Bellovich, K.; Bhat, Z.; Gadegbeku, C.; et al. Unsupervised machine learning for identifying important visual features through bag-of-words using histopathology data from chronic kidney disease. *Sci. Rep.* **2022**, *12*, 4832. [CrossRef] [PubMed]
45. Ahamed, S.B.; Shamsudheen, S.; Balobaid, A.S. Deep Learning Approaches, Algorithms, and Applications in Bioinformatics. In *Applications of Machine Learning and Deep Learning on Biological Data*; Taylor & Francis: Abingdon, UK, 2023; p. 1.
46. Bilal, M.; Nimir, M.; Snead, D.; Taylor, G.S.; Rajpoot, N. Role of AI and digital pathology for colorectal immuno-oncology. *Br. J. Cancer* **2022**, *128*, 3–11. [CrossRef] [PubMed]
47. Banerji, S.; Mitra, S. Deep learning in histopathology: A review. *Wiley Interdiscip. Rev. Data Min. Knowl. Discov.* **2022**, *12*, e1439. [CrossRef]
48. Lu, Z.; Xu, S.; Shao, W.; Wu, Y.; Zhang, J.; Han, Z.; Feng, Q.; Huang, K. Deep-learning–based characterization of tumor-infiltrating lymphocytes in breast cancers from histopathology images and multiomics data. *JCO Clin. Cancer Inform.* **2020**, *4*, 480–490. [CrossRef]
49. Subramanian, H.; Subramanian, S. Improving diagnosis through digital pathology: Proof-of-concept implementation using smart contracts and decentralized file storage. *J. Med. Internet Res.* **2022**, *24*, e34207. [CrossRef]
50. Han, Z.; Wei, B.; Zheng, Y.; Yin, Y.; Li, K.; Li, S. Breast cancer multi-classification from histopathological images with structured deep learning model. *Sci Rep.* **2017**, *7*, 4172. [CrossRef]
51. Ahmedt-Aristizabal, D.; Armin, M.A.; Denman, S.; Fookes, C.; Petersson, L. A survey on graph-based deep learning for computational histopathology. *Comput. Med. Imaging Graph.* **2022**, *95*, 102027. [CrossRef] [PubMed]
52. Bouteldja, N.; Klinkhammer, B.M.; Bülow, R.D.; Droste, P.; Otten, S.W.; von Stillfried, S.F.; Moellmann, J.; Sheehan, S.M.; Korstanje, R.; Menzel, S.; et al. Deep learning–based segmentation and quantification in experimental kidney histopathology. *J. Am. Soc. Nephrol.* **2021**, *32*, 52–68. [CrossRef] [PubMed]
53. Chen, M.; Zhang, B.; Topatana, W.; Cao, J.; Zhu, H.; Juengpanich, S.; Mao, Q.; Yu, H.; Cai, X. Classification and mutation prediction based on histopathology H&E images in liver cancer using deep learning. *NPJ Precis. Oncol.* **2020**, *4*, 14. [PubMed]
54. Schaer, R.; Otálora, S.; Jimenez-del-Toro, O.; Atzori, M.; Müller, H. Deep learning-based retrieval system for gigapixel histopathology cases and the open access literature. *J. Pathol. Inform.* **2019**, *10*, 19. [CrossRef]
55. Chaunzwa, T.L.; Hosny, A.; Xu, Y.; Shafer, A.; Diao, N.; Lanuti, M.; Christiani, D.C.; Mak, R.H.; Aerts, H.J. Deep learning classification of lung cancer histology using CT images. *Sci. Rep.* **2021**, *11*, 5471. [CrossRef]
56. Mahesh, B. Machine learning algorithms-a review. *Int. J. Sci. Res. IJSR* **2020**, *9*, 381–386.
57. Sari, C.T.; Gunduz-Demir, C. Unsupervised feature extraction via deep learning for histopathological classification of colon tissue images. *IEEE Trans. Med. Imaging* **2018**, *38*, 1139–1149. [CrossRef]
58. Huss, R.; Coupland, S.E. Software-assisted decision support in digital histopathology. *J. Pathol.* **2020**, *250*, 685–692. [CrossRef]
59. Ciga, O.; Xu, T.; Martel, A.L. Self supervised contrastive learning for digital histopathology. *Mach. Learn. Appl.* **2022**, *7*, 100198. [CrossRef]
60. Byra, M.; Jarosik, P.; Szubert, A.; Galperin, M.; Ojeda-Fournier, H.; Olson, L.; O'Boyle, M.; Comstock, C.; Andre, M. Breast mass segmentation in ultrasound with selective kernel U-Net convolutional neural network. *Biomed. Signal Process. Control.* **2020**, *61*, 102027. [CrossRef]

61. Jiang, Y.; Sui, X.; Ding, Y.; Xiao, W.; Zheng, Y.; Zhang, Y. A semi-supervised learning approach with consistency regularization for tumor histopathological images analysis. *Front. Oncol.* **2022**, *12*, 7200. [CrossRef]
62. Nugroho, A.; Suhartanto, H. Hyper-parameter tuning based on random search for densenet optimization. In Proceedings of the 2020 7th International Conference on Information Technology, Computer, and Electrical Engineering (ICITACEE), Semarang, Indonesia, 24–25 September 2020; pp. 96–99.
63. Khanam, J.J.; Foo, S.Y. A comparison of machine learning algorithms for diabetes prediction. *ICT Express* **2021**, *7*, 432–439. [CrossRef]
64. Li, Y.; Wei, C.; Ma, T. Towards explaining the regularization effect of initial large learning rate in training neural networks. In Proceedings of the NIPS'19: Proceedings of the 33rd International Conference on Neural Information Processing Systems, Vancouver, BC, Canada, 8–14 December 2019.
65. Chikontwe, P.; Sung, H.J.; Jeong, J.; Kim, M.; Go, H.; Nam, S.J.; Park, S.H. Weakly supervised segmentation on neural compressed histopathology with self-equivariant regularization. *Med. Image Anal.* **2022**, *80*, 102482. [CrossRef]
66. Buddhavarapu, V.G. An experimental study on classification of thyroid histopathology images using transfer learning. *Pattern Recognit. Lett.* **2020**, *140*, 1–9. [CrossRef]
67. Kumar, S.K. On weight initialization in deep neural networks. *arXiv* **2017**, arXiv:1704.08863.
68. Zhang, H.; Feng, L.; Zhang, X.; Yang, Y.; Li, J. Necessary conditions for convergence of CNNs and initialization of convolution kernels. *Digit. Signal Process.* **2022**, *123*, 103397. [CrossRef]
69. Singh, P.; Muchahari, M.K. Solving multi-objective optimization problem of convolutional neural network using fast forward quantum optimization algorithm: Application in digital image classification. *Adv. Eng. Softw.* **2023**, *176*, 103370. [CrossRef]
70. Srikantamurthy, M.M.; Rallabandi, V.P.; Dudekula, D.B.; Natarajan, S.; Park, J. Classification of benign and malignant subtypes of breast cancer histopathology imaging using hybrid CNN-LSTM based transfer learning. *BMC Med. Imaging* **2023**, *23*, 19. [CrossRef]
71. Gour, M.; Jain, S.; Shankar, U. Application of Deep Learning Techniques for Prostate Cancer Grading Using Histopathological Images. In *Computer Vision and Image Processing: 6th International Conference, CVIP 2021, Rupnagar, India, December 3–5, 2021, Revised Selected Papers, Part I*; Springer International Publishing: Cham, Switzerland, 2022; pp. 83–94.
72. Krishna, S.; Krishnamoorthy, S.; Bhavsar, A. Stain normalized breast histopathology image recognition using convolutional neural networks for cancer detection. *arXiv* **2022**, arXiv:2201.00957.
73. Uthatham, A.; Yodrabum, N.; Sinmaroeng, C.; Titijaroonroj, T. Automatic Lymph Node Classification with Convolutional Neural Network. In Proceedings of the 2022 14th International Conference on Information Technology and Electrical Engineering (ICITEE), Yogyakarta, Indonesia, 18–19 October 2022; pp. 1–6.
74. Li, X.; Cen, M.; Xu, J.; Zhang, H.; Xu, X.S. Improving feature extraction from histopathological images through a fine-tuning ImageNet model. *J. Pathol. Inform.* **2022**, *13*, 100115. [CrossRef]
75. Wu, C.T.; Lin, P.H.; Huang, S.Y.; Tseng, Y.J.; Chang, H.T.; Li, S.Y.; Yen, H.W. Revisiting alloy design of low-modulus biomedical β-Ti alloys using an artificial neural network. *Materialia* **2022**, *21*, 101313. [CrossRef]
76. Wright, L.; Demeure, N. Ranger21: A synergistic deep learning optimizer. *arXiv* **2021**, arXiv:2106.13731.
77. Wang, P.; Li, P.; Li, Y.; Wang, J.; Xu, J. Histopathological image classification based on cross-domain deep transferred feature fusion. *Biomed. Signal Process. Control.* **2021**, *68*, 102705. [CrossRef]
78. Akossi, A.; Wang, F.; Teodoro, G.; Kong, J. Image registration with optimal regularization parameter selection by learned auto encoder features. In Proceedings of the 2021 IEEE 18th International Symposium on Biomedical Imaging (ISBI), Nice, France, 13–16 April 2021; pp. 702–705.
79. Moshkov, N.; Mathe, B.; Kertesz-Farkas, A.; Hollandi, R.; Horvath, P. Test-time augmentation for deep learning-based cell segmentation on microscopy images. *Sci. Rep.* **2020**, *10*, 5068. [CrossRef] [PubMed]
80. Nguyen, C.P.; Vo, A.H.; Nguyen, B.T. Breast cancer histology image classification using deep learning. In Proceedings of the 2019 19th International Symposium on Communications and Information Technologies (ISCIT), Ho Chi Minh City, Vietnam, 25–27 September 2019; pp. 366–370.

applied sciences

MDPI

Article

Thalamus Segmentation Using Deep Learning with Diffusion MRI Data: An Open Benchmark

Gustavo Retuci Pinheiro [1,*], Lorenza Brusini [2], Diedre Carmo [1], Renata Prôa [1,3], Thays Abreu [1], Simone Appenzeller [4], Gloria Menegaz [2] and Leticia Rittner [1]

1 School of Electrical and Computing Engineering, University of Campinas, Campinas 13083-852, Brazil
2 Department of Computer Science, University of Verona, 37129 Verona, Italy
3 Institute of Mathematics and Statistic, University of São Paulo, São Paulo 14887-900, Brazil
4 School of Medical Science, University of Campinas, Campinas 13083-887, Brazil
* Correspondence: g162793@dac.unicamp.br

Abstract: The thalamus is a subcortical brain structure linked to the motor system. Since certain changes within this structure are related to diseases, such as multiple sclerosis and Parkinson's, the characterization of the thalamus—e.g., shape assessment—is a crucial step in relevant studies and applications, including medical research and surgical planning. A robust and reliable thalamus-segmentation method is therefore, required to meet these demands. Despite presenting low contrast for this particular structure, T1-weighted imaging is still the most common MRI sequence for thalamus segmentation. However, diffusion MRI (dMRI) captures different micro-structural details of the biological tissue and reveals more contrast of the thalamic borders, thereby serving as a better candidate for thalamus-segmentation methods. Accordingly, we propose a baseline multimodality thalamus-segmentation pipeline that combines dMRI and T1-weighted images within a CNN approach, achieving state-of-the-art levels of Dice overlap. Furthermore, we are hosting an open benchmark with a large, preprocessed, publicly available dataset that includes co-registered, T1-weighted, dMRI, manual thalamic masks; masks generated by three distinct automated methods; and a STAPLE consensus of the masks. The dataset, code, environment, and instructions for the benchmark leaderboard can be found on our GitHub and CodaLab.

Keywords: thalamus; segmentation; diffusion MRI; public dataset; deep learning; benchmark

1. Introduction

The thalamus (Figure 1) is a bilateral subcortical brain structure. Each of its two parts measure on average 20 mm in the left–right direction (radiological convention) and 30 mm in the anterior–posterior direction [1]. It is located in the central region of the brain, below the ventricles and fornix, and above the hypothalamus (Figures 1 and 2). Despite its relatively small volume, the thalamus can be further divided into nuclei depending on the cytological differences existing across different regions of the same structure [1]. The thalamus also has a central physiological role in the nervous system, functioning as a signal transponder owing to the white matter connecting it to a wide area of the cortex. Furthermore, it is involved in other functions, including the regulation of sleep, alertness, motor functions, and spoken language [1,2].

Many neurological disorders are associated with thalamic changes. This region of the brain includes targets for deep-brain stimulation and stereotactic ablation for the treatment of symptoms of conditions such as Parkinson's disease, essential tremors, epilepsy, chronic pain syndrome, and multiple sclerosis [3,4]. In the context of surgical planning, accurate segmentation is essential for the success of therapy. Relevant surgical approaches include focused ultrasound thalamotomy, where the segmentation requirement is the rapidity of its estimation for improving operation efficacy [5]. Accurate segmentation is also highly desirable in the follow-ups and studies of the as-of-yet unclear mechanisms driving these diseases [6].

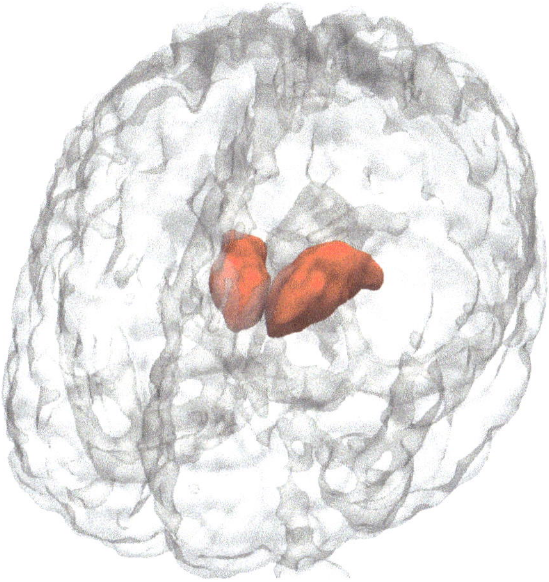

Figure 1. The thalamus's structure and location in the brain.

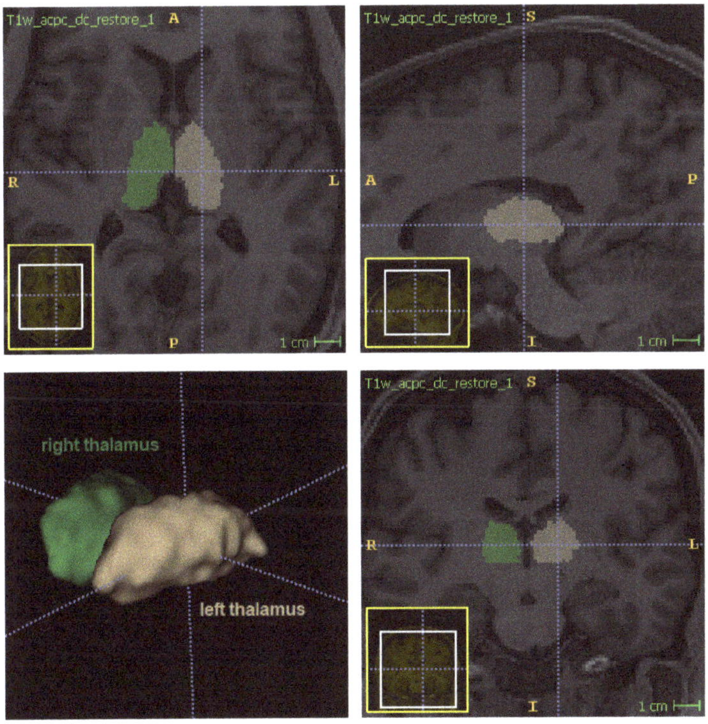

Figure 2. Location of thalamus in orthogonal views: left thalamus in beige (label 10 in FreeSurferColorLUT) and right thalamus in green (label 49 in FreeSurferColorLUT).

Magnetic resonance imaging (MRI) is frequently employed to visualize the thalamus, as it enables the non-invasive observation of in vivo deep brain structures under safe conditions for the patient. A wide variety of automated tools are available for MRI-based thalamus segmentation. Nonetheless, manual segmentation is still considered the "gold standard", as it overcomes the low contrast and resolution achievable in standard 1.5 and 3T T1-weighted acquisitions [7]. In fact, these limitations in contrast and resolution may constitute a bias, thereby yielding suboptimal segmentation results. Unfortunately, manual segmentation has its own limitations: discrepancies owing to the scarcity of protocols [8–10]; the need for trained raters; and an excessively large execution time [7], especially for larger datasets. Consequently, the development of faster and more robust automatic thalamus-segmentation methods is crucial.

The T1-weighted scan is one of the most widespread MRI sequences owing to the rapidity and relative simplicity of its acquisition, visual similarity with anatomical slices, and good spatial resolution [11,12]. For these reasons, it is also one of the most used MRI types with both manual and automated segmentation methods. In the field of neurological structures, existing automated segmentation methods can be primarily categorized as atlas-based or deep-learning-based.

As atlas-based methods, the `fsl_anat` [13] tool of the FSL software and FreeSurfer [14] represent atlas-guided thalamus segmentation approaches, serving as the most popular automated tools, despite their time-intensive underlying algorithms [15] and tendency to overestimate the thalamic shape compared to manual segmentation [7]. Recently, a less common structural acquisition of white-matter-nulled MP-RAGE images has been employed to collect data using a 7T MRI scanner, leading to the development of Thalamus-Optimized Multi-Atlas Segmentation (THOMAS) [1]. Theoretically, such a sequence would enhance the thalamic contrast on a 7T MRI scanner. THOMAS has been successfully used to segment 12 thalamic nuclei with Dice coefficients of 0.85 and 0.7 for large and small nuclei, respectively. Unfortunately, only qualitative results were produced for its feasibility on 3T MRI, whereas quantitative validation is necessary given the known complexity of the task [4,16].

Methods built upon deep learning strategies allow for fast thalamic segmentation, at the cost of requiring a large quantity of data for training in order to avoid overfitting [17,18]. Some exceptional methods [6,19,20] can obtain good segmentation results even with smaller datasets by using artifices such as multi-scale patches. However, generalizability cannot be ensured given an insufficient test set.

One of the most recent and high-performing deep learning techniques is QuickNAT [17], which employs a Bayesian fully-convolutional neural network to estimate the thalamus shape from T1-weighted MR images, requiring only 20 s when using a GPU. This method uses multiple large datasets to ensure consistency across different MRI data.

The advantages derived from multimodality warrant further investigation. Indeed, the multimodality of MRI has enabled highly accurate performance, reaching Dice coefficients of 0.878 and 0.890 for the two thalami when calculated against manual segmentation [21]. Specifically, the random forest algorithm was employed to generate predictions based on structural (T1 and T2-weighted) and diffusion-weighted MRI. In particular, diffusion MRI (dMRI) alone has been frequently employed in prior studies to perform this task [21–23].

Among the most recently proposed works, Battistella et al. [24] took advantage of the orientation-distribution functions calculated using the spherical harmonic model to detect and characterize the thalamus with satisfactory performance. In fact, the inherent cytological differences within the thalamus serve as the basis for the hypothesis of dMRI's sensitivity to the microstructural modulations of this structure. By relying on the Fourier transform that relates the dMRI signal to the propagator from which the orientation-distribution function is calculated, information regarding the brain tissue architecture can be inferred for each voxel [25]. This is possible because the propagator represents the probability that the water volume inside the brain undergoes displacement r in diffusion time τ, which reflects the diffusion process constrained by the walls of the compartment therein (e.g., the white matter axon). The use of dMRI to obtain microstructural details of brain tissue offers the potential to enable more robust and accurate segmentation procedures.

Despite the significant potential of deep learning methods and the use of diffusion data for thalamus segmentation, few attempts have been made to combine the two approaches for that purpose [26,27]. One reason behind the scarcity of research pertaining to this subject is the complexity of using multimodality on CNNs, specifically with dMRI. Additional steps demanded by the use of dMRI data with CNNs include: fitting a diffusion model and computation of diffusion tensor maps; complex registration processes among different MRI sequences; changes in the CNN architecture to handle multiple inputs; manipulation of diffusion tensor maps. All of these steps require a rigorous methodology to express the advantages of diffusion data. Additional challenges, such as the scarcity of large datasets and ground truth (manually annotated segmentations), are more pronounced in dMRI, as the acquisition is more costly and the interpretation of diffusion data is not as trivial as it is on T1-weighted images [28].

The primary objectives of this study were to provide a benchmark for the development of more precise thalamus-segmentation methods, taking advantage of diffusion MRI data; promote fair comparisons among different methods; and interpret the contribution of dMRI to the segmentation task. The main contributions of this work are: a large processed benchmark dataset composed of annotated co-registered T1-weighted and diffusion MRI; a set of different thalamic masks for each subject computed using atlas- and CNN-based methods and statistically-combined masks; manual ground-truth data provided by experts; a baseline framework useful in the processing of diffusion data and additional training of CNNs for thalamus segmentation; and an ablation study on the contribution of dMRI to this task.

Motivation

As mentioned previously, the vast majority of thalamus-segmentation methods use exclusively T1-weighted images [6,15–20,29], an MR sequence that fails to present a good contrast on the thalamus borders (Figure 3-T1). In contrast, diffusion MRI naturally accounts for the different properties of the brain's microstructure [28,30–33], leading to higher contrast for certain sub-cortical structures, and consequently greater potential as a tool for segmentation problems.

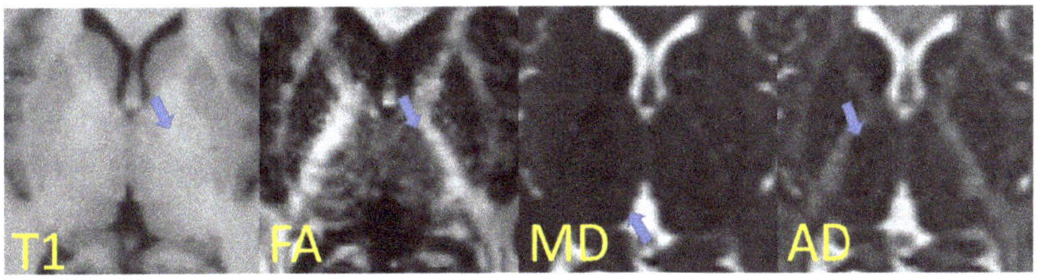

Figure 3. Axial slices in the thalamus region with thalamic borders highlighted (areas pointed by the arrows): T1-weighted image and examples of diffusion indices (fractional anisotropy, mean diffusivity, and axial diffusivity) from diffusion tensor imaging. Adapted with permission from Ref. [26]. 2021 Society of Photo-Optical Instrumentation Engineers (SPIE).

For example, when visualizing scalar maps computed from diffusion tensor imaging (Figure 3), the frontiers of the thalamus with other structures are clearly visible: on FA maps, for instance, the boundary between the thalamus and internal capsule is shown with a higher contrast due to the differing anisotropic diffusivity of these structures.

Another indicator of the potential of dMRI for thalamus segmentation is the use of diffusion indices to parcel the thalamus [2,24,34]. In summary, the parcellation of thalamic nuclei is reliable only when using diffusion MRI.

Considering that dMRI can highlight more differences between the thalamus and its neighboring structures than other MRI contrasts, it may even lead to a more appropriate delineation of the actual structure, thereby pushing the theoretical limits of segmentation performance for both manual and automatic methods.

Despite being able to carry a higher contrast for certain brain structures, dMRI presents some disadvantages, including: an excessive acquisition time in the MR scanner; typically lower spatial resolution compared to T1-weighted images; a high computational complexity owing to multiple diffusion directions; complex registration in cases where T1-weighted images or T1-derived annotations are needed simultaneously; and extra non-trivial processing steps [31,32], as in the cases of geometrical corrections and model fitting.

One of the primary motivations for the use of CNNs is a significant decrease in prediction time compared to other available methods. For instance, the segmentation of a whole brain can be achieved in a matter of seconds—i.e., QuickNAT requires 20 s when using a GPU—whereas atlas-based methods usually demand hours. Furthermore, the latest CNN methods represent the current state-of-the-art in terms of overlap metrics for segmenting brain structures [17,35].

The main downside of these approaches is the requirement for sufficiently large annotated datasets. Furthermore, the performance of these methods is closely linked to the quality of the data labels [36]. In addition, the input data must be diverse and consistent to ensure satisfactory CNN performance. Specifically, the data and labels require appropriate standardization, especially when working with multimodal data [37].

Despite the high performance of segmentation methods using T1-weighted images, prior studies have demonstrated the great potential of dMRI for improving the quality of thalamic segmentation [2,24,26,34]. However, preparing the dMRI to be used in conjunction with CNNs for this purpose is not a trivial task. Accordingly, a primary motivation of this work is the need for an appropriate dMRI processing pipeline for CNN approaches, and there are the additional objectives of providing the preprocessing methodology, preprocessed data, and a benchmark test set to facilitate comparisons with future works.

2. Materials and Methods

The following subsections provide details pertaining to the method's pipeline (Figure 4), including the preprocessing and organizational stages and the segmentation methods and CNN framework.

The processed dataset used for training, testing, and benchmarking throughout this study has been made publicly available. Additional details regarding the folder and file tree are available in the GitHub repository (https://github.com/MICLab-Unicamp/thalamus_benchmark_diffusion) (accessed on 20 April 2023).

2.1. Dataset

The Human Connectome Project (HCP) [38] is a consortium that studies brain connectivity in healthy adults and releases all relevant data. It provides MR images collected in many modalities, including the structural T1 and diffusion-weighted images employed throughout this study. HCP T1-weighted acquisition was performed using a 3D magnetization-prepared rapid acquisition gradient echo (MPRAGE) sequence (repetition time (TR)/echo time (TE) = 2400/2.14 ms, flip angle (FA) = 8°, field of view (FOV) = 224 mm, 0.7 mm isotropic resolution, 256 slices), whereas the diffusion-weighted images were acquired using a Stejskal–Tanner monopolar diffusion-encoding scheme (TR/TE = 5500/89 ms, FA = 160°, FOV = 210 mm, 1.25 mm isotropic resolution, 111 slices, b-values = 1000/2000/3000 s/mm^2 with 90 non-collinear gradient directions for each b-value and 18 b0 volumes) [38]. The consortium provides minimally pre-processed data for both modalities [39]. T1-weighted MRI data were corrected for gradient, readout, and bias field distortions, whereas dMRI data includes b0 intensity normalization and correction for susceptibility-induced b0 fields, eddy current, subject motion, and gradient distortions.

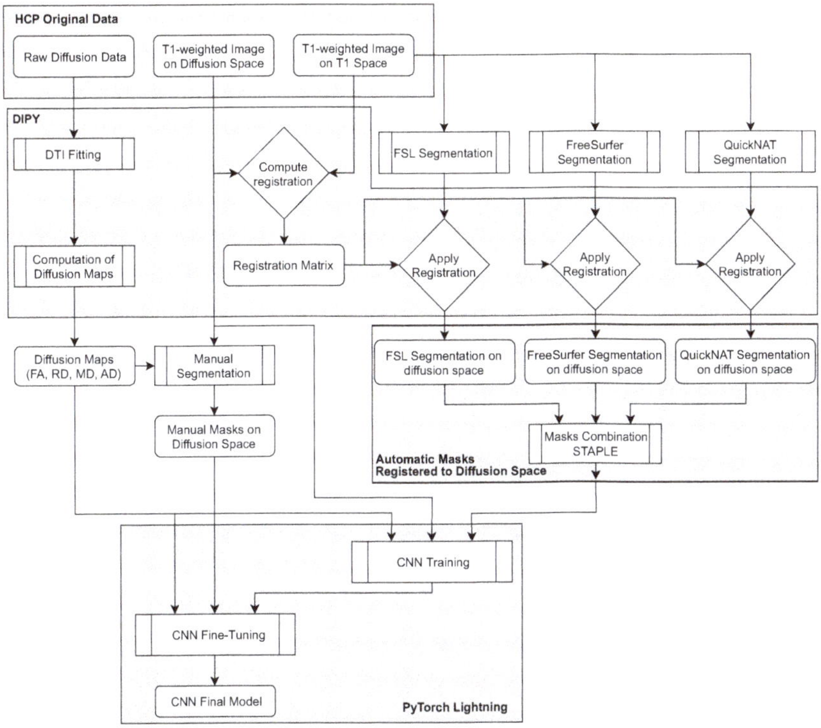

Figure 4. Overview of data processing pipeline and its use for model training: Computation of diffusion tensor maps, registration of images to diffusion space, automated and manual mask generation, registration of masks to diffusion space, CNN training, and fine-tuning.

Although the HCP dataset encompasses data from more than 1200 subjects, a total of 1065 subjects had scans for both diffusion- and T1-weighted MRI. As 2 subjects were discarded due to issues with the registration process, the dataset used throughout this study includes 1063 subjects.

The dataset is fairly balanced with respect to subjects' sex, and has an age distribution from 22 to 35 years (Figure 5).

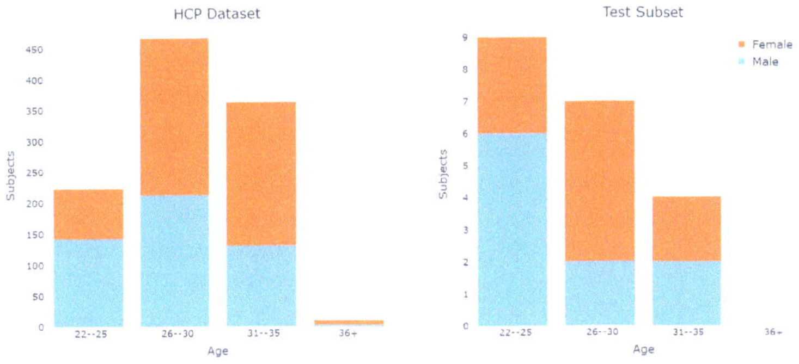

Figure 5. Age range and sex distributions for HCP dataset and test subset.

2.2. Silver Standard Creation

Since the use of manually annotated masks (ground truth) is impractical for a large dataset, a silver standard may be employed instead. The silver standard is a non-ideal mask, generated by automatic or semi-automatic methods, that may substitute the gold standard for specific purposes, as in the case of CNN training prior to fine-tuning.

To generate a silver standard for each subject, three automatic segmentations were obtained through three different algorithms: FreeSurfer [14] (Figure 6A), `fsl_anat` [13] (Figure 6B), and QuickNAT (Figure 6C). This was achieved using only T1-weighted images (in T1 space), as the methods are optimized to work with this specific MRI sequence. Finally, the silver standard was generated using the STAPLE method [40,41] to statistically combine the three segmentations (Figure 6). This procedure was performed for all subjects in the dataset.

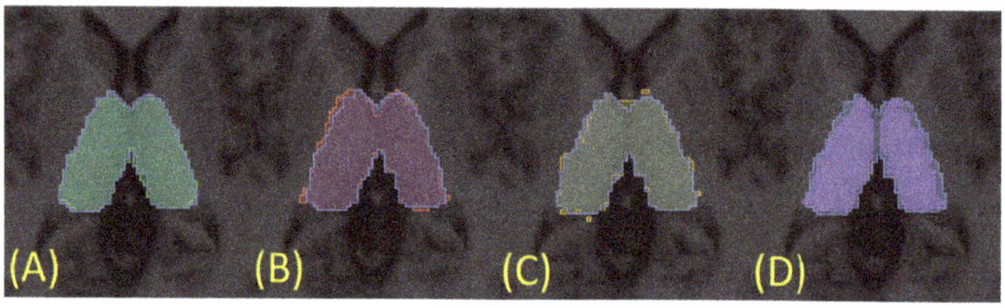

Figure 6. Axial view of the thalamic masks generated by different methods overlaid on silver standard (in blue): (**A**) FSL—green; (**B**) FreeSurfer—red; (**C**) QuickNAT—yellow; (**D**) manual segmentation—purple.

2.3. Manual Segmentation

All manual segmentations were generated following the protocol described in the supplementary material, which uses the T1-weighted images and diffusion tensor maps simultaneously, thereby circumventing the low contrast limitation and achieving a more reliable segmentation of the thalamus.

In summary, the thalamus manual segmentation protocol employed in this work considers the T1-weighted image and diffusion tensor maps, and the three views (axial, coronal, and sagittal), to facilitate specialized decision-making processes. It also used the ITK-SNAP software [42] to simultaneously display multiple grayscale images (e.g., T1-weighted and FA) along with the segmentation.

The proposed manual segmentation protocol was designed to facilitate the task and stabilize the segmentation considering the relatively high inter- and intra-rater variability in thalamic manual segmentation for T1 images alone, as demonstrated in [7]. Results of the proposed manual segmentation protocol are not intended to differ from the segmentation in T1, as they refer to the same structure.

Of the 60 subjects examined in the manual segmentation task, 16 were classified by a non-expert rater, and the remaining 44 by a physician with 15 years of experience in brain structure and manual segmentation on MRI. All manual segmentations performed by the non-expert also followed protocol and were used only to fine-tune the CNN. Only manual segmentations were considered for model evaluation, with a total of 20 subjects.

To evaluate the variability of segmentation between the expert and non-expert raters, five additional subjects were segmented by the latter, and certain metrics were computed (Section 2.7). The comparison (Table 1) indicates that the manual segmentations from the two raters are closer to each other than to the proposed silver standard, especially when considering the overlap (Dice coefficient) and volumetric similarity.

Table 1. Inter rater comparison: DC—Dice coefficient; FNR—false negative ratio; VS—volumetric similarity; AHD—average Hausdorff distance (in voxel size).

Comparison	DC (SD)	FNR	FPR	VS	AHD (SD)
expert vs. non-expert	0.8022 (0.0804)	0.1228	0.2472	0.1555	0.2501 (0.0573)
expert vs. STAPLE	0.7880 (0.0310)	0.0070	0.3459	0.4128	0.2190 (0.0340)
non-expert vs. STAPLE	0.7108 (0.0655)	0.0129	0.4397	0.5577	0.3685 (0.0971)

2.4. Data Processing

The HCP dataset was processed to ensure its compatibility with CNN training. Specifically, minimal steps were taken to standardize and organize the data for use. The processed benchmark dataset was subsequently released for public access.

Indices describing the brain microstructure were derived from the dMRI data by reconstructing signals using a diffusion tensor imaging (DTI) model [43]. These models are frequently employed in clinical activity under the assumption that each diffusion signal coming from the brain tissue can be described by a Gaussian function. The dMRI signal fitting is therefore obtained by calculating the tensor, a symmetric 3×3 matrix whose parameters can be derived from the MR volumes acquired in different gradient directions. Such a tensor is a representation of the 3D diffusion process for any voxel of the 3D volume, and can be expressed via eigenvalue and eigenvector formulation.

The microstructural indices [44,45] used throughout this study were computed from such eigenvalues. These indices were: axial diffusivity (AD), radial diffusivity (RD), mean diffusivity (MD), and fractional anisotropy (FA). All relevant computations were performed using the DIPY library [46] with the weighted least squares method. Only those dMRI volume images corresponding to a b-value of 1000 s/mm^2 (single shell DTI model) were selected. This process generated four 3D volumes, one for each microstructural index, for all subjects of the cohort.

Another crucial process applied to the data is the registration, which placed the diffusion- and T1-weighted images, and the masks, within a single space, allowing them to be simultaneously used by the CNN.

Although the HCP dataset comes with a T1w image registered to a diffusion space, it does not provide an appropriate affine matrix. Therefore, we computed the registration matrix (rigid transformation) using the T1w images on the T1 and diffusion spaces. Subsequently, the matrix was used to translate the masks to the diffusion space. It is important to emphasize that the registration was visually inspected in 20% of the dataset, including all subjects with manual segmentation. Likewise, all registration logs were inspected; the two discarded subjects were flagged.

The decision to transport the T1-weighted images to the diffusion space, rather than the other way around, was made because the scalar T1-weighted images do not suffer as much from voxel interpolation during the registration process as tensor images would. Since the masks are integer values representing structures of the brain, they were interpolated with the nearest-neighbor technique.

2.5. Data Organization

From the 1065 subjects selected for the dataset, the registration algorithm could not converge for 2 subjects, which were discarded. Subsequently, 963 subjects containing only silver-standard masks were allocated to the training set. From the remaining 100 subjects, 60 were manually segmented and used for fine-tuning and testing. A set composed of 40 subjects was reserved to increase the test set in the future (Table 2).

Table 2. Dataset for benchmark, its division for CNN model development and evaluation, and available labels. Manual labels for the testing set exist but are not publicly available on the benchmark platform.

Dataset	Subjects	Labels				
		Freesurfer	fsl_anat	QuickNAT	STAPLE	Manual
Training	963	yes	yes	yes	yes	no
Fine-tuning	16	yes	yes	yes	yes	yes (non-expert)
	24	yes	yes	yes	yes	yes
Testing	20	yes	yes	yes	yes	yes (benchmarking)
Reserved	40	yes	yes	yes	yes	no

All subject recruitment procedures and informed consent forms, including consent to share de-identified data, were approved by the Washington University Institutional Review Board (IRB) [47]. Permission for using open-access data in the present study was obtained from the HCP.

2.6. Segmentation Method

Despite frequent proposals of newer architectures and frameworks, current state-of-the-art deep-learning-based methods, including QuickNAT [17] and nnU-Net [35], are based on the U-Net architecture, one of the most popular CNN architectures for medical imaging. We also employed the U-Net [48] architecture to segment the thalamus, as it represents a baseline segmentation result for the proposed benchmark.

To segment the thalamus using a multimodality dataset, the U-Net model was trained with a multichannel input: each channel received T1w or diffusion images (Figure 7). This is the standard U-Net architecture, which is able to handle any amount of input channels by changing the corresponding hyperparameter [49–53]. When using more than one channel, the U-Net fuses all input channels in the first convolutional layer, transferring features extracted from all inputs to the inner layers.

We used image patches throughout the training and fine-tuning procedures, as U-Net is a fully-convolutional neural network (FCNN) [54], whose training and prediction phases do not require images of the same size. This is advantageous for many reasons: it increases the amount of training data; it makes the model more immune to location variance, as the thalamus may be present anywhere within a patch; it balances the amounts of background and foreground present during training; and it simplifies the extraction of 2D images from the 3D MRI to feed the 2D CNN architecture.

For the output, we employed a softmax activation with two channels for the background and thalamus (foreground), respectively. The target for the output was the thalamus segmentation mask, guided by a soft Dice loss [55]. During fine-tuning, we exploited the encoder-decoder nature of the U-Net, freezing the pre-trained encoder and updating only the decoder weights.

The aforementioned training strategy can be applied to multiple models. We used a multi-view 2D approach to obtain a volumetric thalamus segmentation (Figure 7). First, we predicted the volumetric segmentation three times using different 2D CNN models trained for each respective slicing orientation (axial, sagittal, and coronal). Subsequently, the three volumetric predictions were combined into a single final prediction volume as follows: $Seg = ((A + S + C)/3) > 0.5$. Here, A, S, and C denote the activations for the axial, sagittal, and coronal networks, respectively. Although such a view aggregation requires more computation than a single-view 2D CNN, it significantly improves segmentation quality, primarily by eliminating low-confidence misclassified voxels from the predictions [56]. Furthermore, it requires considerably less computational resources than an equivalent 3D approach. The latter does not guarantee superior performance to the single-view 2D approach [57]. In fact, prior studies have shown equivalent results when comparing 2D view aggregation with the 3D convolutional approach [17,52,58,59].

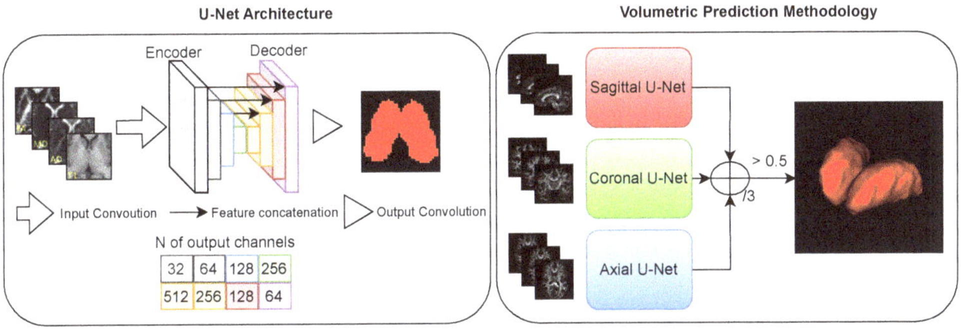

Figure 7. Thalamus segmentation framework: standard U-Net trained with multi-channel patches, and aggregation of multiple models for final prediction.

2.7. Evaluating Metrics

The following metrics were used to evaluate segmentation performance on the test set, with the manual segmentation done by a specialist used as ground truth: Dice coefficient, false negative error, false positive error, Jaccard coefficient, and average Hausdorff distance. However, we focused solely on the Dice coefficient and average Hausdorff distance, as they will be used for the purpose of an open benchmark.

The requirement for different metrics to evaluate segmentation results arises from the complementarity of these metrics in comparing method output to the ground truth. For example, whereas the Dice coefficient evaluates the overall accordance between two objects, the average Hausdorff distance indicates the behavior of agreement in the shells of the volumes [60].

To define some of the metrics used in this study, we consider the four basic cardinalities of the confusion matrix that indicate overlap between the two masks. *True positives* (*TP*): number of positive voxels included in both the automatic segmentation and ground-truth mask; *false positives* (*FP*): number of positive voxels included in the automatic segmentation but not in the ground-truth mask; *true negatives* (*TN*): number of voxels taken as negative (background) in both the automatic segmentation and ground-truth mask; *false negatives* (*FN*): number of positive voxels in the ground-truth mask that were not included in the automatic segmentation.

The *Dice similarity coefficient*, or *Dice coefficient* (*DC*), is a spatial overlap index that ranges from 0 to 1, denoting zero overlap and complete overlap, respectively, [61].

$$DC = \frac{2TP}{2TP + FP + FN}$$

The *Hausdorff distance* (*HD*) is a measure of dissimilarity comparing image segmentations [62]. Given the set of voxels V_A of mask A and the set of voxels V_B of mask B the *Hausdorff distance* is such that

$$HD(V_A, V_B) = max(h(V_A, V_B), h(V_B, V_A))$$

where $h(V_A, V_B)$ is the directed Hausdorff distance given by

$$h(V_A, V_B) = max_{x \in V_A}\{min_{y \in V_B}\{||x - y||\}\}$$

where $||x - y||$ is an arbitrary norm (in our case, Euclidean distance). In this work, the dimension of the Hausdorff distance is expressed in voxel size.

The *average Hausdorff distance (AHD)*, or simply *average distance*, is more stable and less sensitive to outliers than the conventional *HD*, representing the mean *HD* over all points

$$AHD(V_A, V_B) = max(d(V_A, V_B), d(V_B, V_A))$$

2.8. Computational Framework

To conduct the training process, we employed Python Jupyter Notebooks and PyTorch Lightning, a wrapper of the PyTorch library that facilitates the "software engineering" stages of the training process—e.g., logging, data loading, model checkpointing, and the training loop. Training was performed on an Nvidia RTX 2080 Ti GPU (11 GB GDDR6 and 4352 CUDA cores), i9-9900K CPU @ 3.60 GHz, and 64 GB of RAM.

With this setup, the training and fine-tuning, described in Sections 2.6 and 3.3, require for each CNN model about 60 min and 15 min, respectively. The segmentation prediction for each CNN model takes less than 5 s. Among all processes described in this work, only training, fine-tuning, and prediction ran on the GPU, as they are the only ones designed to use CUDA cores.

2.9. Leaderboard Platform

For the benchmark, we are hosting a competition on the CodaLab platform [63], where participants may submit their segmented data to be automatically evaluated and entered in the leaderboard. Our competition can be found at https://codalab.lisn.upsaclay.fr/competitions/8329 (accessed on 20 April 2023).

The evaluation criteria are based on the Dice coefficient score, computed using the complete testing dataset. Individuals and groups can submit their segmented data directly on the platform, with a limitation of two submissions per day. To appropriately submit segmented data, detailed information can be found on our CodaLab page.

Our GitHub (https://github.com/MICLab-Unicamp/thalamus_benchmark_diffusion) (accessed on 20 April 2023) offers the baseline for CNN training, and all necessary code to process and organize the data prior to submission.

3. Experiments and Results

The following subsections present the experiments conducted throughout this study, and their results.

3.1. Data Preparation for CNN Training and Predicting

The first step encompasses the filtering and normalization of data. The T1-weighted MR, AD, RD, MD, and FA images were all normalized between zero and one to be used as input for the CNN. Prior to that, a percentile filter was applied to eliminate 0.2% of the highest values in each channel, as defined in preliminary experiments. This step is necessary to eliminate any spurious voxel values and keep all input channels within the same normalized range. Failure to follow this step may result in suboptimal performance, as high-value voxels and discrepancies among the maximum values of each map may obscure brain tissue information from the CNN, and any comparison study would not be valid.

The next step is to generate patches from the images to be used for training. Patches were extracted for the three data views, allowing three corresponding models to be trained and combined. Of the 60 patches extracted for each subject, all were randomly selected; however, 50 were centered inside the thalamus to ensure good balancing of the amounts of voxels inside and outside the segmenting structure. We stress that all input channels and masks must be taken to have exactly the same size and coordinates for each patch to maintain the alignment of input data.

Data were subsequently allocated among training, validation, fine-tuning, and testing subsets. The testing set comprised the data of 20 subjects, for whom manual segmentation was performed by the specialist. For the training phase, 963 subjects (Table 2) were split among the training and validation sets according to an 80:20 ratio.

A data augmentation method was also applied during model training. This augmentation was not performed on the raw diffusion or tensorial data, but on the scalar maps computed from the DTI models, as the interpolation of tensors is not as straightforward as that of scalar maps. Two data augmentation techniques were applied to the images: rotation constrained by limits of -5° to $+5^\circ$ with a random distribution, and horizontal reflection. We note that the latter does not apply to the sagittal view, which does not exhibit lateral symmetry. Furthermore, the masks and input channels must undergo identical transformations to keep them aligned. Data augmentations such as translations were not used, as the patching also functions as an augmentation method to make the CNN more generalizable to translations.

Finally, the training masks were appropriately standardized, as the automated segmentation methods (FSL, FreeSurfer, QuickNAT, and STAPLE) assign different labels to each thalamus with respect to laterality. The standardization consists of setting the background and structures to zero and one, respectively, (we employed a single label for both thalami). Nonetheless, the offered framework supports multiple labels, allowing for multi-structure segmentation as necessary.

3.2. Setting Hyperparameters

The hyperparameters for the training were obtained from preliminary experiments. Patch sizes of 64×64 were chosen based on the optimal balance, training time, and data storage. The learning rate was defined as 10^{-3}, with a decay factor of 0.1 for every time the validation loss function did not yield a significant improvement for 20 epochs. We defined an offset of 30 epochs for training to terminate in the absence of improvement. Adam was selected as the optimizer, as it yields substantially faster convergence and better quantitative results than SGD [64].

The preliminary experiments also helped to define the approach regarding single or multiple views. Using all available channels as input, the dice metrics of the test dataset (Figure 8) indicate that the sagittal and axial views led to the worst results, whereas the coronal and combined views led to the best results. We also note that the aggregated view yielded the best AHD in terms of both average and standard deviation, indicating better and more stable segmentation behavior. This occurred because the aggregation of views corrects any misclassified voxels that appear far from the segmented thalamus. Accordingly, view aggregation was chosen as the approach to be used.

3.3. Gaining Performance by Fine-Tuning

As the silver-standard mask was computed by combining three other automatic segmentations, the CNNs were not initially fit to the manual segmentation protocol. Instead, the CNN models were replicating the segmentation resulted from the STAPLE method. To make the CNN model replicate the manual segmentation (ground truth), fine-tuning was conducted with manually annotated data, presenting a substantial improvement (Table 3).

Table 3. Dice coefficient (DC), average Hausdorff distance (AHD) in voxel size, and their respective standard deviations (sd) for the test dataset before and after fine-tuning.

	Not Fine-Tuned				Fine-Tuned			
Input Maps	**DC**	**sd DC**	**AHD**	**sd AHD**	**DC**	**sd DC**	**AHD**	**sd AHD**
FA, MD, RD, AD, T1	0.7775	0.0223	0.2320	0.0253	0.8970	0.0116	0.1102	0.0129
FA, MD, RD, AD	0.7721	0.0229	0.2389	0.0259	0.8904	0.0100	0.1158	0.0105
T1	0.7676	0.0242	0.2440	0.0272	0.8904	0.0154	0.1158	0.0157

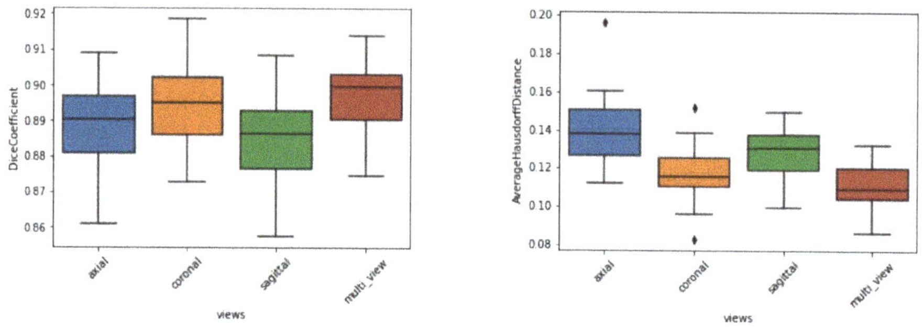

Figure 8. Dice and average Hausdorff coefficients for each automatic segmentation method evaluated on the test set.

Fine-tuning was performed by freezing the encoder component of U-Net and training solely the decoder component. Conceptually, the feature extraction of the CNN model was kept intact, and the reconstruction of the segmentation was adjusted to the manual label. The same training hyper-parameters from the training phase were used during the fine-tuning phase.

During the fine-tuning phase, 40 subjects with manual segmentation as ground truth were used (Table 2). The input configuration (input channels and their order) was kept identical.

3.4. Input Maps Ablation Study

As our primary hypothesis assumed that diffusion tensor maps can improve the quality of thalamus segmentation, the performances of models trained with each input map individually were compared to those of models trained with a combination of input maps. All models were trained using the data distribution described in Section 3.1. The reported results are the average metrics among the 20 subjects from the test set.

The results (Table 4) indicate that the model trained on T1-weighted images yielded the worst results for every computed metric. While they are still within state-of-the-art levels, the worst Dice coefficients were obtained when the T1-weighted image was the only input channel (DC of 0.8837). The same consideration is valid for the average Hausdorff distance (AHD of 0.1230).

In contrast, models trained using diffusion tensor maps as input (single or combined maps) exhibited improvements in Dice score. In fact, the worst result presented by a model trained with a single diffusion map was a Dice coefficient of 0.8925 (AD), and the only combined-channel model that yielded a Dice coefficient below 0.89 was that trained on MD and T1. Furthermore, all combined models produced superior results to those of the model using solely T1 images.

Noteworthy results were also obtained by the model trained on the combination of all available maps. This combination, which can be regarded as the addition of T1 to the combination of all diffusion maps, improved the DC from 0.8904 to 0.8970. Nonetheless, if we consider the addition of diffusion indices to T1, the DC increases from 0.8837 to 0.8970, representing a much more substantial improvement. Regardless of interpretation, this combination yielded the best performance in terms of the evaluation metrics, indicating that the segmentation that uses all input channels exhibited more agreement with the ground truth. This result is intriguing, as T1 images were associated with decreased performance when combined with singular diffusion maps (FA and MD).

Table 4. Evaluation metrics for each CNN input map combination on the test set: DC—Dice coefficient; FNR—false negative ratio; FPR—false positive ratio; JAC—Jaccard coefficient; VS—volumetric similarity; AHD—average Hausdorff distance (in voxel size). The best and worst DC and AHD results are in **bold**.

Fine-Tuned	DC (SD)	FNR	FPR	JAC	VS	AHD (SD)
T1	**0.8837** (0.0154)	0.1649	0.0596	0.7920	−0.1193	**0.1230** (0.0157)
FA	0.8945 (0.0089)	0.1390	0.0677	0.8092	−0.0795	0.1116 (0.0097)
MD	0.8931 (0.0122)	0.1326	0.0776	0.8071	−0.0615	0.1143 (0.0133)
RD	0.8935 (0.0115)	0.1364	0.0724	0.8077	−0.0715	0.1137 (0.0134)
AD	0.8925 (0.0131)	0.1419	0.0680	0.8061	−0.0829	0.1143 (0.0142)
FA, T1	0.8943 (0.0107)	0.1373	0.0700	0.8090	−0.0754	0.1119 (0.0112)
FA, MD	0.8943 (0.0113)	0.1327	0.0754	0.8089	−0.0638	0.1126 (0.0136)
MD, T1	0.8882 (0.0136)	0.1462	0.0716	0.7992	−0.0842	0.1185 (0.0132)
FA, MD, RD, AD	0.8904 (0.0100)	0.1509	0.0623	0.8026	−0.0994	0.1158 (0.0105)
FA, MD, RD, AD, T1	**0.8970** (0.0116)	0.1182	0.0853	0.8135	−0.0367	**0.1102** (0.0129)

Furthermore, results regarding the standard deviation reflect the segmentation stability for each map and certain combinations (Figure 9). Again, we note that models trained on T1-weighted images exhibited the highest dispersion in both DC and AHD. Nevertheless, among the models trained with a single input, that trained with FA, produced the best average and dispersion results.

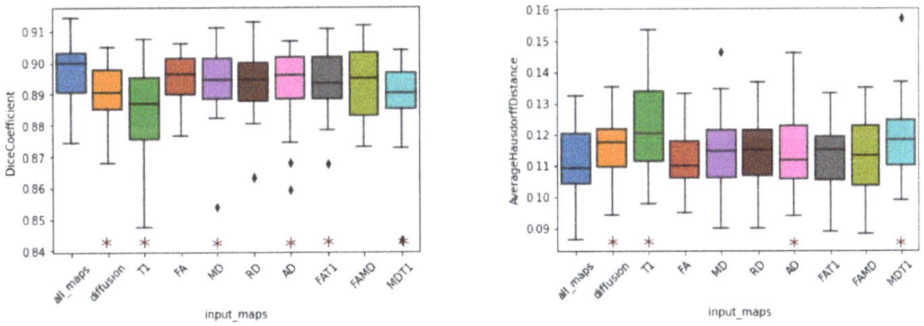

Figure 9. Dice coefficient and average Hausdorff coefficient for each input map combination evaluated on the test set. Star (∗) denotes statistical significance ($p < 0.05$) when compared to our best model (all_maps). All p-values were estimated using a two-sided Wilcoxon signed-rank test.

A statistical analysis was conducted through a two-sided Wilcoxon signed-rank test to compare the CNN models (Figure 9) and other methods (Figure 10) in terms of performance against our best model, namely, the model that used all diffusion maps in conjunction with T1-w images as input. We note that in addition to exhibiting better metrics when compared to other methods, our approach's results are significantly different, statistically. Identical analyses were performed to compare every CNN model with a single input channel (Table 5) to interpret their equivalences. From these tests, it is apparent that the statistical differences between the T1 models and any of the diffusion models are much more significant than those between models that use diffusion maps as input. This implies that any of the tested CNN models that use diffusion maps as input produce different results when compared to a CNN with T1w images as input. Simultaneously, it is apparent that all CNN models using single diffusion maps as input produced mutually similar results.

Table 5. Analysis of statistical significance between CNN models through two-sided Wilcoxon signed-rank test on the test set, considering only models with a single input channel. Star (*) indicates that the pair exhibits mutual statistical significance ($p < 0.05$).

	Dice Coefficient—DC				Average Hausdorff Distance—AHD			
	FA	MD	RD	AD	FA	MD	RD	AD
T1	* 0.0020	* 0.0056	* 0.0083	* 0.0014	* 0.0023	* 0.0153	* 0.0172	* 0.0094
FA		0.4524	0.6742	0.3683		0.0973	0.2611	0.2774
MD			0.7012	0.8983			0.8983	0.4749
RD				0.7285				1.0000

3.5. Comparison with Existing Segmentation Tools

The results achieved by the proposed pipeline were compared to those of common methods. Tools that are easy to use and well-validated in the thalamus-segmentation task were selected for reproducibility purposes. To maximize diversity and generalizability, two classes of segmentation methods were employed: atlas-based and CNN-based.

This comparison may be considered somewhat biased, as the ground-truth was generated with a combination of T1-weighted images and dMRI, whereas all other methods only used T1. However, the masks generated with the assistance of dMRI are assumed to be equivalent to those generated only on T1, as both represent the same structure.

FSL and FreeSurfer were evaluated as representative atlas-based methods. Their segmentations were computed in the T1 original space, and subsequently registered to the diffusion space to be compared against manual segmentation.

The QuickNAT framework was evaluated as an off-the-shelf CNN-based method. Although the original QuickNAT weights were not fine-tuned to this specific dataset, all input data were normalized according to the author's requirements (FreeSurfer's *mri_convert –conform* command).

The results (Figure 10) indicate that the best evaluating metrics, excluding those exhibited by our method, were obtained by FSL. All other methods, including STAPLE, exhibited considerable differences in performance compared to the proposed method. While these methods exhibited Dice coefficients in the range of 0.75 to 0.78, our CNN model achieved DC values exceeding 0.9.

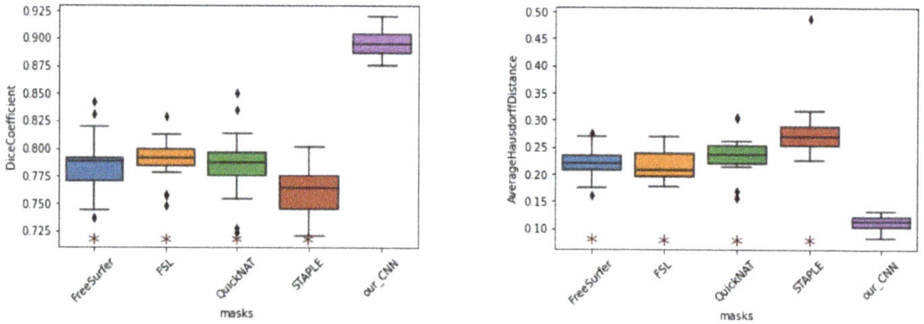

Figure 10. Dice and average Hausdorff coefficients for each segmentation method evaluated on the test set. Star (∗) denotes statistical significance ($p < 0.05$) when compared to our optimal CNN model (all_maps). All p-values were estimated using a two-sided Wilcoxon signed-rank test.

3.6. Qualitative Results

A visualization of the 3D segmentations is used to display the similarities and differences between the ground-truth and each method's results (Figure 11).

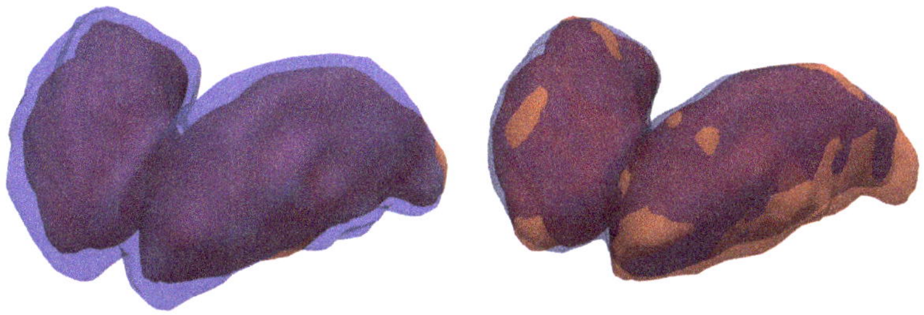

Figure 11. Thalamus segmentation: ground truth (manual segmentation) in red, silver standard (STAPLE) in blue on the (**left**), and CNN prediction (with the best model—all input channels combined) in blue on the (**right**).

When comparing the manual annotation with the silver-standard mask, is is apparent that the latter considers the thalamus a much broader structure than the former. Other studies [7] have observed similar results. Another important consideration is that the segmentation performed by the model after fine-tuning exhibits only minor differences when compared with the specialist's annotation, with only a few voxels misclassified the borders of the thalami.

4. Discussion

Fine-tuning represents an effective approach when adjusting a model to manually segmented data. Prior to fine-tuning, our CNN models produced inferior results compared to those achieved by the atlas-based methods and QuickNAT segmentation. However, the fine-tuning process yielded an absolute improvement of approximately 0.12 in the Dice coefficient. It is important to remember that the encoder was frozen throughout the fine-tuning phase, and only the decoder weights that reconstructed the segmentation were trained.

Although minor differences in metrics were observed when aggregating all input, the diffusion indices computed from DTI clearly improved the quality of thalamus segmentation when used as input channels to the CNN. These differences in metrics were more significant for the FA map and combination of all available maps when compared to the case of using T1-weighted images alone as input. Further improvements may be obtained by extending the proposed approach to other microstructural indices [65], especially when multi-shell data, such as NODDI and MAP-MRI, are available, as for HCP.

As a single-input channel, T1-weighted achieved a Dice coefficient of approximately 0.88, representing the current state-of-the-art in thalamus segmentation, as reported in the original QuickNAT work [17]. Therefore, the proposed method surpasses state-of-the-art performance by incorporating dMRI, showing that aggregated multimodal information is beneficial for the thalamus-segmentation task.

The DC attained by our reproduction of the QuickNAT was in the range of 0.79, as opposed to the result of 0.88 reported by [17]. However, we stress that the QuickNAT model was not fine-tuned to this specific dataset, and the only addition to the framework was the "FreeSurfer conform", as it is a requirement for the QuickNAT pipeline.

Among the three possible views, the sagittal view yielded the lowest dice coefficient. A possible reason for this occurrence is the lack of thalamus symmetry under this view, which restricts the horizontal-reflection technique. Furthermore, the thalamus shape is more elongated in the anteroposterior axis, favoring the partial volume issue being more pronounced in this view. This also explains the best segmentation quality in the coronal view, where the thalamus exhibits the smallest cross section.

Our best results were obtained when using all input maps simultaneously (diffusion combined with T1). However, certain specific combinations unexpectedly led to deteriorated performance; i.e., the combination of the FA and MD yielded worse results than either of its constituent maps. We hypothesize that the aggregation of maps with small statistical differences is disadvantageous for the CNN model, as the resultant increase in information does not outweigh the increase in complexity. However, further investigation is required to understand this mechanism and determine the optimal map combinations for this task.

Although the FSL masks yield better validation metrics compared to other automatic masks, they were not selected as the silver standard during the training phase. Instead, the masks created by combining FSL, FreeSurfer, and QuickNAT via STAPLE were used for this purpose, as the combination of atlas- and CNN-based methods is more likely to eliminate model bias.

As all CNN models used and shared throughout this study were trained and evaluated on these specific benchmark data, we do not expect identical results if they are applied directly to other datasets. This is one of the limitations of the presented method. To successfully use our models and framework with other data, we recommended retraining or fine-tuning the models in the new data domain. With appropriate fine-tuning, the model is expected to yield comparable performance irrespective of dataset.

Additionally, our method was not tested on data from patients. Thus, in the presence of disease, the performance of the method cannot be ensured. Actually, the performance is expected to decrease if the model is not fine-tuned to adverse conditions.

The only segmented structure considered throughout this study was the thalamus. However, the framework proposed here also offers the possibility of working with other structures—such as the caudate, hippocampus, and putamen—as the dataset is published with a variety of pre-segmented structures.

Future work will focus on segmenting the thalamus nuclei. The presented framework is also able to perform structure parcellation—e.g., thalamus parcellation into nuclei—if the proper ground truth is available. For this purpose, other diffusion maps, such as the tensorial morphological gradient [22], could be beneficial to achieving optimal results.

5. Conclusions

This study presents a ready-to-use framework for the development of thalamus-segmentation methods, comprising a processed multimodal dataset, code for reproducing the baseline model, and a test set for benchmarking. The dataset, based on the HCP data, encompasses a total of 1063 processed subjects with diffusion data, T1-weighted images, segmentation masks from FSL, FreeSurfer, QuickNAT, and a combination of the aforementioned masks through the STAPLE method. Furthermore, the dataset includes a subset with professionally segmented images.

For benchmarking purposes, researchers can submit their predictions to a leaderboard made available on our Codalab platform. A complete framework for training a CNN model is also available on our GitHub for other researchers to build upon.

Our proposed method combines T1-weighted images with diffusion MRI, representing a valid option for accurate segmentation of the thalamic structure. We demonstrated that the addition of diffusion MRI yields improvements in thalamus segmentation. Comparisons with existing state-of-the-art methods indicate the superiority of our approach, although a more fair comparison would demand the fine-tuning of QuickNAT using our manual masks.

The automatic generation of silver-standard masks circumvented the lack of a large volume of manually annotated data. The model, pre-trained on the silver-standard mask and fine-tuned on a small quantity of manual masks, led to an absolute improvement of 0.122 in the Dice coefficient.

Supplementary Materials: The file describing the thalamus manual segmentation protocol can be downloaded at: https://www.mdpi.com/article/10.3390/app13095284/s1. The dataset, code, environment, and instructions for the benchmark leaderboard can be found at https://github.com/MICLab-Unicamp/thalamus_benchmark_diffusion and https://codalab.lisn.upsaclay.fr/competitions/8329 (accessed on 20 April 2023).

Author Contributions: G.R.P. defined the project pipeline and experiments, implemented the code for data processing and CNN training, made the figures, and helped with the manual segmentation protocol. L.B. was responsible for the data processing, data organization, and literature review. D.C. helped with the experimental planning, Python codes, and benchmark environment. R.P. helped with the data and evaluation metrics. T.A. performed all statistical analyses. S.A. performed manual data annotation and helped with the manual segmentation protocol. G.M. supervised the methods and data processing. L.R. supervised the overall development of the project. All authors have read and agreed to the published version of the manuscript.

Funding: This project was partially supported by COOPERINT program, by the São Paulo Research Foundation (FAPESP–process 2013/07559-3), and by the National Council for Scientific and Technological Development (CNPq 313598/2020-7). Gustavo R. Pinheiro was supported by CNPq (National Council for Scientific and Technological Development). Diedre Carmo appreciates grant #2019/21964-4, São Paulo Research Foundation (FAPESP).

Institutional Review Board Statement: Ethical review and approval were waived for this study since it uses a public dataset.

Informed Consent Statement: All subject recruitment procedures and informed consent forms, including consent to share de-identified data, were approved by the Washington University Institutional Review Board (IRB) [47]. Permission for using the Open Access data in the present study was obtained from the HCP.

Data Availability Statement: Raw data used for the present study are available for download from the Human Connectome Project (www.humanconnectome.org) (accessed on 20 April 2023): WU-Minn Consortium (principal investigators: David Van Essen and Kamil Ugurbil; 1U54MH091657) funded by the 16 NIH Institutes and Centers that support the NIH Blueprint for Neuroscience Research; and by the McDonnell Center for Systems Neuroscience at Washington University. All processed and organized data can be found at https://www.ccdataset.com/thalamus-benchmark (accessed on 20 April 2023). Code for data processing, training, and analysis is provided as part of the reproducibility package, including a Docker image for the reproduction of the environment. It is available at https://github.com/MICLab-Unicamp/thalamus_benchmark_diffusion (accessed on 20 April 2023). The imaging data used for the testing set of 20 subjects (Table 2) are provided without the specialist labels, as they are used to construct the leaderboard. Instructions on how to submit your segmentation results for this test set are provided at https://www.ccdataset.com/thalamus-benchmark (accessed on 20 April 2023). We will evaluate all the submitted results and present a leaderboard on the GitHub repository.

Acknowledgments: We would like to thank Livia Rodrigues and Roberto Medeiros de Souza for helping organize and host the data on the server. We also thank HCP for sharing the raw and pre-processed data, and for allowing us to use and share it.

Conflicts of Interest: The authors declare that the research was conducted in the absence of any commercial or financial relationships that could be construed as a potential conflict of interest.

References

1. Su, J.H.; Thomas, F.T.; Kasoff, W.S.; Tourdias, T.; Choi, E.Y.; Rutt, B.K.; Saranathan, M. Thalamus Optimized Multi Atlas Segmentation (THOMAS): Fast, fully automated segmentation of thalamic nuclei from structural MRI. *NeuroImage* **2019**, *194*, 272–282. [CrossRef]
2. Iglesias, J.E.; Insausti, R.; Lerma-Usabiaga, G.; Bocchetta, M.; Van Leemput, K.; Greve, D.N.; Van der Kouwe, A.; Fischl, B.; Caballero-Gaudes, C.; Paz-Alonso, P.M.; et al. A probabilistic atlas of the human thalamic nuclei combining ex vivo MRI and histology. *Neuroimage* **2018**, *183*, 314–326. [CrossRef] [PubMed]
3. Akram, H.; Dayal, V.; Mahlknecht, P.; Georgiev, D.; Hyam, J.; Foltynie, T.; Limousin, P.; De Vita, E.; Jahanshahi, M.; Ashburner, J.; et al. Connectivity derived thalamic segmentation in deep brain stimulation for tremor. *Neuroimage Clin.* **2018**, *18*, 130–142. [CrossRef]
4. Liu, Y.; D'Haese, P.F.; Newton, A.T.; Dawant, B.M. Generation of human thalamus atlases from 7 T data and application to intrathalamic nuclei segmentation in clinical 3 T T1-weighted images. *Magn. Reson. Imaging* **2020**, *65*, 114–128. [CrossRef]
5. Elias, W.J.; Huss, D.; Voss, T.; Loomba, J.; Khaled, M.; Zadicario, E.; Frysinger, R.C.; Sperling, S.A.; Wylie, S.; Monteith, S.J.; et al. A pilot study of focused ultrasound thalamotomy for essential tremor. *N. Engl. J. Med.* **2013**, *369*, 640–648. [CrossRef] [PubMed]
6. Dolz, J.; Desrosiers, C.; Ayed, I.B. 3D fully convolutional networks for subcortical segmentation in MRI: A large-scale study. *NeuroImage* **2018**, *170*, 456–470. [CrossRef] [PubMed]

7. Makowski, C.; Béland, S.; Kostopoulos, P.; Bhagwat, N.; Devenyi, G.A.; Malla, A.K.; Joober, R.; Lepage, M.; Chakravarty, M.M. Evaluating accuracy of striatal, pallidal, and thalamic segmentation methods: Comparing automated approaches to manual delineation. *Neuroimage* **2018**, *170*, 182–198. [CrossRef]
8. Neuromorphometrics, I. Segmentation: Thalamus, 2005. Available online: http://neuromorphometrics.com/Seg/html/segmentation/thalamus.html (accessed on 20 April 2023)
9. Power, B.D.; Wilkes, F.A.; Hunter-Dickson, M.; van Westen, D.; Santillo, A.F.; Walterfang, M.; Nilsson, C.; Velakoulis, D.; Looi, J.C. Validation of a protocol for manual segmentation of the thalamus on magnetic resonance imaging scans. *Psychiatry Res. Neuroimaging* **2015**, *232*, 98–105. [CrossRef]
10. Burggraaff, J.; Liu, Y.; Prieto, J.C.; Simoes, J.; de Sitter, A.; Ruggieri, S.; Brouwer, I.; Lissenberg-Witte, B.I.; Rocca, M.A.; Valsasina, P.; et al. Manual and automated tissue segmentation confirm the impact of thalamus atrophy on cognition in multiple sclerosis: A multicenter study. *Neuroimage Clin.* **2021**, *29*, 102549. [CrossRef]
11. Bitar, R.; Leung, G.; Perng, R.; Tadros, S.; Moody, A.R.; Sarrazin, J.; McGregor, C.; Christakis, M.; Symons, S.; Nelson, A.; et al. MR pulse sequences: What every radiologist wants to know but is afraid to ask. *Radiographics* **2006**, *26*, 513–537. [CrossRef]
12. Chen, Y.; Almarzouqi, S.J.; Morgan, M.L.; Lee, A.G. T1-weighted image. In *Encyclopedia of Ophthalmology*; JB Metzler: Stuttgart, Germany, 2018; pp. 1747–1750.
13. Patenaude, B.; Smith, S.M.; Kennedy, D.N.; Jenkinson, M. A Bayesian model of shape and appearance for subcortical brain segmentation. *Neuroimage* **2011**, *56*, 907–922. [CrossRef] [PubMed]
14. Bruce, F. Freesurfer. *NeuroImage* **2012**, *62*, 774–781.
15. Hannoun, S.; Tutunji, R.; El Homsi, M.; Saaybi, S.; Hourani, R. Automatic thalamus segmentation on unenhanced 3D T1 weighted images: Comparison of publicly available segmentation methods in a pediatric population. *Neuroinformatics* **2019**, *17*, 443–450. [CrossRef] [PubMed]
16. Liu, Y.; D'Haese, P.F.; Newton, A.T.; Dawant, B.M. Thalamic nuclei segmentation in clinical 3T T1-weighted Images using high-resolution 7T shape models. In Proceedings of the Medical Imaging 2015: Image-Guided Procedures, Robotic Interventions, and Modeling. International Society for Optics and Photonics, Orlando, FL, USA, 18 March 2015; Volume 9415, p. 94150E.
17. Roy, A.G.; Conjeti, S.; Navab, N.; Wachinger, C.; Alzheimer's Disease Neuroimaging Initiative. QuickNAT: A fully convolutional network for quick and accurate segmentation of neuroanatomy. *NeuroImage* **2019**, *186*, 713–727.
18. Wachinger, C.; Reuter, M.; Klein, T. DeepNAT: Deep convolutional neural network for segmenting neuroanatomy. *NeuroImage* **2018**, *170*, 434–445. [CrossRef] [PubMed]
19. Wu, J.; Tang, X. Brain segmentation based on multi-atlas and diffeomorphism guided 3D fully convolutional network ensembles. *Pattern Recognit.* **2021**, *115*, 107904. [CrossRef]
20. Shakeri, M.; Tsogkas, S.; Ferrante, E.; Lippe, S.; Kadoury, S.; Paragios, N.; Kokkinos, I. Sub-cortical brain structure segmentation using F-CNN's. In Proceedings of the 2016 IEEE 13th International Symposium on Biomedical Imaging (ISBI), Prague, Czech Republic, 13–16 April 2016; pp. 269–272.
21. Glaister, J.; Carass, A.; NessAiver, T.; Stough, J.V.; Saidha, S.; Calabresi, P.A.; Prince, J.L. Thalamus segmentation using multi-modal feature classification: Validation and pilot study of an age-matched cohort. *NeuroImage* **2017**, *158*, 430–440. [CrossRef]
22. Rittner, L.; Lotufo, R.A.; Campbell, J.; Pike, G.B. Segmentation of thalamic nuclei based on tensorial morphological gradient of diffusion tensor fields. In Proceedings of the 2010 IEEE International Symposium on Biomedical Imaging: From Nano to Macro, Rotterdam, The Netherlands, 14–17 April 2010; pp. 1173–1176.
23. Mang, S.C.; Busza, A.; Reiterer, S.; Grodd, W.; Klose, U. Thalamus segmentation based on the local diffusion direction: A group study. *Magn. Reson. Med.* **2012**, *67*, 118–126. [CrossRef] [PubMed]
24. Battistella, G.; Najdenovska, E.; Maeder, P.; Ghazaleh, N.; Daducci, A.; Thiran, J.P.; Jacquemont, S.; Tuleasca, C.; Levivier, M.; Bach Cuadra, M.; et al. Robust thalamic nuclei segmentation method based on local diffusion magnetic resonance properties. *Brain Struct. Funct.* **2017**, *222*, 2203–2216. [CrossRef]
25. Stejskal, E.O.; Tanner, J.E. Spin diffusion measurements: Spin echoes in the presence of a time-dependent field gradient. *J. Chem. Phys.* **1965**, *42*, 288–292. [CrossRef]
26. Pinheiro, G.; Brusini, L.; Bajrami, A.; Pizzini, F.; Calabrese, M.; Reis, F.; Appenzeller, S.; Menegaz, G.; Rittner, L. Diffusion MRI and silver standard masks to improve CNN-based thalamus segmentation. In Proceedings of the Medical Imaging 2021: Image Processing, San Diego, CA, USA, 14–18 February 2021; International Society for Optics and Photonics: Bellingham, WA, USA, 2021; Volume 11596, p. 115962L.
27. Wang, S.L.; Han, S.; Carass, A.; Zhuo, J.; Roys, S.; Gullapalli, R.P.; Jiang, L.; Prince, J.L. Thalamus segmentation using convolutional neural networks. In Proceedings of the Medical Imaging 2021: Image Processing, San Diego, CA, USA, 14–18 February 2021; International Society for Optics and Photonics: Bellingham, WA, USA, 2021; Volume 11596, p. 1159634.
28. Le Bihan, D.; Johansen-Berg, H. Diffusion MRI at 25: Exploring brain tissue structure and function. *Neuroimage* **2012**, *61*, 324–341. [CrossRef] [PubMed]
29. Traynor, C.R.; Barker, G.J.; Crum, W.R.; Williams, S.C.; Richardson, M.P. Segmentation of the thalamus in MRI based on T1 and T2. *Neuroimage* **2011**, *56*, 939–950. [CrossRef] [PubMed]
30. Le Bihan, D. Diffusion MRI: What water tells us about the brain. *EMBO Mol. Med.* **2014**, *6*, 569–573. [CrossRef]
31. Tournier, J.D.; Mori, S.; Leemans, A. Diffusion tensor imaging and beyond. *Magn. Reson. Med.* **2011**, *65*, 1532. [CrossRef]

32. Assaf, Y.; Alexander, D.C.; Jones, D.K.; Bizzi, A.; Behrens, T.E.; Clark, C.A.; Cohen, Y.; Dyrby, T.B.; Huppi, P.S.; Knoesche, T.R.; et al. The CONNECT project: Combining macro-and micro-structure. *Neuroimage* **2013**, *80*, 273–282. [CrossRef]
33. Cruciani, F.; Brusini, L.; Zucchelli, M.; Retuci Pinheiro, G.; Setti, F.; Boscolo Galazzo, I.; Deriche, R.; Rittner, L.; Calabrese, M.; Menegaz, G. Interpretable deep learning as a means for decrypting disease signature in multiple sclerosis. *J. Neural Eng.* **2021**, *18*, 0460a6. [CrossRef] [PubMed]
34. Najdenovska, E.; Alemán-Gómez, Y.; Battistella, G.; Descoteaux, M.; Hagmann, P.; Jacquemont, S.; Maeder, P.; Thiran, J.P.; Fornari, E.; Cuadra, M.B. In-vivo probabilistic atlas of human thalamic nuclei based on diffusion-weighted magnetic resonance imaging. *Sci. Data* **2018**, *5*, 180270. [CrossRef] [PubMed]
35. Isensee, F.; Jaeger, P.F.; Kohl, S.A.; Petersen, J.; Maier-Hein, K.H. nnU-Net: A self-configuring method for deep learning-based biomedical image segmentation. *Nat. Methods* **2021**, *18*, 203–211. [CrossRef]
36. Munappy, A.; Bosch, J.; Olsson, H.H.; Arpteg, A.; Brinne, B. Data management challenges for deep learning. In Proceedings of the 2019 45th Euromicro Conference on Software Engineering and Advanced Applications (SEAA), Kallithea, Greece, 28–30 August 2019; pp. 140–147.
37. Menze, B.H.; Jakab, A.; Bauer, S.; Kalpathy-Cramer, J.; Farahani, K.; Kirby, J.; Burren, Y.; Porz, N.; Slotboom, J.; Wiest, R.; et al. The multimodal brain tumor image segmentation benchmark (BRATS). *IEEE Trans. Med. Imaging* **2014**, *34*, 1993–2024. [CrossRef]
38. Van Essen, D.C.; Smith, S.M.; Barch, D.M.; Behrens, T.E.; Yacoub, E.; Ugurbil, K.; the WU-Minn HCP Consortium. The WU-Minn human connectome project: An overview. *Neuroimage* **2013**, *80*, 62–79. [CrossRef]
39. Glasser, M.F.; Sotiropoulos, S.N.; Wilson, J.A.; Coalson, T.S.; Fischl, B.; Andersson, J.L.; Xu, J.; Jbabdi, S.; Webster, M.; Polimeni, J.R.; et al. The minimal preprocessing pipelines for the Human Connectome Project. *Neuroimage* **2013**, *80*, 105–124. [CrossRef]
40. Warfield, S.K.; Zou, K.H.; Wells, W.M. Validation of image segmentation and expert quality with an expectation-maximization algorithm. In Proceedings of the Medical Image Computing and Computer-Assisted Intervention—MICCAI 2002, Tokyo, Japan, 25–28 September 2002; Springer: Berlin/Heidelberg, Germany, 2002; pp. 298–306.
41. Warfield, S.; Zou, K.; Wells, W.M. Simultaneous truth and performance level estimation (STAPLE): An algorithm for the validation of image segmentation. *IEEE Trans. Med. Imaging* **2004**, *23*, 903–921. [CrossRef]
42. Yushkevich, P.A.; Piven, J.; Cody Hazlett, H.; Gimpel Smith, R.; Ho, S.; Gee, J.C.; Gerig, G. User-Guided 3D Active Contour Segmentation of Anatomical Structures: Significantly Improved Efficiency and Reliability. *Neuroimage* **2006**, *31*, 1116–1128. [CrossRef] [PubMed]
43. Basser, P.J.; Mattiello, J.; LeBihan, D. Estimation of the effective self-diffusion tensor from the NMR spin echo. *J. Magn. Reson. Ser. B* **1994**, *103*, 247–254. [CrossRef] [PubMed]
44. Pierpaoli, C.; Basser, P.J. Toward a quantitative assessment of diffusion anisotropy. *Magn. Reson. Med.* **1996**, *36*, 893–906. [CrossRef]
45. Peeters, T.; Rodrigues, P.; Vilanova, A.; ter Haar Romeny, B. Analysis of distance/similarity measures for diffusion tensor imaging. In *Visualization and Processing of Tensor Fields*; Springer: Berlin/Heidelberg, Germany, 2009; pp. 113–136.
46. Garyfallidis, E.; Brett, M.; Amirbekian, B.; Rokem, A.; Van Der Walt, S.; Descoteaux, M.; Nimmo-Smith, I. Dipy, a library for the analysis of diffusion MRI data. *Front. Neuroinform.* **2014**, *8*, 8. [CrossRef]
47. Glasser, M.F.; Smith, S.M.; Marcus, D.S.; Andersson, J.L.; Auerbach, E.J.; Behrens, T.E.; Coalson, T.S.; Harms, M.P.; Jenkinson, M.; Moeller, S.; et al. The human connectome project's neuroimaging approach. *Nat. Neurosci.* **2016**, *19*, 1175–1187. [CrossRef] [PubMed]
48. Ronneberger, O.; Fischer, P.; Brox, T. U-net: Convolutional networks for biomedical image segmentation. In Proceedings of the MICCAI, Munich, Germany, 5–9 October 2015; Springer: Cham, Switzerland, 2015; pp. 234–241.
49. Xu, F.; Ma, H.; Sun, J.; Wu, R.; Liu, X.; Kong, Y. Lstm multi-modal unet for brain tumor segmentation. In Proceedings of the 2019 IEEE 4th International Conference on Image, Vision and Computing (ICIVC), Xiamen, China, 5–7 July 2019; pp. 236–240.
50. Rodrigues, J.; Pinheiro, G.; Carmo, D.; Rittner, L. Volumetric segmentation of the corpus callosum: Training a deep learning model on diffusion MRI. In Proceedings of the 17th International Symposium on Medical Information Processing and Analysis, Campinas, Brazil, 17–19 November 2021; Volume 12088, pp. 198–207.
51. Buda, M.; Saha, A.; Mazurowski, M.A. Association of genomic subtypes of lower-grade gliomas with shape features automatically extracted by a deep learning algorithm. *Comput. Biol. Med.* **2019**, *109*, 218–225. [CrossRef] [PubMed]
52. Pinheiro, G.R.; Voltoline, R.; Bento, M.; Rittner, L. V-Net and U-Net for ischemic stroke lesion segmentation in a small dataset of perfusion data. In Proceedings of the International MICCAI Brainlesion Workshop, Granada, Spain, 16–20 September 2018; Springer: Cham, Switzerland, 2018; pp. 301–309.
53. Pinheiro, G.; Carmo, D.; Yasuda, C.; Lotufo, R.; Rittner, L. Convolutional Neural Network on DTI Data for Sub-cortical Brain Structure Segmentation. In *Computational Diffusion MRI*; Springer: Berlin/Heidelberg, Germany, 2020; pp. 135–146.
54. Long, J.; Shelhamer, E.; Darrell, T. Fully convolutional networks for semantic segmentation. In Proceedings of the IEEE Conference on Computer Vision and Pattern Recognition, Boston, MA, USA, 7–12 June 2015; pp. 3431–3440.
55. Sudre, C.H.; Li, W.; Vercauteren, T.; Ourselin, S.; Cardoso, M.J. Generalised dice overlap as a deep learning loss function for highly unbalanced segmentations. In *Deep Learning in Medical Image Analysis and Multimodal Learning for Clinical Decision Support*; Springer: Berlin/Heidelberg, Germany, 2017; pp. 240–248.

56. Carmo, D.; Silva, B.; Yasuda, C.; Rittner, L.; Lotufo, R.; Alzheimer's Disease Neuroimaging Initiative. Hippocampus segmentation on epilepsy and Alzheimer's disease studies with multiple convolutional neural networks. *Heliyon* **2021**, *7*, e06226. [CrossRef] [PubMed]
57. Zettler, N.; Mastmeyer, A. Comparison of 2D vs. 3D U-Net Organ Segmentation in abdominal 3D CT images. *arXiv* **2021**, arXiv:2107.04062.
58. Carmo, D.; Silva, B.; Yasuda, C.; Rittner, L.; Lotufo, R. Extended 2D consensus hippocampus segmentation. *arXiv* **2019**, arXiv:1902.04487.
59. Lucena, O.; Souza, R.; Rittner, L.; Frayne, R.; Lotufo, R. Silver standard masks for data augmentation applied to deep-learning-based skull-stripping. In Proceedings of the 2018 IEEE 15th International Symposium on Biomedical Imaging (ISBI 2018), Washington, DC, USA, 4–7 April 2018; pp. 1114–1117.
60. Taha, A.A.; Hanbury, A. Metrics for evaluating 3D medical image segmentation: Analysis, selection, and tool. *BMC Med. Imaging* **2015**, *15*, 29. [CrossRef] [PubMed]
61. Zou, K.H.; Warfield, S.K.; Bharatha, A.; Tempany, C.M.; Kaus, M.R.; Haker, S.J.; Wells, W.M.; Jolesz, F.A.; Kikinis, R. Statistical validation of image segmentation quality based on a spatial overlap index: Scientific reports. *Acad. Radiol.* **2004**, *11*, 178–189. [CrossRef] [PubMed]
62. Taha, A.A.; Hanbury, A. An efficient algorithm for calculating the exact Hausdorff distance. *IEEE Trans. Pattern Anal. Mach. Intell.* **2015**, *37*, 2153–2163. [CrossRef]
63. Pavao, A.; Guyon, I.; Letournel, A.C.; Baró, X.; Escalante, H.; Escalera, S.; Thomas, T.; Xu, Z. *CodaLab Competitions: An Open Source Platform to Organize Scientific Challenges*; Technical Report; Université Paris-Saclay: Gif-sur-Yvette, France, 2022.
64. Kingma, D.P.; Ba, J. Adam: A method for stochastic optimization. *arXiv* **2014**, arXiv:1412.6980.
65. Brusini, L.; Obertino, S.; Boscolo Galazzo, I.; Zucchelli, M.; Crueger, G.; Granziera, C.; Menegaz, G. Ensemble average propagator-based detection of microstructural alterations after stroke. *Int. J. Comput. Assist. Radiol. Surg.* **2016**, *11*, 1585–1597. [CrossRef]

applied sciences

MDPI

Article

Semi-Supervised Medical Image Classification Combined with Unsupervised Deep Clustering

Bang Xiao and Chunyue Lu *

Digital Design and Intelligent Manufacturing Laboratory, North University of China, Taiyuan 030051, China; s202102015@st.nuc.edu.cn
* Correspondence: luchunyue@nuc.edu.cn; Tel.: +86-136-0351-4911

Abstract: An effective way to improve the performance of deep neural networks in most computer vision tasks is to improve the quantity of labeled data and the quality of labels. However, in the analysis and processing of medical images, high-quality annotation depends on the experience and professional knowledge of experts, which makes it very difficult to obtain a large number of high-quality annotations. Therefore, we propose a new semi-supervised framework for medical image classification. It combines semi-supervised classification with unsupervised deep clustering. Spreading label information to unlabeled data by alternately running two tasks helps the model to extract semantic information from unlabeled data, and prevents the model from overfitting to a small amount of labeled data. Compared with current methods, our framework enhances the robustness of the model and reduces the influence of outliers. We conducted a comparative experiment on the public benchmark medical image dataset to verify our method. On the ISIC 2018 Dataset, our method surpasses other methods by more than 0.85% on AUC and 1.08% on Sensitivity. On the ICIAR BACH 2018 dataset, our method achieved 94.12% AUC, 77.92% F1-score, 77.69% Recall, and 78.16% Precision. The error rate is at least 1.76% lower than that of other methods. The result shows the effectiveness of our method in medical image classification.

Keywords: medical image classification; semi-supervised learning; unsupervised learning; deep clustering; overclustering

1. Introduction

With the development of deep learning technology, deep neural networks have become widely used in medical image analysis and processing. However, due to the need for professional knowledge, it is difficult to manually label medical images on a large scale. At the same time, there are constantly unlabeled data being generated in the clinical medical process, which results in a small number of labeled images and a large number of unlabeled images being generated. In this case, semi-supervised learning [1,2], which can use both labeled data and unlabeled data, has certain advantages. In this paper, we propose a semi-supervised learning framework combined with unsupervised learning [3–5], which can enhance the model's ability to extract information from unlabeled data, reduce the risk of overfitting, and effectively reduce the impact of outlier data.

Slight disturbances in an image do not affect a human's basic judgment of the image's semantics. Based on this feature, people apply the consistency regularization method [6–8] to semi-supervised learning, and generate different samples by adding different disturbances (such as Gaussian noise, flipping, cropping, etc.) to the input samples, and then encourage the model to generate similar predictions for the different disturbed versions of the same input. Theoretically, a good model can eliminate the influence of disturbance and make self-consistent predictions. For example, in the π-model [6], for any input x_i, the model generates two different disturbances and inputs them into the feature extraction network to obtain two predictions. The differences between these predictions are then used as the objective function to optimize the model. The TE model [6] takes the EMA (exponential moving average) predictions in different epochs as the comparison target. The MT (mean teacher) model [7] has two parallel feature extraction networks, and different disturbance samples are input into different networks, in which the teacher network uses the EMA weight of the student network, and the output results of the two networks are regarded as the consistency target. However, the current semi-supervised method also has some limitations. For example, the unsupervised phase of the model depends on the label information of supervised learning, and it is difficult to avoid over-fitting when the scale of labeled data is small. For example, most semi-supervised methods assume that labeled data and unlabeled data obey the same distribution and have the same label space, which makes the occasional outlier in medical images (including instrument failure, improper operation, diseases that are not within the prediction range, etc.) often have negative effects on the quality of prediction.

In this paper, we introduce an unsupervised learning process that is completely independent of semi-supervised learning, which ensures that this part of the training is not affected by supervised learning, so we can produce pseudo-labels [9] that are not affected by label information. As shown in Figure 1, we represent the model as two phases: a semi-supervised phase and an unsupervised phase, which share the feature extraction network. Among them, the semi-supervised phase is the main task to perform the image classification task, and the unsupervised phase is the secondary task to cluster the data [10–13]. Our semi-supervised network architecture is based on the basic architecture of FixMatch [14]. Our work focuses on the unsupervised clustering phase.

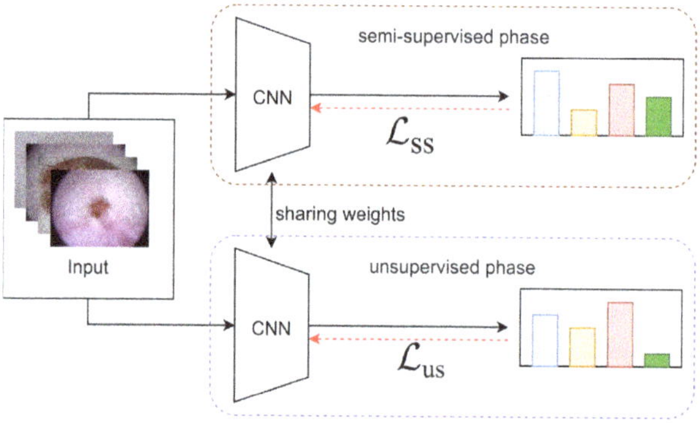

Figure 1. Overview of our two-phase framework for medical image classification. A semi-supervised phase and an unsupervised phase run alternately, and the feature extraction networks of the two phases share weights. In the semi-supervised phase, all data information is used to calculate the semi-supervised loss (L_{SS}), and in the unsupervised phase, all data without label information is used to calculate the unsupervised loss (L_{US}).

In order to prevent cluster degradation in the iterative process, we design a network structure similar to a Siamese Network and update the weights by momentum [15]. At the same time, the auxiliary overclustering method [16] is adopted to make the outliers less likely to affect the clustering results. Our main contributions are as follows:

1. We proposed a new semi-supervised learning framework to improve the classification performance of the semi-supervised model by introducing an unsupervised deep clustering algorithm.
2. Based on consistency regularization, a new objective function was designed to cross-verify different augmentations of the same image, and use an auxiliary overclustering method in the clustering process to reduce the influence of outliers on model training and ensure intra-class consistency in feature space.

3. We conducted experiments on two medical datasets, and the results show that our method is effective. Compared with the current semi-supervised medical image classification methods, our method has better performance.

2. Related Work

In this section, we review some basic methods related to our work and the recent developments in these fields. This includes semi-supervised learning in the field of medical image analysis, data augmentation methods, and deep clustering [17,18].

2.1. *Semi-Supervised Learning in Medical Image Analysis*

The characteristics of semi-supervised learning make it particularly advantageous for medical image analysis. In fact, the research on semi-supervised learning in this field [19–22] has been carried out for a long time. The tasks of semi-supervised learning in the field of medical image analysis can be divided into image classification [23,24] and semantic segmentation [25–28]. Methodologically, the field of medical image analysis mainly includes methods based on confrontation and methods based on consistency regularization.

In the field of medical image segmentation, Zhao et al. proposed a pseudo supervision method based on consistency regularization and uncertainty evaluation [29], which reduced the influence of the potential noise of pseudo-labels on segmentation results in semi-supervised learning. Dong et al. [30] proposed an unsupervised domain adaptive framework based on an antagonistic network, and applied it to semi-supervised learning on the JSRT (Japanese Society of Radiological Technology) datasets.

In the field of medical image classification, Liu et al. [31] put forward sample relation consistency on the basis of consistency regularization, so that the semi-supervised model can obtain more semantic information from unlabeled data. Pang et al. [32] proposed a data augmentation method based on a GAN (generative adversarial network) for semi-supervised learning.

2.2. *Data Augmentation Methods*

At present, there are many semi-supervised works based on consistency regularization, which improve the performance of the model by adding different disturbances to the same target and encouraging the model to generate consistent prediction. Although good results have been achieved, their methods of adding disturbances are still relatively primary, and most of them are based on Gaussian noise, dropout noise, or adversarial noise. Obviously, there are reasons for the complexity of data and training cost, but the effect of data augmentation is obviously not fully exerted. Some targeted data augmentation strategies have been proved to be effective in supervised learning. At present, data augmentation is also one of the keys to improving the model's performance in the field of semi-supervised learning. The data augmentation strategy of Mixup proposed by Berthelot et al. in [1] significantly enhances the robustness and generalization ability of the model and improves the model's performance. The AutoAugment strategy proposed by Cubuk et al. in [33] "Learning Augmentation Policies from Data," improves the data augmentation method through automatic search, and achieves better results in the same semi-supervised framework in multiple datasets. Subsequently, on the basis of AutoAugment, RandAugment [34] changed the search strategy and reduced the parameter space of data augmentation, and achieved better results while the complexity and training cost were significantly reduced.

2.3. *Deep Clustering*

Clustering is a widely used unsupervised algorithm, which divides a group of data into different clusters according to certain standards, so that the data in the same cluster are as similar as possible and the data in different clusters are as dissimilar as possible. Different clustering algorithms are based on different assumptions and data distribution, and the same group of data can also use different clustering methods, such as partition-based clustering methods such as k-means, density-based clustering methods such as DBSCAN

(Density-Based Spatial Clustering of Applications with Noise) [35], and distribution-based clustering methods such as Gaussian Mixture [36]. With the increase in data complexity, the effect of these traditional clustering algorithms is gradually declining. To solve this problem, Caron et al. put forward the concept of deep clustering in [17], that is, combining deep learning with clustering, and its basic framework is shown in Figure 2.

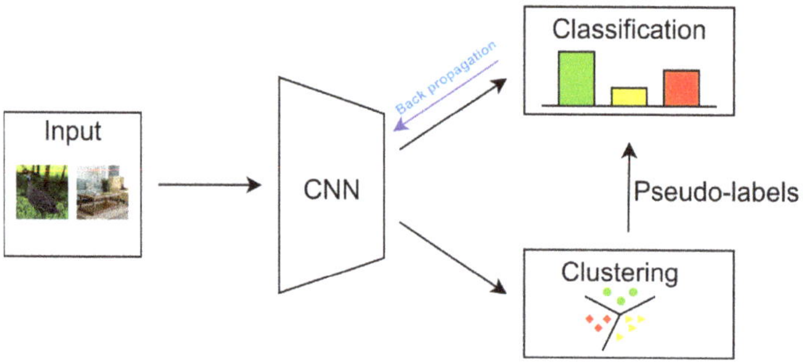

Figure 2. Overall process of deep clustering.

The deep clustering model firstly clusters the features, then generates pseudo-labels based on the clustering results, updating the parameters of the network, and making the network predict these pseudo-labels. These two processes are alternately carried out. Many excellent works have been improved on this basis. Joint Unsupervised Learning [37] proposes a cyclic framework of joint unsupervised learning for depth representation and image clustering, which updates network parameters in a hierarchical way. The learning presentation for clustering via prototype patterning and positive sampling [38] firstly maximizes the distance between different prototypes, and then closes the distance of samples in the same clustering center to improve the clustering effect. Its model takes into account both Contrastive Learning and non-Contrastive Learning, and trains in an end-to-end manner. Invariant information clustering (IIC) [16] maximizes the mutual information between two different augmentations of the same image and generates clustering of the data based on mutual information loss.

3. Method

In this paper, we propose a semi-supervised classification framework that combines unsupervised learning. As shown in Figure 1, our method includes two tasks: unsupervised clustering and semi-supervised classification. These tasks are carried out alternately in the training process. The semi-supervised learning phase uses all data containing label information, while the unsupervised phase uses all data without label information. When the number of labels is small, this method can effectively prevent the model from overfitting and improve its generalization ability.

This paper focuses on unsupervised clustering. We design an unsupervised clustering framework based on the basic framework of deep clustering and propose an objective function that is more conducive to clustering. This allows the unsupervised part to reduce the influence of outliers on the model and enhance its ability to extract semantic information from unlabeled data.

3.1. Semi-Supervised Phase

In the semi-supervised phase, we adopt the FixMatch semi-supervised framework, which is based on consistency regularization and pseudo-labeling. It combines and simplifies advanced ideas and methods used in models such as UDA (unsupervised data augmentation) [39] and ReMixMatch [40], and has achieved good results on massive datasets.

3.1.1. Data Augmentation Method

We use weak augmentation for labeled data and strong augmentation for unlabeled data. Weak augmentation is a standard flip-and-shift augmentation strategy that flips with a 50% probability and shifts with a 12.5% probability in both horizontal and vertical directions. Strong augmentation mainly applies two strategies: RandAugment and CTAugment, followed by Cutout [41].

3.1.2. Semi-Supervised Loss Function and Details

In the semi-supervised phase, we adopt different augmentation methods for labeled and unlabeled data (as shown in Figure 3).

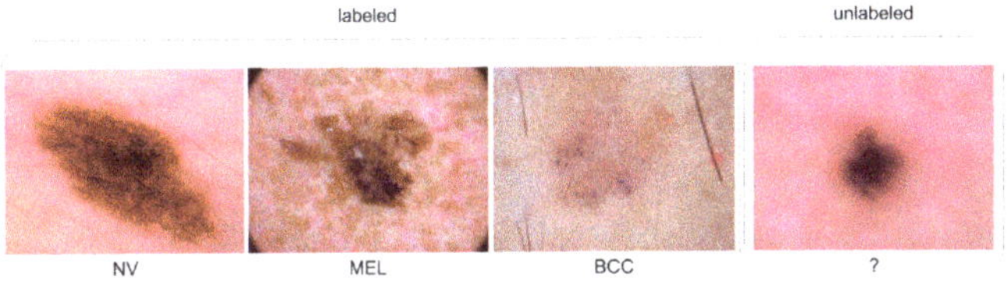

Figure 3. The type of input data divided into two categories according to whether they are labeled or not.

Specifically, labeled images are represented as $x = \{x_1, \ldots, x_n\}$, and their labels are represented as $y = \{y_1, \ldots, y_n\}$. The unlabeled images are represented as $u = \{u_1, \ldots, u_{\mu n}\}$, and the network is represented as f_θ. $\mathrm{A}(\cdot)$ represents a strong augmentation function and $\mathrm{a}(\cdot)$ represents a weak augmentation function. The loss of annotation data can be expressed as:

$$\mathcal{L}_s = \frac{1}{n}\sum_{i=1}^{n} \mathrm{H}(f_\theta(\mathrm{a}(x_i)), y_i) \tag{1}$$

The Pseudo-labels of unlabeled data can be expressed as:

$$y_i' = \mathrm{argmax}(f_\theta(\mathrm{A}(u_i)) \tag{2}$$

The loss of unlabeled data can be expressed as:

$$\mathcal{L}_u = \frac{1}{\mu n}\sum_{i=1}^{\mu n} 1(\max(f_\theta(\mathrm{A}(u_i)) \geq \tau)\mathrm{H}(f_\theta(\mathrm{A}(u_i)), y_i') \tag{3}$$

where μ represents the ratio of unlabeled data to labeled data; $\mathrm{H}(\cdot,\cdot)$ represents cross entropy loss; τ is a scalar hyperparameter denouncing the threshold, and when the confidence exceeds the threshold, the pseudo-label is retained. Therefore, the final loss in the semi-supervised phase can be expressed as:

$$\mathcal{L}_{ss} = \mathcal{L}_s + \lambda_u \mathcal{L}_u \tag{4}$$

Among them, the hyperparameter λ_u is the relative weight of unsupervised loss, which is used to balance supervised loss and unsupervised loss (use the same hyperparameter settings as FixMatch did in most datasets).

3.2. Unsupervised Phase

In this paper, we use a clustering method for unsupervised learning. There are many kinds of clustering algorithms, and their results vary when used alone. However, considering that different clustering algorithms are similar within the framework of deep clustering, we adopt the standard k-means clustering algorithm to reduce computational complexity and shorten iteration time. In this section, we describe the unsupervised algorithm framework used in this paper and introduce the total loss function in the unsupervised phase.

3.2.1. Unsupervised Clustering Framework

Figure 4 describes our basic process in the unsupervised learning phase. Different augmentations of the same image are input into the network, and then the output results are clustered separately. The clustering results are used as pseudo-labels to update the network parameters. Our framework regularizes the centroid distribution of different clusters to improve the clustering effect and make better use of unlabeled data.

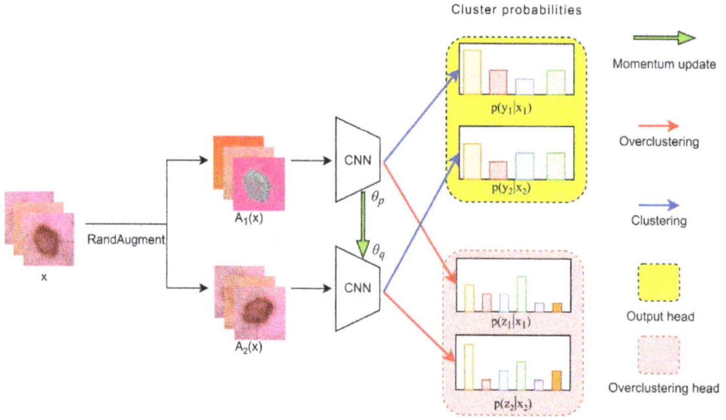

Figure 4. Overview of our unsupervised deep clustering framework. $A_1(x)$ and $A_2(x)$ are the outputs of x after augmentation. $p(y_1|x_1)$ and $p(y_2|x_2)$ are the results of clustering. $p(z_1|x_1)$ and $p(z_1|x_1)$ are the results of overclustering. The online network (above) and the target network (below) update the parameters in momentum. Image feature representation is clustered by the k-means method to get the pseudo-label. The over-clustering head is used to assist the training process, and only the output head is used in the test.

We denote unlabeled data as $x = \{x_1, \ldots, x_N\}$, $y_i (i = 1, 2, \ldots N)$ represents the corresponding pseudo-label, f_θ represents the parameterized model, $A'(\cdot)$ represents the augmentation function, and η represents the clustering center. We adopt the RandAugment [34] augmentation method in the unsupervised phase (parameters settings are the same as the experiment on cifar10). The optimization goal can be expressed as:

$$\min_{\theta} \sum_{i} \mathcal{L}(f_\theta(A(x_i)), y_i, \eta)$$
$$\mathcal{L}(f_\theta(x_i), y_i, \eta) = -\log\left(\frac{e^{-d(f_\theta(x_i), \eta y_i)}}{\sum_j e^{-d(f_\theta(x_i), \eta_j)}}\right) \tag{5}$$

Here $d(\cdot,\cdot)$ represents cosine distance.

We design a parallel network structure consisting of an online network and a target network. Two different augmentations of the same image are input into the online network and target network. The obtained vectors are then clustered, and a clustering center is assigned to each image xi. This process does not depend on labels at all. Usually, unsupervised models eventually collapse into prone mode and output invalid solutions without any constraints. To prevent this situation, the usual practice is to add reconstruction loss [42,43], or explicitly constrain the uniform distribution of samples of all kinds [17]. Inspired by Contrastive Learning [15,44], we make the online network and target network not share weights but update their parameters by momentum. This keeps differences between them at all times, providing motivation for continuous updating. Specifically, the parameters of the two networks are recorded as θ_p and θ_q, and we update θ_q by:

$$\theta_q \leftarrow m\theta_q + (1-m)\theta_p \tag{6}$$

where m is a hyperparameter representing momentum. The greater the value of m, the slower the updating speed. In our experiment, m = 0.99.

3.2.2. Loss Function in Unsupervised Phase

Formally, for any picture x_i, the model generates two feature vectors $v_i^{(1)}$ and $v_i^{(2)}$:

$$\begin{aligned} v_i^{(1)} &= f_{\theta p}(\mathrm{A}'(x_i)) \\ v_i^{(2)} &= f_{\theta q}(\mathrm{A}'(x_i)) \end{aligned} \tag{7}$$

By clustering these two feature vectors, respectively, we can get two groups of pseudo-labels and centroids:

$$\begin{aligned} \mathbf{y}^{(1)}, \eta^{(1)} &= \underset{\mathbf{y},\eta}{\operatorname{argmin}} \textstyle\sum_i \parallel v_i^{(1)} - \eta_{y_i} \parallel^2 \\ \mathbf{y}^{(2)}, \eta^{(2)} &= \underset{\mathbf{y},\eta}{\operatorname{argmin}} \textstyle\sum_i \parallel v_i^{(2)} - \eta_{y_i} \parallel^2 \end{aligned} \tag{8}$$

We hope that the clustering label is consistent with its corresponding input, so we first calculate the internal loss of the same picture:

$$\mathcal{L}_{inward} = \sum_i \mathcal{L}(v_i^{(1)}, y_i^{(1)}, \eta^{(1)}) + \mathcal{L}(v_i^{(2)}, y_i^{(2)}, \eta^{(2)}) \tag{9}$$

At the same time, according to the principle of semantic consistency of the same picture, different augmentations will not change the semantic information, so we can also match the pseudo-label and centroid with different views:

$$\mathcal{L}_{cross} = \sum_i \mathcal{L}(v_i^{(1)}, y_i^{(2)}, \eta^{(2)}) + \mathcal{L}(v_i^{(2)}, y_i^{(1)}, \eta^{(1)}) \tag{10}$$

The final loss of clustering process $\mathrm{L_C}$ can be simply expressed as:

$$\mathcal{L}_C = \frac{1}{\mathrm{N}}(\mathcal{L}_{inward} + \mathcal{L}_{cross}) \tag{11}$$

To improve the generalization ability of the network and reduce the influence of outliers, we add an overclustering head to the network. We use k clustering centroids in the output head and $\mathrm{k} + \lceil \mathrm{k}/2 \rceil$ clustering centers in the overclustering head. Some data or outliers with low confidence will be divided into additional clustering centers during overclustering. The output head still maintains the same number of predictions as the actual category, improving the model's utilization efficiency for unlabeled data and increasing expressiveness in the learned feature representation. Similar to the previous clustering process, we obtain two groups of pseudo-labels and clustering centroids $\left(z^{(1)}, \rho^{(1)}\right)$, $\left(z^{(2)}, \rho^{(2)}\right)$ in the overclustering process. The loss can be calculated in the same way:

$$\mathcal{L}'_{inward} = \sum_i \mathcal{L}(v_i^{(1)}, z_i^{(1)}, \rho^{(1)}) + \mathcal{L}(v_i^{(2)}, z_i^{(2)}, \rho^{(2)}) \tag{12}$$

$$\mathcal{L}'_{cross} = \sum_i \mathcal{L}(v_i^{(1)}, z_i^{(2)}, \rho^{(2)}) + \mathcal{L}(v_i^{(2)}, z_i^{(1)}, \rho^{(1)}) \tag{13}$$

The final loss of the over-clustering process $\mathcal{L}_{OC}$ is expressed as:

$$\mathcal{L}_{OC} = \frac{1}{\mathrm{N}}(\mathcal{L}'_{inward} + \mathcal{L}'_{cross}) \tag{14}$$

Finally, we express the loss function of the unsupervised phase as:

$$\mathcal{L}_{US} = \mathcal{L}_C + \mathcal{L}_{OC} \quad (15)$$

3.3. *Semi-Supervised Classification Method Combined with Unsupervised Learning*

In both the unsupervised and semi-supervised phases, we use the same feature extraction network. The model alternates between semi-supervised classification and unsupervised clustering. In the semi-supervised learning phase, unsupervised clustering becomes easier by spreading label information. In the unsupervised phase, by ignoring label information, the model can obtain stronger generalization performance and avoid overfitting a small amount of labeled data. At the same time, using an overclustering method reduces the influence of low-confidence targets or outliers on network parameters. After trying different hyperparameters and based on final experimental results, we set the model to perform semi-supervised training four times first and then unsupervised training once.

4. Experiments

In this section, we evaluate our method on two large public datasets (the ISIC 2018 Dataset and the ICIAR BACH 2018 dataset) and compare it with state-of-the-art methods.

4.1. *Datasets*

4.1.1. ISIC 2018

The ISIC 2018 dataset [45] contains 10,015 skin lesion detection images marked as 7 common skin lesion types. The images in the ISIC 2018 dataset are dermoscopy images taken with a dermatoscope. Dermoscopy images provide more details and features of skin lesions than conventional photography, such as colors, patterns, and structures. The images in the dataset come from different sources and have varying resolutions, formats, and quality. We resize the image to 224×224 and normalize them using statistical data based on the ImageNet dataset. We divide the dataset into training, validation, and test sets in a 7:1:2 ratio. The number of clustering centers k is 7, and the number of overclustering centers is 10.

4.1.2. ICIAR BACH 2018

The ICIAR BACH 2018 [46] dataset contains hematoxylin and eosin-stained images of breast tissue commonly used for histopathological diagnosis of breast cancer. The images are divided into two types: microscopy images and whole-slide images. Microscopy images are 2048×1536 pixels in size and are extracted from different regions of interest within whole-slide images. Whole-slide images are very large (typically over $100{,}000 \times 100{,}000$ pixels) and contain multiple tissue samples. The images are annotated with four classes: normal, benign, in situ, and invasive. To eliminate overfitting, we augment the original dataset and adopt a nucleus-based patch extraction approach to extract 21,705 non-overlapping nucleus patches (a total of 22,105 non-overlapping nucleus patches are extracted), including 13,026 cancerous nucleus patches and 8679 non-cancerous nucleus patches. We divide the dataset into training, validation, and test sets in a 7:1:2 ratio. The number of clustering centers k is 4, and the number of overclustering centers is 6.

4.2. *Metrics*

For the ISIC 2018 dataset, our evaluation indicators include AUC (Area Under Curve), accuracy, sensitivity, and specificity.

For the ICIAR BACH 2018 dataset, our evaluation indicators include AUC, Error rate, Precision, Recall, and F1-score.

4.3. *Implementation Details*

We use Wide-ResNet-28-2 pre-trained on ImageNET as the backbone network of all experiments and use the same parameter settings as FixMatch in the semi-supervised phase. In the unsupervised clustering phase, we use the SGD (stochastic gradient descent) optimizer with a batch size of 64. The learning rate and weight decay are set to 0.01 and 0.0002, respectively. All methods train for 100 epochs on the ISIC 2018 dataset (our method trains for 80 epochs in the semi-supervised phase and 20 epochs in the unsupervised phase) and 20 epochs on the ICIAR BACH 2018 dataset (our method trains for 16 epochs in the semi-supervised phase and 4 epochs in the unsupervised phase).

4.4. Results

We compare our method with current semi-supervised methods, including TCSE (transformation consistent self-ensembling) [47] (based on Pi-Model), Temporal Ensembling [6], MT [7], UDA [39], and the original FixMatch [14] framework to evaluate its effectiveness.

4.4.1. Comparison on ISIC 2018 Dataset

To clarify the actual effect of semi-supervised learning, we use a fully supervised model trained with 10% labeled data as a comparison baseline. We test the performance of these semi-supervised methods with 10% labeled data. As shown in Table 1, the performance of all models is significantly better than the reference baseline. The performance of the TE model is slightly better than that of the TCSE model because it integrates predictions from different periods and uses them as consistency targets, significantly reducing the model's calculation cost. Compared with the TE and TCSE models, the performance of the MT model is further improved thanks to its network structure and consistent target design. The good performance of the UDA model and FixMatch model proves that the advanced data augmentation method has obvious effects on improving the performance of the model. In addition, our method is better than FixMatch in all indicators, which shows that our proposed method can make better use of unlabeled data.

Table 1. Comparison with different semi-supervised learning methods on ISIC 2018 Dataset.

Method	Metrics			
	AUC	Accuracy	Sensitivity	Specificity
Baseline	85.17	89.42	63.11	87.25
TCSE	87.15	89.91	65.56	90.05
TE	87.23	90.05	65.69	90.14
MT	89.56	91.36	67.35	91.22
UDA	91.04	91.45	68.89	92.56
FixMatch	91.56	91.87	68.36	92.36
ours	92.41	92.16	69.44	92.45

At the same time, we also tested the actual performance of various methods with less labeled data. As shown in Table 2, under the condition of using 2% and 4% labeled data, our method shows more obvious advantages, and the indexes drop less than other methods, which further proves that our method can still perform well with less labeled data.

4.4.2. Comparison on ICIAR BACH 2018 Dataset

We trained a fully supervised model with all labeled data as the upper benchmark and a fully supervised model with 10% labeled data as the lower benchmark. Table 3 shows the comparison of various methods under different percentages of labeled data, and it can be observed that the model with more advanced data augmentation strategies (Auto Augment, CT Augment, Rand Augment, etc.) can perform better. At the same time, it can be noted that with the decrease in labeled data, the performance attenuation of our method is the least obvious, which reflects that our method has better generalization performance than the pure semi-supervised method and is more robust in the face of the fluctuation of labeled data.

Table 2. Performance comparison of different methods under different scale labeled data.

Method	Labeled	Metrics			
		AUC	Accuracy	Sensitivity	Specificity
TCSE	2%	84.12	84.36	63.14	85.21
	4%	85.25	86.12	64.21	86.31
TE	2%	84.32	86.14	63.07	85.16
	4%	85.36	87.12	64.22	86.33
MT	2%	87.23	89.75	63.89	89.24
	4%	88.45	90.11	65.14	90.13
UDA	2%	89.36	91.07	66.19	91.14
	4%	90.71	91.34	67.33	91.79
FixMatch	2%	90.13	91.03	66.24	91.45
	4%	90.69	91.25	67.39	92.07
ours	2%	92.04	91.89	68.86	92.14
	4%	92.27	92.11	69.13	92.30

Table 3. Comparison of different semi-supervised methods under different scale labeled data.

Method	Labeled	Metrics			
		Error Rate	Precision	Recall	F1-Score
supervised	100%	21.23	81.25	81.69	81.46
	10%	36.24	59.41	56.36	57.84
TCSE	10%	32.51	64.17	63.21	63.69
	20%	30.09	68.45	66.31	67.36
	40%	28.72	71.84	68.34	70.05
TE	10%	31.21	68.19	67.23	67.71
	20%	28.74	70.13	68.14	69.12
	40%	27.55	72.54	70.04	71.27
MT	10%	30.11	70.88	68.91	69.88
	20%	27.52	72.18	70.21	71.18
	40%	26.25	74.89	72.14	73.49
UDA	10%	27.51	75.14	74.10	74.62
	20%	26.24	76.14	76.33	76.23
	40%	26.03	77.23	76.89	77.06
FixMatch	10%	28.72	73.16	72.89	73.02
	20%	26.27	75.21	74.01	74.61
	40%	25.06	77.14	77.07	77.10
ours	10%	26.11	76.13	76.22	76.17
	20%	25.08	77.89	77.24	77.56
	40%	23.39	78.16	77.69	77.92

We also compare the specific performance of different methods in terms of AUC. As shown in Table 4, with 40% labeled data, the average AUC of our method reaches 94.12%, ahead of all four categories. This proves the effectiveness of our method. At the same time, we notice that the performance of each model shows a gap in different categories. This may be because labeling noise in datasets reduces the effect of consistency regularization and our unsupervised clustering shows better classification ability in this case. The training method of temporarily ignoring label information in the unsupervised training phase makes it less likely to overfit a small amount of training data.

Table 4. Evaluation of different methods on the ICIAR BACH 2018 dataset with AUC metric.

Method	Labeled	Normal Tissue	Benign Tissue	Ductal Carcinoma in Situ	Invasive Carcinoma	Average AUC
supervised	100%	95.61	94.69	93.16	94.36	94.46
TCSE	40%	89.36	88.12	88.07	88.71	88.57
TE	40%	89.44	87.91	88.26	88.64	88.56
MT	40%	91.12	90.08	89.68	90.11	90.25
UDA	40%	93.11	92.14	90.74	92.07	92.02
FixMatch	40%	94.69	93.25	91.45	93.25	93.16
ours	40%	95.44	94.36	92.89	93.77	94.12

5. Discussion

We designed a semi-supervised classification model with unsupervised learning and compared it with current semi-supervised learning methods on the ISIC 2018 and ICIAR BACH 2018 datasets. On the ISIC 2018 dataset, we achieved significant improvement in AUC and sensitivity. On the ICIAR BACH 2018 dataset, our method performed better on all metrics, especially in AUC and error rate. The results show that our method has stronger classification ability and can distinguish between positive and negative samples more clearly. We believe that this is the result of the combined action of semi-supervised and unsupervised classification mechanisms. When the proportion of labeled data decreases, the advantage of our method becomes more obvious. This shows that intermittently ignoring label information during neural network training can effectively avoid overfitting of the model. We improve the effect of unsupervised clustering by cross-comparison and auxiliary overclustering during unsupervised learning, ultimately improving the performance of the entire model. Considering the high initialization requirement of clustering algorithms, we use a network pre-trained on ImageNet as the feature extraction network. The results of random initialization in our experiments are not ideal, which is a problem that the deep clustering framework needs to address. In future studies, we will try to improve the performance of the model under random initialization and make it have stronger generalization ability.

Semi-supervised learning has great potential in medical image classification. Labeling medical images is often time-consuming and expensive, so semi-supervised learning can leverage large amounts of unlabeled data to improve model accuracy. In reality, a large number of unlabeled medical images are generated every day, making it practical to learn from these data in an unsupervised way. However, current semi-supervised learning methods still have some limitations, such as not adequately addressing the problem of class imbalance or being prone to overfitting when there is insufficient labeled data. We have shown that unsupervised clustering can be combined with semi-supervised learning to improve overall performance. Our work focuses on extracting meaningful semantic information from a large number of unlabeled data and dividing the same category into the same cluster to help the semi-supervised model classify better. In general, our method can be considered a supplementary means of semi-supervised learning, and we hope to reduce the model's dependence on manually labeled data.

6. Conclusions

In this paper, we study the problem of semi-supervised medical image classification with the aim of better utilizing medical images without labels. We propose a new learning framework that combines semi-supervised learning with unsupervised clustering.

The model alternates between semi-supervised and unsupervised learning. During the semi-supervised learning phase, the model propagates label information to accelerate the convergence speed of unsupervised clustering. In the unsupervised learning phase, the model ignores label information to reduce the risk of overfitting. Our experiments on two datasets have achieved better metrics, with a significant lead in AUC, indicating that our proposed method has stronger classification ability. When reducing the ratio of labeled data, our method has more obvious advantages in all metrics, indicating that it can still perform well with less labeled data. We have tried training the model without pre-training, but the overall effect was not satisfactory. Additionally, the unsupervised phase takes quite a long time, which lead to an increase in training costs. In future studies, we will continue to improve our methods so that they can still perform well under random initialization and lower training costs.

Author Contributions: Conceptualization, B.X.; methodology, B.X. and C.L.; software, B.X. and C.L.; validation, B.X.; writing—original draft preparation, B.X. All authors have read and agreed to the published version of the manuscript.

Funding: This research received no external funding.

Institutional Review Board Statement: Not applicable.

Informed Consent Statement: Not applicable.

Data Availability Statement: Not applicable.

Conflicts of Interest: The authors declare no conflict of interest.

References

1. Berthelot, D.; Carlini, N.; Goodfellow, I.; Papernot, N.; Oliver, A.; Raffel, C.A. Mixmatch: A holistic approach to semi-supervised learning. *Adv. Neural Inf. Process. Syst.* **2019**, *32*. [CrossRef]
2. Van Engelen, J.E.; Hoos, H.H. A survey on semi-supervised learning. *Mach. Learn.* **2020**, *109*, 373–440. [CrossRef]
3. Barlow, H.B. Unsupervised learning. *Neural Comput.* **1989**, *1*, 295–311. [CrossRef]
4. Ghahramani, Z. Unsupervised learning. In *Advanced Lectures on Machine Learning: ML Summer Schools 2003*; Revised Lectures; Springer: Berlin/Heidelberg, Germany, 2004; pp. 72–112.
5. Hahne, F.; Huber, W.; Gentleman, R.; Falcon, S.; Gentleman, R.; Carey, V. Unsupervised machine learning. In *Bioconductor Case Studies*; Springer: New York, NY, USA, 2008; pp. 137–157.
6. Laine, S.; Aila, T. Temporal Ensembling for Semi-Supervised Learning. In Proceedings of the International Conference on Learning Representations(ICLR), Toulon, France, 24–26 April 2017.
7. Tarvainen, A.; Valpola, H. Mean teachers are better role models: Weight-averaged consistency targets improve semi-supervised deep learning results. *Adv. Neural Inf. Process. Syst.* **2017**, *30*. [CrossRef]
8. Luo, Y.; Zhu, J.; Li, M.; Ren, Y.; Zhang, B. Smooth neighbors on teacher graphs for semi-supervised learning. In Proceedings of the IEEE Conference on Computer Vision and Pattern Recognition, Salt Lake City, UT, USA, 18–22 June 2018; pp. 8896–8905.
9. Lee, D.-H. Pseudo-label: The simple and efficient semi-supervised learning method for deep neural networks. In Proceedings of the Workshop on Challenges in Representation Learning, ICML, Atlanta, GA, USA, 16–21 June 2013; p. 896.
10. Madhulatha, T.S. An overview on clustering methods. *IOSR J. Eng.* **2012**, *2*, 719–725. [CrossRef]
11. Sinaga, K.P.; Yang, M.-S. Unsupervised K-means clustering algorithm. *IEEE Access* **2020**, *8*, 80716–80727. [CrossRef]
12. Murtagh, F.; Contreras, P. Algorithms for hierarchical clustering: An overview. *Wiley Interdiscip. Rev. Data Min. Knowl. Discov.* **2012**, *2*, 86–97. [CrossRef]
13. Vesanto, J.; Alhoniemi, E. Clustering of the self-organizing map. *IEEE Trans. Neural Netw.* **2000**, *11*, 586–600. [CrossRef]
14. Sohn, K.; Berthelot, D.; Carlini, N.; Zhang, Z.; Zhang, H.; Raffel, C.A.; Cubuk, E.D.; Kurakin, A.; Li, C.-L. Fixmatch: Simplifying semi-supervised learning with consistency and confidence. *Adv. Neural Inf. Process. Syst.* **2020**, *33*, 596–608.
15. He, K.; Fan, H.; Wu, Y.; Xie, S.; Girshick, R. Momentum contrast for unsupervised visual representation learning. In Proceedings of the IEEE/CVF Conference on Computer Vision and Pattern Recognition, Seattle, WA, USA, 13–19 June 2020; pp. 9729–9738.
16. Ji, X.; Henriques, J.F.; Vedaldi, A. Invariant information clustering for unsupervised image classification and segmentation. In Proceedings of the IEEE/CVF International Conference on Computer Vision, Seoul, Republic of Korea, 27–28 October 2019; pp. 9865–9874.
17. Caron, M.; Bojanowski, P.; Joulin, A.; Douze, M. Deep clustering for unsupervised learning of visual features. In Proceedings of the European Conference on Computer Vision (ECCV), Munich, Germany, 8–14 September 2018; pp. 132–149.

18. Guo, X.; Liu, X.; Zhu, E.; Yin, J. Deep clustering with convolutional autoencoders. In Proceedings of the Neural Information Processing: 24th International Conference, ICONIP 2017, Guangzhou, China, 14–18 November 2017; Proceedings, Part II 24. Springer: Berlin/Heidelberg, Germany, 2017; pp. 373–382.
19. Cheplygina, V.; de Bruijne, M.; Pluim, J.P. Not-so-supervised: A survey of semi-supervised, multi-instance, and transfer learning in medical image analysis. *Med. Image Anal.* **2019**, *54*, 280–296. [CrossRef]
20. Bai, W.; Oktay, O.; Sinclair, M.; Suzuki, H.; Rajchl, M.; Tarroni, G.; Glocker, B.; King, A.; Matthews, P.M.; Rueckert, D. Semi-supervised learning for network-based cardiac MR image segmentation. In Proceedings of the Medical Image Computing and Computer-Assisted Intervention—MICCAI 2017: 20th International Conference, Quebec City, QC, Canada, 11–13 September 2017; Proceedings, Part II 20. Springer: Berlin/Heidelberg, Germany, 2017; pp. 253–260.
21. Jin, Y.; Cheng, K.; Dou, Q.; Heng, P.-A. Incorporating temporal prior from motion flow for instrument segmentation in minimally invasive surgery video. In Proceedings of the Medical Image Computing and Computer Assisted Intervention—MICCAI 2019: 22nd International Conference, Shenzhen, China, 13–17 October 2019; Proceedings, Part V 22. Springer: Berlin/Heidelberg, Germany, 2019; pp. 440–448.
22. Zhang, Y.; Yang, L.; Chen, J.; Fredericksen, M.; Hughes, D.P.; Chen, D.Z. Deep adversarial networks for biomedical image segmentation utilizing unannotated images. In Proceedings of the Medical Image Computing and Computer Assisted Intervention—MICCAI 2017: 20th International Conference, Quebec City, QC, Canada, 11–13 September 2017; Proceedings, Part III 20. Springer: Berlin/Heidelberg, Germany, 2017; pp. 408–416.
23. Li, Q.; Cai, W.; Wang, X.; Zhou, Y.; Feng, D.D.; Chen, M. Medical image classification with convolutional neural network. In Proceedings of the 2014 13th International Conference on Control Automation Robotics & Vision (ICARCV), Singapore, 10–12 December 2014; IEEE: Piscataway, NJ, USA, 2014; pp. 844–848.
24. Yadav, S.S.; Jadhav, S.M. Deep convolutional neural network based medical image classification for disease diagnosis. *J. Big Data* **2019**, *6*, 113. [CrossRef]
25. Pham, D.L.; Xu, C.; Prince, J.L. Current methods in medical image segmentation. *Annu. Rev. Biomed. Eng.* **2000**, *2*, 315–337. [CrossRef]
26. Norouzi, A.; Rahim, M.S.M.; Altameem, A.; Saba, T.; Rad, A.E.; Rehman, A.; Uddin, M. Medical image segmentation methods, algorithms, and applications. *IETE Tech. Rev.* **2014**, *31*, 199–213. [CrossRef]
27. Chartsias, A.; Joyce, T.; Papanastasiou, G.; Semple, S.; Williams, M.; Newby, D.; Dharmakumar, R.; Tsaftaris, S.A. Factorised spatial representation learning: Application in semi-supervised myocardial segmentation. In Proceedings of the Medical Image Computing and Computer Assisted Intervention–MICCAI 2018: 21st International Conference, Granada, Spain, 16–20 September 2018; Proceedings, Part II 11. Springer: Berlin/Heidelberg, Germany, 2018; pp. 490–498.
28. Nie, D.; Gao, Y.; Wang, L.; Shen, D. ASDNet: Attention based semi-supervised deep networks for medical image segmentation. In Proceedings of the Medical Image Computing and Computer Assisted Intervention–MICCAI 2018: 21st International Conference, Granada, Spain, 16–20 September 2018; Proceedings, Part IV 11. Springer: Berlin/Heidelberg, Germany, 2018; pp. 370–378.
29. Zhao, X.; Qi, Z.; Wang, S.; Wang, Q.; Wu, X.; Mao, Y.; Zhang, L. RCPS: Rectified Contrastive Pseudo Supervision for Semi-Supervised Medical Image Segmentation. *arXiv* **2023**, arXiv:2301.05500.
30. Dong, N.; Kampffmeyer, M.; Liang, X.; Wang, Z.; Dai, W.; Xing, E. Unsupervised domain adaptation for automatic estimation of cardiothoracic ratio. In Proceedings of the Medical Image Computing and Computer Assisted Intervention–MICCAI 2018: 21st International Conference, Granada, Spain, 16–20 September 2018; Proceedings, Part II 11. Springer: Berlin/Heidelberg, Germany, 2018; pp. 544–552.
31. Liu, Q.; Yu, L.; Luo, L.; Dou, Q.; Heng, P.A. Semi-supervised medical image classification with relation-driven self-ensembling model. *IEEE Trans. Med. Imaging* **2020**, *39*, 3429–3440. [CrossRef]
32. Pang, T.; Wong, J.H.D.; Ng, W.L.; Chan, C.S. Semi-supervised GAN-based radiomics model for data augmentation in breast ultrasound mass classification. *Comput. Methods Programs Biomed.* **2021**, *203*, 106018. [CrossRef] [PubMed]
33. Cubuk, E.D.; Zoph, B.; Mane, D.; Vasudevan, V.; Le, Q.V. AutoAugment: Learning Augmentation Policies from Data. In Proceedings of the IEEE/CVF Conference on Computer Vision and Pattern Recognition (CVPR), New Orleans, LA, USA, 18–24 June 2019; pp. 113–123.
34. Cubuk, E.D.; Zoph, B.; Shlens, J.; Le, Q.V. Randaugment: Practical automated data augmentation with a reduced search space. In Proceedings of the IEEE/CVF Conference on Computer Vision and Pattern Recognition (CVPR), Seattle, WA, USA, 13–19 June 2020; pp. 702–703.
35. Ester, M.; Kriegel, H.-P.; Sander, J.; Xu, X. A Density-Based Algorithm for Discovering Clusters in Large Spatial Databases with Noise. kdd, 1996; pp. 226–231. Available online: https://file.biolab.si/papers/1996-DBSCAN-KDD.pdf (accessed on 2 August 1996).
36. Reynolds, D.A. Gaussian mixture models. *Encycl. Biom.* **2009**, *741*. [CrossRef]
37. Yang, J.; Parikh, D.; Batra, D. Joint unsupervised learning of deep representations and image clusters. In Proceedings of the IEEE Conference on Computer Vision and Pattern Recognition, Las Vegas, NV, USA, 27–30 June 2016; pp. 5147–5156.
38. Huang, Z.; Chen, J.; Zhang, J.; Shan, H. Learning Representation for Clustering Via Prototype Scattering and Positive Sampling. *IEEE Trans. Pattern Anal. Mach. Intell* **2022**, 1–16. [CrossRef]
39. Xie, Q.; Dai, Z.; Hovy, E.; Luong, T.; Le, Q. Unsupervised data augmentation for consistency training. *Adv. Neural Inf. Process. Syst.* **2020**, *33*, 6256–6268.

40. Berthelot, D.; Carlini, N.; Cubuk, E.D.; Kurakin, A.; Sohn, K.; Zhang, H.; Raffel, C. ReMixMatch: Semi-Supervised Learning with Distribution Matching and Augmentation Anchoring. In Proceedings of the International Conference on Learning Representations (ICLR), Addis Ababa, Ethiopia, 26–30 April 2020.
41. DeVries, T.; Taylor, G.W. Improved regularization of convolutional neural networks with cutout. *arXiv* **2017**, arXiv:1708.04552.
42. Yang, B.; Fu, X.; Sidiropoulos, N.D.; Hong, M. Towards k-means-friendly spaces: Simultaneous deep learning and clustering. In Proceedings of the International Conference on Machine Learning, PMLR, Sydney, Australia, 6–11 August 2017; pp. 3861–3870.
43. Tian, K.; Zhou, S.; Guan, J. Deepcluster: A general clustering framework based on deep learning. In Proceedings of the Machine Learning and Knowledge Discovery in Databases: European Conference, ECML PKDD 2017, Skopje, Macedonia, 18–22 September 2017; Proceedings, Part II 17. Springer: Berlin/Heidelberg, Germany, 2017; pp. 809–825.
44. Chen, T.; Kornblith, S.; Norouzi, M.; Hinton, G. A simple framework for contrastive learning of visual representations. In Proceedings of the International Conference on Machine Learning, PMLR, Baltimore, MD, USA, 13–18 July 2020; pp. 1597–1607.
45. Codella, N.; Rotemberg, V.; Tschandl, P.; Celebi, M.E.; Dusza, S.; Gutman, D.; Helba, B.; Kalloo, A.; Liopyris, K.; Marchetti, M. Skin lesion analysis toward melanoma detection 2018: A challenge hosted by the international skin imaging collaboration (isic). *arXiv* **2019**, arXiv:1902.03368.
46. Aresta, G.; Araújo, T.; Kwok, S.; Chennamsetty, S.S.; Safwan, M.; Alex, V.; Marami, B.; Prastawa, M.; Chan, M.; Donovan, M. Bach: Grand challenge on breast cancer histology images. *Med. Image Anal.* **2019**, *56*, 122–139. [CrossRef]
47. Li, X.; Yu, L.; Chen, H.; Fu, C.-W.; Heng, P.-A. Semi-supervised skin lesion segmentation via transformation consistent self-ensembling model. In Proceedings of the British Machine Vision Conference 2018 (BMVC 2018), Newcastle upon Tyne, UK, 3–6 September 2018.

applied sciences

MDPI

Article

A Histopathological Image Classification Method Based on Model Fusion in the Weight Space

Gang Zhang [1], Zhi-Fei Lai [2], Yi-Qun Chen [3], Hong-Tao Liu [1] and Wei-Jun Sun [1,*]

1 School of Automation, Guangdong University of Technology, Guangzhou 510006, China; ipx@gdut.edu.cn (G.Z.); liuhongtao@gdut.edu.cn (H.-T.L.)
2 Information Engineering College, Guangzhou Panyu Polytechnic, Guangzhou 511483, China; laizf@gzpyp.edu.cn
3 School of Computer Science, Guangdong University of Education, Guangzhou 510303, China; chenyiqun@gdei.edu.cn
* Correspondence: gdutswj@gdut.edu.cn

Abstract: Automatic classification of histopathological images plays an important role in computer-aided diagnosis systems. The automatic classification model of histopathological images based on deep neural networks has received widespread attention. However, the performance of deep models is affected by many factors, such as training hyperparameters, model structure, dataset quality, and training cost. In order to reduce the impact of the above factors on model training and reduce the training and inference costs of the model, we propose a novel method based on model fusion in the weight space, which is inspired by stochastic weight averaging and model soup. We use the cyclical learning rate (CLR) strategy to fine-tune the ingredient models and propose a ranking strategy based on accuracy and diversity for candidate model selection. Compared to the single model, the weight fusion of ingredient models can obtain a model whose performance is closer to the expected value of the error basin, which may improve the generalization ability of the model. Compared to the ensemble model with n base models, the testing cost of the proposed model is theoretically $1/n$ of that of the ensemble model. Experimental results on two histopathological image datasets show the effectiveness of the proposed model in comparison to baseline ones, including ResNet, VGG, DenseNet, and their ensemble versions.

Keywords: histopathological image classification; model fusion; deep neural network; weight averaging; ensemble learning

1. Introduction

Histopathological images are digital images of tissue sections observed under a microscope, and a large number of studies have shown and verified their important value in biomedicine [1,2]. In particular, histopathological images have been broadly used in the screening of many cancers and are, in fact, considered the gold standard for diagnosing a significant number of cancers. One notable feature of histopathological images is their high information density, which may include microstructures, such as cells, nuclei, stroma, tumors, blood vessels, glands, etc., and histopathological images can be observed at various magnifications, allowing for a multi-scale analysis [3].

The automatic classification of histopathological images plays an important role in computer-aided diagnosis (CAD) systems, which can reduce the burden of pathologists, decrease the influence of human factors in diagnosis, and improve the stability of the results. With the rapid development of deep learning theory and technology [4–7], histopathological image classification models based on convolutional neural networks have exhibited excellent performance in many applications. In order to improve the inference performance of convolutional neural networks, models with a larger number of layers and channels have been designed. For example, in the famous ImageNet image classification challenge [8], the number of parameters of CoAtNet-4+PT-RA-E150 [9], one of the state-of-the-art models at present, reaches 275M. Large-scale models have high requirements when it comes to the size of the training dataset and the capabilities of computer hardware. However, obtaining a large number of histopathological images is not an easy task for certain medical departments. It is also difficult to fully satisfy the computing resources required to train the model.

Different strategies have been proposed to solve the contradiction between the lack of training data and computing resources and the pursuit of model performance. One widely used strategy is transfer learning. It takes the approach of further training (fine-tuning) on top of a well-trained model, e.g., models trained on ImageNet. A common practice is to train only the weights of the last few fully connected layers while fixing the weights of the remaining layers. By using a pre-trained model, one can make full use of its architecture and weights, resulting in significant reductions in the design and training costs of the model. This strategy has been widely used in work on histopathological image analysis [10–15]. However, setting the model hyperparameters becomes a challenge when using this strategy to train or fine-tune the pre-trained model. Common hyperparameters include the learning rate, weight decay rate, batch size, data augmentation strength, etc. Hyperparameters have a direct impact on the training effect of the model. The optimal hyperparameter setting is usually difficult to obtain. Instead, people determine hyperparameter settings based on experience or by using a grid search on a small verification set. However, the grid search requires a lot of computational resources and may not reach global optima. Another strategy is model ensemble. The main idea of model ensemble is to train several base models with diversity, and then perform majority voting or weighted voting on the output of these models to obtain the final results. By using different training sets, changing the training hyperparameters, using different types of optimizers, etc., the diversity between base models can be improved. Model ensemble can combine multiple base models with suboptimal performance into a model with strong overall performance, which can lead to better results than a single model, provided that the diversity among the base models is ensured. Although the model ensemble strategy avoids the computationally expensive hyperparameter search, it greatly increases the inference cost of the model. This is because each test sample needs to be fed to each base model for inference and, hence, the running time is proportional to the number of base models. This limits the application scope of the model ensemble methods, especially in low-specification terminals or mobile devices.

Recently, some studies on model fusion in the weight space have been proposed [16–19]. Researchers proposed different strategies to fuse weights of some trained/pre-trained models to form a single model. Equation (1) shows the weight average strategy for model fusion:

$$f_{fusion}(x, \theta) = f(x, \frac{1}{M} \sum_{k=1}^{M} \theta_k) \tag{1}$$

where $F = \{f(x, \theta_1), f(x, \theta_2), \cdots, f(x, \theta_M)\}$ represents a set of trained models with the same architecture but different weights.

In contrast, model ensemble works in the model space, meaning that it fuses the output of the models to obtain a final result. Equation (2) shows the majority voting strategy on the model set F:

$$f_{ens}(x) = \frac{1}{M} \sum_{k=1}^{M} f(x, \theta_k) \tag{2}$$

It can be seen that the inference cost of f_{fusion} is only $\frac{1}{M}$ of that of f_{ens} while the training costs of both are almost equivalent. The rationale for model fusion in the weight space lies in the relationship between local minima and the global solution. Draxler et al. [20] claimed that the loss minima of a deep neural network are not isolated in a parameter space but rather form a connected manifold. There can be a path between two local minima where the loss does not significantly fluctuate. Izmailov et al. [16] observed that when training a deep neural network using a high-frequency cyclical learning rate (CLR) [21], the model weights corresponding to the periodic minimum learning rate are located on the periphery of the most desirable solutions (global loss minima). Averaging these weights may lead to a solution closer to the optimal solution than the ones located on the periphery. Wortsman et al. [17] extended the weight-averaging method from a single training trajectory to the context of fine-tuning models with different training hyperparameters. Their method can also work in the transfer learning mode.

Inspired by these studies, we propose a novel model-based fusion method for histopathological image classification tasks. Following the work of Wortsman et al. [17], we use the term soup in this paper to refer to the models fused in the weight space, and each model's weights are referred to as the ingredients of the soup. We propose two strategies for constructing soup models: the average strategy and the dominant difference weight-averaging (DDWA) strategy. For DDWA, by drawing on the idea of the selective ensemble [22], we select ingredient models that perform satisfactorily enough on the validation set and have large differences from other models for fusion in the weight space. Compared to the strategy of averaging the weights of all ingredient models, DDWA can produce a fusion model that achieves a loss closer to the optimal expected loss. The proposed method can work either in the fine-tuned model mode or in the full model mode.

The contributions of this paper are two-fold:

- We introduce a weight-based model fusion strategy to solve the problem of histopathological image classification. The strategy significantly reduces the computational complexity of model training and inference.
- We propose the DDWA method to screen the ingredient models, enabling the weight fusion model to achieve a better approximation to the optimal value of the loss function's error basin, thereby improving the generalization ability of the model.

The remainder of this paper is organized as follows. We review some related and important works in Section 2. In Section 3, we present the proposed model and its strategies. The evaluation results are reported and discussed in Section 4. Section 5 discusses the advantages and limitations of the proposed model. The paper is concluded in Section 6.

2. Related Works

The distribution of minima regions in the loss function of deep neural networks has been a subject of study in recent years. Draxler et al. [20] observed that along the paths connecting minima in the weight space, which are unrelated to each other, the training and test loss would remain nearly equal to that of the minima, while the test error slightly increases. Their work revealed that the distribution of local minima in the loss function of deep neural networks has certain characteristics. Smith and Topin [23] explored the topology of the loss function of ResNet-56 on the CIFAR-10 dataset by training with CLR and different fixed learning rates. Their work provides theoretical support for finding the optimal region of the loss function. Garipov et al. [24] further proposed an ensemble framework that consisted of models along high-accuracy paths in the weight space. They proposed a fast geometric ensemble (FGE) strategy, which first trains a model to about 80%, uses CLR or fixed learning rates for further training, records the model weights for every m iteration, and ensembles these recorded models for final results. Izmailov et al. [16] proposed stochastic weight averaging (SWA) by simply averaging the model weights at each recorded point along the trajectory of a stochastic gradient descent (SGD) procedure, with CLR or fixed learning rates. Their work is based on the observation that SGD methods generally converge on the edge of the minima basin. In such cases, weight averaging can lead to a better solution. Jain et al. [25] presented a theoretical analysis of tail-averaging in machine learning models. They presented the generalization error bounds of different weight-averaging strategies in the SGD procedure. Recently, Guo et al. [26] revisited SWA and pointed out that its effectiveness depends on the extent to which the SGD algorithm runs before converging. Their work indicated that fusing models in the weight space can reduce the test variance.

Neyshabur et al. [27] proposed that when a pre-trained model is fine-tuned on a new training dataset using different hyperparameters, the model instances would stay in the same loss landscape basin. Moreover, these fine-tuned instances would be similar in feature spaces and close in parameter spaces. Based on their work, Wortsman et al. [17] proposed model soup, which performs weight fusion over a series of fine-tuned models trained with different hyperparameters. They designed three strategies for weight fusion: average soup, greedy soup, and learned soup. These strategies utilize averaging, selective fusion, and weighted combination to obtain the soup model. For the greedy soup strategy, one would test each ingredient and keep it if its addition improves the performance of the soup model. For the learned soup strategy, one would search for a weighted combination that makes the model perform optimally on the test set. Inspired by their work, in this paper, we introduce the soup model into the histopathological image analysis and propose a novel weight fusion strategy by drawing on the idea of selective ensemble.

As an effective strategy for improving the model performance and reducing variance, ensemble learning has been widely used in histopathological image analysis. Hameed et al. [28] fine-tuned 4 pre-trained models based on VGG16 and VGG19. They then constructed an ensemble model by averaging the prediction probabilities of the 4 models. The ensemble model outperformed the individual models in terms of test loss. Sohail et al. [29] proposed a method based on deep ensemble for the analysis of mitoses in breast histopathology images. First, they selected candidate mitoses via an instance segmentation method based on deep learning. Then a heterogeneous ensemble of deep CNNs was run for mitotic nuclei classification. Kumar et al. [30] proposed the stacked generalized ensemble model for breast cancer classification, which uses 6 deep networks as level-0 models and logistic regression as a level-1 model. The level-1 model acts as an integrator for the outputs of sub-models. Their model achieved competitive results in the invasive ductal carcinoma dataset. Ref. [31] proposed a model that uses a deep transfer learning network to detect COVID-19 from lung CT scan slices, which can make full use of the supervised information in the dataset of the source field, and is more effective for application scenarios where there are inadequate amounts of labeled data in the target fields. Ref. [32] used deep neural networks with different architectures, implemented with contrast-limited adaptive histogram equalization, to detect COVID-19 from CT lung scans. Their work demonstrates the effectiveness of deep neural networks in detecting COVID-19. In [33], the authors designed a weighted average-based heterogeneous network for detecting COVID-19 from chest CT scans and chest X-ray images. They fine-tuned different deep neural networks, such as VGG19, ResNet101, and DenseNet169, as base classifiers, and then integrated the best-performing models to obtain the final results. This work demonstrates that ensemble learning based on model fine-tuning is effective for COVID-19 detection.

In [28–30], it can be seen that the ensemble of different deep neural networks has been extensively utilized in histopathological image analysis. The limitations of these works are listed as follows: (1) They greatly increase the inference costs of the models because they must obtain the results from each model for ensemble learning; (2) different deep neural networks need to be carefully designed to maintain the diversity in ensemble learning, which greatly influences the last outcome. Therefore, the DDWA model is proposed to overcome these limitations. In addition, studies on histopathological image analysis based on model weight fusion are rarely publicly reported. Our study can be used as a complement to the existing work in the field of weight fusion methods for histopathological image analysis to a certain extent.

3. Model Fusion in the Weight Space for Histopathological Image Classification

3.1. Basic Model Training

As indicated by previous studies [16,20,25,27], model fusion in the weight space works well in models from snapshots of the trajectory of an SGD procedure, or from fine-tuned pre-trained models with different hyperparameters. We applied both methods to generate basic models (ingredient models for soup) in this study. Specifically, we used three famous deep convolutional neural network architectures, i.e., ResNet [34], VGG [35], and DenseNet [36], for basic model training. All models were pre-trained on the ImageNet-1000 dataset [8] and, hence, our model works in the fine-tuning mode.

The pre-trained models were fine-tuned with two training settings, i.e., the cyclical learning rate and different training hyperparameters. We saved the model weights in both cases as the potential ingredients for model fusion.

A. Ingredient Model Training with Cyclical Learning Rate

The main idea of the cyclical learning rate (CLR) [21,23,24], which is different from the traditional learning rate-adjusting strategy, which decreases monotonically, is to vary the learning rate cyclically within a proper range as the number of training epochs increases. Let α_1 and α_2 represent the lower and upper bounds of the learning rate; the CLR strategy changes the learning rate according to the iteration number k, as shown in Equations (3) and (4):

$$\alpha(k) = (1 - t_k)\alpha_1 + t_k\alpha_2 \tag{3}$$

$$t_k = \frac{\bmod (k-1, c) + 1}{c} \tag{4}$$

In Equation (4), c represents the length of a cycle. Here, we refer to processing a mini-batch of data at a time as an epoch. At the end of each cycle, i.e., when the learning rate reaches the minimum, the model weights are saved as checkpoints. Note that α_1, α_2, and c are hyperparameters for model training, and have a great impact on the effectiveness of model weight averaging. The maximum learning rate α_2 must be able to jump out of a local minima basin, which determines the exploration ability of the model. In this study, we set α_2 to a slightly larger value than the initial learning rate used in the traditional learning rate decay training strategy. The minimum learning rate α_1 and the length of a cycle c are set according to [24].

B. Ingredient Model Training with Different Training Hyperparameters

In addition to CLR, we also fine-tuned the pre-trained model with different (but constant) learning rates with data augmentation. For constant learning rates, we set the learning rate to 0.0001, 0.0015, and 0.0002, respectively. We used RandAugment [37] for data augmentation, which aims to reduce the parameter space and maintain the diversity of data (images) by using a non-parametric process instead of the learning strategy and probability. There are only two parameters involved when using RandAugment, i.e., the number of transformations N and the degree of augmentation distortion M. RandAugment makes use of a linear scale to represent the intensity of each conversion. Simply put, each transformation is in the integer range of 0 to 10, where 10 represents the maximum range of a given transformation. The larger the values of N and M, the stronger the degree of regularization. We set $N = 9$ and $M = 2$ in all of the experiments in this study.

C. The Effectiveness of Soup Ingredients

The effectiveness of model fusion in the weight space depends on whether the model weights are located in the same loss basin. To show that the ingredients obtained through our two training strategies meet the requirement of fusion in the weight space, we will first provide a formal definition of the loss basin, and then use a linear interpolation method for validation. We use the definition of loss basin proposed in [27], which can be formally written as follows:

Definition 1. *Let $L : R^n \to R^+$ be a loss function and $S \subseteq R^n$ be a closed convex set, then S is a $(\varepsilon, \delta)-$basin for L if and only if the following holds:*

- *Let U_S represent the uniform distribution over S, and $v_{S,L}$ represent the expected value of L on samples drawn from U_S. Then*

$$\mathbb{E}_{w \sim U_S}[|L(w) - v_{S,L}|] \leq \varepsilon \tag{5}$$

- $\forall w_1, w_2 \in S$, *define* $h(w_1, w_2) = w_1 + \tilde{\alpha}(w_2 - w_1)$, *where* $\tilde{\alpha} = \max \alpha | w_1 + \alpha(w_2 - w_1) \in S$. *Then*

$$\mathbb{E}_{w_1,w_2 \sim U_S, p \sim \mathcal{N}(0,(\delta^2/n)I_n)}[L(f(w_1, w_2) + p) - v_{S,L}] \geq 2\varepsilon \quad (6)$$

- *Let* $\kappa(w_1, w_2, p) = f(w_1, w_2) + \frac{p}{\|f(w_1,w_2)-w_1\|_2}(f(w_1, w_2) - w_1)$. *Then*

$$\mathbb{E}_{w_1,w_2 \sim U_S, p \sim \mathcal{N}(0,\delta^2)}[L(\kappa(w_1, w_2, |p|)) - v_{S,L}] \geq 2\varepsilon \quad (7)$$

The definition of basin implies that, on the one hand, a basin should be relatively flat (small variance), and the value of the loss function that corresponds to each point in it should be close to the expected value. On the other hand, the value of the loss function corresponding to the points around the basin should be higher than the expected loss. Specifically, Equation (6) stipulates that the values of the loss function associated with the points within the basin should be higher than the expected values when Gaussian noise is added. Equation (7) stipulates that if a point within the basin is manually pushed away from the basin by a short distance, the value of its loss function should increase.

To validate the effectiveness of the ingredients, we use linear interpolation between two ingredient models parameterized by w_1 and w_2 to generate k middle points $w_i (1 \leq i \leq k)$, where w_i is given by

$$w_i = \gamma_i w_1 + (1 - \gamma_i) w_2 \quad 0 \leq \gamma_i \leq 1 \quad (8)$$

If $L(w_i) - \frac{L(w_1)+L(w_2)}{2} < \tau$ holds for all $w_i (1 \leq i \leq k)$, in which τ is a threshold, it can be inferred that w_1 and w_2 are in the same basin. We report the results of the proposed model in Section 4.

3.2. Soup Strategies

Recent studies have shown that the way in which the model weights are generated and the method used for weight fusion have significant impacts on the performance of the soup model. We collectively refer to the generating and fusing of soup ingredients as soup strategies. We implemented two strategies for building the soup model. The first strategy was averaging the soup, which simply involves averaging the weight of each gradient in the soup. The weight-averaging strategy was applied and proved effective in previous studies. Since models trained using methods such as gradient descent often converge near the edge of the error basin, the use of the averaging strategy holds promise in moving a model closer to the center (expected value) of the error basin, which may have better generalization ability. Fine-tuning a pre-trained model with different training hyperparameters and recording the weights in each case would result in a set of models located in the same low-loss basin. The second strategy involves the use of dominant difference weight averaging (DDWA), which is motivated by the classical ensemble pruning method [38]. According to the classification accuracy *acc* and diversity *div*, DDWA selects the ingredients with better performance to construct the soup model. Let $H = \{h_{w_1}, h_{w_2}, \cdots, h_{w_M}\}$ represent the set of candidate ingredients and $D = \{(x_1, y_1), (x_2, y_2), \cdots, (x_n, y_N)\}$ represent the evaluation dataset, where x_i represents the ith instance and y_i represents the corresponding class label. The ith ingredient's *acc* and *div* are defined as Equations (9) and (10):

$$acc_i = \frac{1}{N} \sum_{j=1}^{N} L(h_{w_i}(x_j), y_j) \quad (9)$$

$$div_i = \frac{\sum_{j=1}^{N} (h_{w_i}(x_j) - avg_j)^2 \cdot \alpha}{N} \quad (10)$$

$$avg_j = \frac{1}{M} \sum_{k=1}^{M} h_{w_k}(x_j) \quad (11)$$

where $L(\cdot,\cdot)$ is a zero-one loss function, avg_j is the averaging output of all candidate ingredients on x_j, and $\alpha = 1$ if $h_{w_i}(x_j)$ equals the ground truth label y_j; otherwise, $\alpha = 0$. div_i evaluates the difference between the ith component and the entire set under the condition of correct classification. We sort all of the ingredients using non-dominated sort (NDS) according to these two indices, and select the top q% of ingredients to build the soup model, as shown in Algorithm 1.

Algorithm 1 Non-dominated sort.

```
Input:
    rank_A: acc ranking of M candidate ingredients
    rank_D: div ranking of M candidate ingredients
    H: candidate ingredients
Output: rank_NDS: NDS ranking of M candidate ingredients
F = ∅, rank_NDS = ∅
for i = 1, 2, ···, M do
    S_i = ∅ , b_i = 0
    for j = i, 2, ···, M do
        if h_i dominates h_j then
            add h_j to S_i
        else if h_j dominates h_i then
            b_i = b_i + 1
        end if
    end for
    if b_i = 0 then
        Add h_i to F
    end if
end for
Ascending sort F according to the sum of rank_A and rank_D
while F ≠ ∅ do
    Q = ∅
    for i = 1, 2, ···, M do
        for all g in S_i do
            if n_g ≠ 0 then
                n_g = n_g − 1
                Addg to Q if n_g = 0
            end if
        end for
    end for
    Ascending sort Q according to the sum of rank_A and rank_D
    Add Q to rank_NDS
end while
return rank_NDS
```

NDS ensures that the selected soup ingredient models have good accuracy and are different from each other, which is in line with the main idea of model soup. Specifically, a higher accuracy means that the selected ingredient model is close to the error basin, while a larger difference ensures that the spatial distribution of the component model maintains a certain distance, both of which make the soup model more effective. Figure 1 shows the resulting models obtained through weight averaging in two cases. The circles represent the performances of the ingredients for constructing the soup model. The triangle represents the performance of the soup model. The sub-figure on the left shows the soup model obtained by averaging 4 ingredients that are close to each other, located in the edge of the error basin. The sub-graph on the right shows the soup model obtained by ingredients that are close to the edge of the error basin but are apart from each other. The latter error loss is closer to the expected value of the basin, showing that the resulting soup model is more efficient.

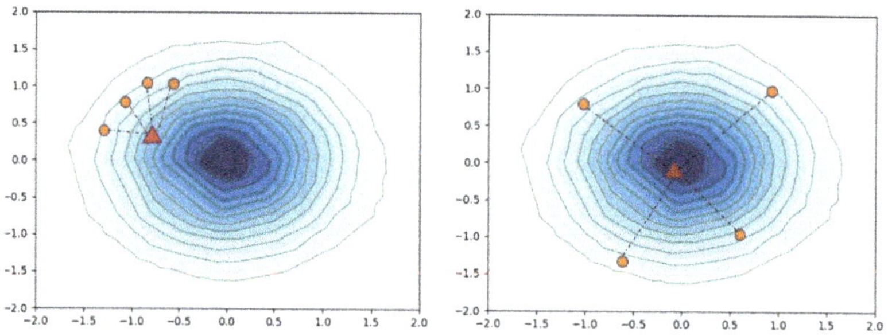

Figure 1. Two cases of weight averaging of soup ingredients.

Finally, we provide a flowchart to present the main steps of the proposed model. See Figure 2.

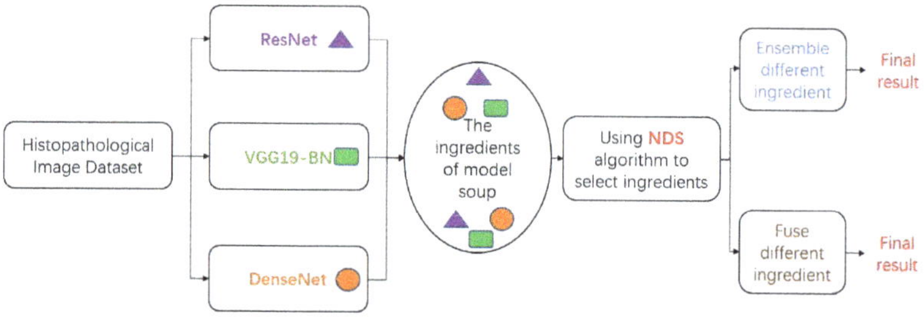

Figure 2. Main steps of the proposed model.

4. Evaluations

4.1. Dataset Description

Two datasets are used for evaluating the proposed model. The first is the SCAN dataset, which contains 270 H&E tissue images from 5 organs, namely the adrenal gland, breast, colon, liver, and prostate. The resolution of each image in the SCAN dataset is 1024×2048. Table 1 shows details of the SCAN dataset.

Table 1. Details of the SCAN dataset.

Tissue	Magnifications	Number of Images
adrenal	$10\times, 20\times$	50
gland	$10\times, 20\times$	50
breast	$20\times, 40\times$	40
colon	$10\times, 20\times, 40\times$	60
prostate	$10\times, 20\times$	70

Figure 3 shows two examples of the SCAN dataset. The left one is a tissue image from the breast and the right one is from the adrenal. The images in SCAN were randomly cropped to 1024×1024 and then resized to 224×224. We combined images of different magnifications during model training to improve the model's ability to obtain scale-independent features.

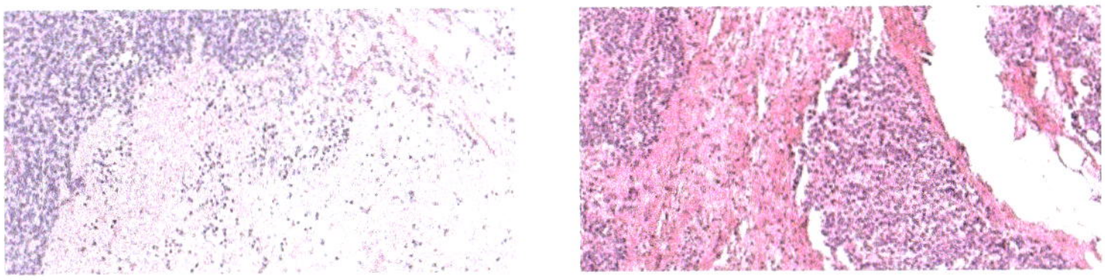

Figure 3. Two examples of the SCAN dataset.

The second dataset is the BreakHis dataset. The breast cancer histopathological image dataset (BreakHis) is composed of 9109 microscopic images, which can be divided into 2 groups: benign tumor and malignant tumor. All images in this dataset were collected from 82 patients and the magnifying factors include 40×, 100×, 200×, and 400×. To date, it contains 2480 benign and 5429 malignant samples. The image has a resolution of 700 × 460, with 3 RGB channels, with an 8-bit depth in each channel, and is in PNG format. Histologically, the term benign refers to a lesion that does not have any criteria associated with malignancy. A malignant tumor is a synonym for cancer; the lesion can invade and destroy adjacent structures (locally invasive) and spread to distant sites (metastasize) to cause death. Table 2 shows the details of the BreakHis dataset.

Table 2. Details of the BreakHis dataset.

Type	Magnifications	Number of Images
benign tumor	10×, 20×, 30×, 40×	2480
malignant tumor	10×, 20×, 30×, 40×	5429

Figure 4 shows two examples of the BreakHis dataset. The left one is a benign tumor and the right one is a malignant tumor. We combined images of varying magnifications during model training. Each image is randomly cropped to 460 × 460 and then resized to 224 × 224.

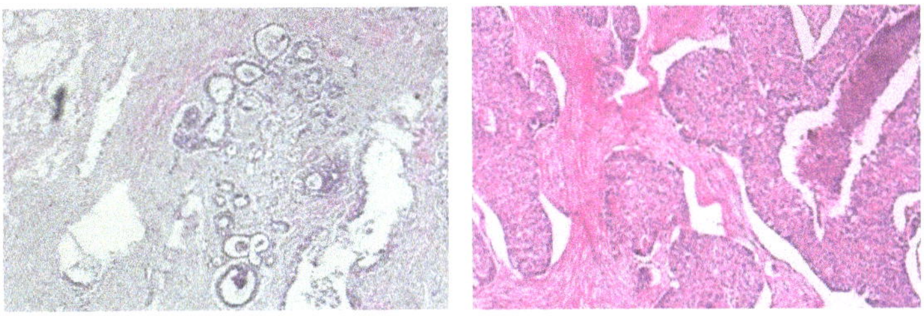

Figure 4. Two examples of the BreakHis dataset.

4.2. Evaluation Environment and Settings

All model training and evaluations were carried out on a server equipped with an Intel (R) Xeon (R) W-2245 CPU @ 3.90 GHz, 64 GB memory, and an NVIDIA GeForce RTX 2080 Ti 12 G graphics card. The evaluation code was implemented in Python, and PyTorch was used to build and train the deep neural networks.

The SCAN dataset is divided into three sets: the training set, validation set, and test set, following an 8:1:1 ratio. Since there are few pictures in the SCAN dataset, in order to fully train the model, it was necessary to use data augmentation methods to expand the training dataset. We used RandAugment [37] for data augmentation after the dataset division. The RandAugment method uses a series of operations for image data augmentation, such as rotating, autoContrast, random cropping, adding Gaussian error, etc., and the number and magnitude of operations for data augmentation are controlled by two parameters (M

and N). For the stability of the evaluation results, the same augmentation settings were applied to the validation and test sets. For model training, the batch size was set to 16. For SWA model training, we set the maximum epoch to 90 and the cyclical learning rate (CLR) to 0.0002. AdamW was used as the optimizer for model training.

4.3. Evaluation Results

In order to evaluate the effectiveness of the proposed model, measures such as $precision$, $recall$, $accuracy$, and $F1score$ are used. The definitions of $precision$, $recall$, $accuracy$, and $F1score$ are as follows:

$$Precision = \frac{TP}{TP + FP} \tag{12}$$

$$Recall = \frac{TP}{TP + FN} \tag{13}$$

$$Accuracy = \frac{TP + TN}{TP + TN + FP + FN} \tag{14}$$

$$F1score = \frac{2 \times recall \times precision}{precision + recall} \tag{15}$$

where TP is true positive, TN is true negative, FP is false positive, and FN is false negative. Precision refers to the proportion of samples that the model predicts as positive examples and that are actually positive examples. Recall refers to the proportion of samples that are actually positive examples and are correctly predicted as positive examples by the model. The F1 score is the harmonic mean of precision and recall, which is used to comprehensively evaluate the performance of the model on imbalanced datasets. The range of the F1 score is between 0 and 1, the closer to 1, the better the model performance. For a detailed description of these evaluation indicators, please refer to [39].

Table 3 shows the precision, recall, and F1 score of the proposed method, as well as the comparison methods, on the SCAN and BreakHis datasets.

The **Model** column represents the base model used to generate soup ingredients and the **Strategy** column represents the strategies used for model training. LR= 0.0001 represents the results obtained by fine-tuning the model using a constant learning rate of 0.0001. LR-ensemble represents the majority voting ensemble of models trained with different LRs, i.e., 0.0001, 0.0015, and 0.0002. LR-Aver-Soup represents the average soup model, where its ingredients are models trained using the aforementioned different learning rates. CLR-Aver-Soup (SWA) represents the model obtained using the random weight-averaging method [16]. CLR-DDWA-Ensemble represents the ensemble model, which is obtained by selecting the checkpoint models using CLR through the DDWA strategy. CLR-DDWA-Soup represents the average soup model, which is obtained by selecting the checkpoint models using CLR through the DDWA strategy.

It can be seen from Table 3 that the model obtained by training with different but fixed LR values demonstrates a relatively similar performance across each evaluation index. Ensemble models trained by different LRs can further improve the performance, showing that the models have diversity. LR-Aver-Soup outperforms LR-Ensemble with a precision improvement ratio of 3.9%. When comparing CLR-Aver-Soup(SWA) and CLR-DDWA-Soup, it can be seen that the latter has better performance, showing the effectiveness of the proposed DDWA ingredient model selection strategy.

Table 3. Precision, recall, and F1 score on the SCAN and BreakHis datasets.

Model	Strategy	SCAN			BreakHis		
		Precision	Recall	F1 Score	Precision	Recall	F1 Score
ResNet	LR = 0.0001	0.888	0.871	0.880	0.952	0.950	0.950
	LR = 0.00015	0.888	0.888	0.888	0.958	0.957	0.957
	LR = 0.0002	0.871	0.854	0.862	0.924	0.923	0.923
	LR-Ensemble	0.877	0.871	0.874	0.958	0.957	0.957
	LR-Aver-Soup	0.911	0.900	0.906	0.950	0.949	0.949
	CLR-Aver-Soup(SWA)	0.901	0.896	0.898	0.957	0.956	0.956
	CLR-DDWA-Ensemble	**0.907**	**0.902**	**0.904**	**0.965**	**0.963**	**0.962**
	CLR-DDWA-Soup	**0.929**	**0.926**	**0.931**	**0.979**	**0.978**	**0.978**
VGG19-BN	LR = 0.0001	0.918	0.917	0.915	0.962	0.961	0.961
	LR = 0.00015	0.925	0.925	0.924	0.972	0.971	0.971
	LR = 0.0002	0.892	0.889	0.887	0.963	0.961	0.961
	LR-Ensemble	0.923	0.921	0.921	0.979	0.978	0.978
	LR-Aver-Soup	0.924	0.960	0.940	0.978	0.978	0.978
	CLR-Aver-Soup(SWA)	0.914	0.948	0.929	0.970	0.969	0.969
	CLR-DDWA-Ensemble	**0.915**	**0.913**	**0.912**	**0.979**	**0.978**	**0.978**
	CLR-DDWA-Soup	**0.947**	**0.969**	**0.958**	**0.985**	**0.984**	**0.984**
DenseNet	LR = 0.0001	0.905	0.906	0.904	0.925	0.921	0.920
	LR = 0.00015	0.916	0.917	0.915	0.918	0.917	0.917
	LR = 0.0002	0.893	0.894	0.892	0.926	0.922	0.921
	LR-Ensemble	0.919	0.918	0.916	0.929	0.924	0.924
	LR-Aver-Soup	0.928	0.925	0.925	0.937	0.934	0.934
	CLR-Aver-Soup(SWA)	0.905	0.904	0.903	0.956	0.956	0.956
	CLR-DDWA-Ensemble	**0.916**	**0.915**	**0.913**	**0.960**	**0.959**	**0.959**
	CLR-DDWA-Soup	**0.931**	**0.931**	**0.931**	**0.971**	**0.971**	**0.971**

Figure 5 shows the confusion matrices of the models based on ResNet.

The values on the diagonal (green) of the confusion matrix indicate the number of correctly classified samples in each class and their proportions relative to the entire dataset. The values in red cells represent the number of misclassified samples and their proportions of the entire dataset. In the last row, the upper value represents the recall of each class. The last column represents the precision corresponding to each class. The most bottom right values represent the accuracy and error rates of the model. It can be seen that the model does not discriminate well between class 1 and class 4 since, for each model, there are samples from class 4 that are misclassified as class 1. Compared with the other models, the CLR-DDWA-Soup model performs better mainly because it has better classification performance in classes 2, 3, and 5, and fewer misclassified samples in class 1 when compared to the other models. Compared with the constant learning rate models, the ensemble-based model (LR-Ensemble) demonstrates a large improvement in the classification accuracy of class 1. We can see that the ensemble model can make good use of the advantages of the three base models. Finally, the CLR-based soup models outperform the models with constant learning rates since their classification performances for class 1 are much better than the other models.

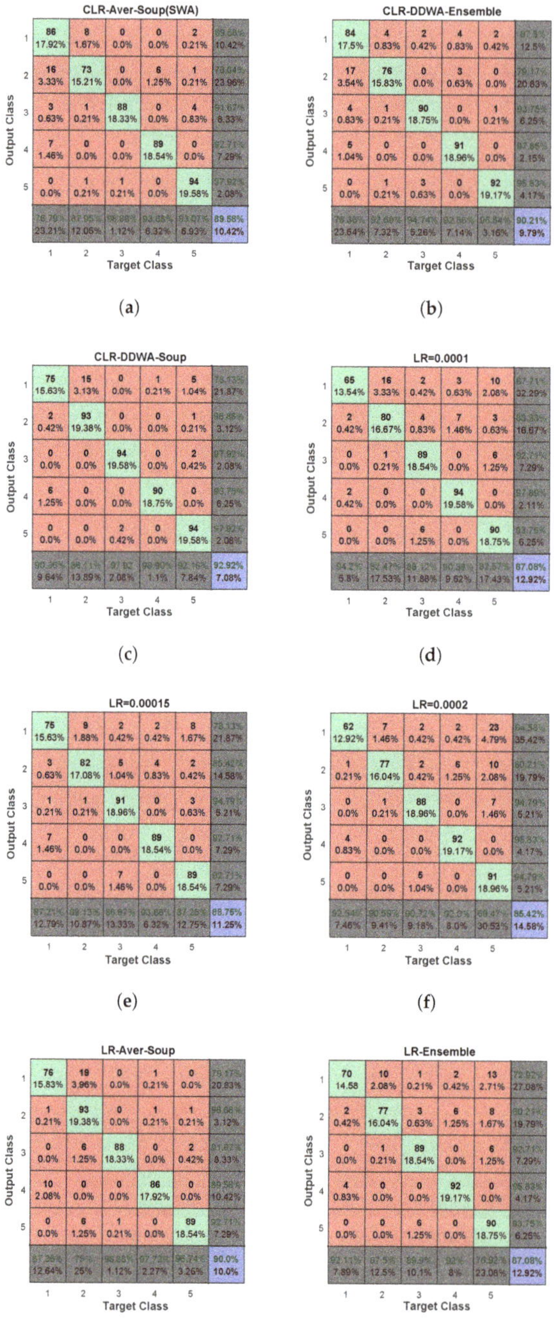

Figure 5. Confusion matrix of the models based on ResNet. (**a**) CLR-Aver-Soup (SWA); (**b**) CLR-DDWA-Ensemble; (**c**) CLR-DDWA-Soup; (**d**) LR = 0.0001; (**e**) LR = 0.00015; (**f**) LR = 0.0002; (**g**) LR-Aver-Soup; (**h**) LR-Ensemble.

We also provide the top 8 ranking ingredient models as well as their accuracy and diversity values, as shown in Table 4.

Table 4. Ranking of the ingredient models on the SCAN dataset.

Model	Acc	Div	$Rank_{Acc}$	$Rank_{Div}$	$Rank_{Final}$
model_84	0.908	0.232	1	1	2
model_51	0.864	0.201	7	3	10
model_60	0.880	0.157	2	8	10
model_57	0.862	0.178	8	5	13
model_27	0.857	0.159	9	6	15
model_87	0.872	0.129	4	11	15
model_75	0.878	0.115	3	12	15
model_30	0.855	0.157	11	7	18

In Tables 4 and 5, the first column represents the names of ingredient models. The second and third columns represent the accuracy and diversity values of each ingredient model, respectively. Moreover, the last three columns represent the ranks of accuracy, diversity, and the final ranking. The final ranking is obtained by simply adding $\mathbf{Rank_{Acc}}$ and $\mathbf{Rank_{Div}}$. We can see from Table 4 that the proposed DDWA method selects ingredient models based on the combination of accuracy and diversity. From the last line of Table 4, it can be seen that even the 11th most accurate ingredient model can be selected by DDWA, which has the advantage of approaching the optimal solution from a wider range.

Table 5. Ranking of the ingredient models on the BreakHis dataset.

Model	Acc	Div	$Rank_{Acc}$	$Rank_{Div}$	$Rank_{Final}$
model_39	0.883	0.049	1	1	2
model_42	0.883	0.047	2	2	4
model_18	0.867	0.044	4	3	7
model_15	0.873	0.043	3	4	7
model_27	0.863	0.043	6	5	11
model_57	0.865	0.041	5	7	12
model_54	0.857	0.041	9	8	17
model_24	0.858	0.040	8	9	17

Figures 6 and 7 show the polylines, representing the accuracies of different models by changing p from 6% to 10% on two datasets. It can be seen that it is not that the more ingredients in the soup, the higher the accuracy; the best classification results can be achieved when the components have the ability to approximate the expected value of the error basin, as depicted in Figure 1.

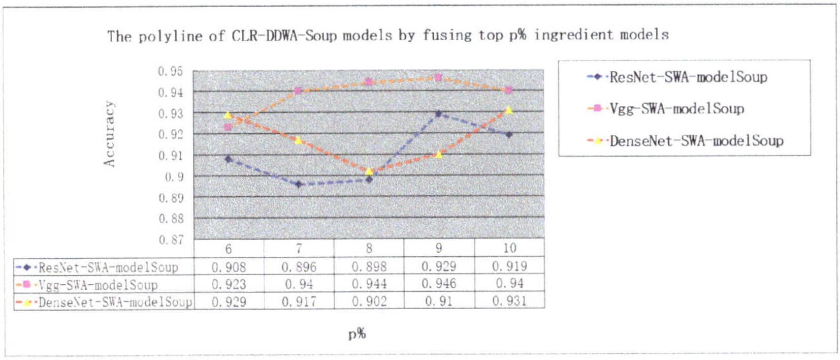

Figure 6. The accuracy of the polyline representing CLR-DDWA-Soup, fusing the top p% ingredient models on the SCAN dataset.

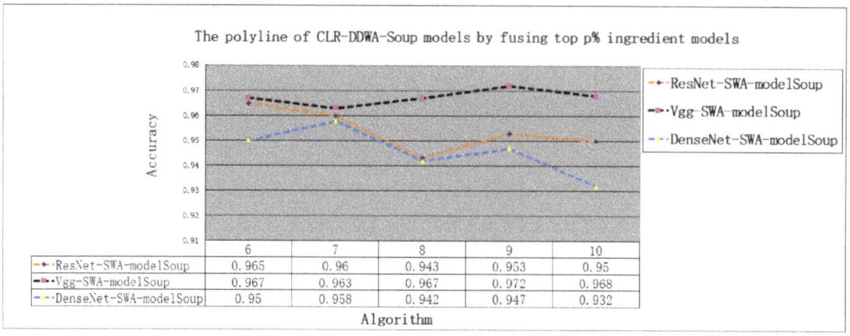

Figure 7. The accuracy of the polyline representing CLR-DDWA-Soup, fusing the top $p\%$ ingredient models on the BreakHis dataset.

Figures 8 and 9 show the accuracies of the SCAN and BreakHis datasets for ensemble and soup models based on different ingredient models, i.e., ResNet, VGG, and DenseNet. It can be seen that no single model can achieve the best classification performance in all ingredient models. For CLR-DDWA-Soup, the soup model based on VGG achieves the best performance. The reason may be that the features of the training images in the SCAN dataset are relatively salient and can be effectively extracted via a relatively standard convolutional neural network. In addition, the soup model based on ResNet and DenseNet demonstrates relatively close classification results, which are greatly improved compared to the standard SWA model and the three models with constant learning rates. The highest increase rate reached 8.78%.

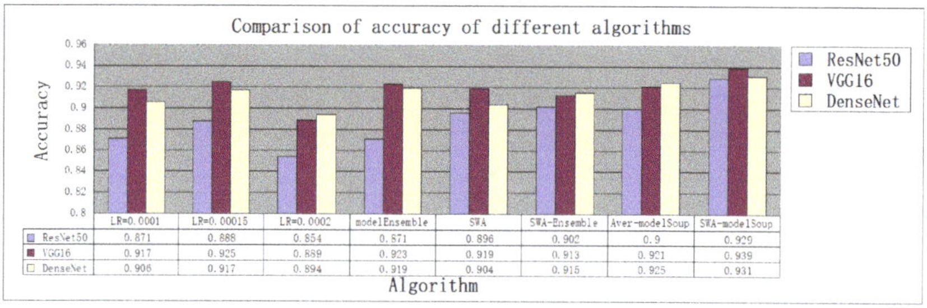

Figure 8. Accuracies of different models on the SCAN dataset.

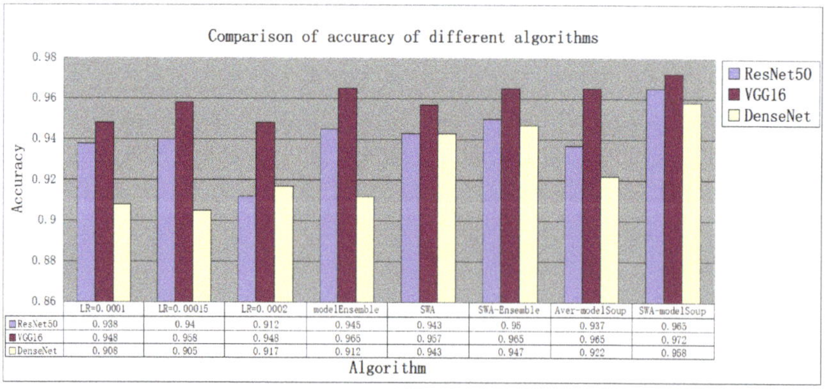

Figure 9. Accuracies of different models on the BreakHis dataset.

Figure 10 shows the receiver operating characteristic (ROC) curves of the models on the BreakHis dataset. It is a curve drawn according to a series of different two-classification methods (cut-off value or determination threshold), with the true positive rate (sensitivity) representing the ordinate and the false positive rate representing the abscissa. The ROC curve can easily determine the ability of a model to recognize samples at a certain threshold. We can see that CLR-DDWA-Soup achieves the largest area under the curve (AUC) among all methods. The larger the AUC, the higher the sensitivity; the lower the misclassification rate, the better the performance of the model.

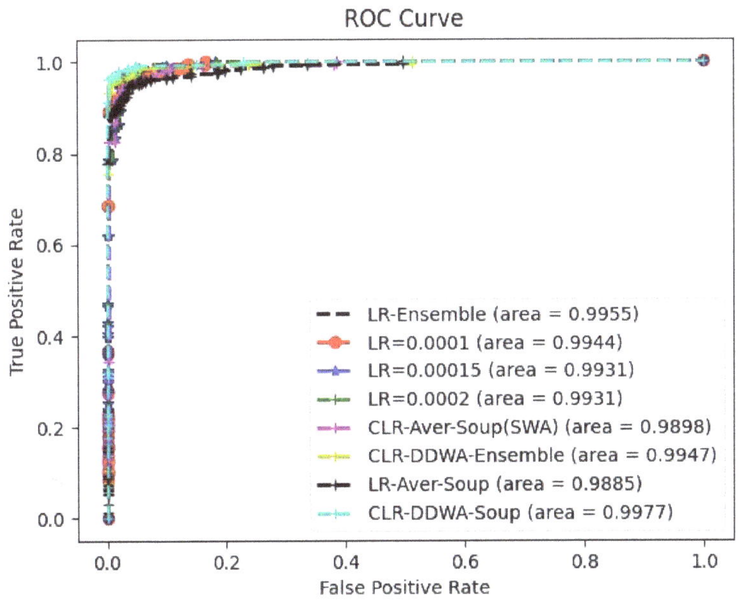

Figure 10. ROC curves of the models on the BreakHis dataset.

As indicated by Figure 1, averaging the weights of the ingredient models that are located on the edge of the error basin and that have large diversity can result in a model whose loss is closer to the expected value of the error basin. We interpolate the weights of the two ingredient models to obtain a path through the error basin according to Equation (8). The interpolation parameter γ is set to $\{0, \frac{1}{4}, \frac{1}{3}, \frac{1}{2}, \frac{2}{3}, \frac{3}{4}, 1\}$. The accuracy of the model with interpolated weights at each point is recorded, as shown in Figure 11. The x-axis coordinates represent various values of γ and the y-axis coordinates represent the model accuracies.

We can see from Figure 11 that for each specific model category (ResNet, VGG, DenseNet), the error variation of the weight interpolation model on the two datasets is always kept within a small fluctuation range, i.e., $\tau \leq 0.017$. This result confirms the conclusion that the model selected by the DDWA strategy is located at the edge of the error basin, which shows its effectiveness.

Finally, we present the results of the Friedman test conducted to evaluate the performance of the methods. The Friedman test [40] is a non-parametric test method that uses rank to realize whether there are significant differences in multiple population distributions. The principle hypothesis is that there is no significant difference in multiple population distributions from multiple paired samples. In the field of machine learning, the Friedman test is often used to compare the performances of multiple algorithms, which can verify whether there are significant differences among multiple learning algorithms as a whole.

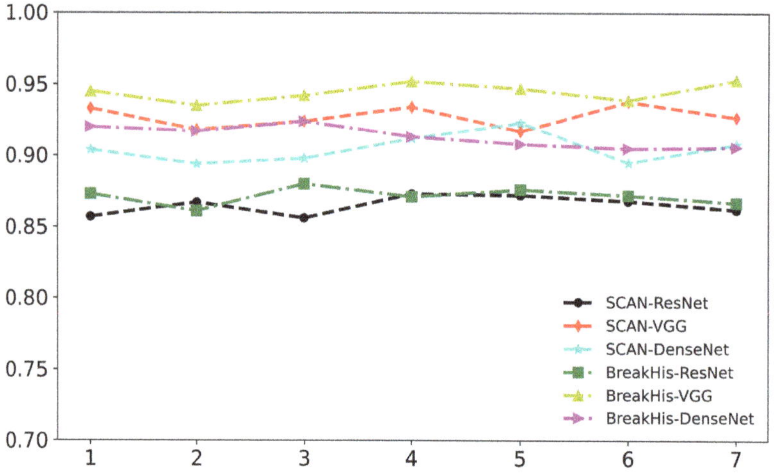

Figure 11. Model losses with interpolated weights on the SCAN and BreakHis datasets.

Let I and J denote the numbers of methods and datasets. In the Friedman test, we first calculate the average accuracy of each algorithm running on different datasets, denoted as $V = (v_{ij})$, where v_{ij} represents the accuracy of the ith model on the jth dataset. We then sort v_{ij} in descending order for each dataset and determine the rank values of each algorithm. So far, the Friedman test involves converting the table representing the original experimental results, denoted as $V = (v_{ij})$, into the rank table $R = (r_{ij})$. In this study, there are 3 base models, 9 methods, and 2 datasets used for the evaluation. We performed the Friedman test on each dataset with different base models. Hence, the size of the ranking matrix R is $(9,3)$, i.e., $I = 3 \times 9$ and $J = 2$. The original hypothesis is that the performances of I different algorithms are similar. The statistic of the Friedman test F_f is defined as follows:

$$F_f = \frac{12 \times J}{I \times (I+1)} \left[\sum_{i=1}^{I} \overline{R}_i^2 - \frac{I \times (I+1)^2}{4} \right] \tag{16}$$

F_f asymptotically obeys the χ^2 distribution with a degree of freedom $I-1$ when $I > 5$ and $J > 10$. The corresponding value of p is defined as:

$$p = P(\chi^2_{I-1} \geq F_f) \tag{17}$$

When the p-value is less than the given significance level α, we reject the original hypothesis, meaning that the I algorithms have significant differences in the performance. Otherwise, we accept the original hypothesis, meaning that the I algorithms have no significant differences in performance.

Table 6 shows the ranking of the models on both datasets in a Friedman test. There are three values in each cell, representing the average ranking of the method on the SCAN dataset, the average ranking on the BreakHis dataset, and the average ranking of the model on the two datasets. The last column is the total ranking, which is obtained by averaging the rankings on two datasets and three base models. In our study, $I = 3 \times 9$ and $J = 2$, meaning that the values do not meet the requirements of Equation (17). Therefore, it is necessary to look up the table to determine the value of p. Thus, we have $p = 0.006$. In the field of machine learning, we usually presuppose that α ranges from 0.05 to 0.1. Since the p-value is less than α, we need to reject the original hypothesis, which suggests that there are significant differences in the performances among the I algorithms being compared across the datasets.

Table 6. Rankings of the models on SCAN and BreakHis in a Friedman test (SCAN/BreakHis/dataset average).

Model	ResNet	VGG	DenseNet	Average
LR = 0.0001	23.0/17.0/20.0	9.5/10.5/10.0	13.0/23.0/18.0	16.0
LR = 0.00015	24.0/16.0/20.0	3.5/7.0/5.25	9.5/24.0/16.75	14.0
LR = 0.0002	21.5/21.5/21.5	16.0/10.5/13.25	15.0/20.0/17.5	17.4
LR-Ensemble	21.5/13.0/17.25	5.0/3.5/4.25	7.0/21.5/14.25	11.9
LR-Aver-Soup	19.0/18.0/18.5	6.0/3.5/4.75	3.5/19.0/11.25	11.5
CLR-Aver-Soup(SWA)	18.0/14.5/16.25	8.0/8.0/8.0	14.0/14.5/14.25	12.8
CLR-DDWA-Ensemble	20.0/9.0/14.5	12.0/3.5/7.75	11.0/12.0/11.5	11.25
CLR-DDWA-Soup	**17.0/3.5/10.25**	**1.0/1.0/1.0**	**2.0/6.0/4.0**	**5.08**

The smaller the rank value of the model, the better the classification effect. We highlight the smallest rank value in each column in Table 6. It can be seen that the proposed CLR-DDWA-Soup model achieves the best results, which shows its effectiveness.

4.4. Model Complexity

The computational complexity of the proposed model includes three aspects. The first is the computational complexity of training the component models. The component model mainly consists of ResNet50, VGG19, and DenseNet121, and the computational complexity of fine-tuning them is related to the size of the model parameters. Please refer to [34–36] for the model parameter information and computational complexity. The second aspect is the computational complexity of ingredient model fusion. For a simple weight-averaging fusion strategy, the weights of each ingredient model are simply averaged. For DDWA, the NDS algorithm needs to be used to sort the ingredient models, resulting in a total computational complexity of $o(n \log n)$, where n is the number of ingredient models to be sorted. The third is the time complexity of inference. Since the model in this paper is a single model after fusion, the computational complexity of inference remains the same as that of a single ingredient model.

5. Discussion

Our rationale for proposing that the model performs well can be attributed to the following factors. On the one hand, during the training of ingredient models, different hyperparameters are fully utilized. Averaging the model weights in different training stages can result in a model that is closer to the optimal solution. On the other hand, using the DDWA model selection strategy to rank and select the ingredient models, we can further improve the performance of the weight fusion model.

Compared to ensemble learning and other model fusion strategies, the proposed model soup has the following advantages. Firstly, in terms of training and inference costs, model soup has certain advantages. In terms of training costs, the training strategy used by model soup is to fine-tune models with different training parameters. Each ingredient model is further trained on a pre-trained model, so the overall training cost is much smaller than starting from scratch. In terms of inference costs, the model soup approach involves averaging, selectively averaging, or weighted averaging the weights of all ingredient models, ultimately resulting in a single model. On the other hand, ensemble learning performs voting or selectively weighting the inference results of n different models, so the inference cost is n times that of model soup. Secondly, in terms of model interpretability, model soup requires the weight structure of the model to be consistent, and its optimal solution estimate is supported by the error basin theory of the loss functions, which has good interpretability. However, for ensemble learning strategies, the component models have different structures and mainly estimate the error bound of the ensemble model through the diversity and accuracy of the component models, so the interpretability is not as good as model soup.

The proposed model has the following limitations. First, the premise of merging ingredient models in the weight space is that the weight structures of each model must be consistent, which limits the diversity of ingredient models, including structural diversity and model type diversity. This kind of model diversity is good at preventing over-fitting during training. Secondly, limited by the error basin minimization theory of the loss function, the model soup proposed in this paper seems to perform better when fine-tuning the pre-training model, and model fine-tuning is easier to satisfy the condition that each component model is located at the edge of the error basin; moreover, the essence of the model soup involves the estimation of the optimal point in the error basin. For ingredient models trained from scratch, the model soup strategy does not lead to significant performance gains. Thirdly, in order to improve the diversity of component models, the model fine-tuning process relies heavily on the adjustment of training parameters, such as CLR, the type and strength of data enhancement, and the optimizer choice, which will increase the training workload and make it challenging to achieve the best training plan.

6. Conclusions

In this paper, we propose a model fusion method in the weight space with a ranking-based model selection strategy. The DDWA strategy selects ingredient models based on accuracy and diversity, causing the selected models to scatter around the edge of the error basin, which makes the weight averaging of the model more efficient. The proposed method can be used in model training or fine-tuning tasks and is especially suitable for medical image classification scenarios with only a small number of training samples. At the same time, compared with ensemble models, our model has lower inference overhead, which is especially suitable for application scenarios with limited computing resources.

Upcoming research will focus on two key areas. The initial aspect will aim to implement the ensemble strategy into the proposed weight fusion model. The second aspect will involve the theoretical derivation of error bounds for the ensemble weight fusion model, considering different strategies.

Author Contributions: Conceptualization, G.Z. and Z.-F.L.; methodology, Z.-F.L.; software, Y.-Q.C.; formal analysis, G.Z.; investigation, Y.-Q.C.; resources, H.-T.L.; original draft preparation, G.Z.; review and editing, G.Z. and Z.-F.L.; visualization, H.-T.L.; project administration, G.Z. and W.-J.S. All authors have read and agreed to the published version of the manuscript.

Funding: This work was funded by the National Natural Science Foundation of China (NSFC) under grant 81573827 and 81373883, the Basic Research Project (Dengfeng hospital) jointly Funded by Guangzhou City and the School under grant 202201020586, the Science and Technology Projects in Guangzhou under grant 202102080252, and the Key Platforms and Scientific Research Projects in Universities in Guangdong Province under grant 2020KCXTD053.

Data Availability Statement: No new data were created or analyzed in this study. Data sharing is not applicable to this article.

Conflicts of Interest: The authors declare no conflict of interest.

References

1. Snead, D.R.; Tsang, Y.W.; Meskiri, A.; Kimani, P.K.; Crossman, R.; Rajpoot, N.M.; Blessing, E.; Chen, K.; Gopalakrishnan, K.; Matthews, P.; et al. Validation of digital pathology imaging for primary histopathological diagnosis. *Histopathology* **2016**, *68*, 1063–1072. [CrossRef]
2. Saltz, J.; Gupta, R.; Hou, L.; Kurc, T.; Singh, P.; Nguyen, V.; Samaras, D.; Shroyer, K.R.; Zhao, T.; Batiste, R.; et al. Spatial organization and molecular correlation of tumor-infiltrating lymphocytes using deep learning on pathology images. *Cell Rep.* **2018**, *23*, 181–193. [CrossRef]
3. Panayides, A.S.; Amini, A.; Filipovic, N.D.; Sharma, A.; Tsaftaris, S.A.; Young, A.; Foran, D.; Do, N.; Golemati, S.; Kurc, T.; et al. AI in medical imaging informatics: Current challenges and future directions. *IEEE J. Biomed. Health Inform.* **2020**, *24*, 1837–1857. [CrossRef] [PubMed]
4. LeCun, Y.; Bengio, Y.; Hinton, G. Deep learning. *Nature* **2015**, *521*, 436–444. [CrossRef]
5. Shinde, P.P.; Shah, S. A review of machine learning and deep learning applications. In Proceedings of the 2018 Fourth International Conference on Computing Communication Control and Automation (ICCUBEA), Pune, India, 16–18 August 2018; pp. 1–6.
6. Li, Y.; Huang, C.; Ding, L.; Li, Z.; Pan, Y.; Gao, X. Deep learning in bioinformatics: Introduction, application, and perspective in the big data era. *Methods* **2019**, *166*, 4–21. [CrossRef]
7. Nichita, A. A Series-Based Deep Learning Approach to Lung Nodule Image Classification. *Cancers* **2023**, *15*, 843.

8. Deng, J.; Dong, W.; Socher, R.; Li, L.J.; Li, K.; Fei-Fei, L. Imagenet: A large-scale hierarchical image database. In Proceedings of the 2009 IEEE Conference on Computer Vision and Pattern Recognition, Miami, FL, USA, 20–25 June 2009; pp. 248–255.
9. Dai, Z.; Liu, H.; Le, Q.V.; Tan, M. CoAtNet: Marrying Convolution and Attention for All Data Sizes. *arXiv* **2021**, arXiv:2106.04803.
10. Hu, L.S.; Yoon, H.; Eschbacher, J.M.; Baxter, L.C.; Dueck, A.C.; Nespodzany, A.; Smith, K.A.; Nakaji, P.; Xu, Y.; Wang, L.; et al. Accurate patient-specific machine learning models of glioblastoma invasion using transfer learning. *Am. J. Neuroradiol.* **2019**, *40*, 418–425. [CrossRef]
11. Sheehan, S.; Mawe, S.; Cianciolo, R.E.; Korstanje, R.; Mahoney, J.M. Detection and classification of novel renal histologic phenotypes using deep neural networks. *Am. J. Pathol.* **2019**, *189*, 1786–1796. [CrossRef]
12. Roster, K.; Connaughton, C.; Rodrigues, F.A. Forecasting new diseases in low-datasettings using transfer learning. *arXiv* **2022**, arXiv:2204.05059.
13. Han, W.; Johnson, C.; Gaed, M.; Gómez, J.A.; Moussa, M.; Chin, J.L.; Pautler, S.; Bauman, G.S.; Ward, A.D. Histologic tissue components provide major cues for machine learning-based prostate cancer detection and grading on prostatectomy specimens. *Sci. Rep.* **2020**, *10*, 9911. [CrossRef]
14. Hassan, S.A.; Sayed, M.S.; Abdalla, M.I.; Rashwan, M.A. Breast cancer masses classification using deep convolutional neural networks and transfer learning. *Multimed. Tools Appl.* **2020**, *79*, 30735–30768. [CrossRef]
15. Liu, W.; Mo, J.; Zhong, F. Class Imbalanced Medical Image Classification Based on Semi-Supervised Federated Learning. *Appl. Sci.* **2023**, *13*, 2109. [CrossRef]
16. Izmailov, P.; Podoprikhin, D.; Garipov, T.; Vetrov, D.; Wilson, A.G. Averaging weights leads to wider optima and better generalization. *arXiv* **2018**, arXiv:1803.05407.
17. Wortsman, M.; Ilharco, G.; Gadre, S.Y.; Roelofs, R.; Gontijo-Lopes, R.; Morcos, A.S.; Namkoong, H.; Farhadi, A.; Carmon, Y.; Kornblith, S.; et al. Model soups: Averaging weights of multiple fine-tuned models improves accuracy without increasing inference time. *arXiv* **2022**, arXiv:2203.05482.
18. Choshen, L.; Venezian, E.; Slonim, N.; Katz, Y. Fusing finetuned models for better pretraining. *arXiv* **2022**, arXiv:2204.03044.
19. Dansereau, C.; Sobral, M.; Bhogal, M.; Zalai, M. Model soups to increase inference without increasing compute time. *arXiv* **2023**, arXiv:2301.10092.
20. Draxler, F.; Veschgini, K.; Salmhofer, M.; Hamprecht, F. Essentially no barriers in neural network energy landscape. In Proceedings of the 35th International Conference on Machine Learning, Stockholm, Sweden, 10–15 July 2018.
21. Smith, L.N. Cyclical learning rates for training neural networks. In Proceedings of the 2017 IEEE Winter Conference on Applications of Computer Vision (WACV), Santa Rosa, CA, USA, 24–31 March 2017.
22. Wei, L.; Wan, S.; Guo, J.; Wong, K.K. A novel hierarchical selective ensemble classifier with bioinformatics application. *Artif. Intell. Med.* **2017**, *83*, 82–90. [CrossRef]
23. Smith, L.N.; Topin, N. Exploring loss function topology with cyclical learning rates. *arXiv* **2017**, arXiv:1702.04283.
24. Garipov, T.; Izmailov, P.; Podoprikhin, D.; Vetrov, D.P.; Wilson, A.G. Loss Surfaces, Mode Connectivity, and Fast Ensembling of DNNs. In Proceedings of the Advances in Neural Information Processing Systems 31 (NeurIPS 2018), Montreal, QC, Canada, 3–8 December 2018.
25. Jain, P.; Kakade, S.M.; Kidambi, R.; Netrapalli, P.; Sidford, A. Parallelizing Stochastic Gradient Descent for Least Squares Regression: Mini-batching, Averaging, and Model Misspecification. *J. Mach. Learn. Res.* **2018**, *18*, 1–42.
26. Guo, H.; Jin, J.; Liu, B. Stochastic Weight Averaging Revisited. *Appl. Sci.* **2023**, *13*, 2935.
27. Neyshabur, B.; Sedghi, H.; Zhang, C. What is being transferred in transfer learning? *Adv. Neural Inf. Process. Syst.* **2020**, *33*, 512–523.
28. Hameed, Z.; Zahia, S.; Garcia-Zapirain, B.; Javier Aguirre, J.; María Vanegas, A. Breast cancer histopathology image classification using an ensemble of deep learning models. *Sensors* **2020**, *20*, 4373. [CrossRef] [PubMed]
29. Sohail, A.; Khan, A.; Nisar, H.; Tabassum, S.; Zameer, A. Mitotic nuclei analysis in breast cancer histopathology images using deep ensemble classifier. *Med. Image Anal.* **2021**, *72*, 102121. [CrossRef]
30. Kumar, D.; Batra, U. Classification of Invasive Ductal Carcinoma from histopathology breast cancer images using Stacked Generalized Ensemble. *J. Intell. Fuzzy Syst.* **2021**, *40*, 4919–4934. [CrossRef]
31. Ahuja, S.; Panigrahi, B.K.; Dey, N.; Rajinikanth, V.; Gandhi, T.K. Deep transfer learning-based automated detection of COVID-19 from lung CT scan slices. *Appl. Intell.* **2021**, *51*, 571–585. [CrossRef] [PubMed]
32. Lawton, S.; Viriri, S. Detection of COVID-19 from CT Lung Scans Using Transfer Learning. *Comput. Intell. Neurosci.* **2021**, *2021*, 5527923. [CrossRef]
33. Jangam, E.; Barreto, A.A.D.; Annavarapu, C.S.R. Automatic detection of COVID-19 from chest CT scan and chest X-Rays images using deep learning, transfer learning and stacking. *Appl. Intell.* **2022**, *52*, 2243–2259. [CrossRef]
34. He, K.; Zhang, X.; Ren, S.; Sun, J. Deep residual learning for image recognition. In Proceedings of the IEEE Conference on Computer Vision and Pattern Recognition, Las Vegas, NV, USA, 27–30 June 2016; pp. 770–778.
35. Simonyan, K.; Zisserman, A. Very deep convolutional networks for large-scale image recognition. *arXiv* **2014**, arXiv:1409.1556.
36. Huang, G.; Liu, Z.; van der Maaten, L.; Weinberger, K.Q. Densenet: Densely connected convolutional networks. In Proceedings of the IEEE Computer Society Conference on Computer Vision and Pattern Recognition, Honolulu, HI, USA, 21–26 July 2017; Volume 30, pp. 82–84.

37. Cubuk, E.D.; Zoph, B.; Shlens, J.; Le, Q.V. RandAugment: Practical automated data augmentation with a reduced search space. In Proceedings of the IEEE/CVF Conference on Computer Vision and Pattern Recognition Workshops, Seattle, WA, USA, 14–19 June 2020; pp. 702–703.
38. Lu, Z.; Wu, X.; Zhu, X.; Bongard, J. Ensemble pruning via individual contribution ordering. In Proceedings of the 16th ACM SIGKDD International Conference on Knowledge Discovery and Data Mining, Washington, DC, USA, 25–28 July 2010; pp. 871–880.
39. Sahu, A.K.; Sahu, M.; Patro, P.; Sahu, G.; Nayak, S.R. Dual image-based reversible fragile watermarking scheme for tamper detection and localization. *Pattern Anal. Appl.* **2023**, *26*, 571–590. [CrossRef]
40. Demiar, J.; Schuurmans, D. Statistical Comparisons of Classifiers over Multiple Data Sets. *J. Mach. Learn. Res.* **2006**, *7*, 1–30.

applied sciences

MDPI

Article

Enhancing an Imbalanced Lung Disease X-ray Image Classification with the CNN-LSTM Model

Julio Fachrel [1], Anindya Apriliyanti Pravitasari [1,*], Intan Nurma Yulita [2], Mulya Nurmansyah Ardhisasmita [3] and Fajar Indrayatna [1]

1 Department of Statistics, Faculty of Mathematics and Natural Sciences, Universitas Padjadjaran, Bandung 45363, Indonesia; julio19001@mail.unpad.ac.id (J.F.); fajar.indrayatna@unpad.ac.id (F.I.)
2 Department of Computer Science, Faculty of Mathematics and Natural Sciences, Universitas Padjadjaran, Bandung 45363, Indonesia; intan.nurma@unpad.ac.id
3 Department of Public Health, Faculty of Medicine, Universitas Padjadjaran, Bandung 45363, Indonesia; mulya@unpad.ac.id
* Correspondence: anindya.apriliyanti@unpad.ac.id

Abstract: Lung diseases have a significant impact on respiratory health, causing various symptoms and posing challenges in diagnosis and treatment. This research presents a methodology for classifying lung diseases using chest X-ray images, specifically focusing on COVID-19, pneumonia, and normal cases. The study introduces an optimal architecture for convolutional neural network (CNN) and long short-term memory (LSTM) models, considering evaluation metrics and training efficiency. Furthermore, the issue of imbalanced datasets is addressed through the application of some image augmentation techniques to enhance model performance. The most effective model comprises five convolutional blocks, two LSTM layers, and no augmentation, achieving an impressive F1 score of 0.9887 with a training duration of 91 s per epoch. Misclassifications primarily occurred in normal cases, accounting for only 3.05% of COVID-19 data. The pneumonia class demonstrated excellent precision, while the normal class exhibited high recall and an F1 score. Comparatively, the CNN-LSTM model outperformed the CNN model in accurately classifying chest X-ray images and identifying infected lungs. This research provides valuable insights for improving lung disease diagnosis, enabling timely and accurate identification of lung diseases, and ultimately enhancing patients' outcomes.

Keywords: lung diseases; COVID-19; pneumonia; X-ray; convolutional neural networks; long short-term memory

1. Introduction

Lung diseases encompass a wide range of disorders that are prevalent and linked to significant morbidity and mortality [1]. These disorders can significantly impact the respiratory system, including the lungs, airways, and pulmonary blood vessels. As critical organs responsible for the respiration process, the lungs play an essential role in providing oxygen to the body and eliminating carbon dioxide. However, lung diseases can interrupt this vital process, causing uncomfortable symptoms, such as fatigue, shortness of breath, wheezing, coughing, and chest pain. Diagnosing and treating lung diseases can be challenging due to the wide range of possible causes and symptoms [2]. Nevertheless, it is critical to identify and treat them early to enhance patient outcomes and lessen the burden of these conditions on society. With ongoing research and advances in technology, there is optimism for improving our understanding and management of various lung diseases.

One of the most widely discussed topics in the field of lung diseases today is COVID-19. The global impact of COVID-19 on lung health has been significant, resulting in a large number of hospitalizations and fatalities worldwide. COVID-19 has served as a painful reminder of the importance of respiratory health and the need for continued study, preparation, and cooperation to successfully handle lung diseases. The global response to the COVID-19 pandemic has stressed the interconnectedness between lung health and public health, pressing on the importance of ongoing study and joint efforts in the field of lung diseases. It is worth mentioning that many people who died from COVID-19 had severe chest congestion and a consequent large decrease in oxygen levels, which raised the risk of massive heart attacks [3]. On another note, pneumonia is also a type of lung disease characterized by inflammation in the small air sacs within the lungs. It can be caused by different pathogens, including bacteria, viruses, or fungi [4]. Interestingly, the signs and symptoms of pneumonia have similarities with COVID-19 [5]. Given this similarity and the fact that different diseases require different treatments [6], it becomes crucial to accurately identify specific diseases. This ensures that appropriate and distinct treatment approaches can be employed based on the specific lung disease. Because of that, this research aims to identify the classes as COVID-19, pneumonia, and normal.

Radiological images of the lungs provide an alternative approach to diagnosing lung infections. Clinical diagnostic tools, such as X-rays and computed tomography (CT), can effectively assess and describe the condition of the lungs. Although CT scans offer better detection sensitivity, X-ray radiography is more commonly utilized in clinical settings due to its advantages and conveniences, including lower cost and widespread availability in general hospitals [7]. Thus, X-ray radiography is preferred in many cases, serving as a practical and efficient method for diagnosing lung infections.

Detecting and classifying lung diseases using chest X-ray images is a challenging and complex task. To aid radiologists and accelerate the identification process, researchers have developed deep-learning models [8–10]. These models utilize advanced machine learning algorithms and neural networks to analyze and categorize X-ray images based on distinct patterns and features associated with various lung diseases. Furthermore, the emergence of COVID-19 has significantly increased the patient load, placing additional demands on radiologists to accurately identify and diagnose cases. This surge in cases has necessitated more time and energy from radiologists, highlighting the need for efficient and effective diagnostic tools. Deep learning is hoped to be a valuable tool in this context, enabling radiologists to handle the growing workload.

The goal of this study is to create an image classification model that uses deep-learning techniques to speed up the identification of lung diseases, thereby reducing the effort and time involved in the diagnostic process. This model will aid in effectively identifying patients exposed to COVID-19 and those with pneumonia. The major objective is to reduce mistakes and misdiagnoses in lung disease treatment, thereby improving patient care and outcomes. By enhancing the accuracy and efficiency of disease detection, this study endeavors to contribute to the overall optimization of lung disease management and reduce the potential for mishandling of such conditions.

The main contributions of this research are two-fold:

1. Implementation and selection of the optimal architecture of convolutional neural network (CNN) and long short-term memory (LSTM) deep-learning models for the classification of lung diseases using chest X-ray images. The selection process is based on evaluation metrics and training time, ensuring that the models are efficient and effective in accurately identifying different lung diseases;
2. Addressing the challenge of an imbalanced dataset by applying various image augmentation techniques. Imbalanced datasets, where certain classes have significantly fewer samples than others, can pose challenges in model training. By employing appropriate image augmentation methods, this research aims to improve the performance of the deep-learning models by artificially expanding the dataset and creating a more balanced representation of different lung diseases.

The remainder of this paper is structured as follows. Section 2 provides a comprehensive review of the existing scientific literature related to this research. Section 3 outlines the methodology employed in this research, including the collection and splitting of the dataset. Section 4 presents the results obtained from the experiments conducted in this study. Section 5 offers a comprehensive discussion of the findings, conclusions, and recommendations for future research.

2. The Literature Review

Tekerek and Al-Rawe [11] introduced a classification method based on deep learning to identify lung diseases from chest X-ray images, with a specific emphasis on detecting COVID-19. This approach aims to categorize chest X-ray images into three groups: normal; COVID-19; and viral pneumonia. It employs an eight-layer convolutional neural network that combines MobileNet [12] and DenseNet [13] models. The research findings indicate a precision value of 1.00 for COVID-19 and normal cases while achieving a precision of 0.79 for viral pneumonia. The recall values are 1.00 for normal and viral pneumonia and 0.69 for COVID-19. The F1 score is found to be 1.00 for normal, 0.79 for COVID-19, and 0.85 for viral pneumonia. The proposed method achieves an impressive accuracy of 96% and a ROC AUC score of 0.94. These outcomes showcase the remarkable accuracy of the proposed approach in diagnosing and classifying chest X-ray images, surpassing the performance of traditional CNN and MobileNet methods. The method's high precision and F1 score are particularly important for minimizing false negatives, thereby aiding in the prevention of disease transmission.

Gupta et al. [14] presented a method that uses deep-learning models, pre-processing techniques, and lung segmentation to improve the precision of COVID-19 detection in chest X-ray images. The study uses InceptionV3 [15] and U-Net [16], which are deep-learning models, to process and identify chest X-ray images as either COVID-19-negative or positive. By adding lung segmentation during pre-processing, this study aims to remove irrelevant surrounding information that could introduce bias and create inaccurate results. The results of this study show an amazing accuracy rate of approximately 99% for the most effective models in spotting COVID-19. However, this study also shows the effect of visual noise on model bias and underscores the value of lung segmentation in reducing bias and ensuring more consistent results. This study admits that the current models strongly rely on visible abnormalities in the lungs as signs of COVID-19, and further improvements are necessary to address this weakness.

Badrahadipura et al. [17] conducted a study utilizing the Inception ResNet-v2 [18] architecture and transfer learning to classify chest X-ray images into three categories: normal; viral pneumonia; and COVID-19. The dataset consisted of 3616 COVID-19 cases, 10,192 of normal cases, and 1345 cases of viral pneumonia. The model underwent two rounds of training. Initially, the Inception ResNet-v2 layers were frozen, preserving the weights and biases learned from the ImageNet dataset. Only the additional layers were added after the Inception ResNet-v2 was trained. In the second training phase, all layers were unfrozen, allowing for further fine-tuning of the entire model. This research highlighted that the model performed better in classifying images belonging to viral pneumonia and normal classes compared to the COVID-19 class, as indicated by higher precision, recall, and F1 scores. The overall accuracy of the model was reported to be 0.966, with an F1 score of 0.97. These findings demonstrate the potential of using the Inception ResNet-v2 architecture and transfer learning for accurate classification of chest X-ray images, particularly in distinguishing between viral pneumonia, normal, and COVID-19 cases, contributing to advancements in medical imaging and healthcare applications.

Abbas et al. [19] conducted a study to investigate the application of transfer learning using the DeTraC (Decompose, Transfer, and Compose) deep CNN architecture for COVID-19 chest X-ray classification. DeTraC incorporates a class decomposition mechanism to address irregularities presented in the image dataset. This study demonstrates the effectiveness of DeTraC in accurately classifying COVID-19 cases while also showcasing its robustness in handling data irregularities and the limited availability of training images. Through validation experiments with various pre-trained CNN models, VGG19 [20] emerged as the most successful model within the DeTraC framework. The experimental results highlight the impressive performance of DeTraC in detecting COVID-19 cases, achieving an accuracy of 93.1% with a sensitivity of 100% in accurately distinguishing COVID-19 X-ray images from both normal and severe acute respiratory syndrome cases.

Goyal and Singh [5] proposed a framework for detecting COVID-19 and pneumonia in chest X-ray images. The framework is divided into multiple steps, which include dataset gathering, picture quality improvement, ROI estimation, feature extraction, and illness classification. Two publicly accessible chest X-ray datasets are used, and picture quality is improved by utilizing such techniques as median filtering and histogram equalization. Various characteristics, such as visual, shape, texture, and intensity, are retrieved and normalized from each ROI picture. Soft computing approaches, such as ANN [21], SVM [22], KNN [23], ensemble classifiers [24], and a deep-learning classifier dubbed F-RNN-LSTM, are used for classification. The F-RNN-LSTM deep-learning architecture combines RNN and LSTM for enhanced disease categorization. Experiment findings show that the suggested framework is successful. When compared to previous approaches, the F-RNN-LSTM model achieves an accuracy of roughly 95% while requiring less computing effort.

Demir [25] introduced an innovative method for detecting COVID-19 from X-ray images by utilizing a deep LSTM model. The model is developed from scratch, offering a unique architecture specifically designed for this purpose. To enhance the model's performance, the study incorporates such pre-processing techniques as the Sobel gradient and marker-controlled watershed segmentation. This research conducts experiments on a combined public dataset consisting of 361 COVID-19, 500 pneumonia, and 200 normal chest X-ray images. The dataset is divided randomly into training and testing sets, with different ratios tested. The most favorable results are obtained when using an 80% training and 20% testing split. Impressively, the proposed model achieves a perfect 100% success rate across all performance metrics, including accuracy, sensitivity, specificity, and F-score. These findings are particularly remarkable considering the small size of the dataset used in the study.

Pustokhin et al. [26] introduced the RCAL-BiLSTM model, which combines ResNet [27], a class attention layer (CAL) [28], and a Bi-LSTM. The model comprises several stages, including preprocessing, using bilateral filtering [29], feature extraction, using RCAL-BiLSTM, and classification employing SoftMax. Feature extraction involves ResNet for extracting features, CAL for capturing discriminative class-based features, and Bi-LSTM for modeling class dependencies in both directions. The SoftMax layer is then used to classify the feature vectors into their respective feature maps. Experimental validation is performed on a dataset of chest X-ray images, and the results illustrate the superior performance of the RCAL-BiLSTM model. It achieves high sensitivity (93.28%), specificity (94.61%), precision (94.90%), accuracy (94.88%), F-score (93.10%), and kappa value (91.40%), highlighting the effectiveness of the proposed model for COVID-19 diagnosis.

Hamza et al. [30] proposed a CNN-LSTM architecture combined with an improved optimization algorithm to address the challenges of multisource fusion and redundant features. The dataset consisted of four classes: COVID-19; normal, viral pneumonia, and lung opacity. The framework includes contrast enhancement and data augmentation to improve the quality and quantity of training samples. Deep transfer learning is utilized in training a CNN-LSTM model and fine-tuning an EfficientNet [31] model for feature extraction. The overall accuracy achieved was 98.5%.

Fachrel et al. [32] compared two deep-learning models, namely, convolutional neural networks (CNN) and a combination of CNN and long short-term memory (LSTM). The dataset consists of 4095 CXR images (1400 of normal conditions, 1350 of COVID-19, and 1345 of pneumonia). Both CNN and CNN-LSTM models are evaluated using a confusion matrix and compared in terms of performance. The experimental results demonstrate that the CNN-LSTM model outperforms the CNN model, achieving an overall accuracy of approximately 98.78%. It also exhibits high precision and recall, reaching 99% and 98%, respectively. These findings suggest that the proposed CNN-LSTM model can contribute to fast and accurate COVID-19 detection.

The previous studies primarily focused on the development of deep-learning algorithms and certain preprocessing methods to classify lung diseases. Furthermore, the utilization of LSTM networks has been recognized as an effective approach to achieving higher performance scores [5,25,26,30,32]. To the best of our knowledge, the problem of imbalanced datasets has been given limited consideration in these studies. Therefore, our research aims to address this gap by focusing on selecting the optimal architecture for the CNN-LSTM model and tackling the challenges associated with imbalanced datasets. We plan to employ various image augmentation techniques to improve the model's performance and enhance its ability to handle imbalanced data.

3. Materials and Methods

In this section, we will provide a description of the dataset utilized, the models employed, the experimental setup, and the evaluation metrics used to assess the performance of the models.

3.1. Dataset

This study used a dataset from Kaggle [33,34] that contained three classes (COVID-19, normal, and pneumonia) shown in Figure 1. A total of 15,153 images (10,912 normal; 3616 COVID-19; and 1345 pneumonia) were used in this study, with 90% used for training and 10% used for validation. The proportion of splitting data can be seen in Table 1.

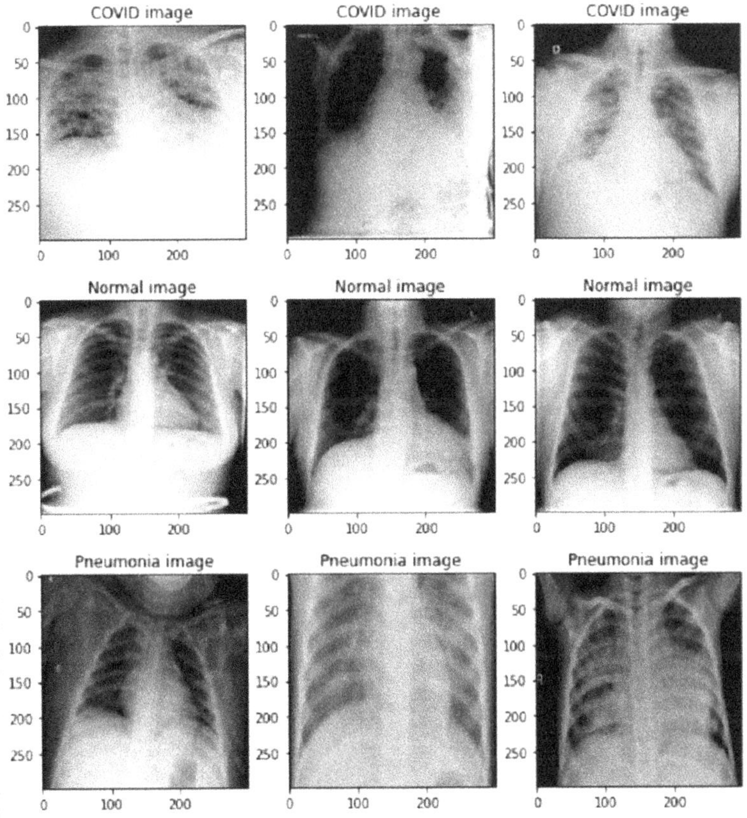

Figure 1. Images of normal, COVID-19, and pneumonia.

Table 1. Separating training and test data for each class.

	Normal	COVID-19	Pneumonia	Total
Training	9173	3255	1211	13,639
Validation	1019	361	134	1514
Total	10,912	3616	1345	15,153

3.2. Convolutional and Recurrent Networks: CNN and LSTM

The convolutional neural network (CNN) is a widely used algorithm for processing image data. It employs mathematical operations to learn from a network called a "convolution" [35]. The convolution layer, which is a crucial component of CNN, plays a vital role in feature extraction by utilizing local connections and shared characteristic weights [36]. It consists of linear and non-linear operations that work together to extract meaningful patterns from the input data [37]. The convolution layer's ability to extract important features is a key reason why CNN is well-suited for image data. Multiple filters within the convolution layer learn distinct features through a variety of weights [38]. These filters can be represented mathematically as $n \times n$ matrices, where each element corresponds to a weight. The filtering process is illustrated in Figure 2, where each pair of elements in the filter is multiplied and added to generate a single output value. This process is repeated for each filter, resulting in a "feature map" that highlights specific features in the input data. By employing multiple filters with different weights, the convolution layer effectively learns a diverse set of features, enabling it to identify and differentiate various objects or patterns in the input data.

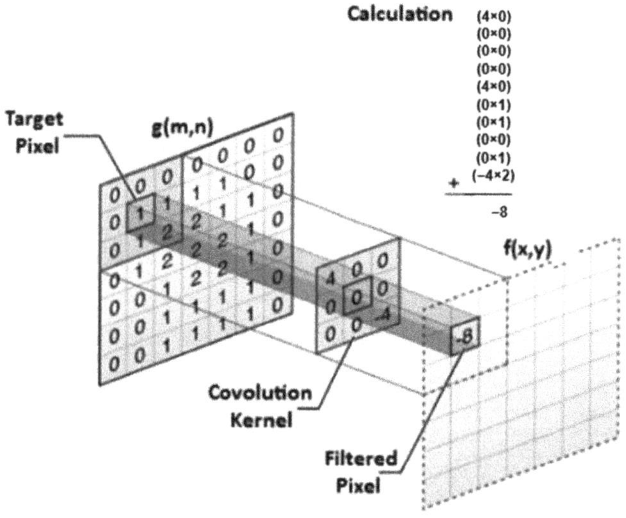

Figure 2. Illustration of the filtering process on the convolution layer (modified from [39]).

LSTM, a type of recurrent neural network (RNN), can effectively retain information over long periods and learn from inputs that are widely separated in time [40]. Unlike traditional RNNs, LSTM overcomes the problem of vanishing gradients and captures long-term dependencies by employing memory cells with specialized gating mechanisms [41]. Figure 3 illustrates the architecture of LSTM, where each memory cell consists of three types of gates (forget, input, and output) that control the information flow. The forget gate filters out small values, the input gate determines new information to be added to the memory, and the output gate determines whether to output the stored value. Additionally, each memory cell incorporates three sigmoid activation functions and one tanh activation function [42]. The tanh function maintains values within the range from -1 to 1, while the sigmoid function transforms the range from −1 to 1 to 0 to 1, preventing zero values from entering the memory cells. For a more detailed explanation of LSTM, refer to [43].

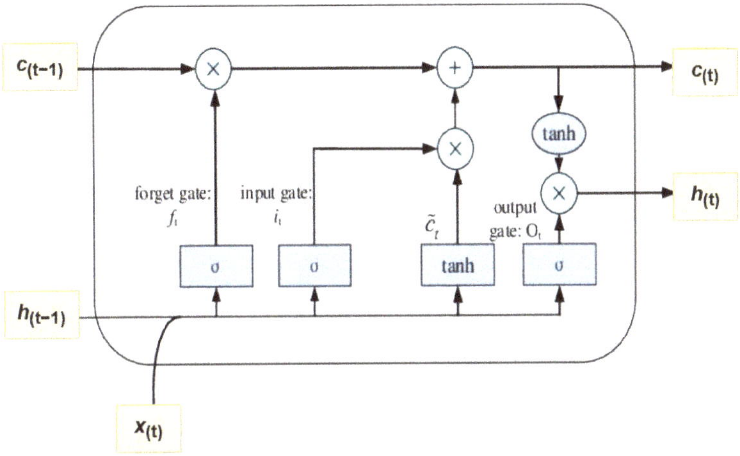

Figure 3. The architecture of the long short-term memory (LSTM) (modified from [44]).

3.3. CNN-LSTM Architecture

In the CNN-LSTM architecture, CNN is used to extract important features from an image, while LSTM replaces the fully connected role, which is to classify based on the features that have been extracted by CNN. By combining CNN and LSTM networks in this way, the CNN-LSTM architecture can handle both spatial and temporal information in an image, making it useful for classification. Figure 4 shows the architecture of the CNN-LSTM, where the LSTM layer is placed after the convolution layer and receives the output value from the last convolution layer for further classification.

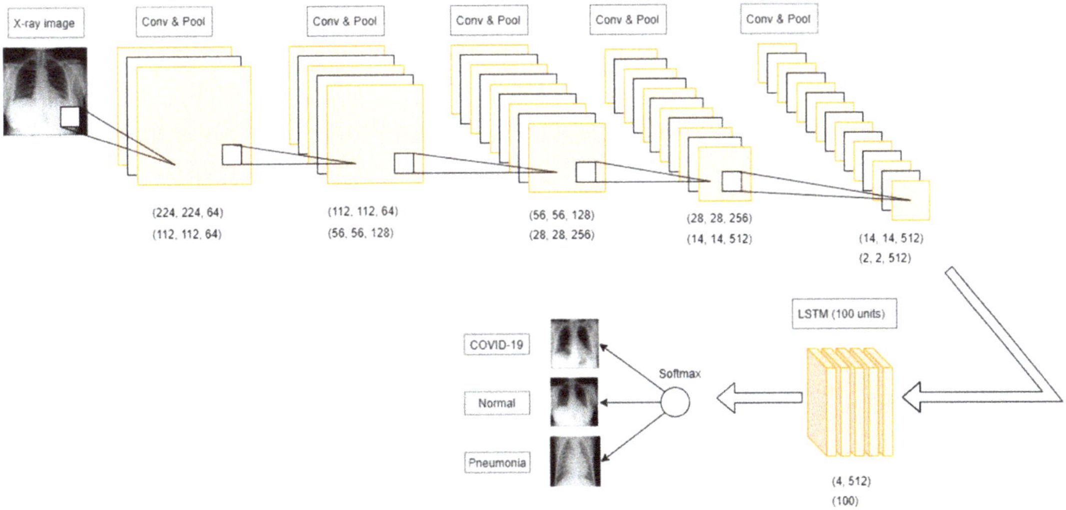

Figure 4. The architecture of CNN-LSTM.

In a fully connected layer, the connections between nodes in different layers are not specific to any particular sequence of inputs, and each node can only process one input at a time. On the other hand, the nodes in an LSTM layer are connected along the sequence of inputs, allowing the network to capture dependencies between elements in the sequence [45]. Additionally, LSTM employs a gating mechanism that enables it to selectively recall or forget information from previous time steps, allowing it to simulate long-term dependencies in the input sequence effectively. Furthermore, because of its ability to manage the problem of vanishing gradients (gradients that become very small during backpropagation), LSTM is more easily optimized than typical fully-connected networks [46].

3.4. Evaluation

3.4.1. Confusion Matrix

Confusion matrix is a method for evaluating the performance of a classification model in making predictions [47]. The confusion matrix generates scores for accuracy, precision, recall, and F1 score. This score is used to assess the model's performance. Predicted and actual classifications are shown in a $n \times n$ confusion matrix, where n is the number of classes [48]. There were three classes employed in this study: normal, COVID-19, and pneumonia. The form of the confusion matrix for the three classes can be seen in Table 2.

Table 2. Confusion matrix for three classes.

Actual	Predict		
	A	B	C
A	T_{AA}	F_{BA}	F_{CA}
B	F_{AB}	T_{BB}	F_{CB}
C	F_{AC}	F_{BC}	T_{CC}

In the three-class confusion matrix, there is a slight difference in calculating true positive, true negative, false positive, and false negative. In the context of class A in Table 2, the calculations for those values are as follows:

$$True\ Positive = T_{AA} \tag{1}$$

$$True\ Negative = T_{BB} + T_{CC} + F_{BC} + F_{CB} \tag{2}$$

$$False\ Positive = F_{AB} + F_{AC} \tag{3}$$

$$False\ Negative = F_{BA} + F_{CA} \tag{4}$$

From the confusion matrix, we can calculate the evaluation metric as follows:

$$\text{precision} = \frac{TP}{TP + FP} \tag{5}$$

$$\text{recall} = \frac{TP}{TP + FN} \tag{6}$$

$$\text{F1 score} = 2 \times \frac{\text{precision} \times \text{recall}}{\text{precision} + \text{recall}} = \frac{TP}{TP + \frac{1}{2}(FP + FN)} \tag{7}$$

In this case, we did not use accuracy because, when dealing with imbalanced data, where one class has significantly fewer instances than the others, accuracy can be misleading. In such cases, the F1 score is a more suitable evaluation metric as it takes into account both precision and recall. The F1 score is particularly useful in cases of unbalanced data. This is because the F1 score considers both false positives and false negatives, which are crucial in such cases to identify the model's performance in correctly predicting the minority class [49].

3.4.2. K-Fold Cross-Validation

K-fold cross-validation means performing data splits repeatedly k times. In this method, the data is first partitioned into k segments. Then k training iterations were carried out, and validation was carried out in such a way that in each iteration, there were k different test data conditions [50]. An illustration of the k-fold cross-validation process can be seen in Figure 5.

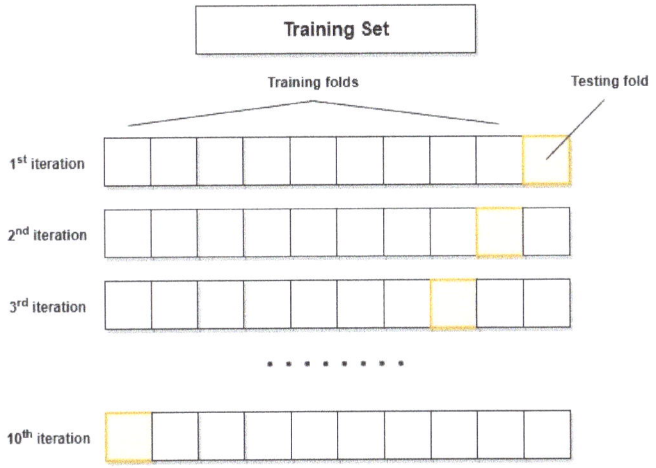

Figure 5. Illustration of K-fold cross-validation.

3.5. Experimental Setup

As shown in Figure 6, this study consists of several steps, including pre-processing, dataset splitting, selecting an appropriate architecture, and evaluating the best architecture. To ensure accurate and reliable predictions from a machine learning model, it is crucial to perform data pre-processing before training the model. This process involves transforming the data into a format suitable for the machine learning model. In this specific research, the images are resized to 224 × 224 pixels, and the pixel values are normalized by dividing them by 255. This transformation converts the range from 0–255 to 0–1, preparing the data for the model.

This research aims to explain the process of training a model to achieve accurate classification of X-ray images. The training will be conducted in two phases:

1. Determining the optimal number of deep-learning layers;
2. Applying image augmentation techniques.

To select the optimal method for achieving high classification accuracy, both stages will be evaluated using the F1-score metric. The experiment will maintain the same setup as presented in Table 3, with 65 epochs and a batch size of 32, ensuring consistency. Additionally, the Adam optimizer will be used with an initial learning rate of 5×10^{-6}. These hyperparameters were chosen based on previous experimentation and have been found to be effective for the task at hand [32]. By maintaining consistent hyperparameters across experiments, the obtained results can be easily compared and evaluated, leading to more reliable and accurate conclusions.

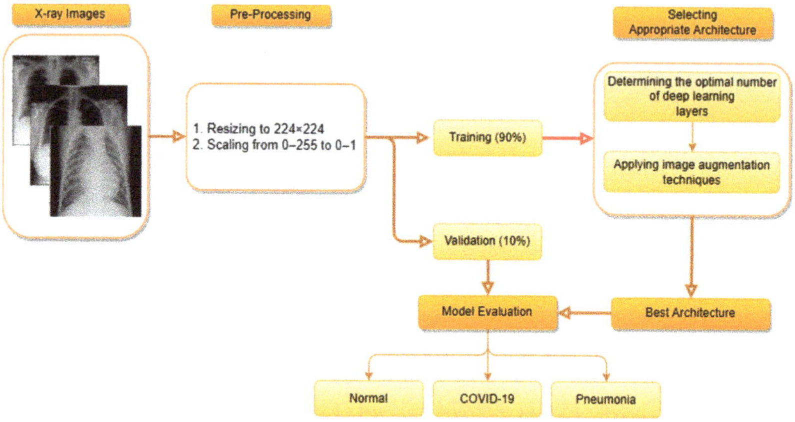

Figure 6. Research scheme.

Table 3. Hyperparameters Setup.

Hyperparameters	
Batch Size	32
Optimizer	Adam
Learning rate	5×10^{-6}
Epochs	65

In the first stage, experiments with various layer configurations will be conducted to establish the ideal number of deep-learning layers. This will involve building models with different numbers of layers. To increase the diversity of the training data, image augmentation techniques will be applied in the second step to the X-ray images. This will include transformations, such as rotation, flipping, and cropping, to generate new versions of the images for the model to learn from. The best augmentation techniques will be selected for use in the final model. Our aim is to develop a highly accurate model for X-ray image classification that can support medical diagnosis by incorporating the outcomes of both training phases.

4. Results and Discussion

4.1. Determining the Optimal Number of Deep-Learning Layers

In this section, there are two processes, determining the number of convolutional blocks and the number of LSTM layers. Two training scenarios were employed to determine the optimal number of convolutional blocks: one with four convolutional blocks and another with five convolutional blocks. Each convolutional block in this study consisted of two convolutional layers with a kernel size of 3 × 3. Following the convolution-al layers, there was one layer of batch normalization and, subsequently, a layer of max pooling with a pool size of 2 × 2. Additionally, a dropout layer with a parameter of 0.5 was added to the output layer in both scenarios.

Figure 7 illustrates the architecture consisting of four convolutional blocks, with each block employing a distinct number of convolutional filters. Specifically, the convolutional filters used were 64, 128, 256, and 512 for the corresponding blocks. Figure 8 illustrates the architecture with five convolutional blocks. This architecture is similar to the one with four convolutional blocks, with the addition of an extra block that has a convolutional filter size of 512.

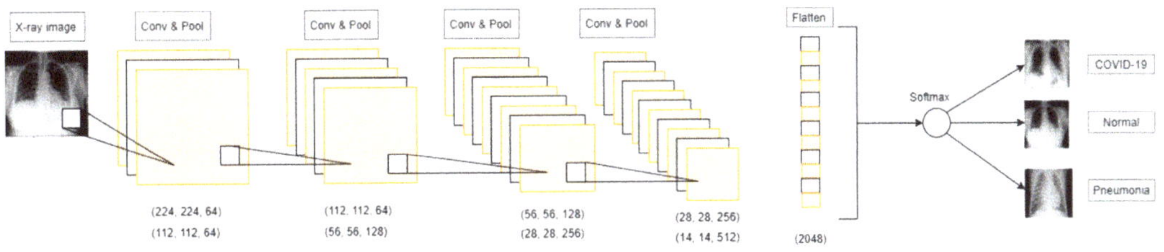

Figure 7. Convolutional neural network with 4 convolution blocks.

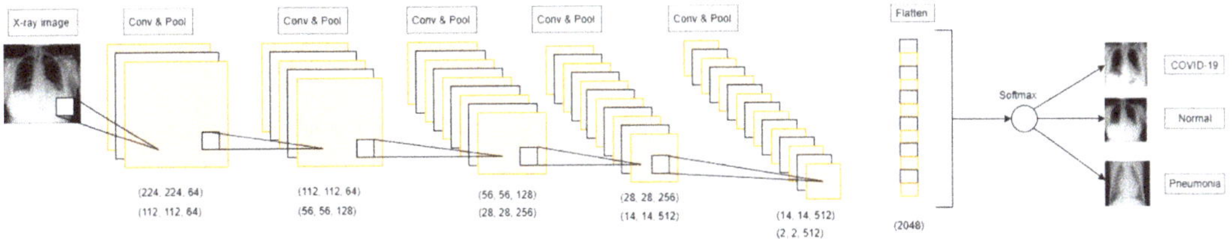

Figure 8. Convolutional neural network with 5 convolution blocks.

From Table 4, it can be concluded that the second scenario, which utilizes a convolutional neural network with five convolutional blocks, achieves better performance than scenario 1, with an F1 score of 0.97. This indicates that increasing the number of convolutional blocks in the model allows for deeper and more comprehensive learning of the input data, resulting in improved performance. As the best scenario involves using five convolutional blocks, for the next step, which is determining the number of LSTM layers, we will proceed with the five convolutional layers in the model.

Table 4. Results for the Number of Convolution Blocks.

Scenario	F1 Score
4 convolutional blocks	0.96
5 convolutional blocks	0.97

The next step involves determining the optimal number of LSTM layers. Two scenarios are conducted, one with one LSTM layer and another with two LSTM layers. Since the LSTM layer accepts two-dimensional input while the output of the convolutional layer is three-dimensional, we need to reshape the convolutional output value to match the input shape required by the LSTM layer. The output value of the initial convolution, which is (2, 2, 512), is reshaped (4, 512) to serve as the input for the LSTM layer.

Figure 9 presents the architecture of the CNN-LSTM model with one layer of LSTM. This architecture utilizes five convolutional blocks and incorporates an additional layer of LSTM with a unit size of 100. Consequently, the output shape of this model will be (100). Figure 10 presents the architecture with two layers of LSTM. This architecture is similar to the one with one layer of LSTM but includes an additional LSTM layer with a unit size of 50. As a result, the output shape will be (50).

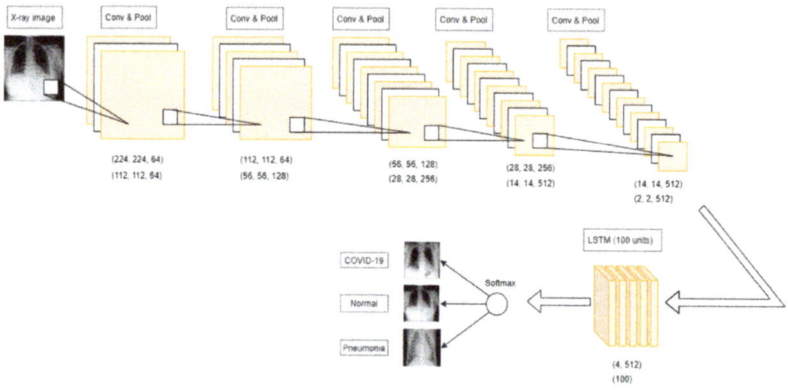

Figure 9. CNN-LSTM with 1 LSTM Layer.

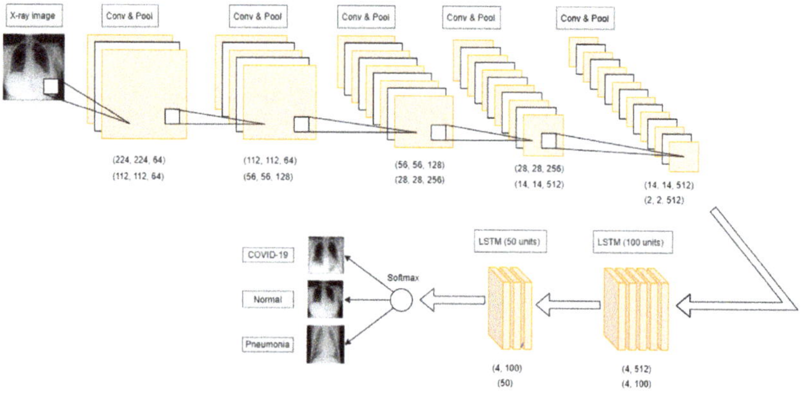

Figure 10. CNN-LSTM with 2 LSTM Layer.

Based on the findings presented in Table 5, it can be concluded that using two layers of LSTM leads to improved performance compared to using only one layer. The model with two LSTM layers achieves an F1 score of 0.99, indicating its effectiveness. This suggests that the deeper architecture with two layers of LSTM enables the model to capture more complex patterns and dependencies in the data, resulting in higher accuracy in classifying lung diseases. The additional layer allows for a more comprehensive analysis of sequential information and enhances the model's ability to make accurate predictions. Therefore, at this stage, it can be inferred that the optimal model utilizes five convolutional blocks and two LSTM layers.

Table 5. Results for the Number of LSTM layers.

Scenario	F1 Score
1 layer of LSTM	0.96
2 layers of LSTM	0.99

4.2. Applying Image Augmentation Techniques

This stage will involve model training by applying image augmentation techniques. Image augmentation is a method used to perform oversampling, which helps address imbalanced datasets by resampling the imbalanced classes [51]. In this study, the following three types of augmentations will be applied: rotation; shifting; and zooming.

The test results were obtained by applying image augmentation techniques, as shown in Table 6. Three augmentations yielded the best results. Firstly, a rotation of five degrees achieved an F1 score of 0.98. Secondly, a height shift, which involves vertically moving the image with a range of 0.1 (10% of the size of the image height), resulted in an F1 score of 0.98. Thirdly, a width shift, which involves horizontally shifting the image with a range of 0.1 (10% of the size of the image width), yielded an F1 score value of 0.98.

Table 6. Image augmentation test results.

Augmentation	F1 Score
Without augmentation	0.99
Rotate (5)	0.98
Rotate (10)	0.97
Rotate (15)	0.97
Zoom (0.1)	0.95
Zoom (0.2)	0.91
Heigh Shift (0.1)	0.98
Width Shift (0.1)	0.98

After obtaining the best augmentation results, we attempted to combine the three augmentations and recorded the results in Table 7. Surprisingly, the model without augmentation yielded better results than the augmented model, with an F1 score of 0.99. This could be attributed to the fact that the augmented model requires more training to achieve high accuracy. By examining the training process depicted in Figures 11 and 12, it is evident that the model without augmentation achieved higher accuracy and lower loss within the same number of epochs. On the other hand, the augmented model shows potential for improved results if trained for a greater number of epochs.

Table 7. Result of combined augmentation.

Augmentation	F1 Score
Without augmentation	0.99
Rotate (5) Heigh Shift (0.1) Width Shift (0.1)	0.92

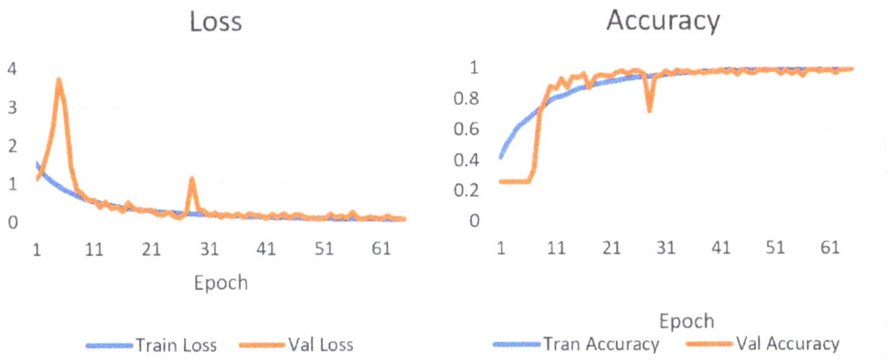

Figure 11. Loss and accuracy model without augmentation.

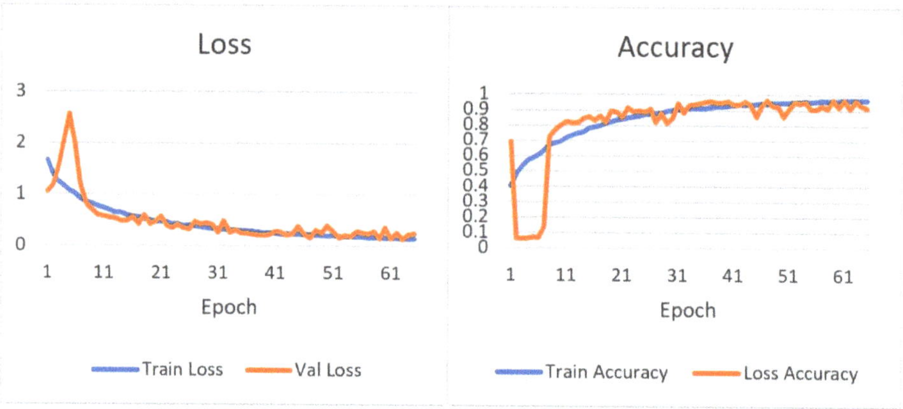

Figure 12. Loss and accuracy model with augmentation.

To further investigate this, an experiment was conducted by training the augmented model for 85 epochs. The findings, illustrated in Figure 13, indicate that increasing the number of epochs only benefits the training data, as the loss consistently decreases while accuracy steadily increases. However, there is no significant difference observed in the validation data when compared to the 65-epoch model. The graph of the validation data exhibits fluctuations and even shows signs of overfitting around the 80th epoch. This observation may be attributed to the lack of variation in the dataset and the standardized format of many X-ray datasets, rendering augmentation unnecessary.

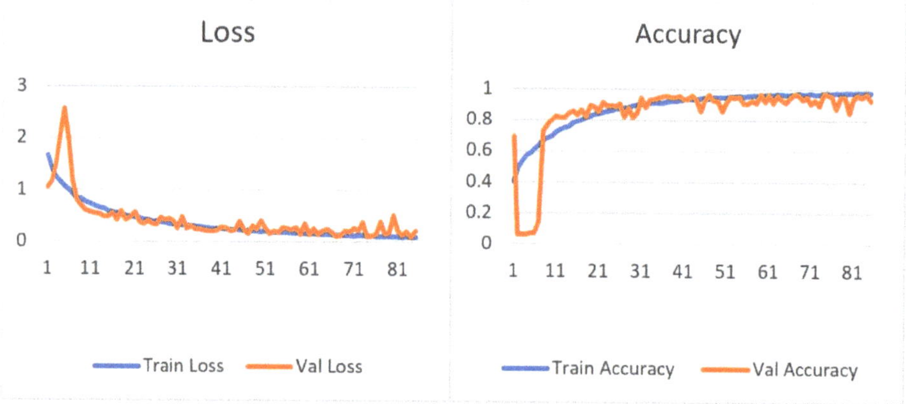

Figure 13. Loss and accuracy model with augmentation and an epoch of 85.

Models with augmentation also require a longer training time. Table 8 presents a comparison of the training process time using the same machine on Kaggle and the GPU P100 accelerator. It turns out that the model without augmentation has the fastest training process, with a duration of 91 s per epoch.

The most optimal model, based on the findings of stages 1 and 2, consists of five convolutional blocks and two layers of LSTM. Interestingly, this model achieves outstanding accuracy and also boasts the fastest training process.

Table 8. Comparison of model training time.

Augmentation	F1 Score	Training Time (s/Epoch)
Without augmentation	0.99	91
Rotate (5)	0.98	199
Heigh Shift (0.1)	0.98	199
Width Shift (0.1)	0.98	199
Rotate (5) Heigh Shift (0.1) Width Shift (0.1)	0.92	202

4.3. Evaluation

An evaluation was conducted to assess the performance of the optimal model. The model was validated using a dataset of 1514 observations, including 361 for the COVID-19 class, 1019 for the normal class, and 134 for the pneumonia class. The classification results are presented in Table 9, demonstrating that the model performs well in accurately classifying X-ray images, with a significant number of correct classifications. Out of the total 1514 images, 1497 were classified correctly, resulting in an overall accuracy of 98.88% (1497/1514). However, some errors were observed in the COVID-19 class, with 11 images misclassified as normal. Figure 14 displays the misclassified images for the COVID-19 class, highlighting that some of these images do not meet the required standards, such as being too small, leading to their misclassification.

Table 9. Confusion matrix.

Actual	Predict		
	COVID-19	Normal	Pneumonia
COVID-19	350	11	0
Normal	2	1017	0
Pneumonia	0	4	130

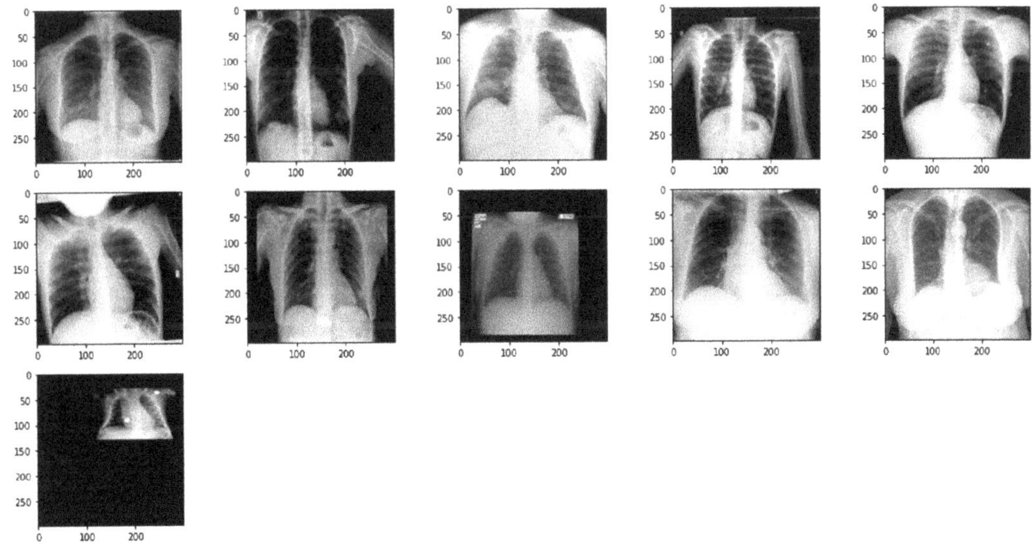

Figure 14. Image of COVID-19 misclassified as normal.

The classification report is presented in Table 10, revealing that the CNN-LSTM model effectively classifies X-ray images of the lungs with an overall F1 score of 0.99. The precision score for the pneumonia class was found to be the highest at 1.00, indicating a low probability of misclassifying COVID-19 or normal images as pneumonia. On the other hand, the recall score for the normal class was the highest at 1.00, indicating a low error rate in misclassifying normal images into other classes. The F1 score for the normal class was also the highest at 0.99, demonstrating that the CNN-LSTM model performs exceptionally well in predicting the normal class compared to the other two classes. These findings suggest that the CNN-LSTM model exhibits a high level of accuracy in classifying X-ray images of the lungs, which could potentially assist medical professionals in diagnosing respiratory diseases.

Table 10. Classification report.

	Precision	Recall	F1 Score
COVID-19	0.99	0.97	0.98
Normal	0.99	1.00	0.99
Pneumonia	1.00	0.97	0.98
Accuracy			0.99

To validate the performance of the constructed model architecture, the k-fold cross-validation method will be employed. This method aims to assess the model's performance when tested with different datasets. In this study, the test was conducted 10 times using 10 different validation data sets. The results, as presented in Table 11, indicate an average precision value of 0.97, a recall value of 0.96, and an F1 score of 0.9776.

Table 11. Results using k-fold cross-validation.

Fold	Precision	Recall	F1 Score
1	0.99	0.97	0.9887
2	0.96	0.95	0.9788
3	0.95	0.99	0.9808
4	0.99	0.96	0.9854
5	0.98	0.94	0.9739
6	0.94	0.98	0.9764
7	0.99	0.96	0.9874
8	0.96	0.98	0.9835
9	0.97	0.96	0.9614
10	0.99	0.92	0.9592
Average	0.97	0.96	0.9776

To assess the performance of our proposed model, we conducted a thorough comparison with other existing models using the same dataset. Table 12 presents a comparison of different architectures for the classification of lung diseases using chest X-ray images. Our proposed architecture (CNN-LSTM) outperforms the other architectures with an impressive F1 score of 0.9887. Despite having a similar training time of 91 s per epoch, the CNN-LSTM model demonstrates superior classification performance in accurately identifying lung diseases. These results highlight the potential of deep-learning models, particularly CNN-LSTM, in improving the accuracy of lung disease classification. The findings of this research emphasize the importance of selecting appropriate architectures for specific tasks and underscore the benefits of utilizing CNN-LSTM models in the field of medical image analysis.

Table 12. Comparison of the proposed architectures with existing architectures.

Architectures	F1 Score	Training Time (s/Epoch)
Inception-ResNet-v2 [18]	0.8687	147
ResNet-50 [27]	0.9485	82
VGG16 [20]	0.9728	93
VGG19 [20]	0.9679	109
CNN (5 convolutional blocks)	0.9721	92
Proposed architectures (CNN-LSTM)	0.9887	91

5. Conclusions

The analysis of chest X-ray images for COVID-19, pneumonia, and normal cases was conducted using a combination of convolutional neural network (CNN) and long short-term memory (LSTM) models. These findings highlight the significant potential of deep-learning models, particularly the CNN-LSTM architecture, in greatly enhancing the accuracy of lung disease classification. This research emphasizes the critical importance of selecting appropriate architectures tailored to specific tasks and underscores the numerous advantages of employing CNN-LSTM models in medical image analysis.

Among the evaluated models, the one with five convolutional blocks, two LSTM layers, and no augmentation emerged as the most effective, achieving an impressive F1 score of 0.9887 with a training duration of 91 s per epoch. It is worth noting that the main source of misclassifications was observed in 11 COVID-19 datasets mistakenly labeled as normal, accounting for 3.05% of the COVID-19 data. The pneumonia class demonstrated the highest precision (1.00), while the normal class exhibited the highest recall (1.00) and F1 score (0.99). Through k-fold cross-validation with 10 folds, the average precision, recall, and F1 score were calculated to be 0.97, 0.96, and 0.9776, respectively. Overall, incorporating an LSTM layer into the CNN model can improve the classification of chest X-ray images and effectively identify infected lungs. The addition of the LSTM layer allows the model to capture temporal dependencies and effectively model sequential information present in the images. By considering both spatial and temporal information, the CNN-LSTM architecture enhances the accuracy and robustness of the classification task. This combination of CNN and LSTM networks proves to be valuable in medical image analysis, particularly for the detection and diagnosis of lung diseases.

The results of this research provide valuable insights for future studies. To improve the accuracy and reliability of the model, it is recommended that the next study focus on cleaning and organizing the data prior to modeling. This step can help reduce misclassification and enhance the model's performance. Additionally, for further development and to broaden the scope of the study, it is suggested to include more types of lung data, such as lung cancer and tuberculosis. This would enable the model to identify a wider range of lung diseases and provide more comprehensive and accurate results.

Author Contributions: J.F., A.A.P., I.N.Y., M.N.A. and F.I., understood and designed this research; J.F. analyzed the data and drafted this paper. All authors critically read and revised the draft and approved the final paper. All authors have read and agreed to the published version of the manuscript.

Funding: The authors are grateful to the Directorate for Research and Community Service (DRPM) Universitas Padjadjaran, which supports this research under RPLK Grant no. 2203/UN6.3.1/PT.00/2022.

Institutional Review Board Statement: Not applicable.

Informed Consent Statement: Not applicable.

Data Availability Statement: Data is available at Kaggle [33,34]. The source code of this study is available at https://www.kaggle.com/code/jfachrel/covid19-detection-from-chest-x-ray-images-cnn-lstm, accessed on 5 July 2022.

Acknowledgments: The authors would like to thank the Artificial Intelligence and Big Data Research Center of Universitas Padjadjaran for the facilities provided to carry out this study. We would also like to acknowledge Mohammad Hamid Asnawi for his valuable contribution in reviewing and editing the manuscript.

Conflicts of Interest: The authors declare no conflict of interest.

References

1. Antoniou, K.M.; Margaritopoulos, G.A.; Tomassetti, S.; Bonella, F.; Costabel, U.; Poletti, V. Interstitial Lung Disease. *Eur. Respir. Rev.* **2014**, *23*, 40–54. [CrossRef] [PubMed]
2. Postow, L.; Noel, P.; Lin, S.; Zhou, G.; Fessel, J.; Kiley, J.P. Diagnosing and Treating Lung Disease at the Cellular Level. *Am. J. Physiol.-Lung Cell. Mol. Physiol.* **2020**, *319*, L541–L544. [CrossRef] [PubMed]
3. Chen, X.; Laurent, S.; Onur, O.A.; Kleineberg, N.N.; Fink, G.R.; Schweitzer, F.; Warnke, C. A Systematic Review of Neurological Symptoms and Complications of COVID-19. *J. Neurol.* **2021**, *268*, 392–402. [CrossRef] [PubMed]
4. McIntosh, K. Community-Acquired Pneumonia in Children. *N. Engl. J. Med.* **2002**, *346*, 429–437. [CrossRef] [PubMed]
5. Goyal, S.; Singh, R. Detection and Classification of Lung Diseases for Pneumonia and COVID-19 Using Machine and Deep Learning Techniques. *J. Ambient. Intell. Humaniz. Comput.* **2021**, *14*, 3239–3259. [CrossRef]
6. Gattinoni, L.; Chiumello, D.; Caironi, P.; Busana, M.; Romitti, F.; Brazzi, L.; Camporota, L. COVID-19 Pneumonia: Different Respiratory Treatments for Different Phenotypes? *Intensive Care Med.* **2020**, *46*, 1099–1102. [CrossRef] [PubMed]
7. Narin, A.; Kaya, C.; Pamuk, Z. Automatic Detection of Coronavirus Disease (COVID-19) Using X-ray Images and Deep Convolutional Neural Networks. *Pattern Anal. Appl.* **2021**, *24*, 1207–1220. [CrossRef]
8. Reshi, A.A.; Rustam, F.; Mehmood, A.; Alhossan, A.; Alrabiah, Z.; Ahmad, A.; Alsuwailem, H.; Choi, G.S. An Efficient CNN Model for COVID-19 Disease Detection Based on X-ray Image Classification. *Complexity* **2021**, *2021*, 6621607. [CrossRef]
9. Salman, F.M.; Abu-Naser, S.S.; Alajrami, E.; Abu-Nasser, B.S.; Ashqar, B.A.M. COVID-19 Detection Using Artificial Intelligence. *Int. J. Acad. Eng. Res.* **2020**, *4*, 18–25.
10. Gilanie, G.; Bajwa, U.I.; Waraich, M.M.; Asghar, M.; Kousar, R.; Kashif, A.; Aslam, R.S.; Qasim, M.M.; Rafique, H. Coronavirus (COVID-19) Detection from Chest Radiology Images Using Convolutional Neural Networks. *Biomed. Signal Process. Control* **2021**, *66*, 102490. [CrossRef]
11. Tekerek, A.; Al-Rawe, I.A.M. A Novel Approach for Prediction of Lung Disease Using Chest X-ray Images Based on DenseNet and MobileNet. *Wirel. Pers. Commun.* **2023**, *12*, 1–15. [CrossRef] [PubMed]
12. Howard, A.G.; Zhu, M.; Chen, B.; Kalenichenko, D.; Wang, W.; Weyand, T.; Andreetto, M.; Adam, H. MobileNets: Efficient Convolutional Neural Networks for Mobile Vision Applications. *arXiv* **2017**, arXiv:1704.04861.
13. Huang, G.; Liu, Z.; van der Maaten, L.; Weinberger, K.Q. Densely Connected Convolutional Networks. *arXiv* **2016**, arXiv:1608.06993.
14. Gupta, A.; Mishra, S.; Sahu, S.C.; Srinivasarao, U.; Naik, K.J. Application of Convolutional Neural Networks for COVID-19 Detection in X-ray Images Using InceptionV3 and U-Net. *New Gener. Comput.* **2023**, *41*, 475–502. [CrossRef]
15. Szegedy, C.; Vanhoucke, V.; Ioffe, S.; Shlens, J.; Wojna, Z. Rethinking the Inception Architecture for Computer Vision. *arXiv* **2015**, arXiv:1512.00567.
16. Ronneberger, O.; Fischer, P.; Brox, T. U-Net: Convolutional Networks for Biomedical Image Segmentation. *arXiv* **2015**, arXiv:1505.04597.
17. Badrahadipura, R.; Nur Septi, S.Q.; Fachrel, J.; Yulita, I.N.; Pravitasari, A.A.; Agustian, D. COVID-19 Detection in Chest X-rays Using Inception Resnet-V2. In Proceedings of the 2021 International Conference on Artificial Intelligence and Big Data Analytics, ICAIBDA 2021, Bandung, Indonesia, 27–29 October 2021. [CrossRef]
18. Szegedy, C.; Ioffe, S.; Vanhoucke, V.; Alemi, A.A. Inception-v4, Inception-ResNet and the Impact of Residual Connections on Learning. In Proceedings of the 31st AAAI Conference on Artificial Intelligence, AAAI 2017, San Francisco, CA, USA, 4–9 February 2017. [CrossRef]
19. Abbas, A.; Abdelsamea, M.M.; Gaber, M.M. Classification of COVID-19 in Chest X-ray Images Using DeTraC Deep Convolutional Neural Network. *Appl. Intell.* **2021**, *51*, 854–864. [CrossRef]
20. Simonyan, K.; Zisserman, A. Very Deep Convolutional Networks for Large-Scale Image Recognition. In Proceedings of the 3rd International Conference on Learning Representations, ICLR 2015-Conference Track Proceedings, San Diego, CA, USA, 7–9 May 2015.
21. Priddy, K.L.; Paul, E. *Keller. Artificial Neural Networks: An Introduction*; SPIE Press: Bellingham, WC, USA, 2005; Volume 68.
22. Boser, B.E.; Guyon, I.M.; Vapnik, V.N. Training Algorithm for Optimal Margin Classifiers. In Proceedings of the Fifth Annual ACM Workshop on Computational Learning Theory, Pittsburgh, PA, USA, 27–29 July 1992. [CrossRef]
23. Cover, T.; Hart, P. Nearest Neighbor Pattern Classification. *IEEE Trans. Inf. Theory* **1967**, *13*, 21–27. [CrossRef]
24. Rahman, A.; Tasnim, S. Ensemble Classifiers and Their Applications: A Review. *arXiv Prepr.* **2014**, arXiv:1404.4088. [CrossRef]
25. Demir, F. DeepCoroNet: A Deep LSTM Approach for Automated Detection of COVID-19 Cases from Chest X-ray Images. *Appl. Soft. Comput.* **2021**, *103*, 107160. [CrossRef]

26. Pustokhin, D.A.; Pustokhina, I.V.; Dinh, P.N.; Phan, S.V.; Nguyen, G.N.; Joshi, G.P.; Shankar, K. An Effective Deep Residual Network Based Class Attention Layer with Bidirectional LSTM for Diagnosis and Classification of COVID-19. *J. Appl. Stat.* **2023**, *50*, 477–494. [CrossRef]
27. He, K.; Zhang, X.; Ren, S.; Sun, J. Deep Residual Learning for Image Recognition. In Proceedings of the IEEE Computer Society Conference on Computer Vision and Pattern Recognition (CVPR), Las Vegas, NV, USA, 27–30 June 2016.
28. Touvron, H.; Cord, M.; Sablayrolles, A.; Synnaeve, G.; Jégou, H. Going Deeper with Image Transformers. In Proceedings of the IEEE International Conference on Computer Vision, Montreal, QC, Canada, 11–17 October 2021. [CrossRef]
29. Paris, S.; Kornprobst, P.; Tumblin, J.; Durand, F. Bilateral Filtering: Theory and Applications. *Found. Trends Comput. Graph. Vis.* **2009**, *4*, 1–73. [CrossRef]
30. Hamza, A.; Attique Khan, M.; Wang, S.-H.; Alqahtani, A.; Alsubai, S.; Binbusayyis, A.; Hussein, H.S.; Martinetz, T.M.; Alshazly, H. COVID-19 Classification Using Chest X-ray Images: A Framework of CNN-LSTM and Improved Max Value Moth Flame Optimization. *Front. Public Health* **2022**, *10*, 948205. [CrossRef] [PubMed]
31. Tan, M.; Le, Q.V. EfficientNet: Rethinking Model Scaling for Convolutional Neural Networks. In Proceedings of the 36th International Conference on Machine Learning, ICML 2019, Long Beach, CA, USA, 9–15 June 2019; Volume 2019.
32. Fachrel, J.; Pravitasari, A.A.; Yulita, I.N.; Ardhisasmita, M.N.; Indrayatna, F. A Comparison between CNN and Combined CNN-LSTM for Chest X-ray Based COVID-19 Detection. *Decis. Sci. Lett.* **2023**, *12*, 199–210. [CrossRef]
33. Chowdhury, M.E.H.; Rahman, T.; Khandakar, A.; Mazhar, R.; Kadir, M.A.; Bin Mahbub, Z.; Islam, K.R.; Khan, M.S.; Iqbal, A.; Al Emadi, N.; et al. Can AI Help in Screening Viral and COVID-19 Pneumonia? *IEEE Access* **2020**, *8*, 132665–132676. [CrossRef]
34. Rahman, T.; Khandakar, A.; Qiblawey, Y.; Tahir, A.; Kiranyaz, S.; Kashem, S.B.A.; Islam, M.T.; Al Maadeed, S.; Zughaier, S.M.; Khan, M.S.; et al. Exploring the Effect of Image Enhancement Techniques on COVID-19 Detection Using Chest X-ray Images. *Comput. Biol. Med.* **2021**, *132*, 104319. [CrossRef]
35. Goodfellow, I.; Bengio, Y.; Courville, A. *Deep Learning*; MIT Press: Cambridge, MA, USA, 2016.
36. Guo, T.; Dong, J.; Li, H.; Gao, Y. Simple Convolutional Neural Network on Image Classification. In Proceedings of the 2017 IEEE 2nd International Conference on Big Data Analysis, ICBDA 2017, Beijing, China, 10–12 March 2017. [CrossRef]
37. Yamashita, R.; Nishio, M.; Do, R.K.G.; Togashi, K. Convolutional Neural Networks: An Overview and Application in Radiology. *Insights Imaging* **2018**, *9*, 611–629. [CrossRef]
38. Lee, H.; Song, J. Introduction to Convolutional Neural Network Using Keras; An Understanding from a Statistician. *Commun. Stat. Appl. Methods* **2019**, *26*, 591–610. [CrossRef]
39. Aparna, S.; Ekambaram Naidu, M. Applying FIR and IIR Digital Filters over Video Image Processing. *Int. J. Appl. Eng. Res.* **2016**, *11*, 7624–7632.
40. Yadav, A.; Jha, C.K.; Sharan, A. Optimizing LSTM for Time Series Prediction in Indian Stock Market. *Procedia Comput. Sci.* **2020**, *167*, 2091–2100. [CrossRef]
41. Liu, Y.; Yu, X.; Wu, Y.; Song, S. Forecasting Variation Trends of Stocks via Multiscale Feature Fusion and Long Short-Term Memory Learning. *Sci. Program* **2021**, *2021*, 5113151. [CrossRef]
42. Qiu, J.; Wang, B.; Zhou, C. Forecasting Stock Prices with Long-Short Term Memory Neural Network Based on Attention Mechanism. *PLoS ONE* **2020**, *15*, e0227222. [CrossRef]
43. Hochreiter, S.; Schmidhuber, J. Long Short-Term Memory. *Neural Comput.* **1997**, *9*, 1735–1780. [CrossRef] [PubMed]
44. Taroon, G.; Tomar, A.; Manjunath, C.; Balamurugan, M.; Ghosh, B.; Krishna, A.V.N. Employing Deep Learning in Intraday Stock Trading. In Proceedings of the 2020 5th International Conference on Research in Computational Intelligence and Communication Networks, ICRCICN 2020, Bangalore, India, 26–27 November 2020. [CrossRef]
45. Wang, Y.; Wu, Q.; Dey, N.; Fong, S.; Ashour, A.S. Deep Back Propagation–Long Short-Term Memory Network Based Upper-Limb SEMG Signal Classification for Automated Rehabilitation. *Biocybern. Biomed. Eng.* **2020**, *40*, 987–1001. [CrossRef]
46. Sagheer, A.; Kotb, M. Unsupervised Pre-Training of a Deep LSTM-Based Stacked Autoencoder for Multivariate Time Series Forecasting Problems. *Sci. Rep.* **2019**, *9*, 19038. [CrossRef] [PubMed]
47. Ting, K.M. Confusion Matrix. In *Encyclopedia of Machine Learning and Data Mining*; Springer: Boston, MA, USA, 2017; p. 260. [CrossRef]
48. Visa, S.; Ramsay, B.; Ralescu, A.; Van Der Knaap, E. Confusion Matrix-Based Feature Selection. *Maics* **2011**, *710*, 120–127.
49. Ibrahim, M.; Torki, M.; El-Makky, N. Imbalanced Toxic Comments Classification Using Data Augmentation and Deep Learning. In Proceedings of the 17th IEEE International Conference on Machine Learning and Applications, ICMLA 2018, Orlando, FL, USA, 17–20 December 2018. [CrossRef]
50. Refaeilzadeh, P.; Tang, L.; Liu, H. Cross-Validation. In *Encyclopedia of Database Systems*; Springer: Boston, MA, USA, 2009; pp. 532–538. [CrossRef]
51. Shorten, C.; Khoshgoftaar, T.M. A Survey on Image Data Augmentation for Deep Learning. *J. Big Data* **2019**, *6*, 1–48. [CrossRef]

applied sciences

MDPI

Article

Fully Automatic Thoracic Cavity Segmentation in Dynamic Contrast Enhanced Breast MRI Using Deep Convolutional Neural Networks

Marco Berchiolli [1,*], Susann Wolfram [2,3], Wamadeva Balachandran [4] and Tat-Hean Gan [1]

1. Brunel Innovation Centre, Brunel University London, Uxbridge UB8 3PH, UK; tat-hean.gan@brunel.ac.uk
2. Healthcare Innovation Centre, Teesside University, Middlesbrough TS1 3BX, UK
3. School of Kinesiology, University of Michigan, Ann Arbor, MI 48109, USA
4. Electronic and Computer Engineering Department, Brunel University London, Uxbridge UB8 3PH, UK; wamadeva.balachandran@brunel.ac.uk

* Correspondence: marco.berchiolli@brunel.ac.uk

Abstract: Dynamic Contrast Enhanced Magnetic Resonance Imaging (DCE-MRI) is regarded as one of the main diagnostic tools for breast cancer. Several methodologies have been developed to automatically localize suspected malignant breast lesions. Changes in tissue appearance in response to the injection of the contrast agent (CA) are indicative of the presence of malignant breast lesions. However, these changes are extremely similar to the ones of internal organs, such as the heart. Thus, the task of chest cavity segmentation is necessary for the development of lesion detection. In this work, a data-efficient approach is proposed, to automatically segment breast MRI data. Specifically, a study on several UNet-like architectures (Dynamic UNet) based on ResNet is presented. Experiments quantify the impact of several additions to baseline models of varying depth, such as self-attention and the presence of a bottlenecked connection. The proposed methodology is demonstrated to outperform the current state of the art both in terms of data efficiency and in terms of similarity index when compared to manually segmented data.

Keywords: DCE-MRI; breast segmentation; deep learning

1. Introduction

Breast cancer is the most frequent cancer among females, amounting to 24% of all cancer occurrences in 2018 [1], accounting for 684,996 deaths in 2020 worldwide [2]. The World Health Organization indicates screening programs aimed at early detection as one of the key factors in reducing mortality [3]. Magnetic Resonance Imaging (MRI) is an increasingly popular procedure for the screening of high-risk groups [4] and evaluating the response to neo-adjuvant chemotherapy [5]. MRI has several benefits over X-ray mammography; it does not utilize ionizing radiation, generates high-resolution images and contains dynamic information. Moreover, recent developments in MRI image processing [6] indicate that MRI is gaining popularity even with its major drawbacks (time-consuming, stressful and costly) and is actively being targeted by the research community.

Dynamic Contrast Enhanced MRI (DCE-MRI) outputs four-dimensional data (three spatial dimensions + one temporal dimension), consisting of images acquired before and after the intravenous injection of a contrast agent (CA). The change in tissue appearance in response to the CA is tissue-specific and, therefore, indicative of the presence of malignant breast lesions [7]. These changes in tissue appearance are extremely similar to the ones of the internal organs such as the heart, making automatic lesion detection in breast DCE-MRI sequences challenging. Manual delineation of the chest wall is an extremely time-consuming activity. Therefore, the automatic removal of the internal organs from the images by segmenting the chest cavity is instrumental to the development of an automatic lesion detection methodology. Figure 1 shows the results of an automatic lesion detection algorithm for a properly segmented image and a poorly segmented image of a breast DCE-MRI sequence. The algorithm is based on the statistical properties of the whole sequence and indicates areas with a high likelihood of containing a lesion, with red indicating the most likely candidate area. By not excluding the chest cavity, the system evaluates the heart as an area of high likelihood. As the chest cavity is segmented, the actual lesion is correctly highlighted.

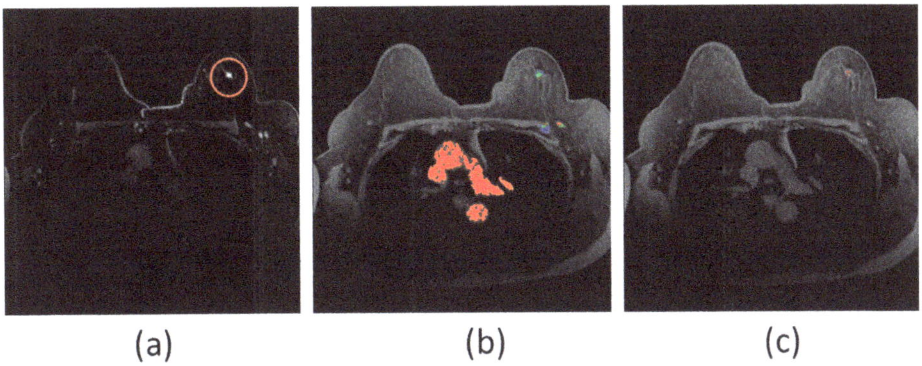

Figure 1. Results of an automatic lesion detection algorithm on a lesion. The original image with the lesion is visible in (**a**), with the lesion highlighted in the red circle. The coloring scheme of the other images (**b**,**c**) is based on statistical properties of the full breast volume. Red represents high likelihood of a lesion, while green and blue represent lower likelihood. In (**b**), the chest cavity is incorrectly segmented, and the lesion detection algorithm identifies the heart as an area of high likelihood to be a lesion. In (**c**), the chest cavity is correctly segmented, and the area of high likelihood to contain a lesion is correctly identified.

The current state of the art addresses the challenge by training a three-dimensional cluster of 2D UNets [8]. We argue that implementing more recent deep learning (DL) techniques can lead to better results and generalization performance.

In this study, a novel, DL-based methodology for the segmentation of the chest cavity from breast DCE-MRI scans is proposed. The solution aims to address the main challenges in chest cavity segmentation, especially sternum detection, by using a data-based approach. To showcase the potential of the solution, the target area to segment is selected to be the upper half of the chest cavity.

The paper is organized as follows. In Section 2, a selection of previous studies with relative contributions is presented; in Section 3, the proposal is presented in detail; in Section 4, the results of the experiments are presented and discussed; finally, in Section 6, conclusions and suggestions for further work are presented.

2. Related Work

Given the importance of the task and its complexity, there have been numerous approaches proposed in the published literature. In line with Marrone et al. [9], DL-based approaches are also included in the following overview. While the DL category has limited representation at present, it currently represents the state of the art. Moreover, it is expected that the popularity of this subfield will increase due to the vast representation of DL-based techniques in parallel fields, such as hand and brain segmentation [10]. For these reasons, the section dedicated to DL approaches is given higher importance.

2.1. Pixel-Based Approaches

Approaches in this category rely on classifying pixels or voxels individually, or with simple computations on the surrounding pixels [11,12]. Results are not always fully automatic and tend to be suboptimal, especially the boundary between the sternum and the internal organ, which is often wrongly segmented. On the other hand, they require minimal computational costs. For example, in the approach of Vignati et al. [13], the images are processed using Otsu's thresholding and a sequence of dilations and erosions. Results show good breast parenchyma segmentation performance. However, the limitations become apparent as the examples provided show imprecise chest wall segmentation, as specified by the authors, and require the aid of fat-saturated images or an atlas-based segmentation. The study demonstrates that segmentation of the outer boundary of the breast is achievable by computationally efficient methodologies, while chest cavity segmentation would require more complex solutions. Given the importance of minimizing the presence of internal organs (see Figure 1), specifically the heart, chest cavity segmentation is fundamental in the development of lesion detection systems for DCE-MRI. Future studies should then focus on the detection of the chest wall.

2.2. Atlas-Based Approaches

The solutions in this category are generated by comparing the anatomical atlas generated by manually segmented data [12,14–17]. The approaches usually require a high number of instances in the atlas to guarantee generalizability to different anatomical features and acquisition protocols. The size of the atlas, however, is directly linked to an increased computational cost. To counteract such limitations, the solutions are often restricted to a specific anatomical part. An example of such an application is provided by Fooladivanda et al. [18], in which the authors use an atlas-based approach to segment the pectoral muscle, relying on a simpler pixel-based approach to segment the chest wall edge.

2.3. Geometrical-Based Approaches

The proposed solutions within the category revolve around constraining the segmentation results to predetermined anatomical and physiological characteristics. Their most common usage is as a refinement to pixel-based approaches [19,20]. The main criticisms of the techniques are the extreme computational costs and extremely poor generalization performance. Notable examples come from Wu et al. [20], in which the authors propose a methodology to extract the chest wall line from sagittal breast MRI.

Results are based on the refinement of edge detection via enforcing geometrical constraints and are extremely effective. The fundamental assumptions, however, highlight the limitations in generalizability, as the methodology does not account for the edge detection algorithm failing. This limits the potential application in a contrast-enhanced MRI environment, as post-enhancement images usually feature high-intensity chest wall and heart regions, as shown in Figure 2.

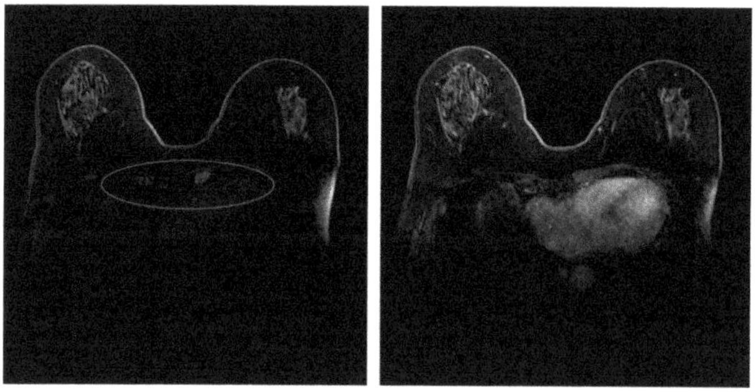

Figure 2. Pre-enhancement and post-enhancement (6 min after CA injection) images of a central slice of the breast. The area of the sternum highlighted in the picture on the left is not clearly defined through an edge detection algorithm in the picture on the right.

2.4. Deep Learning-Based Approaches

Deep learning-based solutions allow for the creation of fully automated segmentation methodologies by exploiting previous examples in the form of manually segmented data. The limitations of the approaches consist in the training process, for which large quantities of data and computational resources are needed. The techniques have been applied with great success to an increasing amount of research problems in recent years [21].

The pioneering solution is attributable to Dalmis et al. [22], in which the authors propose automated breast and fibroglandular tissue (FGT) segmentation using a UNet approach [23]. They obtained considerable improvements in accuracy over the state of the art at that time in terms of Dice Similarity Coefficient (DSC), achieving a DSC of 0.944 against 0.863 from the previous reported state of the art [12,15]. The current state of the art is attributable to Piantadosi et al. [8], who implemented a multi-planar UNet approach, obtaining some improvements over Dalmis et al. [23]. The methodology uses three discrete UNets on the transverse, sagittal and coronal planes instead of a three-dimensional (3D) UNet, to increase the computational efficiency for the solution. The 3D aspect of the network, however, effectively triples the computational cost. Moreover, the current state of the art [8] was trained on a dataset composed of fully labeled data from 117 patients, well above the data available to many developers. As the labeling process is the most time-consuming aspect of the development, solutions should aim at maximizing performance with a minimal amount of data. To this end, novel techniques need to be employed, both architecturally and from a data pre-processing point of view.

Given the limitations of the approaches presented and their advantages, the convolutional neural network (CNN) methodologies are the most applicable for problems in computer-aided diagnostics (CAD). However, all DL approaches available in the literature fail to address the most limiting aspect of the issue, which is data availability. The proposed solution aims to improve the current state of the art by focusing on data efficiency, by employing architectures that are less prone to overfitting and behave better in transfer learning scenarios. Moreover, recent advancements in DL research, such as self-attention [24], have the potential to further improve upon the state of the art. In addition, computational efforts need to be compliant with the hardware that is potentially available in a hospital; hence, the algorithms should process patient data in a two-dimensional fashion, as 3D data can be generated if needed.

The current paper reports on improvements to the current state of the art by employing several techniques that have been successful in parallel fields. To this end, a total of 18 configurations were evaluated, corresponding to the combination of three different architectures and three different techniques to be applied.

3. Methodology

3.1. Introduction

The proposed automatic chest cavity segmentation algorithm is composed of two main parts. In the first part, the volume is sliced in its transverse plane images, and it is inputted in a Dynamic UNet (fast.ai, n.d.), inspired by [25].

Figure 3 shows the schematic of the solution, with an image being inputted in the DL model to generate a mask. The mask is then applied to the input image.

3.2. Dataset and Labeling Strategy

A dataset consisting of breast DCE-MRI data from 44 patients was used for the training and testing of the proposed segmentation model. Data were acquired on a 1.5 T scanner (MAGNETOM Avanto, Siemens Healthcare GmbH, Erlangen, Germany) with the patient positioned lying face down. The TR/TE/flip angle was 4.33 s/1.32 s/10° for each scan, with a slice thickness of 1.1 mm, with no gaps between slices. The resolution of each slice was 448×448 pixels. Each breast DCE-MRI protocol consisted of one pre-contrast T1-weighted sequence and seven post-contrast T1-weighted sequences collected at intervals of 1:01 min between sequences.

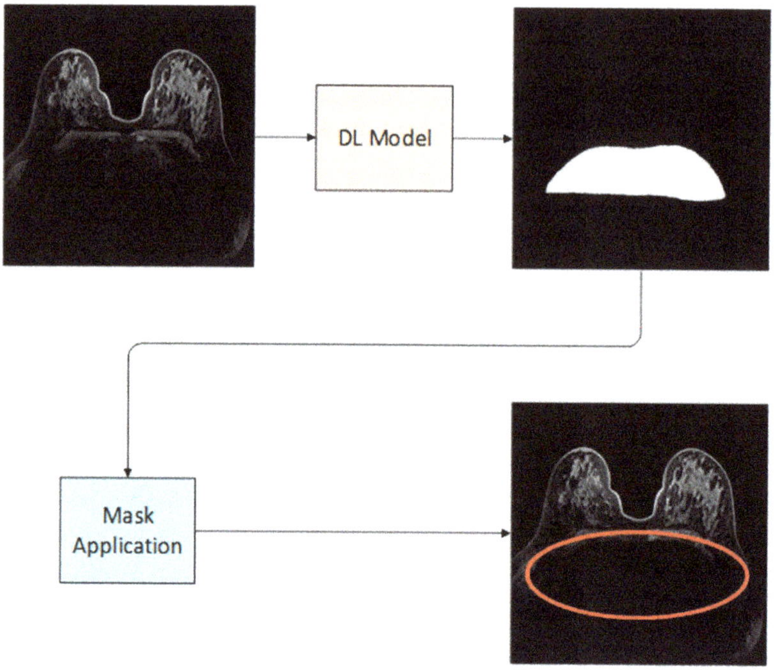

Figure 3. Schematic of the proposed solution. The input image is inputted in a deep learning model, which outputs a generated mask. The segmentation mask is then applied to the input image. Notably, the upper part of the internal organs is removed, as highlighted by the red circle.

A subset of the slices of each sequence was manually segmented, and the segmentation was checked for accuracy by a breast radiologist. Before manual segmentation, the slices were cropped to size to remove the posterior half of the thorax. In this developmental phase of the segmentation, the bottom row of 131 pixels was removed as this gave the best cropping result for our dataset. For manual segmentation, eleven evenly spaced slices throughout the central 70 slices of the scan volume of the pre-contrast sequence were selected to address anatomical variations along the upper body. To address changes in tissue brightness because of CA injection, the six central slices of the pre-contrast sequence were also manually segmented. The manual segmentation of these slices was repeated for the corresponding slices in all seven post-contrast sequences. A total of 2552 slices were manually segmented. Segmented slices from 37 patients (n = 2146 slices) were used for the training of the model. The model was tested with segmented slices from the remaining seven patients (n = 406 slices).

3.3. Deep Learning Model

The segmentation model is based on a Dynamic UNet with a pre-trained ResNet encoder. A transfer learning approach was utilized with a pre-trained ResNet encoder to address the challenge of insufficient training data. Transfer learning [26] is a widely used technique in computer vision tasks outside of medical image segmentation [27,28]. In order to leverage transfer learning, the technique employed in the proposed solution is the Dynamic UNet (fast.ai, n.d.), based on the original Unet proposed by Ronneberger et al. [23]. A UNet architecture was chosen as it is the best methodology in terms of overall performance in medical imaging applications [21,29]. The flexibility derived from using custom encoders provided by Dynamic UNet allows for a much greater degree of exploitation of transfer learning.

The original UNet architecture can be divided into an encoding part, or "downsampling", and a decoding part, or "upsampling". The encoding side performs a similar task to a conventional CNN, with regular downsampling steps performed through the maxpool operation. At the same time, the decoding path follows a symmetrical structure, with the upsampling steps performed through a fractionally strided convolution layer. The symmetry allows for the activations of the downsampling layers to be concatenated to the activations of the upsampling layers. This offers better retention of spatial information throughout the upsampling path.

The Dynamic UNet architecture was originally presented by Iglovikov and Shvets [25]. It follows the same basic architecture as the original UNet but adds a pre-trained model as the encoder. The approach not only achieves considerable improvements over the traditional UNet, but it also allows one to experiment with a variety of pre-trained encoders. In this study, the ResNet encoders were used, as it has been demonstrated that they reduce the reliance on regularization techniques [30].

ResNets were first introduced in 2015 [31] to counteract the vanishing/exploding gradient problem in deeper networks, which had been a mainstay challenge in the deep learning research field since the inception of ConvNets [32]. The fundamental component of a ResNet is the residual block, which incorporates a "skip connection". The input to the block is passed through an identity mapping and is summed to the activation of a series of convolutional layers. ResNets can reach theoretically infinite depths, due to the self-regularization method provided by the identity mapping [31]. The flexibility of ResNets allows training for longer (more epochs), thus reducing the likelihood of overfitting [31].

3.4. Model Configuration

In addition to the novel application of the Dynamic UNet in this field, several architectural configurations were added to the models. These model configurations further improve upon the current state of the art. The configurations introduced to the model were (Figure 4).

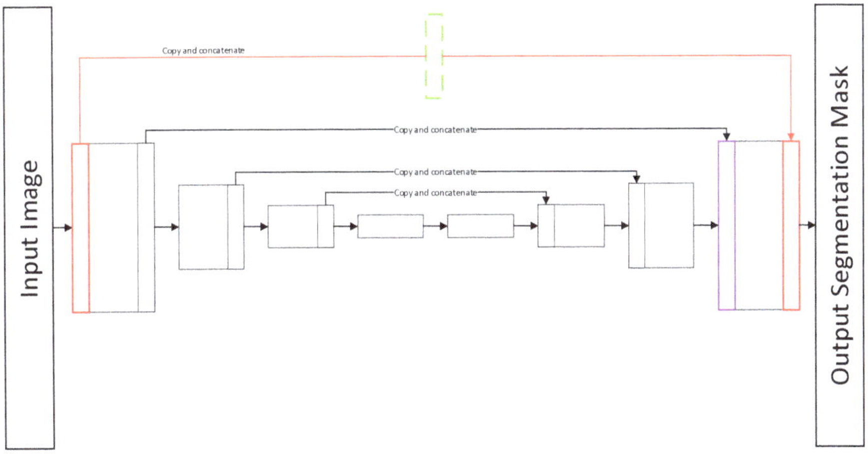

Figure 4. Experimental layout. Purple represents the location of the self-attention layer (here represented in a simplified view of a ResNet18). Red represents the skip connection from the first to last layer. Green is the bottlenecked connection.

- ResNet encoders;
- A self-attention layer as part of the upsampling path of the model;
- A blurring algorithm to avoid checkerboard artefacts;
- A bottleneck connection from input to output.

3.4.1. ResNet Encoders

The chosen encoder architectures were ResNet18, ResNet34 and ResNet50 [31]. It was important to convey the effect of architectural scaling on performance, and ResNets have been demonstrated to be an excellent choice for medical imaging work [33,34]. While the number of training parameters is considerably higher than in most other solutions, the increased transferability of ResNets allows for improved results with lower amounts of data, thus validating the effort that was put into increasing data efficiency. The choice of not experimenting with larger architectures, such as ResNet101, was made due to insufficient data for such architectures. This assumption was confirmed correct by the results.

3.4.2. Self-Attention Layer

Attention is a mechanism that was introduced by Bahdanau et al. [35] with the aim of improving neural machine translation tasks. Attention layers have since been an integral part of transformer-based models [24]. Attention-based models have been shown to excel in all contexts in which capturing global dependencies is necessary, including hybrid text–image tasks [36,37] and computer vision tasks [38]. Self-attention consists of a block of layers that outputs the attention feature maps of an input sequence with each element of the same sequence. Self-attention has been featured in promising research within CAD [39], with the usage of self-attention as a region-of-interest detection tool, thus allowing one to obtain a cropped local image in which to perform a classification. The experiments were run with the implementation described by Zhang et al. [40], who introduced a ResNet-like approach to self-attention by including a skip connection within the final output of a layer y_i:

$$y_i = \gamma o_i + x_i$$

where γ is a learnable parameter that scales the output of a self-attention layer and x_i is the input of the layer. The approach results in greater spatial awareness by the model, a trait that is highly desirable in medical imaging, as images often present themselves with a pseudo-symmetrical and repetitive structure.

3.4.3. Blurring

To counteract the natural occurrence of checkerboard artefacts in CNNs [41], a blurring mechanism was introduced. An average pooling layer with 2×2 dimensions and the unit stride was added after each activation in the upsampling path of the Dynamic UNet.

3.4.4. Bottlenecked Connection

The original UNet architecture did not feature any direct connection between the input and the final layer, opting instead for a concatenation of the activation of the third layer and the activation of the last deconvolution layer [23]. Adding an even less processed pass-through could lead to better spatial awareness and improved performance. In this work, a bottlenecked connection is included, aiming at forcing the model to synthetize the input information by using a bottleneck within the residual block, which halves the number of features in the convolutional path of the block.

3.5. Training of the Models

3.5.1. Data Augmentation

In addition to transfer learning, we further address the issue of insufficient training data by employing a more aggressive data augmentation strategy compared to the published literature. Data augmentation is an ensemble of techniques that are employed to artificially increase the amount of available data with the aim of reducing overfitting and improving generalization [42]. Specifically, in computer vision, images are slightly altered through affine or lighting transformations. These can include rotations, cropping, contrast and color correction. By heavily employing data augmentation, the chances of overfitting are drastically lowered, allowing for improved performance with data being equal (by employing a larger architecture), or by achieving similar results with lower amounts of data, as presented by Wong et al. [43].

We employed several augmentation strategies (summarized in Table 1), and augmented images were used for all model configurations. All transformations were performed with a reflection padding mode, mirroring the pixel values along the image border to fill the shape. Examples of augmented data can be seen in Figure 5. The combined probability of a transformation to a specific feature is

$$p = 1 - \prod(1 - p_i)$$

where p_i is the probability of the transformations that affect the specific feature to occur. The dataset was then composed of ~99.95% data-augmented images. The perfectly horizontal edge of the manually segmented mask was impacted by the perspective warp and the rotation transformation. This led to an overwhelming imbalance in the dataset, with ~93.75% of the images featuring an inclined mask as ground truth.

Table 1. Data augmentation overview. The probability column refers to the likelihood of any transformation occurring.

Transformation	Parameters	Probability
Horizontal flip	N/A	0.5
Rotation	±10°	0.75
Cropping	1.1 magnification	0.75
Contrast adjustment	±20%	0.75
Brightness adjustment	±10%	0.75
Perspective warp	±20% position of the observation plane	0.75

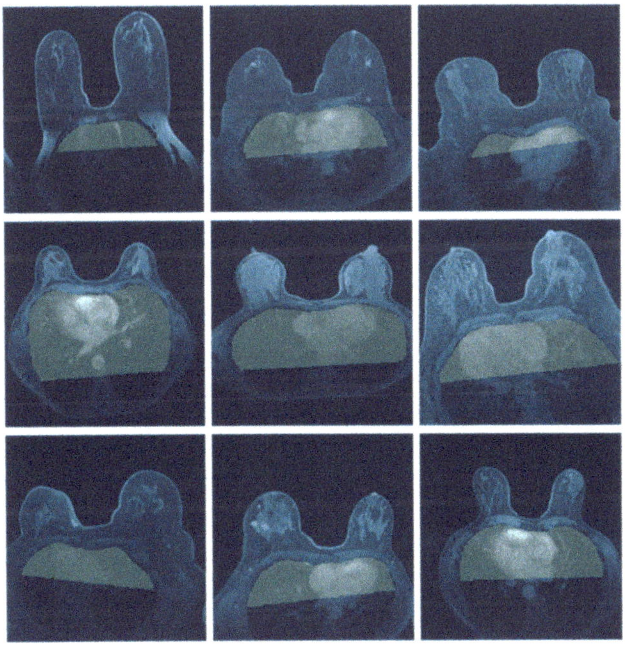

Figure 5. Example of data augmentation on a small batch of data. The reflection padding can be seen in the top left corner. All images have their manually labeled ground truth featuring a straight line at the bottom of the mask.

3.5.2. Hyperparameters

To identify the best segmentation model for the segmentation task, a total of 18 different segmentation models were trained, each with a different combination of the configurations described above. The same training datasets (2146 images from 37 patients) were used for the training of all model configurations. Every model was trained with three distinct random seeds to ensure minimal stochastic noise in the results.

The optimizer for the training was Adam [44], with β_1 of 0.9 and β_2 of 0.99. The optimal learning rate for each architecture was found as shown by Smith [45], resulting in an optimal theorical learning rate of 1×10^{-4} for all configurations. The training phase featured learning rate annealing, as described by the 1-cycle policy [46]. All trainings were performed with weight decay of 0.01.

The models were trained using an NVIDIA P40 with 24 GB of VRAM. Batch sizes were chosen empirically, with ResNet18 models having 64 (31,208,178 parameters), ResNet34 having 32 (41,316,338 parameters) and ResNet50 having 8 (341,254,226 parameters).

3.5.3. Experiments

The performance of each of the 18 different models was tested with images from seven patients not used for training. The computational demand of each model was evaluated by calculating inference times for segmentation. Inference times were calculated for each individual image and for all images of the DCE-MRI sequence of each patient (n = 1260).

The segmentation result of each model was compared to 406 images (58 images per patient) that were manually segmented. Comparisons of agreement between the model segmentation and the manual segmentation were made using the DSC and the Jaccard Similarity Coefficient (JSC):

$$DSC = \frac{2|X \cap Y|}{|X| + |Y|}$$

$$JSC = \frac{|X \cap Y|}{|X \cup Y|}$$

where X is the number of pixels inside the thoracic cavity that are part of the manual segmentation and Y is the number of pixels inside the thoracic cavity that are part of the model segmentation. The DSC represents the mean overlap and the JSC represents the union overlap of pixels that are common to both the manual and automatic segmentation. For each model, DSC and JSC were determined for each image and the mean $\pm$ standard deviation (SD) of each coefficient was calculated for all 406 images.

4. Results

The DSC and JSC for each model are summarized in Table 2. Inference times are summarized in Table 3. The best agreement between model segmentation and manual segmentation was found for the ResNet34 model configuration with self-attention, the bottlenecked connection and the blurring mechanism. It achieved a DSC of 0.9359, JSC of 0.8874 and inference times of 33.56 ms/image and 42.3 s for all 1260 images of one DCE sequence. The worst agreement between model segmentation and manual segmentation was found for the ResNet50 with self-attention model configuration, with a DSC of 0.9210, JSC of 0.8670 and inference times of 194.8 ms/image and 245.2 s for all 1260 images of one DCE sequence.

Upon visual inspection of the model segmentation results, it was found in all models that the lower edge of the segmented area was not straight, which influenced the results of the similarity coefficients. This phenomenon was an artefact caused by the data augmentation strategy, which allowed for reduced overfitting and better training outcomes. The training data were rarely not augmented before being inputted into the models, resulting in the horizontal line at the bottom of the manually segmented mask being interpreted as always inclined. A simple adjustment step was then taken to ensure the real-world usability metrics of the methodology. The refinement algorithm consists of a simple loop over the columns of the output of the model, forcing any pixel between the highest true value in a column and the 131st from the bottom to be true. In other words, the generated masks are refined to only allow for pixels above the height of 131 from the bottom of the image to be true. The updated schematic of the solution can be seen below in Figure 6.

Table 2. Similarity coefficients for all models. The similarity coefficients are represented as mean ± standard deviation. The best performing model was the ResNet34 model with a self-attention layer, bottleneck connection and blurring mechanism, which is highlighted in bold. Abbreviations: BC—bottleneck connection, BL—blurring mechanism, DSC—DSC Similarity Coefficient, JSC—Jaccard Similarity Coefficient, SA—self-attention layer, SD—standard deviation.

Model Configuration	Mean DSC ± SD	Mean JSC ± SD
Resnet18	0.9253 ± 0.1034	0.8760 ± 0.0758
ResNet18 + SA	0.9296 ± 0.1028	0.8757 ± 0.0765
ResNet18 + BL	0.9273 ± 0.1033	0.8795 ± 0.0764
ResNet18 + BC	0.9283 ± 0.1045	0.8742 ± 0.0763
ResNet18 + SA + BL	0.9348 ± 0.1045	0.8846 ± 0.0760
ResNet18 + SA +BL + BC	0.9293 ± 0.1036	0.8755 ± 0.0765
Resnet34	0.9244 ± 0.1017	0.8721 ± 0.0756
ResNet34 + SA	0.9230 ± 0.1012	0.8652 ± 0.0752
ResNet34 + BL	0.9227 ± 0.1015	0.8714 ± 0.0749
ResNet34 + BC	0.9292 ± 0.1009	0.8754 ± 0.0755
ResNet34 + SA + BL	0.9337 ± 0.1008	0.8780 ± 0.0750
ResNet34 + SA + BL + BC	**0.9359 ± 0.1004**	**0.8874 ± 0.0748**
Resnet50	0.9240 ± 0.1055	0.8717 ± 0.0781
ResNet50 + SA	0.9210 ± 0.1069	0.8670 ± 0.0790
ResNet50 + BL	0.9233 ± 0.1063	0.8708 ± 0.0777
ResNet50 + BC	0.9257 ± 0.1059	0.8730 ± 0.0775
ResNet50 + SA + BL	0.9278 ± 0.1061	0.8727 ± 0.0766
ResNet50 + SA +BL + BC	0.9289 ± 0.1053	0.8740 ± 0.0770

Table 3. Inference times for all models. Times are represented in ms/image for single image processing, and in seconds for batch processing. The best performing model was the ResNet18 with no additions, which is highlighted in bold. Abbreviations: BC—bottleneck connection, BL—blurring mechanism, DSC—DSC Similarity Coefficient, JSC—Jaccard Similarity Coefficient, SA—self-attention layer.

Model Configuration	Inference Time (ms/Image)	Batch Inference Time (1260 Images) (s)
Resnet18	**26.83**	**30.0**
ResNet18 + SA	33.56	42.3
ResNet18 + BL	31.88	40.2
ResNet18 + BC	27.68	34.9
ResNet18 + SA + BL	33.56	42.3
ResNet18 + SA +BL + BC	33.56	42.3
Resnet34	31.88	40.2
ResNet34 + SA	33.56	42.3
ResNet34 + BL	33.56	42.3
ResNet34 + BC	30.2	38.1
ResNet34 + SA + BL	33.56	42.3
ResNet34 + SA + BL + BC	33.56	42.3
Resnet50	179.5	226.2
ResNet50 + SA	194.6	245.2
ResNet50 + BL	196.3	247.3
ResNet50 + BC	194.6	245.2
ResNet50 + SA + BL	196.3	247.3
ResNet50 + SA +BL + BC	198	249.5

The sole purpose of the refinement algorithm is to remove the bias inserted into the training process by the aggressive data augmentation strategy. Such an algorithm would not be used in a workflow for lesion detection, or in clinical practice, as it aims at improving performance in areas that result in no additional value in CAD or diagnosis. The performance metrics of the refined masks should then be interpreted as directly correlated with the actual capability of models to segment the chest cavity.

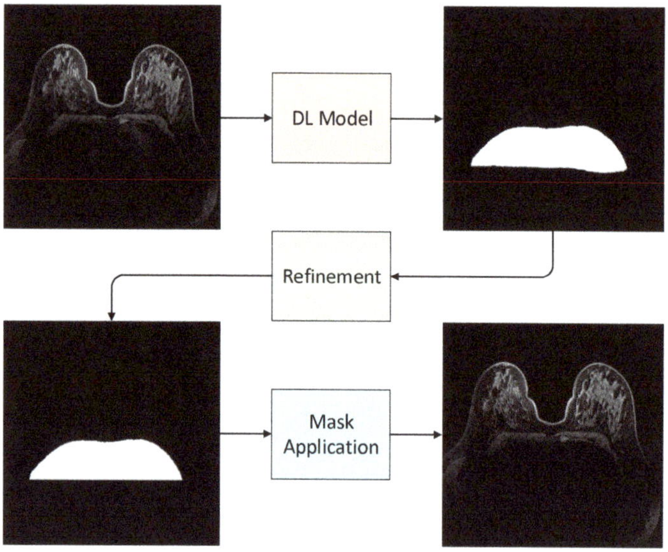

Figure 6. Schematic of the solution. The input image is inputted in a deep learning model, which outputs a generated mask. A refinement algorithm then removes the bottom part of the mask. The segmentation mask is then applied to the input image.

The application of the refinement algorithm led to considerable improvements in the similarity coefficients, but with a slight increase in inference times (Tables 4 and 5). The best agreement between model segmentation and manual segmentation was again found for the ResNet34 model with self-attention, bottlenecked connection and blurring mechanism model configuration. It achieved a DSC of 0.9612 and JSC of 0.9789, with inference times of 98.99 ms/image. The worst agreement between model segmentation and manual segmentation was found for the ResNet50 with self-attention model configuration, with a DSC of 0.9465 and JSC of 0.9708, with inference times of 261.7 ms/image.

Table 4. Similarity coefficients for all models after refinement algorithm. The similarity coefficients are represented as mean ± standard deviation. The best performing model was the ResNet34 model with a self-attention layer, bottleneck connection and blurring mechanism, which is highlighted in bold. Abbreviations: BC—bottleneck connection, BL—blurring mechanism, DSC—DSC Similarity Coefficient, JSC—Jaccard Similarity Coefficient, SA—self-attention layer.

Model Configuration	DSC ± SD (n = 406)	JSC ± SD (n = 406)
Resnet18	0.9750 ± 0.0451	0.9552 ± 0.0667
ResNet18 + SA	0.9731 ± 0.0449	0.9552 ± 0.0669
ResNet18 + BL	0.9739 ± 0.0447	0.9536 ± 0.0701
ResNet18 + BC	0.9717 ± 0.0450	0.9497 ± 0.0670
ResNet18 + SA + BL	0.9751 ± 0.0448	0.9556 ± 0.0665
ResNet18 + SA +BL + BC	0.9737 ± 0.0447	0.9533 ± 0.0674
Resnet34	0.9744 ± 0.0420	0.9541 ± 0.0682
ResNet34 + SA	0.9734 ± 0.0419	0.9527 ± 0.0628
ResNet34 + BL	0.9698 ± 0.0417	0.9512 ± 0.0642

Table 4. *Cont.*

Model Configuration	DSC ± SD (n = 406)	JSC ± SD (n = 406)
ResNet34 + BC	0.9766 ± 0.0422	0.9577 ± 0.0677
ResNet34 + SA + BL	0.9775 ± 0.0425	0.9584 ± 0.0633
ResNet34 + SA + BL + BC	**0.9789 ± 0.0411**	**0.9612 ± 0.0621**
Resnet50	0.9718 ± 0.0493	0.9541 ± 0.0627
ResNet50 + SA	0.9665 ± 0.0502	0.9538 ± 0.0721
ResNet50 + BL	0.9708 ± 0.0488	0.9465 ± 0.0704
ResNet50 + BC	0.9732 ± 0.0499	0.9526 ± 0.0706
ResNet50 + SA + BL	0.9712 ± 0.0501	0.9532 ± 0.0710
ResNet50 + SA +BL + BC	0.9766 ± 0.0497	0.9577 ± 0.0708

Table 5. Inference times for all models with subsequent refinement algorithm. Times are represented in ms/image for single image processing, and in seconds for batch processing. The best performing model was the ResNet18 with no additions, which is highlighted in bold. Abbreviations: BC—bottleneck connection, BL—blurring mechanism, DSC—DSC Similarity Coefficient, JSC—Jaccard Similarity Coefficient, SA—self-attention layer.

Model Configuration	Inference Time (ms/Image)	Batch Inference Time (1260 Images) (s)
Resnet18	**92.28**	**116.3**
ResNet18 + SA	93.96	118.4
ResNet18 + BL	92.28	116.3
ResNet18 + BC	92.28	116.3
ResNet18 + SA + BL	95.64	120.5
ResNet18 + SA +BL + BC	95.64	120.5
Resnet34	90.6	114.2
ResNet34 + SA	95.64	120.5
ResNet34 + BL	95.64	120.5
ResNet34 + BC	92.28	116.3
ResNet34 + SA + BL	97.32	122.6
ResNet34 + SA + BL + BC	98.99	124.7
Resnet50	258.4	325.6
ResNet50 + SA	263.4	331.9
ResNet50 + BL	261.7	329.7
ResNet50 + BC	260.1	327.7
ResNet50 + SA + BL	261.7	329.7
ResNet50 + SA +BL + BC	266.8	336.2

5. Discussion

The main aim of this work was to develop a fully automatic methodology for the segmentation of the chest cavity to use for the development of automatic lesion detection systems. All 18 models showed excellent agreement with the manual segmentation, with DSCs of over 0.92 and JSCs of over 0.86. After the introduction of a refinement algorithm to compensate for artefacts due to the aggressive data augmentation strategy, the DSCs and JSCs improved to over 0.95 and 0.96, respectively. The best performing model was found to be the ResNet34 model with the self-attention layer, blurring mechanism and bottleneck connection, resulting in very high agreement with manual segmentation, with a DSC of 0.9612 and a JSC of 0.9789.

Overall, the techniques proposed show a significant improvement over the current state of the art [8], which features a DSC of 0.9660 on full breast segmentation. While the tasks are not directly comparable, body–air segmentation has been shown to achieve more than optimal results in the past [20], hence highlighting the need for novelty solely in chest cavity segmentation. Moreover, the DSC is expected to be lower with smaller regions to segment. Hence, it is reasonable to assume that the cost to the DSC and JSC of generating incorrect chest wall segmentation is lower, as shown in Piantadosi et al. [8].

The best configuration also improves inference timings, matching the previous state of the art after post-processing on comparable hardware, but dramatically improving on it without. As previously mentioned, the post-processing algorithm is solely used to highlight the validity of the proposed solution and is not meant to be included in any CAD workflow.

The agreement between the model segmentation and the manual segmentation was very good to excellent for all model configurations. The addition of each proposed improvement to the models provided marginal improvements for all architectures. However, the models with all configurations added consistently resulted in higher performance. This improvement was particularly striking for the ResNet 34 encoder, which showed an increase in the DSC from 0.9541 (ResNet34 only) to 0.9612 (ResNet34 with self-attention layer, blurring and bottleneck). However, adding to the complexity of the model comes with an increased computational cost, especially when adding the self-attention layer. For example, the inference time for the entire DCE image sequence is 114.2 s for ResNet34 only, but this increases by 6.3 s when adding the self-attention layer, while adding the bottleneck connection causes an increase of only 2.1 s (Table 5). The best performing model before post-processing is the ResNet34 featuring all proposed additions. The considerable improvement in segmentation accuracy over a standard ResNet encoder may justify the additional computational cost. ResNet50 configurations performed worse than the smaller ResNet34 architectures. This is likely due to underfitting, and having access to more data would be extremely beneficial and most likely would lead to better performance than ResNet34 on larger training datasets. The difference between the worst performing architecture (ResNet18 with bottleneck connection) and the best performing architecture (ResNet34 with all proposed additions) can be seen in Figure 7 below.

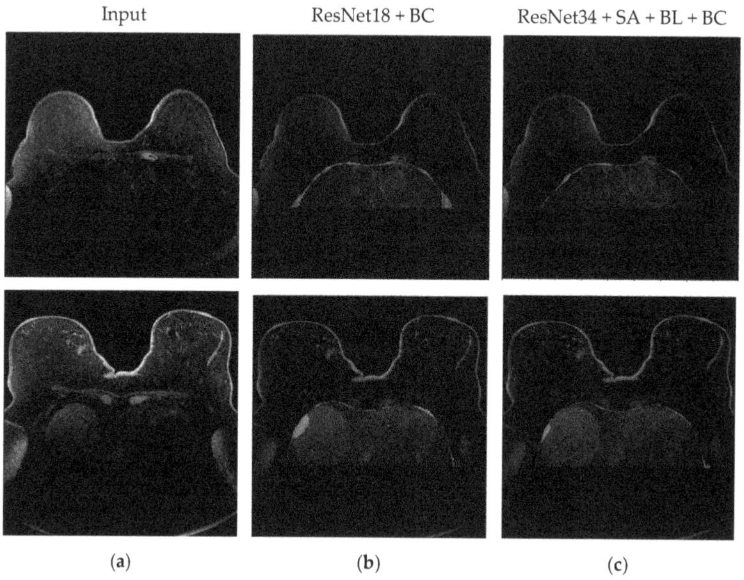

Figure 7. Comparison of results. The input images to the algorithms (**a**); the results from the worst performing algorithm (ResNet18 with bottleneck connection) (**b**); the results from the best performing architecture (**c**). The generated masks are purple, while the yellow coloring represents the areas of disagreement with the manual labeling. Abbreviations: BC—bottleneck connection, BL—blurring mechanism, SA—self-attention layer.

In cases of limited computational resources, both at training time and at inference time, the ResNet18 configurations would be the recommendation.

As the refinement algorithm is applied, improvements can be uniformly observed across all model configurations. By removing the bottom boundaries of the generated masks, the mean JSC is increased by 0.098, and the average DSC is increased by 0.026. The low variance of both similarity coefficients corroborates the observation that aggressive data augmentation is one of the main causes of irregularities in the generated masks (Table 4).

6. Conclusions

In this work, a series of experiments were run on Dynamic UNet architectures to determine their performance in chest cavity segmentation, achieving the best performance with a ResNet34 downsampling path, a self-attention layer, a blurring mechanism and a bottlenecked connection between the activation of the first block and the last block of the model. The average model performance without any post-processing achieved a DSC of 0.9359 and a JSC of 0.8874. Applying a simple algorithm aimed at correcting artefacts that were generated by aggressive data augmentation yielded an average DSC of 0.9612 and JSC 0.9789, achieving a new state of the art.

While the results are a significant step in the direction of clinical usability, future research should aim to expand the overall training datasets, as well as test the solution with different acquisition protocols and/or tasks.

Author Contributions: Conceptualization: M.B.; Methodology: M.B.; Software: M.B.; Validation: M.B., S.W. and W.B.; Investigation: M.B.; Data curation: S.W.; Writing: M.B., S.W. and W.B.; Visualization: M.B.; Reviewing and Editing: S.W. and W.B.; Supervision: T.-H.G. and W.B. All authors have read and agreed to the published version of the manuscript.

Funding: The authors declare that Marco Berchiolli and Susann Wolfram received financial support provided by UK Research and Innovation (project reference: 104192). UK Research and Innovation did not have any involvement in the study design; in the collection, analysis and interpretation of data; in the writing of the manuscript; or in the decision to submit the manuscript for publication. The APC was funded by Brunel University London.

Institutional Review Board Statement: The study was conducted in accordance with the Declaration of Helsinki and approved by the Institutional Review Board of HRA and HCRW (IRAS project ID 258617; latest amendment date: 18 December 2020).

Informed Consent Statement: Patient consent was waived due to the data collected being anonymized.

Data Availability Statement: The data presented in this study are available on request from the corresponding author. The data are not publicly available due to ethical restrictions.

Conflicts of Interest: None top declare.

References

1. Bray, F.; Ferlay, J.; Soerjomataram, I.; Siegel, R.L.; Torre, L.A.; Jemal, A. Global cancer statistics 2018: GLOBOCAN estimates of incidence and mortality worldwide for 36 cancers in 185 countries. *CA Cancer J. Clin.* **2018**, *68*, 394–424. [CrossRef]
2. Sung, H.; Ferlay, J.; Siegel, R.L.; Laversanne, M.; Soerjomataram, I.; Jemal, A.; Bray, F. Global Cancer Statistics 2020: GLOBOCAN Estimates of Incidence and Mortality Worldwide for 36 Cancers in 185 Countries. *CA Cancer J. Clin.* **2021**, *71*, 209–249. [CrossRef]
3. Ferlay, J.; Soerjomataram, I.; Dikshit, R.; Eser, S.; Mathers, C.; Rebelo, M.; Parkin, D.M.; Forman, D. Bray, Cancer incidence and mortality worldwide: Sources, methods and major patterns in GLOBOCAN 2012. *Int. J. Cancer* **2014**, *136*, 359–386. [CrossRef]
4. Vinnicombe, S. How I report breast magnetic resonance imaging studies for breast cancer staging and screening. *Cancer Imaging* **2016**, *16*, 1–14. [CrossRef]
5. Cho, N.; Im, S.-A.; Park, I.-A.; Lee, K.-H.; Li, M.; Han, W.; Noh, D.-Y.; Moon, W.K. Breast cancer: Early prediction of response to neoadjuvant chemotherapy using parametric response maps for MR imaging. *Radiology* **2014**, *272*, 385–396. [CrossRef]
6. Zbontar, J.; Knoll, F.; Sriram, A.; Murrell, T.; Huang, Z.; Muckley, M.J.; Defazio, A.; Stern, R.; Johnson, P.; Bruno, M.; et al. fastMRI: An Open Dataset and Benchmarks for Accelerated MRI. *arXiv* **2018**, arXiv:1811.08839. [CrossRef]
7. Chang, Y.-C.; Huang, Y.-H.; Huang, C.-S.; Chang, P.-K.; Chen, J.-H.; Chang, R.-F. Magnetic Resonance Spectroscopy and Imaging Guidance in Molecular Medicine: Targeting and Monitoring of Choline and Glucose Metabolism in Cancer. *Magn. Reson. Imaging* **2012**, *30*, 312–322. [CrossRef] [PubMed]
8. Piantadosi, G.; Sansone, M.; Fusco, R.; Sansone, C. Multi-planar 3D breast segmentation in MRI via deep convolutional neural networks. *Artif. Intell. Med.* **2020**, *103*, 101781. [CrossRef] [PubMed]

9. Marrone, S.; Piantadosi, G.; Fusco, R.; Petrillo, A.; Sansone, M.; Sansone, C. Breast segmentation using Fuzzy C-Means and anatomical priors in DCE-MRI. In Proceedings of the 23rd IEEE International Conference on Pattern Recognition (ICPR), Cancun, Mexico, 4–8 December 2016; pp. 1472–1477.
10. Kayalibay, B.; Jensen, G.; van der Smagt, P. CNN-based Segmentation of Medical Imaging Data. *arXiv* **2017**, arXiv:1701.03056. [CrossRef]
11. Alshanbari, H.S.; Amin, S.; Shuttleworth, J.; Slman, K.A.; Muslam, S. Automatic Segmentation in Breast Cancer Using Watershed Algorithm. *Int. J. Biomed. Eng.* **2015**, *2*, 1–6.
12. Wang, L.; Platel, B.; Ivanovskaya, T.; Harz, M.; Hahn, H.K. Fully automatic breast segmentation in 3D breast MRI. In Proceedings of the 9th IEEE International Symposium on Biomedical Imaging (ISBI), Barcelona, Spain, 2–5 May 2012.
13. Vignati, A.; Giannini, V.; de Luca, M.; Morra, L.; Persano, D.; Carbonaro, L.A.; Bertotto, I.; Martincich, L.; Regge, D.; Bert, A.; et al. Performance of a Fully Automatic Lesion Detection System for Breast DCE-MRI. *J. Magn. Reson. Imaging* **2011**, *34*, 1341–1351. [CrossRef]
14. Gallego Ortiz, C.; Martel, A.L. Automatic atlas-based segmentation of the breast in MRI for 3D breast volume computation. *Med. Phys.* **2012**, *39*, 5835–5848. [CrossRef]
15. Gubern-Mérida, A.; Kallenberg, M.; Mann, R.M.; Martí, R.; Karssemeijer, N. Breast segmentation and density estimation in breast MRI: A fully automatic framework. *IEEE J. Biomed. Health Inform.* **2015**, *19*, 349–357. [CrossRef] [PubMed]
16. Khalvati, F.; Gallego-Ortiz, C.; Balasingham, S.; Martel, A.L. Automated Segmentation of Breast in 3D MR Images Using a Robust Atlas. *IEEE Trans. Med. Imaging* **2015**, *34*, 116–125. [CrossRef]
17. Reed, V.K.; Woodward, W.A.; Zhang, L.; Strom, E.A.; Perkins, G.H.; Tereffe, W.; Oh, J.L.; Yu, T.K.; Bedrosian, I.; Whitman, G.J.; et al. Automatic segmentation of whole breast using atlas approach and deformable image registration. *Int. J. Radiat. Oncol. Biol. Phys.* **2009**, *73*, 1493–1500. [CrossRef]
18. Fooladivanda, A.; Shokouhi, S.B.; Mosavi, M.R.; Ahmadinejad, N. Atlas-based automatic breast MRI segmentation using pectoral muscle and chest region model. In Proceedings of the 21th IEEE Iranian Conference on Biomedical Engineering (ICBME), Tehran, Iran, 26–28 November 2014.
19. Mustra, M.; Bozek, J. Breast border extraction and pectoral muscle detection using wavelet decomposition. In Proceedings of the IEEE EUROCON, St. Petersburg, Russia, 18–23 May 2009.
20. Wu, S.; Weinstein, S.P.; Conant, E.F.; Schnall, M.D.; Kontos, D. Automated chest wall line detection for whole-breast segmentation in sagittal breast MR images. *Med. Phys.* **2013**, *40*, 1–12. [CrossRef]
21. Cai, L.; Gao, J.; Zhao, D. A review of the application of deep learning in medical image classification and segmentation. *Ann. Transl. Med.* **2020**, *8*, 713. [CrossRef]
22. Dalmış, M.; Litjens, G.; Holland, K.; Setio, A.; Mann, R.; Karssemeijer, N.; Gubern-Mérida, A. Using deep learning to segment breast and fibroglandular tissue in MRI volumes. *Med. Phys.* **2017**, *44*, 533–546. [CrossRef]
23. Ronneberger, O.; Fischer, P.; Brox, T. U-Net: Convolutional Networks for Biomedical Image Segmentation. In Proceedings of the Medical Image Computing and Computer-Assisted Intervention–MICCAI 2015: 18th International Conference, Munich, Germany, 5–9 October 2015; pp. 234–241.
24. Vaswani, A.; Shazeer, N.; Parmar, N.; Uszkoreit, J.; Jones, L.; Gomez, A.N.; Kaiser, L.; Polosukhin, I. Attention is All you Need. In Proceedings of the Advances in Neural Information Processing Systems 30 (NIPS 2017), Long Beach, CA, USA, 4–8 December 2017.
25. Iglovikov, V.I. Shvets, TernausNet. In *Computer-Aided Analysis of Gastrointestinal Videos*; Bernal, J., Histace, A., Eds.; Springer: Cham, Switzerland, 2021. [CrossRef]
26. Maitra, D.S.; Bhattacharya, U.; Parui, S.K. CNN based common approach to handwritten character recognition of multiple scripts. In Proceedings of the 13th IEEE International Conference on Document Analysis and Recognition (ICDAR), Tunis, Tunisia, 23–26 August 2015; pp. 1021–1025.
27. Raghu, M.; Zhang, C.; Kleinberg, J.; Bengio, S. Transfusion: Understanding Transfer Learning for Medical Imaging. In Proceedings of the Advances in Neural Information Processing Systems, Vancouver, BC, Canada, 8–14 December 2019.
28. Tan, C.; Sun, F.; Kong, T.; Zhang, W.; Yang, C.; Liu, C. A Survey on Deep Transfer Learning. In Proceedings of the Artificial Neural Networks and Machine Learning—ICANN 2018, Rhodes, Greece, 4–7 October 2018; pp. 270–279.
29. Serte, S.; Serener, A.; Al-Turjman, F. Deep learning in medical imaging: A brief review. *Trans. Emerg. Telecommun. Technol.* **2020**, *33*, e4080. [CrossRef]
30. Zhang, H.; Dauphin, Y.N.; Ma, T. Fixup Initialization: Residual Learning Without Normalization. *arXiv* **2019**, arXiv:1901.09321. [CrossRef]
31. He, K.; Zhang, X.; Ren, S.; Sun, J. Delving deep into rectifiers: Surpassing human-level performance on imagenet classification. In Proceedings of the International Conference on Computer Vision ICCV, Santiago, Chile, 7–13 December 2015.
32. Krizhevsky, A.; Sutskever, I.; Hinton, G.E. ImageNet classification with deep convolutional neural networks. *Commun. ACM* **2017**, *60*, 84–90. [CrossRef]
33. Litjens, G.; Kooi, T.; Bejnordi, B.E.; Setio, A.A.A.; Ciompi, F.; Ghafoorian, M.; van der Laak, J.A.W.M.; van Ginneken, B.; Sánchez, C.I. A survey on deep learning in medical image analysis. *Med. Image Anal.* **2017**, *42*, 60–88. [CrossRef]
34. Razzak, M.I.; Naz, S.; Zaib, A. Deep Learning for Medical Image Processing: Overview, Challenges and the Future. *Classif. BioApps Lect. Notes Comput. Vis. Biomech.* **2017**, *26*, 323–350. [CrossRef]

35. Bahdanau, D.; Cho, K.; Bengio, Y. Neural Machine Translation by Jointly Learning to Align and Translate. In Proceedings of the 2nd International Conference on Learning Representations, Banff, AB, Canada, 14–16 April 2014.
36. Xu, T.; Zhang, P.; Huang, Q.; Zhang, H.; Gan, Z.; Huang, X.; He, X. AttnGAN: Fine-Grained Text to Image Generation with Attentional Generative Adversarial Networks. In Proceedings of the IEEE/CVF Conference on Computer Vision and Pattern Recognition (CVPR), Honolulu, HI, USA, 21–26 July 2017.
37. Yang, Z.; He, X.; Gao, J.; Deng, L.; Smola, A. Stacked attention networks for image question answering. *arXiv* **2015**, arXiv:1511.02274.
38. Gregor, K.; Danihelka, I.; Graves, A.; Rezende, D.J.; Wierstra, D. Draw: A recurrent neural network for image generation. *arXiv* **2015**, arXiv:1502.04623.
39. Guan, Q.; Huang, Y.; Zhong, Z.; Zheng, Z.; Zheng, L.; Yang, Y. Diagnose like a Radiologist: Attention Guided Convolutional Neural Network for Thorax Disease Classification. *arXiv* **2018**, arXiv:1801.09927. [CrossRef]
40. Zhang, H.; Goodfellow, I.; Metaxas, D.; Odena, A. Self-Attention Generative Adversarial Networks. In Proceedings of the 36th International Conference on Machine Learning, Long Beach, CA, USA, 9–15 June 2019; pp. 7354–7363.
41. Odena, A.; Dumoulin, V.; Olah, C. Deconvolution and Checkerboard Artifacts. *Distill* **2016**, *1*, e3. [CrossRef]
42. Mikolajczyk, A.; Grochowski, M. Data augmentation for improving deep learning in image classification problem. In Proceedings of the IEEE International Interdisciplinary PhD Workshop (IIPhDW), Świnoujście, Poland, 9–12 May 2018; pp. 117–122.
43. Wong, S.C.; Gatt, A.; Stamatescu, V.; McDonnell, M.D. Understanding data augmentation for classification: When to warp? In Proceedings of the IEEE International Conference on Digital Image Computing: Techniques and Applications (DICTA), Gold Coast, Australia, 30 November–2 December 2016; pp. 1–6.
44. Kingma, D.P.; Ba, J. A method for stochastic optimization. *arXiv* **2014**, arXiv:1412.6980.
45. Smith, L.N. A disciplined approach to neural network hyper-parameters: Part 1—Learning rate, batch size, momentum, and weight decay. *arXiv* **2018**, arXiv:1803.09820.
46. Smith, L.N. No more pesky learning rate guessing games. *arXiv* **2015**, arXiv:1506.01186.

applied sciences

MDPI

Article

Investigating Effective Data Augmentation Techniques for Accurate Gastric Classification in the Development of a Deep Learning-Based Computer-Aided Diagnosis System

Jae-beom Park [1], Han-sung Lee [1] and Hyun-chong Cho [1,2,*]

[1] Department Graduate Program for BIT Medical Convergence, Kangwon National University, Chuncheon 24341, Republic of Korea
[2] Department of Electronics Engineering, Kangwon National University, Chuncheon 24341, Republic of Korea
* Correspondence: hyuncho@kangwon.ac.kr

Abstract: Gastric cancer is a significant health concern, particularly in Korea, and its accurate detection is crucial for effective treatment. However, a gastroscopic biopsy can be time-consuming and may, thus, delay diagnosis and treatment. Thus, this study proposed a gastric cancer diagnostic method, CADx, to facilitate a more efficient image analysis. Owing to the challenges in collecting medical image data, small datasets are often used in this field. To overcome this limitation, we used AutoAugment's ImageNet policy and applied cut-and-paste techniques using a sliding window algorithm to further increase the size of the dataset. The results showed an accuracy of 0.8317 for T-stage 1 and T-stage 4 image classification and an accuracy of 0.8417 for early gastric cancer and normal image classification, indicating improvements of 7 and 9%, respectively. Furthermore, through the application of test-time augmentation to the early gastric cancer and normal image datasets, the image classification accuracy was improved by 5.8% to 0.9000. Overall, the results of this study demonstrate the effectiveness of the proposed augmentation methods for enhancing gastric cancer classification performance.

Keywords: convolutional neural network; Computer-Aided Diagnosis (CADx); deep learning; gastric cancer; image augmentation

1. Introduction

According to a report released by the International Agency for Research on Cancer in 2020, gastric cancer records indicated 1,089,103 new cases and 769,000 deaths worldwide [1]. Among them, East Asia, including Korea, exhibited a higher incidence rate of 32.5 per 100,000 individuals, which is higher by 15.1 than the value of 17.4 in Eastern Europe, the second highest region. Figure 1 depicts the incidence of gastric cancer among distinct geographical regions, expressed as a percentage per 100,000 individuals, as reported by the International Agency for Research. In addition, the severity of gastric cancer can be confirmed in terms of both incidence and survival. According to the National Cancer Registration Program Annual Report released by the Ministry of Health and Welfare in South Korea in 2021, for stage 1 patients with localized lesions, the 5 y survival rate was relatively high (97%). However, the 5 y survival rate of stage 2–3 patients was only 62.1%. The proportion of patients with late-stage gastric cancer and distant metastases was 6.4%, indicating a rapidly decreasing trend [2].

To improve the early detection rate of gastric cancer, the National Health Insurance Corporation of Korea has implemented a regular gastric endoscopy program every two years for Koreans aged 40 years or older. Therefore, the number of gastroscopies performed in Korea steadily increased from 4,729,407 in 2013 to 7,093,024 in 2019 [3]. The detection and classification of gastric cancer during the gastric endoscopy stage can facilitate the early conduction of additional tests, such as blood tests, radiography, and PET-CT scans. However, with an increase in the number of people undergoing gastroscopy, the workload of specialists also increases, which may result in delays in the examination and biopsy periods.

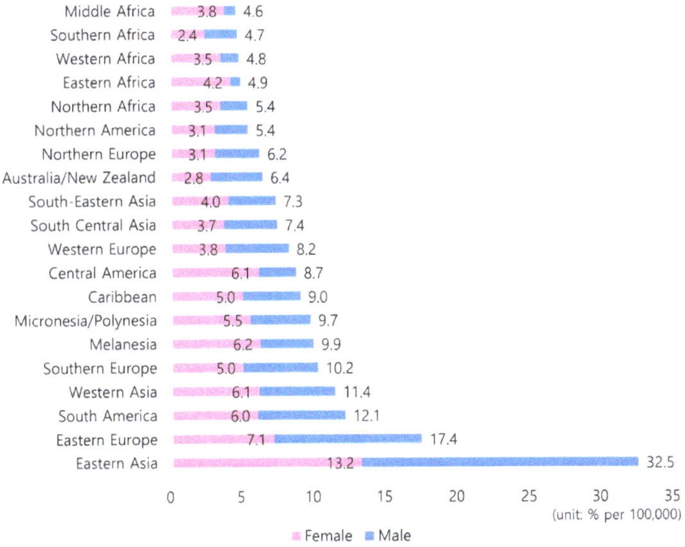

Figure 1. Gastric cancer rates per 100,000 people by region.

Numerous strategies and techniques have been investigated to improve the efficacy of medical procedures [4–6]. In particular, Computer-Aided Diagnosis (CADx), a system designed to support physicians in the diagnostic process across diverse clinical settings, has been a subject of extensive research [7–9]. It can improve the speed and accuracy of diagnoses by providing a consistent second opinion to doctors. Previous studies have demonstrated the practicality of deep learning, and further research is currently being conducted to optimize its performance and efficacy. Li et al. [10] and Li et al. [11] classified gastric cancers using the characteristics learned from gastric endoscopy histopathology slice images. They employed deep learning techniques to develop a model to distinguish between gastric cancer and noncancerous tissues. The results confirmed that CADx could accurately classify gastric cancer, achieving an accuracy of over 96% for slice-based classification. Thus, CADx can potentially improve the accuracy of diagnosis and early detection of gastric cancer, which is crucial for early treatment and improved patient outcomes. In addition to detection using gastric biopsy, detection that identifies the location of lesions using gastric endoscopic imaging has also been studied. Hirasawa et al. [12] conducted a study to detect gastric cancer lesions using gastroscopic imaging. They used data collected from two hospitals in Japan (Cancer Institute Hospital Ariake and Tokatsu-Tsujinaka Hospital) between April 2004 and December 2016, and 13,584 images of 2639 gastric cancer lesions were used as the training dataset. They employed a convolutional neural network (CNN) called the single-shot multibox detector (SSD) as the detection model. The developed CADx exhibited a sensitivity of 92.2% and could detect 70 of 71 lesions with a diameter of 6 mm or greater, as well as all invasive cancers. Yoon et al. [13] studied early gastric cancer (EGC) and invasion depth classifications. They collected data from 800 patients diagnosed with EGC at Gangnam Severance Hospital, Yonsei University College of Medicine in Seoul, South Korea, between January 2012 and March 2018. In total, 11,539 images (896 T1a-EGC, 809 T1b-EGC, and 9834 non-EGC images) were used in this study. Using VGG-16, they achieved detection accuracies of 0.981 for EGC and 0.851 for tumor depth classification. Hu et al. [14] identified EGC using narrow-band magnification images. They collected 1777 magnifying endoscopy with narrow-band imaging (ME-NBI) images from three hospitals in China (Endoscopic Center of Zhongshan Hospital, Affiliated Dongnan Hospital of Xiamen University, and Central Hospital of Wuhan) and used the VGG-19 architecture to identify EGC. The accuracies achieved in this study were 0.808 and 0.813, respectively, similar to those of senior endoscopists. Horiuchi et al. [15] conducted a study using 1492 cancer ME-NBI images and 1078 normal ME-NBI images collected between April 2005 and February 2016. They achieved an accuracy of 0.8684 and compared the results with those determined by 11 doctors for verification. They reported that the CADx system exhibited higher accuracy and sensitivity than those of the experts. However, in contrast to general endoscopes, ME-NBI has an optical system and an imaging system to increase resolution and sharpness, which slows the shooting speed and increases the inspection cost. Consequently, instead of ME-NBI, studies have been conducted using white light endoscopy to segment and classify benign gastric ulcer (BGU), EGC, and advanced gastric cancer (AGC) lesions and to classify T1a and T1b by the depth of invasion through normal gastric endoscopy images. Nam et al. [16] conducted a study classifying gastric mucosal lesions, including BGU, EGC, and AGC, using normal endoscopic images. This study included 1366 patients from two hospitals in Korea (Seoul National University Hospital and Samsung Medical Center). They utilized a CNN model for gastric lesion classification and achieved internal and external verification accuracies of 0.923 and 0.813, respectively. Furthermore, they achieved an internal verification accuracy of 0.77 and an external verification accuracy of 0.72 with the depth of invasion classification performance for T1a and T1b.

A common characteristic of previous studies is that the medical images contain personal patient information, which requires a long time for data collection, resulting in the construction of a small dataset. However, a small dataset size increases the risk of problems such as overfitting or underfitting in the model training owing to the possible requirement of more than one learning process. Data augmentation can ensure diversity in a dataset and facilitate the development of models with improved performance by learning the characteristics of various lesions. Consequently, this could enhance the accuracy and reliability of medical image analysis, ultimately leading to better patient conditions. A study was conducted to classify gastric cancers using data augmentation. Cho et al. [17] studied patients with gastric tumors detected at Chuncheon Sacred Heart Hospital in Gangwon Province, South Korea, between 2010 and 2017. Eventually, 2899 images from 846 patients were included in this study. Among them, images of submucosa-invaded lesions accounted for 34.5% (n = 999), and those of mucosa-confined lesions accounted for 65.5% (n = 1900). The mucosa-confined lesions were rotated by 90° to double their size and overcome data imbalance. The entire image dataset was then augmented four times by flipping it vertically and horizontally. Dense-Net-16 and Inception-ResNet-v2 were used for the training. Overall accuracies of 0.774 and 0.841 were achieved for internal validation, and accuracies of 0.661 and 0.714 were achieved when only classifying the invasion depth of EGC. Further, an external test dataset was constructed by collecting the images of consecutive patients who underwent gastric endoscopy between 2019 and 2020. Overall accuracies of 0.741 and 0.773 were achieved for external validation, and accuracies of 0.650 and 0.672 were achieved when only the invasion depth of the EGC was classified.

Most previous studies only applied simple image augmentation techniques, such as flip and rotation, without the use of additional methods for image augmentation. It is challenging to enhance the diversity of data features by applying simple augmentation techniques only. Therefore, this study used AutoAugment, a technique that adds geometric and color changes to the collected dataset, and introduced the Cut-and-Paste technique, which uses the sliding window algorithm to improve the performance of CADx for gastroscopy classification.

2. Materials and Methods

2.1. Dataset

Early gastric cancer is typically classified as T-stage 1, indicating that the tumor has invaded the mucosal or submucosal layers of the gastric wall. T-stage 4 gastric cancer indicates that the tumor has penetrated the serous layer and invaded significant organs, such as the spleen, transverse colon, liver, diaphragm, pancreas, abdominal wall, adrenal gland, kidney, small intestine, and retroperitoneum. The accurate staging of gastric cancer is crucial for determining the appropriate treatment plan for each patient. This study aimed to improve the performance of the gastric endoscopy diagnostic system through augmentation techniques, and two datasets were utilized to validate the performance of the proposed augmentation method.

The T-stage 1 and T-stage 4 data used in this study were obtained from the AI Hub [18], which provides gastric cancer diagnosis medical images using the tumor–node–metastasis (TNM) staging classification, presented in its 8th edition, of the American Joint Committee on Cancer (AJCC) as a standard for gastric cancer staging [19]. The data were extracted and purified from The Catholic University of Korea, Seoul St. Mary's Hospital electronic medical record (EMR) and picture archiving communication system (PACS), and patient consent and approval were obtained from the Institutional Review Board (IRB). The dataset was verified through three procedures: data collection officers, commentators, and researchers in charge of the participating institutions.

Consequently, an average of 14.5 images were collected per patient for both the T-stage 1 and T-stage 4 datasets. Images obtained from the same patient inherently exhibit similarity. Consequently, we adopted a strategy of partitioning patients into training, validation, and test cohorts to mitigate the risk of assessing the model's performance using substantially similar images. The patient distribution was executed through a random process, which was implemented to bolster the model's overall reliability. In addition, because the number of patients in T-stage 1 and T-stage 4 differed significantly, images of learning patients in T-stage 1 were randomly extracted to match those in T-stage 4. The distribution of the original dataset is presented in Table 1.

Table 1. Original dataset of T-stage 1 and T-stage 4 gastric endoscopy.

		T-Stage 1	T-Stage 4
People	Training	199	35
	Validation	13	13
	Test	13	13
People Total		215	61
Images	Training	512	512
	Validation	190	195
	Test	197	207
Image Total		899	914

Normal and early gastric cancer gastroscopy data were collected by the Department of Gastroenterology at the National Gyeongsang University Hospital in the Republic of Korea. All data were validated by internal medicine specialists and histological examinations were performed to improve the data quality. All data were collected after obtaining patient consent and approval from the IRB. On average, 6.25 images were collected per patient from this dataset. In addition, the patient composition was randomly distributed without duplication in the training, validation, and test datasets. Table 2 presents the distribution of the original dataset.

Table 2. Original dataset of EGC and normal gastric endoscopy.

		EGC	NOR
People	Training	28	28
	Validation	10	10
	Test	10	10
People Total		48	48
Images	Training	180	180
	Validation	60	60
	Test	60	60
Image Total		300	300

2.2. *Effective Augmentation to Gastric Dataset*

High-quality data are essential for accurate feature learning in deep learning models, and the data must satisfy both sufficient quantity and diversity requirements. Such data can improve the convergence speed of the weights and prevent overfitting of the model, thereby improving its performance. However, as observed in previous studies, there are limitations to medical data that satisfy the above conditions because of the time and cost required for the IRB approval process. Therefore, two data augmentation methods were used in this study to overcome these limitations.

2.2.1. AutoAugment

To secure a sufficient dataset for training, we employed data augmentation policies (AutoAugment) to increase the amount of data. AutoAugment is a data augmentation policy developed by Google [20] and comprises 25 subpolicies. Each subpolicy is composed of 2 of 16 image processing methods, such as flip and rotation, along with the probability and intensity of the application of each method. Therefore, the original dataset was expanded 25 times using this augmentation method.

AutoAugment provided optimal augmentation policies for three datasets: Cifar10, ImageNet, and SVHN. Cifar10 is a dataset comprising 32 × 32 images in 10 classes [21]. ImageNet is a dataset with over 1.4 million images and 1000 classes [22]. Finally, SVHN is a dataset of digit images collected from Google Street View and comprises approximately 100,000 images [23]. This study was conducted based on ImageNet, which contains the largest amount of data and classes.

2.2.2. Cut and Paste Using Window Sliding Algorithm

To accurately identify the lesion, a gastroenterology specialist manually confirmed its location and size and labeled the area. The extracted bounding box contained information regarding the size and position of the lesion. The X- and Y-coordinates of the bounding box were calculated to extract only the lesion. To perform augmentation with limited data, a method for pasting the created lesion image into a normal gastric image was used. Variances in the RGB channels of the cut lesion images were calculated to select the appropriate location for pasting. The sliding window algorithm moved normal images along the X- and Y-directions at equal intervals. While moving the virtual window at equal intervals, the lesion image was pasted onto the corresponding region by finding the point where the difference between the image variance of the corresponding region and that of the lesion image was minimized. The following equation was used to calculate the variance of lesion images:

The formula for calculating $\overline{I}_{cut}$, the average of the cut lesions images' RGB channels, is as follows. The size of the lesion image is $w \times h$, and i and j are the pixel coordinates.

$$\overline{I}_{cut} = \frac{1}{wh}\sum_{i=1}^{w}\sum_{j=1}^{h} I_{cut}(i,j) \quad (1)$$

The formula for calculating the variance of a cut image is as follows.

$$\sigma^2{}_{cut} = \frac{1}{wh}\sum_{i=1}^{w}\sum_{j=1}^{h}\left(I_{cut}(i,j) - \overline{I}_{cut}\right)^2 \quad (2)$$

The sliding window algorithm calculates the variance while sequentially moving along the (x, y) area by dividing a normal gastric image of size $w \times h$ into k equal lengths horizontally and vertically.

$$\overline{I}_{slide}(x,y) = \frac{k^2}{wh}\sum_{i=x}^{xw/k}\sum_{j=y}^{yh/k} I_{slide}(i,j) \quad (3)$$

The formula for calculating the variance of each region is as follows.

$$\sigma^2{}_{slide}(x,y) = \frac{k^2}{wh}\sum_{i=x}^{xw/k}\sum_{j=y}^{yh/k}\left(I_{slide}(i,j) - \overline{I}_{slide}(x,y)\right)^2 \quad (4)$$

It sequentially moves the position to determine the (x, y) positions, where the difference between the variances of the area located at (x, y) and the lesion image is the smallest.

$$(x,y) = argmin\left(\left|\sigma^2{}_{slide}(x,y) - \sigma^2{}_{cut}\right|\right) \quad (5)$$

This method was augmented by pasting the lesion image at the (x, y) position. Figure 2 shows an example of a cut-and-pasted image obtained using the sliding window algorithm.

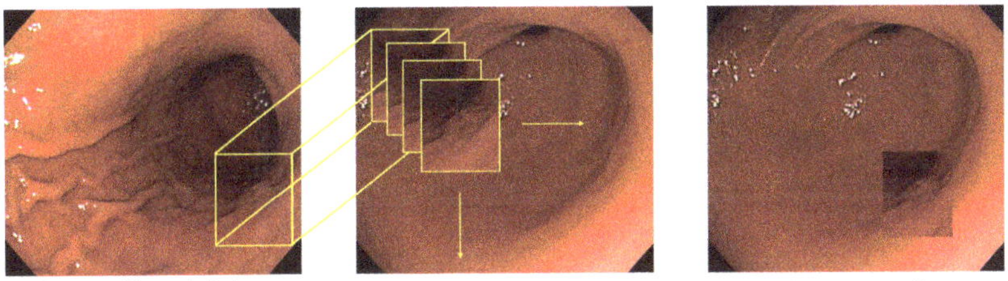

Figure 2. Example of cut-and-pasted image using sliding window algorithm.

2.3. *EfficientNetV2*

This study used a deep learning network with a CNN architecture to learn and diagnose the characteristics of lesions in gastric endoscopic images. With the development of neural architecture search (NAS) through artificial intelligence, networks with high performance and few parameters have been proposed [24]. EfficientNet utilizes a method to optimize three network components, depth, channel width, and input image resolution, to improve the model performance [25]. Moreover, through the application of compound scaling to each component based on a designed base model, EfficientNet facilitates the uniform creation of models of varying sizes.

EfficientNetV1 uses a depth-wise 3 × 3 convolution from MobileNet's MBConvolution in the initial stage [26]. However, this type of convolution causes overhead problems, because it is inefficient for modern accelerators that perform batch operations. To address this issue, EfficientNetV2 uses Fused-MBConv to convert, depth-wise, 3 × 3 convolution and 1 × 1 convolution operations into a regular 3 × 3 convolution to increase the efficiency training speed [27]. In addition, it facilitates effective image learning by utilizing the squeeze-and-excitation (SE) block proposed by SENet to weigh the importance of channels in feature maps during training [28]. Figure 3 shows the architectures of MBconv and Fused-MBConv.

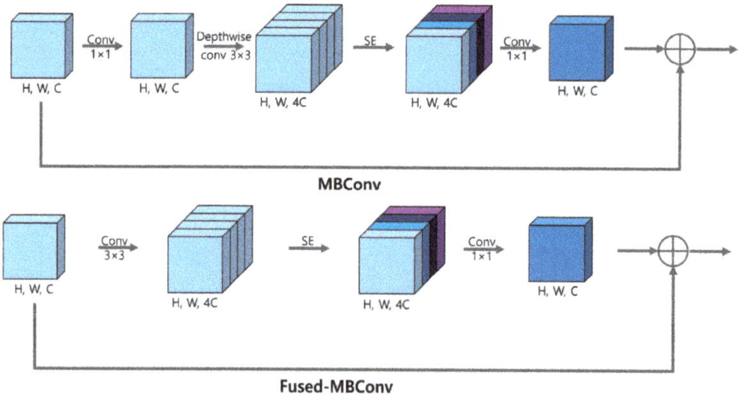

Figure 3. MBConv and Fused-MBConv architectures.

In EfficientNetV2, the maximum resolution of the compound scaling is limited to 480 × 480 for training efficiency, and the number of layers is gradually increased in the later stages. This resulted in the proposal of three models, namely Small, Medium, and Large. The EfficientNetV2-L model trained using the ImageNet21k dataset, which comprises approximately 10 million images and over 22,000 categories, was used in this study.

2.4. Test-Time Augmentation

Test-time augmentation (TTA) is a technique used in machine learning to improve the performance and generalization of a trained model during the inference phase [29]. This method involves the application of various data transformations to the input data and obtaining predictions from the model for each transformed image. The final prediction is determined by aggregating the predictions from the augmented data and computing their averages. Through this process, the TTA utilizes various aspects of the image for prediction, thereby enabling more robust and accurate classification. In addition, TTA can be a useful technique for improving the performance of models during inference, particularly when the test dataset is limited, resulting in low feature distribution and diversity. In this study, the test dataset was increased by 8 times by combining horizontal flip, vertical flip, and rotation (0°, 90°, 180°, and 270°). Figure 4 shows an example of the TTA algorithm.

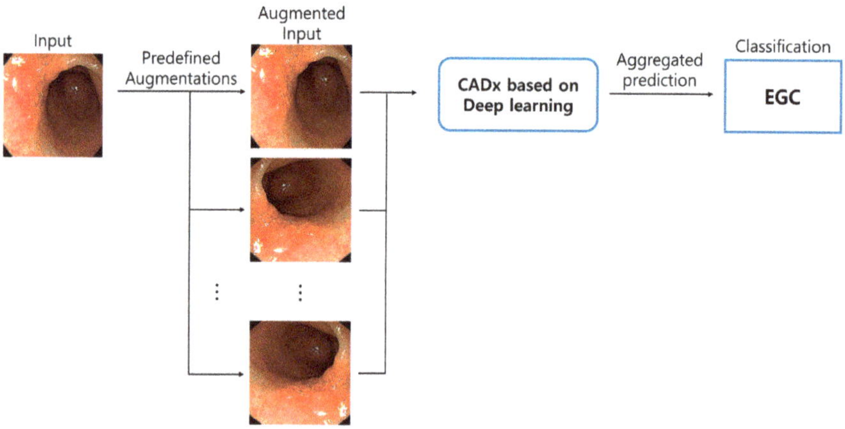

Figure 4. Example of test-time augmentation algorithm.

3. Results

This study aimed to improve the accuracy of gastroscopic classification using a gastric endoscopic image augmentation policy. This effect was confirmed using two datasets. The collected T-stage 1 and T-stage 4 data were used as training (1024 images), validation (385 images), and test (404 images) data. Further, the collected EGC and normal data were used as training (360 images), validation (120 images), and test (120 images) data. AutoAugment generated 25 times more training data images. The lesions were pasted onto normal images using a sliding window algorithm for the Cut-and-Paste technique. The detailed composition of the dataset is presented in Table 3. T-stage 1 and T-stage 4 datasets were defined as Dataset A, and the EGC and normal datasets were defined as Dataset B.

Table 3. Configuration of augmented gastric cancer training datasets.

	Dataset A		Dataset B	
	T-Stage 1	**T-Stage 4**	**EGC**	**NOR**
Original	512	512	180	180
AutoAugment	13,312	13,312	4680	4680
Cut and Paste	166,912	166,912	37,080	4680

The EfficientNetV2-L model was used to evaluate classification network performance. The performance evaluation indices of the trained model were as follows: (1) precision, which is the proportion of predictions that are actually true; (2) sensitivity, which represents the proportion of predictions that are true among those that are actually true; (3) the False Positive Rate (FPR) represents the proportion of true negatives that were inaccurately classified as positives; (4) the F1-score represents the harmonic average of precision and sensitivity; and (5) accuracy, which is the percentage of all predictions that were correctly predicted. The performance of the model for each dataset is summarized in Table 4.

Table 4. Gastric cancer classification results by data augmentation.

	Metrics	**Original**	**AutoAugment**	**Cut and Paste**
Dataset A	Precision	0.7658	0.7936	0.8320
	Sensitivity	0.7655	0.7929	0.8312
	FPR	0.2113	0.1780	0.1737
	F1-score	0.7656	0.7933	0.8316
	Accuracy	0.7649	0.7921	0.8317
Dataset B	Precision	0.7747	0.8114	0.8715
	Sensitivity	0.7500	0.7833	0.8417
	FPR	0.3077	0.2821	0.2338
	F1-score	0.7622	0.7971	0.8563
	Accuracy	0.7500	0.7833	0.8417

Early diagnosis of gastric cancer is essential for improving treatment outcomes and prognosis. For this reason, sensitivity, representing the classification accuracy of gastric cancer images, is a crucial evaluation metric in this study. The results showed that the classification sensitivity using Dataset A improved by 6.5%, from 0.7655 to 0.8312, and that using Dataset B improved by 9.1%, from 0.7500 to 0.8417. The accuracy also exhibited a similar improvement to the sensitivity. The classification accuracy using Dataset A improved by 6.6%, from 0.7649 to 0.8317, and that using Dataset B improved by 9.1%, from 0.7500 to 0.8417.

To address the issue of the limited test dataset in Dataset B, TTA was applied. Consequently, the obtained outcomes were evaluated using a broader data range, which can be considered as an evaluation of enhanced generalization. Table 5 presents the results obtained by applying the TTA algorithm to Dataset B.

Table 5. Gastric cancer classification results using TTA.

	Metrics	Original	AutoAugment	Cut and Paste
Dataset B	Precision	0.7990	0.8683	0.9114
	Sensitivity	0.7750	0.8667	0.9000
	FPR	0.2857	0.1563	0.1571
	F1-score	0.7868	0.8675	0.9057
	Accuracy	0.7750	0.8667	0.9000

The application of the TTA algorithm to Dataset B resulted in an increase in sensitivity compared to when TTA was not applied. Specifically, the sensitivity increased by 2.2% for the original model, 8.3% for the model with only AutoAugment, and 5.8% for the model with Cut-and-Paste augmentation.

4. Discussion

4.1. Comparison with Prior Studies

Comparing our results with previous studies, it becomes evident that data augmentation plays a crucial role in enhancing the performance of CADx systems. Hu et al. [14] showed a performance of a 0.81 AUC and 0.77 accuracy in classifying EGC using narrow-band magnification images. Horiuchi et al. [15] showed an accuracy of 0.87 in classifying EGC using narrow-band magnification images. Nam et al. [16] showed an accuracy of 0.82 in classifying BGU, EGC, AGC. Furthermore, they achieved an external verification accuracy of 0.72 with the depth-of-invasion classification performance for T1a and T1b. Cho et al. [17] used images of lesions that were rotated by 90° to double their size and overcome data imbalance. The entire image dataset was then augmented four times by flipping it vertically and horizontally. Consequently, its study showed an accuracy of 0.77 for external validation in classifying the invasion depth of EGC.

In our study, we achieved an accuracy of 0.83 in classifying T-stages 1 and 4, and an accuracy of 0.90 in distinguishing EGC from normal (NOR) cases. Thus, our study validates the effectiveness of the data augmentation techniques proposed. However, it is important to note that each study varies in terms of data quality, scale, and research objectives. Consequently, the performance figures in each study do not represent absolute values. A comparative overview of the performance of existing studies is presented in Table 6.

Table 6. The performance of previous studies and our study.

	Classification Class	Purpose	Performance
Hu et al. [14]	EGC and NOR	Classification	AUC: 0.81 Acc: 0.77
Horiuchi et al. [15]	EGC and NOR	Classification	Acc: 0.87
Nam et al. [16]	BGU, AGC, EGC Depth of invasion	Classification	Acc: 0.82 Acc: 0.72
Cho et al. [17]	Depth of invasion	Classification	Acc: 0.77
Proposed method	T-stage 1 and 4 EGC and NOR	Classification	Acc: 0.83 Acc: 0.90

4.2. Limitations and Potential

In this study, our Computer-Aided Diagnosis (CADx) system successfully distinguishes between T-stages 1 and 4 of gastric cancer, early gastric cancer, and normal cases. However, it is essential to acknowledge that our system's classification does not encompass the entire spectrum of T-stages, given the intricate nature of cancer staging, which involves factors such as tumor size, depth of invasion, and extent of metastasis. Moreover, the sole reliance on gastroscopy images for staging poses challenges due to the complex interplay of these variables.

The limitations of our current CADx system also pertain to its inability to encompass all possible lesion cases. Notwithstanding these challenges, our research underscores the value of data augmentation techniques, such as Cut and Paste, in improving the performance of the CADx system. This method enables more diverse and comprehensive feature learning by generating gastric cancer tissue samples that faithfully replicate the distinctive characteristics of lesions. These factors collectively contribute to the robust and generalizable performance of our CADx system.

Furthermore, the improved performance of the CADx system holds the potential to offer specialists consistent and highly accurate second opinions. This aspect represents a significant strength of our proposed method in the context of patient care.

5. Conclusions

This study proposed a Cut-and-Paste augmentation technique that can improve gastroscopy classification performance in CADx systems. Data augmentation contributes to performance improvement by enabling deep learning models to learn various characteristics and patterns. Representative augmentation techniques in the field of deep learning include approaches that make geometric changes to images, such as AutoAugment, which was applied in this study. However, when data are augmented, there are factors that may damage the characteristics of the lesion depending on the intensity of the augmentation. From this perspective, the proposed augmentation technique is characterized by the possibility of a large amount of augmentation without damage to the perceptibility of the characteristics of the original lesion. In addition, the effectiveness of these matters was proven by applying the technology to two datasets and improving performance. Furthermore, the problem of a limited test dataset was addressed by applying the TTA algorithm. This allowed the model to obtain more robust results by considering various visual changes and variations.

However, the current lesion images were manually marked and cut into rectangular shapes by a specialist. Rectangular images are likely to include lesions and normal mucosa. In addition, the location and size of the lesion must be known before applying the Cut-and-Paste technique. These issues can be addressed by utilizing Grad-CAM, which visualizes the regions of interest during the decision-making of the deep learning model. Thus, the time and cost required for labeling can be reduced. In future work, we aim to develop a CADx system that can classify all stages from 1 to 4 based on T staging.

Author Contributions: Conceptualization, H.-c.C.; methodology, J.-b.P., H.-s.L. and H.-c.C..; software, J.-b.P.; validation, J.-b.P. and H.-s.L.; formal analysis, J.-b.P.; investigation, J.-b.P.; resources, H.-s.L.; data curation, J.-b.P. and H.-s.L.; writing—original draft preparation, J.-b.P.; writing—review and editing, H.-c.C.; visualization, J.-b.P. and H.-s.L.; supervision, H.-c.C.; project administration, H.-c.C.; funding acquisition, H.-c.C. All authors have read and agreed to the published version of the manuscript.

Funding: This research was supported by Basic Science Research Program through the National Research Foundation of Korea (NRF) funded by the Ministry of Education (No. 2022R1I1A3053872) and was supported by "Regional Innovation Strategy (RIS)" through the National Research Foundation of Korea (NRF) funded by the Ministry of Education (MOE) (2022RIS-005).

Institutional Review Board Statement: This study was conducted according to the guidelines of the Declaration of Helsinki and approved by the Institutional Review Board of Gyeongsang National University Hospital (GNUH 2022-05-033 and 21 June 2022).

Informed Consent Statement: Informed consent was obtained from all subjects involved in the study.

Data Availability Statement: The data presented in this study are available on request from the corresponding author. This needs additional IRB approval.

Conflicts of Interest: The authors declare no conflict of interest.

References

1. Bray, F.; Ferlay, J.; Soerjomataram, I.; Siegel, R.L.; Torre, L.A.; Jemal, A. Global Cancer Statistics 2018: GLOBOCAN Estimates of Incidence and Mortality Worldwide for 36 Cancers in 185 Countries. *Int. J. Cancer* **2018**, *144*, 1941–1953. [CrossRef] [PubMed]
2. Ministry of Health and Welfare. *Annual Report of the National Cancer Registration Program 2020*; Ministry of Health and Welfare: Seoul, Republic of Korea, 2021.
3. National Health Insurance Service. Health Checkup Statistics: Status of Diagnosis Results for Upper Gastrointestinal Contrast and Endoscopic Examinations. 2020. Available online: https://opendata.hira.or.kr/home.do (accessed on 9 March 2023).
4. Alius, C.; Serban, D.; Bratu, D.G.; Tribus, L.C.; Vancea, G.; Stoica, P.L.; Motofei, I.; Tudor, C.; Serboiu, C.; Costea, D.O.; et al. When Critical View of Safety Fails: A Practical Perspective on Difficult Laparoscopic Cholecystectomy. *Medicina* **2023**, *59*, 1491. [CrossRef] [PubMed]
5. Innes, A.L.; Martinez, A.; Gao, X.; Dinh, N.; Hoang, G.L.; Nguyen, T.B.P.; Vu, V.H.; Luu, T.H.T.; Le, T.T.T.; Lebrun, V.; et al. Computer-Aided Detection for Chest Radiography to Improve the Quality of Tuberculosis Diagnosis in Vietnam's District Health Facilities: An Implementation Study. *Trop. Med. Infect. Dis.* **2023**, *8*, 488. [CrossRef]
6. Viknesh, C.K.; Kumar, P.N.; Seetharaman, R.; Anitha, D. Detection and Classification of Melanoma Skin Cancer Using Image Processing Technique. *Diagnostics* **2023**, *13*, 3313. [CrossRef]
7. Ben Ayed, M.; Massaoudi, A.; Alshaya, S.A. Smart Recognition COVID-19 System to Predict Suspicious Persons Based on Face Features. *J. Electr. Eng. Technol.* **2021**, *16*, 1601–1606. [CrossRef]
8. Ramanathan, S.; Ramasundaram, M. Alzheimer's Disease Shape Detection Model in Brain Magnetic Resonance Images Via Whale Optimization with Kernel Support Vector Machine. *J. Electr. Eng. Technol.* **2023**, *18*, 2287–2296. [CrossRef]
9. Saranya, G. Integrated Vision and Sensor Based Analysis for Sleep Apnea Using FeatFaceNet Deep Learning. *J. Electr. Eng. Technol.* **2023**, *18*, 1–10. [CrossRef]
10. Li, Y.; Li, X.; Xie, X.; Shen, L. Deep learning based gastric cancer identification. In Proceedings of the 2018 IEEE 15th International Symposium on Biomedical Imaging (ISBI 2018), Washington, DC, USA, 4–7 April 2018; pp. 182–185. [CrossRef]
11. Li, Y.; Deng, L.; Yang, X.; Liu, Z.; Zhao, X.; Huang, F.; Zhu, S.; Chen, X.; Chen, Z.; Zhang, W. Early diagnosis of gastric cancer based on deep learning combined with the spectral-spatial classification method. *Biomed. Opt. Express* **2019**, *10*, 4999–5014. [CrossRef] [PubMed]
12. Hirasawa, T.; Aoyama, K.; Tanimoto, T.; Ishihara, S.; Shichijo, S.; Ozawa, T.; Fujishiro, M.; Kanesaka, T.; Matsuda, R.; Kobayashi, M.; et al. Application of artificial intelligence using a convolutional neural network for detecting gastric cancer in endoscopic images. *Gastric Cancer* **2018**, *21*, 653–660. [CrossRef]
13. Yoon, H.J.; Kim, S.; Kim, J.-H.; Keum, J.-S.; Oh, S.-I.; Jo, J.; Chun, J.; Youn, Y.H.; Park, H.; Kwon, I.G.; et al. A Lesion-Based Convolutional Neural Network Improves Endoscopic Detection and Depth Prediction of Early Gastric Cancer. *J. Clin. Med.* **2019**, *8*, 1310. [CrossRef] [PubMed]
14. Hu, H.; Gong, L.; Dong, D.; Zhu, L.; Wang, M.; He, J.; Shu, L.; Cai, Y.; Cai, S.; Su, W.; et al. Identifying early gastric cancer under magnifying narrow-band images with deep learning: A multicenter study. *Gastrointest. Endosc.* **2021**, *93*, 1333–1341.e3. [CrossRef] [PubMed]
15. Horiuchi, Y.; Hirasawa, T.; Ishizuka, N.; Tokai, Y.; Namikawa, K.; Yoshimizu, S.; Ishiyama, A.; Yoshio, T.; Tsuchida, T.; Fujisaki, J.; et al. Performance of a computer-aided diagnosis system in diagnosing early gastric cancer using magnifying endoscopy videos with narrow-band imaging (with videos). *Gastrointest. Endosc.* **2020**, *92*, 856–865.e1. [CrossRef] [PubMed]
16. Nam, J.Y.; Chung, H.J.; Choi, K.S.; Lee, H.; Kim, T.J.; Soh, H.; Kang, E.A.; Cho, S.-J.; Ye, J.C.; Im, J.P.; et al. Deep learning model for diagnosing gastric mucosal lesions using endoscopic images: Development, validation, and method comparison. *Gastrointest. Endosc.* **2022**, *95*, 258–268.e10. [CrossRef] [PubMed]
17. Cho, B.J.; Bang, C.S.; Lee, J.J.; Seo, C.W.; Kim, J.H. Prediction of Submucosal Invasion for Gastric Neoplasms in Endoscopic Images Using Deep-Learning. *J. Clin. Med.* **2020**, *9*, 1858. [CrossRef] [PubMed]
18. AI Hub. Medical Imaging for Gastric Cancer Diagnosis. 2021. Available online: https://aihub.or.kr (accessed on 30 June 2021).
19. American Joint Committee on Cancer. *AJCC Cancer Staging Manual*, 8th ed.; Springer: New York, NY, USA, 2017.
20. Cubuk, E.D.; Zoph, B.; Mane, D.; Vasudevan, V.; Le, Q.V. Autoaugment: Learning augmentation strategies from data. In Proceedings of the IEEE/CVF Conference on Computer Vision and Pattern Recognition (CVPR), Long Beach, CA, USA, 15–20 June 2019; pp. 113–123.
21. Krizhevsky, A. *Learning Multiple Layers of Features from Tiny Images*; Technical Report; University of Toronto: Toronto, ON, Canada, 2009.
22. Deng, J.; Dong, W.; Socher, R.; Li, L.-J.; Li, K.; Fei-Fei, L. Imagenet: A large-scale hierarchical image database. In Proceedings of the IEEE Conference on Computer Vision and Pattern Recognition, Miami, FL, USA, 20–25 June 2009; pp. 248–255.
23. Netzer, Y.; Wang, T.; Coates, A.; Bissacco, A.; Wu, B.; Ng, A.Y. Reading Digits in Natural Images with Unsupervised Feature Learning. In Proceedings of the Neural Information Processing Systems (NIPS), Sierra Nevada, Spain, 16–17 December 2011.
24. Zoph, B.; Vasudevan, V.; Shlens, J.; Le, Q.V. Neural Architecture Search with Reinforcement Learning. *arXiv* **2017**, arXiv:1611.01578.
25. Tan, M.; Le, Q.V. EfficientNet: Rethinking Model Scaling for Convolutional Neural Networks. In Proceedings of the 36th International Conference on Machine Learning, PMLR, Long Beach, CA, USA, 10–15 June 2019; pp. 6105–6114.
26. Howard, A.G.; Zhu, M.; Chen, B.; Kalenichenko, D.; Wang, W.; Weyand, T.; Andreetto, M.; Adam, H. MobileNets: Efficient Convolutional Neural Networks for Mobile Vision Applications. *arXiv* **2017**, arXiv:1704.04861.

27. Tan, M.; Huang, R.; Wang, T.; Yang, F.; Duan, J.; Zhang, C.; Huang, Z.; Zhu, M.; Liu, J.; Zhu, J.; et al. EfficientNetV2: Smaller Models and Faster Training. *arXiv* **2021**, arXiv:2104.00298.
28. Jie, Z.; Liang, X.; Feng, J.; Zhao, T.; Liu, S.; Yan, S. Squeeze-and-Excitation Networks. In Proceedings of the IEEE Conference on Computer Vision and Pattern Recognition (CVPR), Salt Lake City, UT, USA, 18–23 June 2018; pp. 7132–7141.
29. Shanmugam, D.; Blalock, D.; Balakrishnan, G.; Guttag, J. Better Aggregation in Test-Time Augmentation. In Proceedings of the IEEE/CVF International Conference on Computer Vision, Montreal, BC, Canada, 11–17 October 2021; pp. 1214–1223.

MDPI AG
Grosspeteranlage 5
4052 Basel
Switzerland
Tel.: +41 61 683 77 34

Applied Sciences Editorial Office
E-mail: applsci@mdpi.com
www.mdpi.com/journal/applsci

www.ingramcontent.com/pod-product-compliance
Lightning Source LLC
LaVergne TN
LVHW070450061126
851858LV00011B/206

* 9 7 8 3 7 2 5 8 8 2 6 7 0 *